THE LEGENDS OF
THE JEWS

THE LEGENDS OF
THE JEWS

BY
LOUIS GINZBERG

TRANSLATED FROM THE GERMAN MANUSCRIPT BY
PAUL RADIN

III

BIBLE TIMES AND CHARACTERS
FROM THE EXODUS TO THE DEATH OF MOSES

PHILADELPHIA
THE JEWISH PUBLICATION SOCIETY OF AMERICA
5728–1968

To
My Mother
On the Occasion of
Her Seventieth Birthday

PREFACE

" When Israel went out of Egypt, the house of Jacob from a people of strange language, Jacob was His sanctuary and Israel His dominion." Jewish legend attempts to describe how God's sanctuary, the religion of Israel and His dominion, the beginnings of Israel as a nation, arose in the time between the Exodus from Egypt and the entrance into the Holy Land.

Moses is regarded not only as the greatest religious guide of Israel, but also as its first national leader; he is " the wisest of the wise, the father of the prophets," as well as " king in Jeshurun, when the heads of the people and the tribes of Israel gathered together." Hence his unique position in Jewish legend, neither Abraham, the friend of God, nor Solomon, the wisest of all men, nor Elijah, the helper in time of need, can lay claim to such a position.

Great religious and national institutions like the Sabbath, the sanctuary, and many other " commandments of God revealed to Moses " stand in a special relation to his life and work. The sanctification of the Sabbath became quite a living thing to him through the miracle of the Manna, and the first sanctuary was actually erected by Moses. The life of Moses ceased, therefore, to be a thing of the past and became closely interwoven with the every-day life of the nation.

The most natural way for the popular mind to connect existing conditions with the past is the symbolic method. The present volume contains, therefore, a number of symbolic explanations of certain laws, as, for instance, the symbolical significance of the Tabernacle, which, properly speaking, do not belong to the domain of legend. The life of Moses, as conceived by Jewish legend, would, however, have been incomplete if the lines between Legend and Symbolism had been kept too strictly. With this exception the arrangement and presentation of the material in the third volume is the same as that in the two preceding ones.

LOUIS GINZBERG.

NEW YORK, *March 2, 1911*

CONTENTS

The Long Route—Pharaoh Pursues the Hebrews—The
Sea Divided—The Passage through the Red Sea—The
Destruction of the Egyptians—The Song at the Sea—The
Awful Desert—The Heavenly Food—The Gathering
of the Manna—Miriam's Well—Amalek's War against
Israel—Amalek Defeated—Jethro—Installation of Elders—
Jethro Rewarded—The Time is at Hand—The Gentiles
Refuse the Torah—The Contest of the Mountains—The
Torah Offered to Israel—Israel Prepares for the Revela-
tion—The Revelation on Mount Sinai—The First Com-
mandment—The Other Commandments Revealed on
Sinai—The Unity of the Ten Commandments—Moses
Chosen as Intermediator—Moses and the Angels Strive
for the Torah—Moses Receives the Torah—The Golden
Calf—Moses Blamed for Israel's Sin—The Punishment
of the Sinners—Moses Intercedes for the People—The
Inscrutable Ways of the Lord—The Thirteen Attributes
of God—The Second Tables—The Census of the Peo-
ple—The Erection of the Tabernacle Commanded—The
Materials for the Construction of the Tabernacle—
Bezalel—The Ark with the Cherubim—The Table and the
Candlestick—The Altar—The Symbolical Significance of
the Tabernacle—The Priestly Robes—The Stones in the
Breastplate—The Completion of the Tabernacle—The
Setting up of the Tabernacle—The Consecration of the
Priests—The Day of the Ten Crowns—The Interrupted
Joy—The Gifts of the Princes—The Revelations in the
Tabernacle—The Cleansing of the Camp—The Lighting
of the Candlestick—The Twelve Princes of the Tribes—
The Census of the Levites—The Four Divisions of the
Levites—The Four Standards—The Camp—The Blas-

Contents

MOSES IN THE WILDERNESS

MOSES IN THE WILDERNESS

The Long Route

The exodus would have been impossible if Joseph's bones had remained behind. Therefore Moses made it his concern to seek their resting-place, while the people had but the one thought of gathering in the treasures of the Egyptians.[1] But it was not an easy matter to find Joseph's body. Moses knew that he had been interred in the mausoleum of the Egyptian kings, but there were so many other bodies there that it was impossible to identify it. Moses' mother Jochebed came to his aid. She led him to the very spot where Joseph's bones lay. As soon as he came near them, he knew them to be what he was seeking, by the fragrance they exhaled and spread around.[2] But his difficulties were not at an end. The question arose, how he was to secure possession of the remains. Joseph's coffin had been sunk far down into the ground, and he knew not how to raise it from the depths. Standing at the edge of the grave, he spoke these words, " Joseph, the time hath come whereof thou didst say, ' God will surely visit you, and ye shall carry up my bones from hence.'" No sooner had this reminder dropped from his lips than the coffin stirred and rose to the surface.

And even yet the difficulties in Moses' way were not removed wholly. The Egyptian magicians had stationed two golden dogs at Joseph's coffin, to keep watch, and they barked vehemently if anyone ventured close to it. The

noise they made was so loud it could be heard throughout
the land, from end to end, a distance equal to a forty days'
journey.   When Moses came near the coffin, the dogs
emitted their warning sound, but he silenced them at once,
with the words, " Come, ye people, and behold the miracle !
The real, live dogs did not bark, and these counterfeit dogs
produced by magic attempt it ! " ³ What he said about real,
live dogs and their refraining from barking had reference
to the fact that the dogs of the Egyptians did not move their
tongues against any of the children of Israel, though they
had barked all the time the people were engaged in burying
the bodies of their smitten first-born.   As a reward God gave
the Israelites the law, to cast to the dogs the flesh they themselves are forbidden to eat, for the Lord withholds due
recompense from none of His creatures.⁴   Indeed, the dogs
received a double reward, for their excrements are used in
tanning the hides from which the Torah scrolls are made, as
well as the Mezuzot and the phylacteries.⁵

Joseph's coffin in the possession of Moses, the march of
the Israelites could begin.   The Egyptians put no manner
of obstacle in their way.   Pharaoh himself accompanied
them, to make sure that they were actually leaving the
land,⁶ and now he was so angry at his counsellors for having advised against letting the Israelites depart that he slew
them.⁷

For several reasons God did not permit the Israelites to
travel along the straight route to the promised land. He desired them to go to Sinai first and take the law upon themselves there, and, besides, the time divinely appointed for
the occupation of the land by the Gentiles had not yet

elapsed. Over and above all this, the long sojourn in the
wilderness was fraught with profit for the Israelites, spiritually and materially. If they had reached Palestine directly
after leaving Egypt, they would have devoted themselves
entirely each to the cultivation of his allotted parcel of
ground, and no time would have been left for the study of
the Torah. In the wilderness they were relieved of the
necessity of providing for their daily wants, and they could
give all their efforts to acquiring the law. On the whole, it
would not have been advantageous to proceed at once to the
Holy Land and take possession thereof, for when the Canaanites heard that the Israelites were making for Palestine,
they burnt the crops, felled the trees, destroyed the buildings, and choked the water springs, all in order to render
the land uninhabitable. Hereupon God spake, and said: " I
did not promise their fathers to give a devastated land unto
their seed, but a land full of all good things. I will lead
them about in the wilderness for forty years, and meanwhile
the Canaanites will have time to repair the damage they
have done." [8] Moreover, the many miracles performed for
the Israelites during the journey through the wilderness had
made their terror to fall upon the other nations, and their
hearts melted, and there remained no more spirit in any
man. They did not venture to attack the Israelites, and the
conquest of the land was all the easier. [9]

Nor does this exhaust the list of reasons for preferring
the longer route through the desert. Abraham had sworn a
solemn oath to live at peace with the Philistines during a
certain period, and the end of the term had not yet arrived.
Besides, there was the fear that the sight of the land of the

Philistines would awaken sad recollections in the Israelites, and drive them back into Egypt speedily, for once upon a time it had been the scene of a bitter disappointment to them. They had spent one hundred and eighty years in Egypt, in peace and prosperity, not in the least molested by the people. Suddenly Ganon came, a descendant of Joseph, of the tribe of Ephraim, and he spake, " The Lord hath appeared unto me, and He bade me lead you forth out of Egypt." The Ephraimites were the only ones to heed his words. Proud of their royal lineage as direct descendants of Joseph, and confident of their valor in war, for they were great heroes, they left the land and betook themselves to Palestine.[10] They carried only weapons and gold and silver. They had taken no provisions, because they expected to buy food and drink on the way or capture them by force if the owners would not part with them for money.

After a day's march they found themselves in the neighborhood of Gath, at the place where the shepherds employed by the residents of the city gathered with the flocks. The Ephraimites asked them to sell them some sheep, which they expected to slaughter in order to satisfy their hunger with them, but the shepherds refused to have business dealings with them, saying, " Are the sheep ours, or does the cattle belong to us, that we could part with them for money?" Seeing that they could not gain their point by kindness, the Ephraimites used force. The outcries of the shepherds brought the people of Gath to their aid. A violent encounter, lasting a whole day, took place between the Israelites and the Philistines. The people of Gath realized that alone they would not be able to offer successful resistance to the

Ephraimites, and they summoned the people of the other
Philistine cities to join them. The following day an army
of forty thousand stood ready to oppose the Ephraimites.
Reduced in strength, as they were, by their three days' fast,
they were exterminated root and branch. Only ten of them
escaped with their bare life, and returned to Egypt, to bring
Ephraim word of the disaster 'that had overtaken his pos-
terity, and he mourned many days.

This abortive attempt of the Ephraimites to leave Egypt
was the first occasion for oppressing Israel. Thereafter the
Egyptians exercised force and vigilance to keep them in
their land. As for the disaster of the Ephraimites, it was
well-merited punishment, because they had paid no heed
to the wish of their father Joseph, who had adjured his
descendants solemnly on his deathbed not to think of quit-
ting the land until the true redeemer should appear. Their
death was followed by disgrace, for their bodies lay unburied for many years on the battlefield near Gath, and the
purpose of God in directing the Israelites to choose the
longer route from Egypt to Canaan, was to spare them the
sight of those dishonored corpses. Their courage might
have deserted them, and out of apprehension of sharing the
fate of their brethren they might have hastened back to the
land of slavery."

PHARAOH PURSUES THE HEBREWS

When Pharaoh permitted Israel to depart, he was under
the impression that they were going only a three days'
journey into the wilderness for the purpose of offering
sacrifices. He sent officers with them, whose duty was to

bring them back at the appointed time. The exodus took place on a Thursday. On the following Sunday the king's watchers noticed that the Israelites, so far from preparing for a return, were making arrangements looking to a long sojourn in the desert. They remonstrated and urged them to go back. The Israelites maintained that Pharaoh had dismissed them for good, but the officers would not be put off with their mere assertions. They said, " Willy-nilly, you will have to do as the powers that be command." To such arrogance the Israelites would not submit, and they fell upon the officers, slaying some and wounding others. The maimed survivors went back to Egypt, and reported the contumacy of the Israelites to Pharaoh. Meantime Moses, who did not desire the departure of his people to have the appearance of flight before the Egyptians, gave the signal to turn back to Pi-hahiroth. Those of little faith among the Israelites tore their hair and their garments in desperation, though Moses assured them that by the word of God they were free men, and no longer slaves to Pharaoh.[12] Accordingly, they retraced their steps to Pi-hahiroth, where two rectangular rocks form an opening, within which the great sanctuary of Baal-zephon was situated. The rocks are shaped like human figures, the one a man and the other a woman, and they were not chiselled by human hands, but by the Creator Himself. The place had been called Pithom in earlier times, but later, on account of the idols set up there, it received the name Hahiroth. Of set purpose God had left Baal-zephon uninjured, alone of all the Egyptian idols. He wanted the Egyptian people to think that this idol was possessed of exceeding might, which it exercised to prevent

the Israelites from journeying on. To confirm them in their
illusory belief, God caused wild beasts to obstruct the road
to the wilderness, and they took it for granted that their
idol Baal-zephon had ordained their appearance.¹³

Pi-hahiroth was famous, besides, on account of the treasures heaped up there. The wealth of the world which Joseph had acquired through the sale of the corn he had stored
up during the seven years of plenty, he had divided into
three parts. The first part he surrendered to Pharaoh. The
second part he concealed in the wilderness, where it was
found by Korah, though it disappeared again, not to come
to view until the Messianic time, and then it will be for the
benefit of the pious. The third part Joseph hid in the sanctuary of Baal-zephon, whence the Hebrews carried it off as
booty.¹⁴

When Amalek and the magicians brought the information
to Pharaoh, that the Israelites had resolved not to return to
Egypt, his heart and the heart of his whole people turned
against them. The very counsellors that had persuaded him
to dismiss the children of Israel spake now as follows: "If
we had only been smitten with the plagues, we could have
resigned ourselves to our fate. Or if, besides being smitten
with the plagues, we had been compelled to let the Hebrews
depart from the land, that, too, we could have borne with
patience. But to be smitten with the plagues, to be compelled to let our slaves depart from us, and to sit by and see
them go off with our riches, that is more than we can
endure."

Now that the children of Israel had gone from them, the
Egyptians recognized how valuable an element they had

been in their country. In general, the time of the exodus of
Israel was disastrous for their former masters. In addition
to losing their dominion over the Israelites, the Egyptians
had to deal with mutinies that broke out among many other
nations tributary to them, for hitherto Pharaoh had been the
ruler of the whole world. The king resorted to blandish-
ments and promises, to induce the people to make war
against the Israelites, saying, " As a rule the army marches
forth first, and the king follows in security, but I will precede you; and as a rule the king has the first choice of the
booty, and as much of it as he desires, but I will take no
more than any one of you, and on my return from the war I
will divide my treasures of silver, gold, and precious stones
among you."

In his zeal Pharaoh did not wait to have his chariot made
ready for him, he did it with his own hands, and his nobles
followed his example.[15] Samael granted Pharaoh assistance,
putting six hundred chariots manned with his own hosts at
his disposal.[16] These formed the vanguard, and they were
joined by all the Egyptians, with their vast assemblages of
chariots and warriors, no less than three hundred of their
men to one of the children of Israel, each equipped with
their different sorts of weapons. The general custom was
for two charioteers to take turns at driving a car, but to
overtake the Israelites more surely and speedily, Pharaoh
ordered three to be assigned to each. The result was that
they covered in one day the ground which it had taken the
Israelites three to traverse.

The mind of the Egyptians was in no wise directed toward
spoil and plunder in this expedition. Their sole and deter-

mined purpose was to exterminate Israel, kith and kin. As
the heathen lay great stress upon omens when they are about
to start out on a campaign, God caused all their preparations
to proceed smoothly, without the slightest untoward circumstance. Everything pointed to a happy issue.[17] Pharaoh,
himself an adept in magic, had a presentiment that dire misfortune would befall the children of Israel in the wilderness,
that they would lose Moses there, and there the whole generation that had departed from Egypt would find its grave.
Therefore he spoke to Dathan and Abiram, who remained
behind in Egypt, saying: " Moses is leading them, but he
himself knows not whither. Verily, the congregation of
Israel will lift up their voice in the wilderness, and cry, and
there they will be destroyed." He thought naturally that
these visions had reference to an imminent future, to the
time of his meeting with his dismissed slaves. But his error
was profound—he was hurrying forward to his own
destruction.[18]

When he reached the sanctuary of Baal-zephon, Pharaoh,
in his joy at finding him spared while all the other idols in
Egypt had been annihilated, lost no time, but hastened to
offer sacrifices to him, and he was comforted, " for," he
said, " Baal-zephon approves my purpose of drowning the
children of Israel in the sea." [19]

When the Israelites beheld the huge detachments of the
Egyptian army moving upon them, and when they considered that in Migdol there were other troops stationed, besides, more, indeed, than their own numbers, men, women,
and children all told, great terror overwhelmed them.[20]
What affrighted them most, was the sight of the Angel of

Egypt darting through the air as he flew to the assistance of the people under his tutelage. They turned to Moses, saying: " What hast thou done to us? Now they will re-quite us for all that hath happened—that their first-born were smitten, and that we ran off with their money, which was thy fault, for thou didst bid us borrow gold and silver from our Egyptian neighbors and depart with their property."

The situation of the Israelites was desperate. Before them was the sea, behind them the Egyptians, on both sides the wild beasts of the desert.[21] The wicked among them spoke to Moses, saying, " While we were in Egypt, we said to thee and to Aaron, ' The Lord look upon you, and judge, because ye have made our savor to be abhorred in the eyes of Pharaoh and in the eyes of his servants, to put a sword in their hand to slay us.' Then there died many of our brethren during the days of darkness, which was worse than the bondage in which the Egyptians kept us. Nevertheless our fate in the desert will be sadder than theirs. They at least were mourned, and their bodies were buried, but our corpses will lie exposed, consumed in the day by drought and by frost in the night."

Moses in his wisdom knew how to pacify the thousands and myriads under his leadership. He impressed them with the words, " Fear ye not, stand still, and see the salvation of the Lord." " When will His salvation come? " questioned the people, and he told them it would appear the following day, but they protested, " We cannot wait until to-morrow." Then Moses prayed to God, and the Lord showed him the angel hosts standing ready to hasten to the assistance of the people.[22]

They were not agreed as to what they were to do. There were four contending parties. The opinion of the first party was that they seek death by drowning in the sea; of the second, that they return to Egypt; the third was in favor of a pitched battle with the enemy, and the fourth thought it would be a good plan to intimidate the Egyptians by noise and a great hubbub. To the first Moses said, " Stand still, and see the salvation of the Lord;" to the second, " The Egyptians whom ye have seen to-day, ye shall see them again no more forever;" to the third, " The Lord shall fight for you;" and to the fourth, " Ye shall hold your peace." " What, then, shall we do? " these asked their leader, and Moses answered them, saying, " Ye shall bless, praise, extol, adore, and glorify Him that is the Lord of war! " Instead of the sword and the five sorts of arms which they bore, they made use of their mouth, and it was of greater avail than all possible weapons of war. The Lord hearkened unto their prayer, for which He had but been waiting.[23]

Moses also addressed himself to God, saying: " O Lord of the world! I am like the shepherd who, having undertaken to pasture a flock, has been heedless enough to drive his sheep to the edge of a precipice, and then is in despair how to get them down again. Pharaoh is behind my flock Israel, in the south is Baal-zephon, in the north Migdol, and before us the sea lies spread out.[24] Thou knowest, O Lord, that it is beyond human strength and human contrivance to surmount the difficulties standing in our way. Thine alone is the work of procuring deliverance for this army, which left Egypt at Thy appointment. We despair of all other assistance or device, and we have recourse only to our hope in Thee. If there be any escape possible, we look up to Thy providence to accomplish it for us." [35] With such words Moses continued to make fervent supplication to God to succor Israel in their need. But God cut short his prayer, saying: "Moses, My children are in distress—the sea blocks the way before them, the enemy is in hot pursuit after them, and thou standest here and prayest. Sometimes long prayer is good, but sometimes it is better to be brief. If I gathered the waters together unto one place, and let the dry land appear for Adam, a single human being, should I not do the same for this holy congregation? I will save them if only for the sake of the merits of Abraham, who stood ready to sacrifice his son Isaac unto Me, and for the sake of My promise to Jacob. The sun and the moon are witnesses that I will cleave the sea for the seed of the children of Israel, who deserve My help for going after Me in the wilderness unquestioningly. Do thou but see to it that they abandon their evil thought of returning to Egypt, and then it will not be necessary to turn to Me and entreat My help." [36]

Moses, however, was still very much troubled in mind, on account of Samael, who had not left off lodging accusations before God against Israel since the exodus from Egypt. The Lord adopted the same procedure in dealing with the accuser as the experienced shepherd, who, at the moment of transferring his sheep across a stream, was faced by a ravening wolf. The shepherd threw a strong ram to the wolf, and while the two engaged in combat, the rest of the flock was carried across the water, and then the shepherd returned and snatched the wolf's supposed prey away from him.

Samael said to the Lord: "Up to this time the children of Israel were idol worshippers, and now Thou proposest so great a thing as dividing the sea for them?" What did the Lord do? He surrendered Job to Samael, saying, "While he busies himself with Job, Israel will pass through the sea unscathed, and as soon as they are in safety, I will rescue Job from the hands of Samael." ³⁷

Israel had other angel adversaries, besides. Uzza, the tutelary Angel of the Egyptians, appeared before God, and said, "O Lord of the world! I have a suit with this nation which Thou hast brought forth out of Egypt. If it seemeth well to Thee, let their angel Michael appear, and contend with me before Thee." The Lord summoned Michael, and Uzza stated his charges against Israel: "O Lord of the world! Thou didst decree concerning this people of Israel that it shall be held in bondage by my people, the Egyptians, for a period of four hundred years. But they had dominion over them only eighty-six years, therefore the time of their going forth hath not yet arrived. If it be Thy will, give me permission to take them back to Egypt, that they may continue in slavery for the three hundred and fourteen years that are left, and Thy word be fulfilled. As Thou art immutable, so let Thy decree be immutable!"

Michael was silent, for he knew not how to controvert these words, and it seemed as if Uzza had won his suit. But the Lord Himself espoused the cause of Israel, and He said to Uzza: "The duty of serving thy nation was laid upon My children only on account of an unseemly word uttered by Abraham. When I spoke to him, saying, 'I am the Lord that brought thee out of Ur of the Chaldees, to give thee this land to inherit it,' he made answer, 'Whereby shall I know that I shall inherit it?' Therefore did I say to him, 'Thy seed shall be a stranger.' But it is well-known and manifest before Me that they were 'strangers' from the day of Isaac's birth, and, reckoning thence, the period of four hundred years has elapsed, and thou hast no right to keep My children in bondage any longer." [28]

THE SEA DIVIDED

God spake to Moses, saying, "Why dost thou stand here praying? My children's prayer has anticipated thine. For thee there is naught to do but lift up thy rod and stretch out thine hand over the sea, and divide it." Moses replied: "Thou commandest me to divide the sea, and lay bare the dry ground in the midst of it, and yet Thou didst Thyself make it a perpetual decree, that the sand shall be placed for the bound of the sea." And again God spake to Moses: "Thou hast not read the beginning of the Torah. I, yea I, did speak, 'Let the waters under the heaven be gathered together unto one place, and let the dry land appear,' and at that time I made the condition that the waters shall divide before Israel. [29] Take the rod that I gave unto thee, and go to the sea upon Mine errand, and speak thus: 'I am the messenger sent by the Creator of the world! Uncover thy paths, O sea, for My children, that they may go through the midst of thee on dry ground.'"

Moses spoke to the sea as God had bidden him, but it replied, "I will not do according to thy words, for thou art only a man born of woman, and, besides, I am three days older than thou, O man, for I was brought forth on the third day of creation, and thou on the sixth." Moses lost no time, but carried back to God the words the sea had spoken, and the Lord said: "Moses, what does a master do with an intractable servant?" "He beats him with a rod," said Moses. "Do thus!" ordered God. "Lift up thy rod, and stretch out thine hand over the sea, and divide it." [80]

Thereupon Moses raised up his rod—the rod that had been created at the very beginning of the world, on which were graven in plain letters the great and exalted Name, the names of the ten plagues inflicted upon the Egyptians, and the names of the three Fathers, the six Mothers, and the twelve tribes of Jacob. This rod he lifted up, and stretched it out over the sea. [81]

The sea, however, continued in its perverseness, and Moses entreated God to give His command direct to it. But God refused, saying: "Were I to command the sea to divide, it would never again return to its former estate. Therefore, do thou convey My order to it, that it be not drained dry forever. But I will let a semblance of My strength accompany thee, and that will compel its obedience." When the sea saw the Strength of God at the right hand of Moses, it spoke to the earth, saying, "Make hollow places for me, that I may hide myself therein before the Lord of all created things, blessed be He." Noticing the terror of the sea, Moses said to it: "For a whole day I spoke to thee at the bidding of the Holy One, who desired thee to divide, but thou didst refuse to pay heed to my words; even when I showed thee my rod, thou didst remain obdurate. What hath happened now that thou skippest hence?" The sea replied, "I am fleeing, not before thee, but before the Lord of all created things, that His Name be magnified in all the earth." [32]   And the waters of the Red Sea divided, and not they alone, but all the water in heaven and on earth, in whatever vessel it was, in cisterns, in wells, in caves, in casks, in pitchers, in drinking cups, and in glasses, and none of these waters returned to their former estate until Israel had passed through the sea on dry land. [33]

The angel Gabriel was eager to drown the Egyptians during the same night, but God bade him wait until early the next day, until the hour of the morning watch, when Abraham had made himself ready to set out for the sacrifice of his son. Gabriel succeeded, however, in holding back the turbulent waters about to sweep over Israel. To the wall of water on the right, he called, " Beware of Israel, who will receive the law in time to come from the right hand of the Lord," and turning to the wall of water on the left, he said, " Beware of Israel, who will wind the phylacteries about their left hand in time to come." The water behind he admonished, " Beware of Israel, who will let the Ẓiẓit drop down upon their back in time to come," and to the water towering in front of them, he called, " Beware of Israel, who bear the sign of the covenant upon their bodies." [34]

God caused the sea to go back by a strong east wind, the wind He always makes use of when He chastises the nations. The same east wind had brought the deluge; it had laid the tower of Babel in ruins; it was to cause the destruction of Samaria, Jerusalem, and Tyre; and it will, in future, be the instrument for castigating Rome drunken with pleasure; and likewise the sinners in Gehenna are punished by means of this east wind. All night long God made it to blow over the sea. To prevent the enemy from inflicting harm upon the Israelites, He enveloped the Egyptians in profound darkness, so impenetrable it could be felt, and none could move or change his posture. He that sat when it fell could not arise from his place, and he that stood could not sit down. Nevertheless, the Egyptians could see that the Israelites were surrounded by bright light, and were enjoying a banquet where they stood, and when they tried to speed darts and arrows against them, the missiles were caught up by the cloud and by the angels hovering between the two camps, and no harm came to Israel.[35]

The Passage through the Red Sea

On the morning after the eventful night, though the sea was not yet made dry land, the Israelites, full of trust in God, were ready to cast themselves into its waters. The tribes contended with one another for the honor of being the first to jump. Without awaiting the outcome of the wordy strife, the tribe of Benjamin sprang in, and the princes of Judah were so incensed at having been deprived of pre-eminence in danger that they pelted the Benjamites with stones. God knew that the Judæans and the Benjamites were animated by a praiseworthy purpose. The ones like the others desired but to magnify the Name of God, and He rewarded both tribes: in Benjamin's allotment the Shekinah took up her residence, and the royalty of Israel was conferred upon Judah.

When God saw the two tribes in the waves of the sea, He called upon Moses, and said: " My beloved are in danger of drowning, and thou standest by and prayest. Bid Israel go forward, and thou lift up thy rod over the sea, and divide it." Thus it happened, and Israel passed through the sea with its waters cleft in twain.

The dividing of the sea was but the first of ten miracles connected with the passage of the Israelites through it. The others were that the waters united in a vault above their heads; twelve paths opened up, one for each of the tribes; the water became as transparent as glass, and each tribe could see the others; the soil underfoot was dry, but it changed into clay when the Egyptians stepped upon it; the walls of water were transformed into rocks, against which the Egyptians were thrown and dashed to death, while before the Israelites they crumbled away into bits. Through the brackish sea flowed a stream of soft water, at which the Israelites could slake their thirst; and, finally, the tenth wonder was, that this drinking water was congealed in the heart of the sea as soon as they had satisfied their need.[36]

And there were other miracles, besides. The sea yielded the Israelites whatever their hearts desired. If a child cried as it lay in the arms of its mother, she needed but to stretch out her hand and pluck an apple or some other fruit and quiet it.[37] The waters were piled up to the height of sixteen hundred miles, and they could be seen by all the nations of the earth.[38]

The great wonder of Israel's passage through the sea took place in the presence of the three Fathers and the six Mothers, for God had fetched them out of their graves to the shores of the Red Sea, to be witnesses of the marvellous deeds wrought in behalf of their children.[39]

Wonderful as were the miracles connected with the rescue

of the Israelites from the waters of the sea, those performed when the Egyptians were drowned were no less remarkable. First of all God felt called upon to defend Israel's cause before Uzza, the Angel of the Egyptians, who would not allow his people to perish in the waters of the sea. He appeared on the spot at the very moment when God wanted to drown the Egyptians, and he spake: "O Lord of the world! Thou art called just and upright, and before Thee there is no wrong, no forgetting, no respecting of persons. Why, then, dost Thou desire to make my children perish in the sea? Canst Thou say that my children drowned or slew a single one of Thine? If it be on account of the rigorous slavery that my children imposed upon Israel, then consider that Thy children have received their wages, in that they took their silver and golden vessels from them."

Then God convoked all the members of His celestial family, and He spake to the angel hosts: " Judge ye in truth between Me and yonder Uzza, the Angel of the Egyptians. At the first I brought a famine upon his people, and I appointed My friend Joseph over them, who saved them through his sagacity, and they all became his slaves. Then My children went down into their land as strangers, in consequence of the famine, and they made the children of Israel to serve with rigor in all manner of hard work there is in the world. They groaned on account of their bitter service, and their cry rose up to Me, and I sent Moses and Aaron, My faithful messengers, to Pharaoh. When they came before the king of Egypt, they spake to him, ' Thus said the Lord, the God of Israel, Let My people go, that they may hold a feast unto Me in the wilderness.' In the presence of the kings of the East and of the West, that sinner began to boast, saying: 'Who is the Lord, that I should hearken unto His voice, to let Israel go? Why comes He not before me, like all the kings of the world, and why doth He not bring me a present like the others? This God of whom you speak, I know Him not at all. Wait and let me search my lists, and see whether I can find His Name.' But his servants said, 'We have heard that He is the son of the wise, the son of ancient kings.' Then Pharaoh asked My messengers, 'What are the works of this God?' and they replied, 'He is the God of gods, the Lord of lords, who created the heaven and the earth.' But Pharaoh doubted their words, and said, 'There is no God in all the world that can accomplish such works beside me, for I made myself, and I made the Nile river.' Because he denied Me thus, I sent ten plagues upon him, and he was compelled to let My children go. Yet, in spite of all, he did not leave off from his wicked ways, and he tried to bring them back under his bondage. Now, seeing all that hath happened to him, and that he will not acknowledge Me as God and Lord, does he not deserve to be drowned in the sea with his host?"

The celestial family called out when the Lord had ended His defense, "Thou hast every right to drown him in the sea!"

Uzza heard their verdict, and he said: "O Lord of all worlds! I know that my people deserve the punishment Thou hast decreed, but may it please Thee to deal with them according to Thy attribute of mercy, and take pity upon the work of Thy hands, for Thy tender mercies are over all Thy works!"

Almost the Lord had yielded to Uzza's entreaties, when Michael gave a sign to Gabriel that made him fly to Egypt swiftly and fetch thence a brick for which a Hebrew child had been used as mortar. Holding this incriminating object in his hand, Gabriel stepped into the presence of God, and said: " O Lord of the world! Wilt Thou have compassion with the accursed nation that has slaughtered Thy children so cruelly? " Then the Lord turned Himself away from His attribute of mercy, and seating Himself upon His throne of justice He resolved to drown the Egyptians in the sea."

The first upon whom judgment was executed was the Angel of Egypt—Uzza was thrown into the sea." A similar fate overtook Rahab, the Angel of the Sea, with his hosts. Rahab had made intercession before God in behalf of the Egyptians. He had said: " Why shouldst Thou drown the Egyptians? Let it suffice the Israelites that Thou hast saved them out of the hand of their masters." At that God dealt Rahab and his army a blow, under which they staggered and fell dead, and then He cast their corpses in the sea, whence its unpleasant odor."

THE DESTRUCTION OF THE EGYPTIANS

At the moment when the last of the Israelites stepped out of the bed of the sea, the first of the Egyptians set foot into it, but in the same instant the waters surged back into their wonted place, and all the Egyptians perished."

But drowning was not the only punishment decreed upon them by God. He undertook a thoroughgoing campaign against them. When Pharaoh was preparing to persecute the Israelites, he asked his army which of the saddle beasts was the swiftest runner, that one he would use, and they said: "There is none swifter than thy piebald mare, whose like is to be found nowhere in the world." Accordingly, Pharaoh mounted the mare, and pursued after the Israelites seaward. And while Pharaoh was inquiring of his army as to the swiftest animal to mount, God was questioning the angels as to the swiftest creature to use to the detriment of Pharaoh. And the angels answered: "O Lord of the world! All things are Thine, and all are Thine handiwork. Thou knowest well, and it is manifest before Thee, that among all Thy creatures there is none so quick as the wind that comes from under the throne of Thy glory," and the Lord flew swiftly upon the wings of the wind."

The angels now advanced to support the Lord in His war against the Egyptians. Some brought swords, some arrows, and some spears. But God warded them off, saying, "Away! I need no help!"" The arrows sped by Pharaoh against the children of Israel were answered by the Lord with fiery darts directed against the Egyptians. Pharaoh's army advanced with gleaming swords, and the Lord sent out lightnings that discomfited the Egyptians. Pharaoh hurled missiles, and the Lord discharged hailstones and coals of fire against him. With trumpets, sackbuts, and horns the Egyptians made their assault, and the Lord thundered in the heavens, and the Most High uttered His voice. In vain the Egyptians marched forward in orderly battle array; the Lord deprived them of their standards, and they were thrown into wild confusion." To lure them into the water, the Lord caused fiery steeds to swim out upon the sea, and the horses of the Egyptians followed them, each with a rider upon his back."

Now the Egyptians tried to flee to their land in their chariots drawn by she-mules. As they had treated the children of Israel in a way contrary to nature, so the Lord treated them now. Not the she-mules pulled the chariots, but the chariots, though fire from heaven had consumed their wheels, dragged the men and the beasts into the water. The chariots were laden with silver, gold, and all sorts of costly things, which the river Pishon, as it flows forth from Paradise, carries down into the Gihon. Thence the treasures float into the Red Sea, and by its waters they were tossed into the chariots of the Egyptians. It was the wish of God that these treasures should come into the possession of Israel, and for this reason He caused the chariots to roll down into the sea, and the sea in turn to cast them out upon the opposite shore, at the feet of the Israelites.[48]

And the Lord fought against the Egyptians also with the pillar of cloud and the pillar of fire. The former made the soil miry, and the mire was heated to the boiling point by the latter, so that the hoofs of the horses dropped from their feet, and they could not budge from the spot.[49]

The anguish and the torture that God brought upon the Egyptians at the Red Sea caused them by far more excruciating pain than the plagues they had endured in Egypt, for at the sea He delivered them into the hands of the Angels of Destruction, who tormented them pitilessly. Had God not endowed the Egyptians with a double portion of strength, they could not have stood the pain a single moment.[50]

The last judgment executed upon the Egyptians corresponded to the wicked designs harbored against Israel by the three different parties among them when they set out in

pursuit of their liberated slaves. The first party had said,
"We will bring Israel back to Egypt;" the second had said,
"We will strip them bare," and the third had said, "We
will slay them all." The Lord blew upon the first with His
breath, and the sea covered them; the second party He shook
into the sea, and the third He pitched into the depths of the
abyss." He tossed them about as lentils are shaken up and
down in a saucepan; the upper ones are made to fall to the
bottom, the lower ones fly to the top. This was the experience of the Egyptians. And worse still, first the rider and
his beast were whisked high up in the air, and then the two
together, the rider sitting upon the back of the beast, were
hurled to the bottom of the sea."

The Egyptians endeavored to save themselves from the
sea by conjuring charms, for they were great magicians.
Of the ten measures of magic allotted to the world, they had
taken nine for themselves. And, indeed, they succeeded for
the moment; they escaped out of the sea. But immediately
the sea said to itself, "How can I allow the pledge entrusted
to me by God to be taken from me?" And the water rushed
after the Egyptians, and dragged back every man of them.

Among the Egyptians were the two arch-magicians
Jannes and Jambres. They made wings for themselves,
with which they flew up to heaven. They also said to Pharaoh: "If God Himself hath done this thing, we can effect
naught. But if this work has been put into the hands of His
angels, then we will shake His lieutenants into the sea."
They proceeded at once to use their magic contrivances,
whereby they dragged the angels down. These cried up to
God: "Save us, O God, for the waters are come in unto

our soul! Speak Thy word that will cause the magicians to
drown in the mighty waters." And Gabriel cried to God,
" By the greatness of Thy glory dash Thy adversaries to
pieces." Hereupon God bade Michael go and execute judgment upon the two magicians. The archangel seized hold of
Jannes and Jambres by the locks of their hair, and he shat-
tered them against the surface of the water.⁵⁶

Thus all the Egyptians were drowned. Only one was
spared—Pharaoh himself. When the children of Israel
raised their voices to sing a song of praise to God at the
shores of the Red Sea, Pharaoh heard it as he was jostled
hither and thither by the billows, and he pointed his finger
heavenward, and called out: " I believe in Thee, O God!
Thou art righteous, and I and My people are wicked, and I
acknowledge now that there is no god in the world beside
Thee." Without a moment's delay, Gabriel descended and
laid an iron chain about Pharaoh's neck, and holding him
securely, he addressed him thus: " Villain! Yesterday
thou didst say, ' Who is the Lord that I should hearken to
His voice?' and now thou sayest, ' The Lord is righteous.' "
With that he let him drop into the depths of the sea, and
there he tortured him for fifty days, to make the power of
God known to him. At the end of the time he installed him
as king of the great city of Nineveh, and after the lapse of
many centuries, when Jonah came to Nineveh, and prophesied the overthrow of the city on account of the evil done by
the people, it was Pharaoh who, seized by fear and terror,
covered himself with sackcloth, and sat in ashes, and with
his own mouth made proclamation and published this decree
through Nineveh: " Let neither man nor beast, herd nor

flock, taste anything; let them not feed nor drink water; for I know there is no god beside Him in all the world, all His words are truth, and all His judgments are true and faithful."

Pharaoh never died, and never will die. He always stands at the portal of hell, and when the kings of the nations enter, he makes the power of God known to them at once, in these words: "O ye fools! Why have ye not learnt knowledge from me? I denied the Lord God, and He brought ten plagues upon me, sent me to the bottom of the sea, kept me there for fifty days, released me then, and brought me up. Thus I could not but believe in Him." [54]

God caused the Egyptians to be washed ashore in their death struggle. There were four reasons for this. The Israelites were not to say that as they themselves had escaped, so also the Egyptians had passed through the sea dryshod, only the latter had gone in another direction, and therefore had vanished from sight. The Egyptians, on the other hand, were not to think that the children of Israel had been drowned in the sea like themselves. In the third place, the Israelites were to have, as their booty, the silver, gold, and other precious things with which the Egyptians were decked; and, finally, the Israelites were to enjoy the satisfaction of seeing their enemies suffer. With their finger they could point them out one by one, saying, "This one was my taskmaster, who beat me with those fists of his at which the dogs are now gnawing, and yonder Egyptian, the dogs are chewing the feet with which he kicked me."

As they lay on the shore in their last agony, they had to witness their own destruction and the victory of the Israelites, and they also beheld the suffering of their brethren that had remained behind in Egypt, for God poured out His punishment over the whole people, whether in Egypt or at the Red Sea.[55] As for the corpses by the shores of the sea, they did not remain unburied, the earth swallowed them, by way of reward for Pharaoh's having acknowledged the justice of the chastisement that had been inflicted upon king and people. Before their corpses had been disposed of in this way, there had been a quarrel between the earth and the sea. The sea said to the earth, "Take thy children unto thyself," and the earth retorted, "Keep those whom thou hast slain." The sea hesitated to do as the earth bade, for fear that God would demand them back on the day of judgment; and the earth hesitated, because it remembered with terror the curse that had been pronounced upon it for having sucked up Abel's blood. Only after God swore an oath, not to punish it for receiving the corpses of the Egyptians, would the earth swallow them.[56]

THE SONG AT THE SEA

Mighty is faith, for the spirit of God came upon the Israelites as a reward for their trust in God, and in His servant Moses; and it was in this exaltation that they sang to the Lord a song[57] that moved Him to grant forgiveness for all their sins.[58] This song was the second of the nine songs that in the course of history Israel sang to their God. They assembled to sing the first in Egypt, on the night when they were freed from captivity; their second was the song of triumph by the Red Sea; their third, when the well sprang up in the wilderness; Moses sang the fourth before his death;

the fifth was Joshua's song after his victory over the five
Amorite kings; Deborah and Barak sang the sixth when they
conquered Sisera; the seventh was David's psalm of thanksgiving to God for his deliverance out of the hand of all his
enemies; the eighth was Solomon's song at the dedication of
the Temple; the ninth Jehoshaphat sang as, trusting in God,
he went to battle against the Moabites and the Ammonites.
The tenth and last song, however, will be that grand and
mighty song, when Israel will raise their voice in triumph at
their future deliverance, for that will be the final release of
Israel for all time.⁵⁹

When Israel prepared to sound their praises to God for
delivering them from destruction in the Red Sea, God, to
show His recognition of Israel's fulfilment of the token of
the Abrahamic covenant, bade the angels who came to intone
their song, wait: "Let My children sing first," He said.
This incident with the angels is like the story of that king
who, upon returning from a victorious campaign, was told
that his son and his servant were waiting with wreaths in
their hands, and were asking who should first crown him.
The king said, "O ye fools, to question if my servant should
walk before my son! No, let my son come first!"

This was the second time that the angels were obliged to
retire before Israel. When Israel stood by the Red Sea,
before them the rolling waters, and behind them the hosts of
Egypt, then, too, the angels appeared, to sing their daily song
of praise to the Lord, but God called to them, "Forbear!
My children are in distress, and you would sing!"

But even after the men had completed their song, it was not
yet given to the angels to raise their voices, for after the men

followed the women of Israel, and only then came the turn of the angels. Then they began to murmur, and said, " Is it not enough that the men have preceded us? Shall the women come before us also? " But God replied, " As surely as ye live, so it is." ⁶⁰

At first Israel requested their leader Moses to begin the song, but he declined, saying, " No, ye shall begin it, for it is a greater mark of honor to be praised by the multitude than by a single one." At once the people sang: " We will glorify the Eternal, for He has shown us signs and tokens. When the Egyptians passed the decree against us, and said, ' Every son that is born ye shall cast into the river,' our mothers went into the field, and Thou didst bid a sleep to fall upon them, and they bore us without any pain; and the angels descended from Heaven, washed and anointed us, and robed us in many-colored silken garments, and placed in our hands two lumps, one of butter and one of honey. When our mothers awoke and saw us washed, anointed, and clothed in silk, then they praised Thee, and said, ' Praised be God who has not turned His grace and His lasting love from the seed of our father Abraham; and now behold! they are in Thy hand, do with them as Thou wilt.' And they departed. When the Egyptians saw us, they approached to kill us, but Thou in Thy great mercy didst bid the earth swallow us and set us in another place, where we were not seen by the Egyptians, and lo! in this way didst Thou save us from their hand. When we grew up, we wandered in troops to Egypt, where each recognized his parents and his family. All this hast Thou done for us, therefore will we sing of Thee."

Thereupon Moses said: "Ye have given thanks to the Holy One, blessed be He, and now I will praise His name, for to me also has He shown signs and tokens. The Lord is my strength and my song, and He is become my salvation; He is my God, and I will prepare Him an habitation; my father's God, and I will exalt Him." [61]

The song by the Red Sea was as much the song of Moses as of all Israel, for the great leader counted as not less than all the other Israelites together, and, besides, [62] he had composed a large portion of the song. In virtue of the spirit of God that possessed them while they sang, Moses and the people mutually supplemented each other, so that, as soon as Moses spoke half the verse, the people repeated it, and linked the second complementary part to it. So Moses began with the half verse, "I will sing unto the Lord, for He hath triumphed gloriously," whereupon the people answered, "The horse and his rider hath He thrown into the sea." And in this wise developed the whole song. [63]

But not alone the adults took part in this song, even the sucklings dropped their mothers' breasts to join in singing; yea, even the embryos in the womb joined the melody, and the angels' voices swelled the song. [64] God so distinguished Israel during the passage through the Red Sea, that even the children beheld His glory, yea, even the woman slave saw more of the presence of God by the Red Sea than the Prophet Ezekiel was ever permitted to behold. [65]

They closed the song with the words: "Let us set the crown of glory upon the head of our Deliverer, who suffers all things to perish, but does not Himself decay, who changes all things, but is Himself unchanged. His is the diadem of

sovereignty, for He is the King of kings in this world, and
His is the sovereignty of the world to come; it is His and
will be His in all eternity." ⁶⁶ Thereupon Moses spake to
Israel, " Ye have seen all the signs, all miracles and works
of glory that the Holy One, blessed be He, hath wrought
for you, but even more will He do for you in the world to
come; for not like unto this world is the world of the hereafter; for in this world war and suffering, evil inclination,
Satan, and the Angel of Death hold sway; but in the future
world, there will be neither suffering nor enmity, neither
Satan nor the Angel of Death, neither groans nor oppression,
nor evil inclination." ⁶⁷

As Moses and the race that wandered from Egypt with
him sang a song to the Lord by the Red Sea, so shall they
sing again in the world to come. In the world to come, all
generations will pass before the Lord and will ask Him who
should first intone the song of praise, whereupon He will
reply: " In the past it was the generation of Moses that
offered up to me a song of praise. Let them do it now once
more, and as Moses conducted the song by the Red Sea, so
shall he do in the world of the hereafter." ⁶⁸

In other respects, too, it shall be in the world to come as
it was at the time of the song by the sea. For when Israel
intoned the song of praise, God put on a festive robe, on
which were embroidered all the promises for a happy future
to Israel. Among them were written: " Then shall thy
light break forth as the morning "; " Then said they among
the heathen. ' The Lord hath done great things for them,' "
and many similar promises. But when Israel sinned, God
rent the festive robe, and He will not restore it, or put it on,
until the coming of the future world. ⁶⁹

After the men had completed the song, the women under the guidance of Miriam sang the same song to the accompaniment of music and dancing. The Israelites had had perfect faith, that God would perform for them miracles and deeds of glory, hence they had provided themselves with timbrels and with flutes, that they might have them at hand to glorify the anticipated miracles.[10] Then Miriam said to the women, " Let us sing unto the Lord, for strength and sublimity are His ; He lords it over the lordly, and He resents presumption. He hurled Pharaoh's horses and chariots into the sea, and drowned them, because wicked Pharaoh in his presumption pursued God's people, Israel." [11]

THE AWFUL DESERT

Just as Israel had displayed sullenness and lack of faith upon approaching the sea, so did they upon leaving it. Hardly had they seen that the Egyptians met death in the waters of the sea, when they spoke to Moses, and said: " God has led us from Egypt only to grant us five tokens: To give us the wealth of Egypt, to let us walk in clouds of glory, to cleave the sea for us, to take vengeance on the Egyptians, and to let us sing Him a song of praise. Now that all this has taken place, let us return to Egypt." Moses answered: " The Eternal said, ' The Egyptians whom ye have seen to-day, ye shall see them again no more forever.' " But the people were not yet content, and said, " Now the Egyptians are all dead, and therefore we can return to Egypt." Then Moses said, " You must now redeem your pledge, for God said, ' When thou hast brought forth the people out of Egypt, ye shall serve God upon this mountain.' " Still the people remained headstrong, and without giving heed to Moses, they set out on the road to Egypt, under the guidance of an idol that they had brought with them out of Egypt, and had even retained during their passage through the sea. Only through sheer force was Moses able to restrain them from their sinful transgression.[12] This was the second of the ten temptations with which Israel tempted God during their wanderings through the desert.[13]

There was one other difficulty with the people that Moses had to overcome: The sea cast up many jewels, pearls, and other treasures that had belonged to the Egyptians, drowned in its waves, and Israel found it hard to tear themselves away from the spot that brought them such riches. Moses, however, said, " Do you really believe that the sea will continue to yield you pearls and jewels? "[14]

From the sea they passed to the desert Shur, a horrible and dreadful wilderness, full of snakes, lizards, and scorpions, extending over hundreds of miles. So deadly is the nature of the snakes that dwell in this desert, that if one of them merely glides over the shadow of a flying bird, the bird falls into pieces.[15] It was in this desert that the following happened to King Shapor: A cohort that he sent through this desert was swallowed by a snake, and the same fate overtook a second and a third cohort. Upon the advice of his sages, he then filled the hides of animals with hot coals wrapped in straw, and had these cast before the snake until it expired.[16]

It was then a proof of Israel's great faith in their God, that they obeyed Moses, and without murmur or delay followed him into this frightful wilderness.[17] Therefore did

God reward them for their trust in Him, for not only were
they not harmed by the snakes and scorpions during their
many years' stay in the desert, but they were even relieved
of the fear of the reptiles, for as soon as the snakes saw the
Israelites, they meekly lay down upon the sand." For three
days they marched through the desert, uncomplaining, but
when their supply of water gave out, the people murmured
against Moses, saying, "What shall we drink?" While
crossing through the Red Sea they had provided themselves
with water, for, miraculously, the sea flowed sweet for them;
and now when the supply was becoming exhausted, they
began to give expression to their dissatisfaction. On this
occasion they again betrayed their faintheartedness, for instead of seeking advice from their leader Moses, they began
to murmur against him and against God, even though at
present they had not yet suffered from lack of water. So
poorly did they stand the test to which God had put them,
for in fact the very ground upon which they trod had
running water beneath it, but they were not aware of this.
God had desired to see how they would act under these
conditions."

The people were all the more exasperated because their
joy, when they sighted the springs and hastened to draw
from them, turned to keenest disappointment when they
tasted of the water and found it bitter. These deluded hopes
cast them down spiritually as well as physically, and grieved
them, not so much for their own sakes as for those of their
young children, to whose pleas for water they could not
listen without tears. Some of the thoughtless and fickle of
faith among them uttered the accusation that even the former

kindness had been granted them not so much as a benefit, but rather with a view to the present and much greater privation. These said that death by the hand of the enemy is to be thrice preferred to perishing by thirst; for by the wise man, speedy and painless departure from life is in no way to be distinguished from immortality; the only real death, however, is slow and painful dying, for the dread lies not in being dead, but in dying.

While they indulged in these lamentations, Moses prayed to God to forgive the faint of heart their unseemly words, and, furthermore, to supply the general want.[60] Mindful of the distress of the people, Moses did not pray long, but uttered his request in a few words; and quickly, as he had prayed, was his prayer answered. God bade him take a piece of a laurel tree, write upon it the great and glorious name of God, and throw it into the water, whereupon the water would become drinkable and sweet.[61]

The ways of the Holy One, blessed be He, differ from the ways of man: Man turns bitter to sweet by the agency of some sweet stuff, but God transformed the bitter water through the bitter laurel tree. When Israel beheld this miracle, they asked forgiveness of their heavenly Father, and said: "O Lord of the world! We sinned against Thee when we murmured about the water."[62] Not through this miracle alone, however, has Marah become a significant spot for Israel, but, especially, because there God gave to Israel important precepts, like the Sabbath rest, marriage and civil laws, and said to the people: "If you will observe these statutes, you will receive many more, the Ten Commandments, the Halakot, and the Haggadot; the Torah, however,

will bring you happiness and life. If you will diligently
endeavor to walk through life uprightly, so that you will be
virtuous in your dealings with men, I will value it as if you
had fulfilled all commandments, and will put upon you none
of those diseases that I brought upon Egypt. If, however,
you will not be mindful of My laws, and will be visited by
diseases, then will I be your physician and will make you
well, for as soon as you will observe the laws, shall the diseases vanish." [83]

The cause for the want of water at Marah had been that
for three days the people had neglected the study of the
Torah, and it was for this reason that the prophets and
elders of Israel instituted the custom of reading from the
Torah on Saturday, Monday, and Thursday, at the public
service, so that three days might never again pass without a
reading from the Torah. [84]

From Marah they moved on to Elim. From a distance
palm trees made the place look inviting enough, but when
the people came close, they were again disappointed; there
were not more than three score and ten palm trees, and
these were of stunted growth owing to a lack of water, for
in spite of the presence of twelve wells of water, the soil was
so barren and sandy that the wells were not sufficient to
water it. [85] Here again the marvellous intercession of God in
favor of the fate of Israel is shown, for the scant supply of
water at Elim, which had hardly sufficed for seventy palm
trees, satisfied sixty myriads of the wandering people that
stayed there for several days. [86]

The men of understanding could at this place see a clear
allusion to the fortune of the people; for there are twelve

tribes of the people, each of which, if it prove God-fearing, will be a well of water, inasmuch as its piety will constantly and continually bring forth beautiful deeds; the leaders of the people, however, are seventy, and they recall the noble palm tree, for in outward appearance as well as in its fruits, it is the most beautiful of trees, whose seat of life does not lie buried deep in the roots, as with other plants, but soars high, set like the heart in the midst of its branches, by which it is surrounded as a queen under the protection of her body-guard. The soul of him who has tasted piety possesses a similar spirit; it has learned to look up and ascend, and itself ever busy with spiritual things and the investigation of Divine beauty, disdains earthly things, and considers them only as childish play, whereas that aspiration alone seems serious.[87]

It was at Elim, where, at the creation of the world, God had made the twelve wells of water, and the seventy palm trees, to correspond to the twelve tribes and the seventy elders of Israel, that Israel first took up the study of the law, for there they studied the laws given them at Marah.[88]

THE HEAVENLY FOOD

The bread which Israel had taken along out of Egypt sufficed for thirty-one days, and when they had consumed it, the whole congregation of the children of Israel murmured against their leader Moses. It was not only immediate want that oppressed them, but despair of a food supply for the future; for when they saw the vast, extensive, utterly barren wilderness before them, their courage gave way, and they said: " We migrated, expecting freedom, and now we are

not even free from the cares of subsistence; we are not, as
our leader promised, the happiest, but in truth the most
unfortunate of men. After our leader's words had keyed us
to the highest pitch of expectation, and had filled our ears
with vain hopes, he tortures us with famine and does not
provide even the necessary food. With the name of a new
settlement he has deceived this great multitude; after he had
succeeded in leading us from a well-known to an uninhabited
land, he now plans to send us to the underworld, the last
road of life." 'Would to God we had died by the hand of the
Lord during the three days of darkness in the land of Egypt,
when we sat by the flesh-pots, and when we did eat bread to
the full.' " In their exasperation they spoke untruths, for in
reality they had suffered from want of food in Egypt, too,
as the Egyptians had not given them enough to eat.⁹⁰

In spite of the railings against him, Moses was not so
much indignant about their words as about the fickleness of
the people. After those many quite extraordinary experiences they had no right to expect merely the natural and
the probable, but should cheerfully have trusted him; for,
truly, in the sight of all, they had been shown the most
tangible proofs of his reliability. When, on the other hand,
Moses considered their distress, he forgave them; for he
told himself that a multitude is by nature fickle, and allows
itself to be easily influenced by impressions of the moment,
which cast the past into oblivion, and engender despair for
the future.⁹¹

God also forgave the unworthy conduct of Israel, and
instead of being angry with them because they murmured
against Him, when it should have been their duty to pray to

Him, He was ready to grant them aid, saying to Moses, " They act according to their lights, and I will act according to Mine; not later than to-morrow morning manna will descend from heaven."

As a reward for Abraham's readiness, in answer to the summons to sacrifice Isaac, when he said, " Here am I," God promised manna to the descendants of Abraham with the same words, " Here am I." In the same way, during their wanderings through the wilderness, God repaid the descendants of Abraham for what their ancestor had done by the angels who visited him. He himself had fetched bread for them, and likewise God Himself caused bread to rain from heaven; he himself ran before them on their way, and likewise God moved before Israel; he had water fetched for them, and likewise God, through Moses, caused water to flow from the rock; he bade them seek shade under the tree, and likewise God had a cloud spread over Israel.[92] Then God spoke to Moses: " I will immediately reveal Myself without delay; mindful of the services of Abraham, Isaac, and Jacob, ' I will rain bread from My treasure in heaven for you; and the people shall go out and gather a certain rate every day.' "

There were good reasons for not exceeding a day's ration in the daily downpour of manna. First, that they might be spared the need of carrying it on their wanderings; secondly, that they might daily receive it hot; and, lastly, that they might day by day depend upon God's aid, and in this way exercise themselves in faith.[93]

While the people were still abed, God fulfilled their desire, and rained down manna for them. For this food had been created on the second day of creation,[94] and ground by the angels, it later descended for the wanderers in the wilderness.[95] The mills are stationed in the third heaven, where manna is constantly being ground for the future use of the pious;[96] for in the future world manna will be set before them.[97] Manna deserves its name, "bread of the angels," not only because it is prepared by them, but because those who partake of it become equal to the angels in strength, and, furthermore, like them, have no need of easing themselves, as manna is entirely dissolved in the body. Not until they sinned, did they have to ease themselves like ordinary mortals.[98]

Manna also showed its heavenly origin in the miraculous flavor it possessed. There was no need of cooking or baking it, nor did it require any other preparation, and still it contained the flavor of every conceivable dish. One had only to desire a certain dish, and no sooner had he thought of it, than manna had the flavor of the dish desired. The same food had a different taste to every one who partook of it, according to his age; to the little children it tasted like milk, to the strong youths like bread, to the old men like honey, to the sick like barley steeped in oil and honey.[99]

As miraculous as the taste of manna was its descent from heaven. First came a north wind to sweep the floor of the desert; then a rain to wash it quite clean; then dew descended upon it, which was congealed into a solid substance by the wind, that it might serve as a table for the heaven-descending manna, and this frozen dew glistened and sparkled like gold.[100] But, that no insects or vermin might settle on the manna, the frozen dew formed not only a tablecloth, but also a cover for the manna, so that it lay enclosed there as in a casket, protected from soiling or pollution above and below.

THE GATHERING OF THE MANNA

With an easy mind every individual might perform his morning prayer in his house and recite the Shema', then betake himself to the entrance of his tent, and gather manna for himself and all his family.[101] The gathering of manna caused little trouble, and those among the people who were too lazy to perform even the slightest work, went out while manna fell, so that it fell straight into their hands.[102] The manna lasted until the fourth hour of the day, when it melted; but even the melted manna was not wasted, for out of it formed the rivers, from which the pious will drink in the hereafter. The heathen even then attempted to drink out of these streams, but the manna that tasted so deliciously to the Jews, had a quite bitter taste in the mouth of the heathen. Only indirectly could they partake of the enjoyment of manna: They used to catch the animals that drank of the melted manna, and even in this form it was so delicious that the heathen cried, " Happy is the people that is in such a case." [103] For the descent of manna was not a secret to the heathen, as it settled at such enormous heights that the kings of the East and of the West could see how Israel received its miraculous food.[104]

The mass of the manna was in proportion to its height, for as much descended day by day, as might have satisfied the wants of sixty myriads of people, through two thousand years.[105] Such profusion of manna fell over the body of Joshua alone, as might have sufficed for the maintenance of the whole congregation.[106] Manna, indeed, had the peculiarity of falling to every individual in the same measure; and when, after gathering, they measured it, they found that there was an omer for every man.

Many lawsuits were amicably decided through the fall of manna. If a married couple came before Moses, each accusing the other of inconstancy, Moses would say to them, "To-morrow morning judgment will be given." If, then, manna descended for the wife before the house of her husband, it was known that he was in the right; but if her share descended before the house of her own parents, she was in the right.[107]

The only days on which manna did not descend were the Sabbaths and the holy days, but then a double portion fell on the preceding day. These days had the further distinction that, while they lasted, the color of the manna sparkled more than usual, and it tasted better than usual. The people, however, were fainthearted, and on the very first Sabbath, they wanted to go out as usual to gather manna in the morning, although announcement had been made that God would send them no food on that day. Moses, however, restrained them. They attempted to do it again toward evening, and again Moses restrained them with the words, "To-day ye shall not find it in the fields." At these words they were greatly alarmed, for they feared that they might not receive it any more at all, but their leader quieted them with the words, "To-day ye shall not find any of it, but assuredly to-morrow; in this world ye shall not receive manna on the Sabbath, but assuredly in the future world."

The unbelieving among them did not hearken to the words

of God, and went out on the Sabbath to find manna. Hereupon God said to Moses: "Announce these words to
Israel: I have led you out of Egypt, have cleft the sea for
you, have sent you manna, have caused the well of water to
spring up for you, have sent the quails to come up for you,
have battled for you against Amalek, and wrought other
miracles for you, and still you do not obey My statutes and
commandments. You have not even the excuse that I imposed full many commandments upon you, for all that I
bade you do at Marah, was to observe the Sabbath, but you
have violated it." " If," continued Moses, " you will observe
the Sabbath, God will give you three festivals in the months
of Nisan, Siwan, and Tishri; and as a reward for the observance of the Sabbath, you will receive six gifts from God:
the land of Israel, the future world, the new world, the
sovereignty of the dynasty of David, the institution of the
priests and the Levites; and, furthermore, as a reward for
the observance of the Sabbath, you shall be freed from the
three great afflictions: from the sufferings of the times of
Gog and Magog, from the travails of the Messianic time,
and from the day of the great Judgment."

When Israel heard these exhortations and promises, they
determined to observe the Sabbath, and did so.[108] They did
not know, to be sure, what they had lost through their viola-
tion of the first Sabbath. Had Israel then observed the Sabbath, no nation would ever have been able to exercise any
authority over them.[109]

This, moreover, was not the only sin that Israel committed
during this time, for some among them also broke the other
commandment in regard to manna, that is, not to store it

away from day to day. These sinners were none other than
the infamous pair, Dathan and Abiram, who did not hearken
to the word of God, but saved the manna for the following
day. But if they fancied they could conceal their sinful
deed, they were mistaken, for great swarms of worms bred
from the manna, and these moved in a long train from their
tents to the other tents, so that everyone perceived what these
two had done.[110]

To serve future generations as a tangible proof of the
infinite power of God, the Lord bade Moses lay an earthen
vessel full of manna before the Holy Ark, and this command
was carried out by Aaron in the second year of the wanderings through the desert. When, many centuries later, the
prophet Jeremiah exhorted his contemporaries to study the
Torah, and they answered his exhortations, saying, "How
shall we then maintain ourselves?" the prophet brought forth
the vessel with manna, and spoke to them, saying: "O
generation, see ye the word of the Lord; see what it was that
served your fathers as food when they applied themselves
to the study of the Torah. You, too, will God support in the
same way, if you will but devote yourselves to the study of
the Torah.[111]

When the imminent destruction of the Temple was announced to King Josiah, he concealed the Holy Ark, and
with it also the vessel with manna, as well as the jug filled
with sacred oil, which was used by Moses for anointing the
sacred implements, and other sacred objects. In the Messianic time the prophet Elijah will restore all these concealed
objects.[112]

Israel received three gifts during their wanderings through

the desert: the well, the clouds of glory, and the manna; the first for the merits of Miriam, the second for those of Aaron, and the third for those of Moses. When Miriam died, the well disappeared for a time, but it reappeared as a reward for the merits of Aaron and Moses; when Aaron died, the clouds of glory disappeared for a time, but reappeared owing to the merits of Moses. But when the last-named died, the well, the clouds of glory, and the manna disappeared forever.[113] Throughout forty years, however, manna served them not only as food, but also as provender for their cattle, for the dew that preceded the fall of manna during the night brought grain for their cattle.[114] Manna also replaced perfume for them, for it shed an excellent fragrance upon those who ate of it.[115]

In spite of all the excellent qualities of manna, they were not satisfied with it, and demanded that Moses and Aaron give them flesh to eat. These replied: " We might put up with you if you murmured only against us, but you murmur against the Eternal. Come forward, that you may hear the judgment of God." At once God appeared to Moses, and said to him: " It is revealed to Me what the congregation of Israel have said, and what they will say, but tell them this: You have demanded two things; you desired bread, and I gave it to you, because man cannot exist without it; but now, filled to satiety, you demand flesh; this also will I give you, so that you might not say if your wish were denied, ' God cannot grant it,' but at some future time you shall make atonement for it; I am a judge and shall assign punishment for this."

In the meantime, however, God granted their wish, and

toward evening thick swarms of quails came up from the
sea, and covered the whole camp, taking their flight quite
low, not two ells above the ground, so that they might be
easily caught. Contrary to the manna, which fell in the
morning, the quails did not come before evenfall; with a
radiant countenance God gave them the former, as their
desire for bread was justified, but with a darkened mien,
under cover of night, He sent the quails.[116] Now, because
the one food came in the morning and the second in the
evening, Moses instituted the custom among his people of
taking two meals a day, one in the morning and one in the
evening; and he set the meal with the use of meat for the
evening.[117] At the same time he taught them the prayer in
which they were to offer thanks after eating manna, which
read: " Blessed be Thou, O God our Lord, King of the
world, who, in Thy bounty, dost provide for all the world;
who, in Thy grace, goodwill, and mercy, dost grant food to
every creature, for Thy grace is everlasting. Thanks to Thy
bounty we have never lacked food, nor ever shall lack it, for
Thy great name's sake. For Thou suppliest and providest
for all; Thou art bountiful, and nourishest all Thy creatures
which Thou hast made. Blessed be Thou, O God, that dost
provide for all." [118]

MIRIAM'S WELL

Relieved as they were of all the cares of subsistence
through the gift of manna, it was plainly the duty of the
Israelites to devote themselves exclusively to the study of
the Torah.[119] When, therefore, they slackened in the performance of this duty, punishment in the form of lack of

water immediately overtook them. This was the first time that they actually experienced this want, for at Marah nothing more than alarm that this need might come upon them, had caused them to murmur and complain. In their distress they once more unreasonably cast reproaches upon their leader, and disputed with him, saying: "Wherefore is this, that thou hast brought us up out of Egypt, to kill us, and our children, and our cattle with thirst?" Moses replied: "As often as you quarrel with me, you tempt God, but God performeth wonders and excellent deeds for you, as often as you dispute with me, that His name may sound in glory throughout the world."

In spite of the injury they had done him, Moses prayed to God that He might aid them in their distress and also stand by him. "O Lord of the world!" said he, "I am surely doomed to die. Thou biddest me not to be offended with them, but if I obey Thy words, I shall certainly be killed by them." God, however, replied: "Try thou to act like Me; as I return good for evil, so do thou return to them good for evil, and forgive their trespass; go on before the people, and We shall see who dares touch thee." [120] Hardly had Moses shown himself to the people, when all of them rose reverently from their seats, whereupon God said to Moses: "How often have I told thee not to be angry with them, but to lead them, as a shepherd leads his flock; it is for their sake that I have set thee on this height, and only for their sake wilt thou find grace, goodwill, and mercy in My sight." [121]

Then God bade him go with some elders to the rock on Horeb, and fetch water out of it. The elders were to accompany him there, that they might be convinced that he was not bringing water from a well, but smiting it from a rock. To accomplish this miracle, God bade him smite the rock with his rod, as the people labored under the impression that this rod could only bring destruction, for through its agency Moses had brought the ten plagues upon the Egyptians in Egypt, and at the Red Sea; now they were to see that it could work good also.[122] Upon God's bidding, Moses told the people to choose from which rock they wished water to flow,[123] and hardly had Moses touched with his sapphire rod the rock which they had chosen, when plenteous water flowed from it. The spot where this occurred, God called Massah, and Meribah, because Israel had there tried their God, saying, " If God is Lord over all, as over us; if He satisfies our need, and will further show us that He knows our thoughts, then will we serve Him, but not otherwise." [124]

The water that flowed for them on this spot served not only as a relief for their present need, but on this occasion there was revealed to them a well of water, which did not abandon them in all their forty years' wandering, but accompanied them on all their marches.[125] God wrought this great miracle for the merits of the prophetess Miriam, wherefore also it was called " Miriam's Well." [126] But this well dates back to the beginning of the world, for God created it on the second day of the creation,[127] and at one time it was in the possession of Abraham. It was this same well that Abraham demanded back from Abimelech, king of the Philistines, after the king's servants had violently taken it away. But when Abimelech pretended not to know anything about it, saying, " I wot not who hath done this thing," Abraham said : " Thou and I will send sheep to the well, and he shall be declared the rightful owner of the well, for whose sheep the water will spout forth to water them. And," continued Abraham, " from that same well shall the seventh generation after me, the wanderers in the desert, draw their supply." [128]

This well was in the shape of a sieve-like rock, out of which water gushes forth as from a spout. It followed them on all their wanderings, up hill and down dale, and wherever they halted, it halted, too, and it settled opposite the Tabernacle. Thereupon the leaders of the twelve tribes would appear, each with his staff and chant these words to the well, " Spring up, O well, sing ye unto it; nobles of the people digged it by the direction of the lawgiver with their staves." Then the water would gush forth from the depths of the well, and shoot up high as pillars, then discharge itself into great streams that were navigable, and on these rivers the Jews sailed to the ocean, and hauled all the treasures of the world therefrom. [129]

The different parts of the camp were separated by these rivers, so that women, visiting each other, were obliged to make use of ships. Then the water discharged itself beyond the encampment, where it surrounded a great plain, in which grew every conceivable kind of plant and tree; [130] and these trees, owing to the miraculous water, daily bore fresh fruits. [131] This well brought fragrant herbs with it, so that the women had no need of perfumes on the march, for the herbs they gathered served this purpose. [132] This well furthermore threw down soft, fragrant kinds of grass that served as pleasant couches for the poor, who had no pillows or bed-clothes. [133] Upon the entrance to the Holy Land this well disappeared and was hidden in a certain spot of the Sea of

Tiberias. Standing upon Carmel, and looking over the sea,
one can notice there a sieve-like rock, and that is the well of
Miriam.¹³⁴ Once upon a time it happened that a leper bathed
at this place of the Sea of Tiberias, and hardly had he come
in contact with the waters of Miriam's well when he was
instantly healed.¹³⁵

Amalek's War Against Israel

As a punishment because they had not had sufficient faith
in God, and had doubted whether He could fulfil all their
wishes, and had grown negligent in the study of the Torah
and in the observance of the laws, God turned Amalek
against them during their sojourn in Rephidim, where they
had committed these sins. God dealt with them as did that
man with his son, whom he bore through the river on his
shoulders. Whenever the child saw something desirable, he
said, " Father, buy it for me," and he fulfilled the child's
wish. After the son had in this way received many beautiful
things from his father, he called to a passing stranger with
these words, " Hast thou perhaps seen my father? " Then,
indignantly, the father said to his son: " O thou fool, that
sittest on my shoulder! All that thou didst desire, did I
procure for thee, and now dost thou ask of that man, ' Hast
thou seen my father? ' " Thereupon the father threw the
child off his shoulder, and a dog came and bit him. So did
Israel fare. When they moved out of Egypt, God enveloped
them in seven clouds of glory; they wished for bread, and
He gave them manna; they wished for flesh, and He gave
them quails. After all their wishes had been granted, they
began to doubt, saying, " Is the Lord among us, or not? "

Then God answered, "You doubt My power; so surely as you live shall you discover it; the dog will soon bite you." Then came Amalek.[136]

This enemy of Israel bore the name Amalek to denote the rapidity with which he moved against Israel, for like a swarm of locusts he flew upon them; and the name furthermore designates the purpose of this enemy, who came to suck the blood of Israel.[137] This Amalek was a son of Eliphaz, the first-born son of Esau, and although the descendants of Jacob had been weaker and more insignificant in earlier times, Amalek had left them in peace, for he had excellent reasons to delay his attack. God had revealed to Abraham that his seed would have to serve in the land of the Egyptians, and had put the payment of this debt upon Isaac, and after his death, upon Jacob and his descendants. The wicked Amalek now said to himself, "If I destroy Jacob and his descendants, God will impose the Egyptian bondage upon me, grandson of Esau, descendant of Abraham." Therefore he kept himself in restraint as long as Israel dwelt in Egypt, but only after the bondage predicted to the seed of Abraham had been served in full, did he set out to accomplish the war of annihilation against Israel, which his grandfather Esau had enjoined upon him.[138]

No sooner had he heard of Israel's departure from Egypt, than he set out against them and met them by the Red Sea. There, indeed, he could work them no ill, for Moses uttered against him the Ineffable Name; and so great was his confusion, that he was forced to retreat without having effected his object.[139] Then, for some time, he tried lying hidden in ambush, and in this wise molesting Israel, but at length he gave up this game of hide-and-seek, and with a bold front revealed himself as the open enemy of Israel. Not alone, however, did he himself declare war upon Israel, but he also seduced all the heathen nations to assist him in his enterprise against Israel. Although these declined to war upon Israel, fearing that they might have to fare like the Egyptians, they agreed to the following plan of Amalek. He said: "Follow my expedition. Should Israel conquer me, there will still be plenty of time for you to flee, but should success crown my attempt, join your fate to mine, in my undertaking against Israel." So Amalek now marched from his settlement in Seir, which was no less than four hundred parasangs away from the encampment of the Jews; and although five nations, the Hittites, the Hivites, the Jebusites, the Amorites, and the Canaanites, had their dwellings between his home and the camp of the Jews, he insisted upon being the first to declare war upon Israel.

God punished Israel, who had shown themselves an ungrateful people, by sending against them an enemy that was ungrateful, too, never recalling that he owed his life to the sons of Jacob, who had had him in their power after their brilliant victory over Esau and his followers.[140]

In his expedition against Israel he made use of his kinship with them, by pretending, at first, to be their friend and kinsman. Before going over to open attack, he lured many unsuspecting Jews to death by his kindly words. He had fetched from Egypt the table of descent of the Jews; for every Jew had there to mark his name on the bricks produced by him, and these lists lay in the Egyptian archives. Familiar with the names of the different Jewish families,

Amalek appeared before the Jewish camp, and calling the people by name, he invited them to leave the camp, and come out to him. " Reuben! Simeon! Levi! etc.," he would call, " come out to me, your brother, and transact business with me."

Those who answered the enticing call, found certain death at his hands ; and not only did Amalek kill them, but he also mutilated their corpses, following the example of his grand-sire Esau, by cutting off a certain part of the body, and throwing it toward heaven with the mocking words, " Here shalt Thou have what Thou desirest." In this way did he jeer at the token of the Abrahamic covenant.

So long as the Jews remained within the encampment, he could, of course, do them no harm, for the cloud enveloped them, and under its shelter they were as well fortified as a city that is surrounded by a solid wall. The cloud, however, covered those only who were pure, but the unclean had to stay beyond it, until they were cleansed by a ritual bath, and these Amalek caught and killed. The sinners, too, particu-larly the tribe of Dan, who were all worshippers of idols, were not protected by the cloud, and therefore exposed to the attacks of Amalek.¹⁴¹

Moses did not himself set out to battle against this dan-gerous foe of Israel, but he sent his servant Joshua, and for good reasons. Moses knew that only a descendant of Rachel, like the Ephraimite Joshua, could conquer the de-scendant of Esau. All the sons of Jacob had taken part in the unbrotherly act of selling Joseph as a slave, hence none of their descendants might stand up in battle against the descendant of Esau; for they who had themselves acted unnaturally to a brother, could hardly hope for God's assistance in a struggle with the unbrotherly Edomites. Only the descendants of Joseph, the man who had been generous and good to his brothers, might hope that God would grant them aid against the unbrotherly descendants of Esau. In many other respects, too, Joseph was the opposite of Esau, and his services stood his descendants in good stead in their battles against the descendants of Esau. Esau was the firstborn of his father, but through his evil deeds he lost his birthright; Joseph, on the other hand, was the youngest of his father's sons, and through his good deeds was he found worthy of enjoying the rights of a firstborn son. Joseph had faith in the resurrection, while Esau denied it; hence God said, " Joseph, the devout, shall be the one to visit merited punishment on Esau, the unbelieving." Joseph associated with two wicked men, Potiphar and Pharaoh, yet he did not follow their example; Esau associated with two pious men, his father and his brother, yet he did not follow their example. " Hence," said God, " Joseph, who did not follow the example of wicked men, shall visit punishment upon him who did not follow the example of pious men." Esau soiled his life with lewdness and murder; Joseph was chaste and shunned bloodshed, hence God delivered Esau's descendants into the hands of Joseph's descendants. And, as in the course of history only the descendants of Joseph were victorious over the descendants of Esau, so will it be in the future, at the final reckoning between the angel of Esau and the angels of the Jews. The angel of Reuben will be rebuffed by the angel of Esau with these words, " You represent one who had illegal relations with his father's wife "; the angels of Simeon and Levi will have to listen to this reproof, " You represent people who slew the inhabitants of Shechem"; the angel of Judah will be repulsed with the words, " Judah had illicit relations with his daughter-in-law." And the angels of the other tribes will be repulsed by Esau's angel, when he points out to them that they all took part in selling Joseph. The only one whom he will not be able to repulse will be Joseph's angel, to whom he will be delivered and by whom he will be destroyed; Joseph will be the flame and Esau the straw burned in the flame.[143]

AMALEK DEFEATED

Moses now instructed Joshua in regard to his campaign against Amalek, saying, " Choose us out men and go out, fight with Amalek." The words " choose us " characterize the modesty of Moses, who treated his disciple Joshua as an equal; in these words he has taught us that the honor of our disciples should stand as high as our own. Joshua did not at first want to expose himself to danger and leave the protection of the cloud, but Moses said to him, " Abandon the cloud and set forth against Amalek, if ever thou dost hope to set the crown upon thy head." He commanded him to choose his warriors from among the pious and God-fearing, and promised him that he would set a fast day for the following day, and implore God, in behalf of the good deeds of the Patriarchs and the wives of the Patriarchs, to stand by Israel in this war.

Joshua acted in accordance with these commands[144] and set out against Amalek, to conquer whom required not only skilful strategy, but also adeptness in the art of magic. For Amalek was a great magician and knew the propitious and the unpropitious hour of each individual, and in this way regulated his attacks against Israel; he attacked that one at night, whose death had been predicted for a night, and him whose death had been preordained for a day did he attack by day.

But in this art, too, Joshua was his match, for he, too, knew how to time properly the attack upon [114] individuals, and he destroyed Amalek, his sons, the armies he himself commanded, and those under the leadership of his sons. But in the very heat of battle, Joshua treated his enemies humanely, he did not repay like with like. Far was it from him to follow Amalek's example in mutilating the corpses of the enemy. Instead with a sharp sword he cut off the enemies' heads, an execution that does not dishonor.

But only through the aid of Moses, did Joshua win his victory. Moses did not go out into battle, but through his prayer and through his influence upon the people in inspiring them with faith, the battle was won. While the battle raged between Israel and Amalek, Moses was stationed on a height, where, supported by the Levite Aaron and the Judean Hur, the representatives of the two noble tribes Levi and Judah, he fervently implored God's aid. He said: "O Lord of the world! Through me hast Thou brought Israel out of Egypt, through me hast Thou cleft the sea, and through me hast Thou wrought miracles; so do Thou now work miracles for me, and lend victory to Israel, for I well know that while all other nations fight only to the sixth hour of the day, this sinful nation stand in battle ranks till sunset." Moses did not consider it sufficient to pray alone to God, but he raised his hands toward heaven as a signal for the whole nation to follow his example and trust in God. As often as he then raised his hands to heaven and the people prayed with him, trusting that God would lend them victory, they were indeed victorious; as often, however, as Moses let down his hands and the people ceased prayer, weakening in their faith in God, Amalek conquered. But it was hard for Moses constantly to raise his hands. This was God's way of punishing him for being somewhat negligent in the preparations for the war against Amalek. Hence Aaron and Hur were obliged to hold up his arms and assist him in his prayer. As, furthermore, he was unable to stand all that time, he seated himself on a stone, disdaining a soft and comfortable seat, saying, " So long as Israel is in distress, I shall share it with them." [145]

At evenfall, the battle was not yet decided, therefore Moses prayed to God that He might stay the setting of the sun and thus enable Israel to draw the battle to a close. God granted this prayer, for the sun did not set until Israel had completely destroyed their enemy. Thereupon Moses blessed Joshua with the words, " Some day the sun shall stand still for thy sake, as it did to-day for mine," and this blessing was later fulfilled at Gibeon, when the sun stood still to help Joshua in his battle against the Amorites. [146]

Although Amalek had now received the merited punishment from the hands of Joshua, still his enterprise against Israel had not been entirely unavailing. The miraculous exodus of Israel out of Egypt, and especially the cleaving of the sea, had created such alarm among the heathens, that

none among them had dared to approach Israel. But this
fear vanished as soon as Amalek attempted to compete in
battle with Israel. Although he was terribly beaten, still the
fear of the inaccessibility of Israel was gone. It was with
Amalek as with that foolhardy wight who plunged into a
scalding-hot tub. He scalded himself terribly, yet the tub
became a little cooled through his plunge into it. Hence
God was not content with the punishment Amalek received
in the time of Moses, but swore by His throne and by His
right hand that He would never forget Amalek's misdeeds,
that in this world as well as in the time of the Messiah He
would visit punishment upon him, and would completely
exterminate him in the future world. So long as the seed
of Amalek exist, the face of God is, as it were, covered, and
will only then come to view, when the seed of Amalek shall
have been entirely exterminated.

God had at first left the war against Amalek in the hands
of His people, therefore He bade Joshua, the future leader
of the people, never to forget the war against Amalek; and
if Moses had listened intently, he would have perceived from
this command of God that Joshua was destined to lead the
people into the promised land. But later, when Amalek took
part in the destruction of Jerusalem, God Himself took up
the war against Amalek, saying, " By My throne I vow not
to leave a single descendant of Amalek under the heavens,
yea, no one shall even be able to say that this sheep or that
wether belonged to an Amalekite." [147]

God bade Moses impress upon the Jews to repulse no
heathen should he desire conversion, but never to accept an
Amalekite as a proselyte. It was in consideration of this

word of God that David slew the Amalekite, who announced
to him the death of Saul and Jonathan; for he saw in him
only a heathen, although he appeared in the guise of a Jew.[148]
Part of the blame for the destruction of Amalek falls upon
his father, Eliphaz. He used to say to Amalek: " My son,
dost thou indeed know who will possess this world and the
future world?" Amalek paid no attention to this allusion
to the future fortune of Israel, and his father urged it no
more strongly upon him, although it would have been his
duty to instruct his son clearly and fully. He should have
said to him: " My son, Israel will possess this world as well
as the future world; dig wells then for their use and build
roads for them, so that thou mayest be judged worthy to
share in the future world." But as Amalek had not been
sufficiently instructed by his father, in his wantonness he
undertook to destroy the whole world. God, who tries the
reins and the heart, said to him: " O thou fool, I created
thee after all the seventy nations, but for thy sins thou shalt
be the first to descend into hell." [149]

To glorify the victory over Amalek, Moses built an altar,
which God called " My Miracle," for the miracle God
wrought against Amalek in the war of Israel was, as it were,
a miracle for God. For so long as the Israelites dwell in
sorrow, God feels with them, and a joy for Israel is a joy
for God, hence, too, the miraculous victory over Israel's foe
was a victory for God.[150]

JETHRO

" Smite a scorner, and the simple will beware." The destruction of Amalek brought Jethro to his senses. Jethro

was originally in the same plot with Amalek, both having incited Pharaoh against Israel, but when he saw that Amalek lost this world and the other, he repented of his sinful ways, saying: " There is nothing left to me but to go over to the God of Israel "; [151] and although he dwelt in the greatest wealth and honor, he determined to set out for the desert, to Moses and his God.[152] Arrived at the camp of Israel, he could not enter it, for it was enveloped by a cloud that none could pierce, hence he wrote a letter to Moses and shot it off with an arrow, so that it fell into the camp.[153] The letter read: " I adjure thee, by thy two sons and by thy God, to come to meet me and receive me kindly. If thou wilt not do it for my sake, do it for thy wife's sake; and if thou wilt not do it for her sake, do it for thy sons' sake." For Jethro brought with him his daughter Zipporah, from whom Moses had been divorced, as well as her two sons, her only children, for after her separation from Moses, she had wed no other man.

At first Moses was inclined to give no ear to this letter, but God said to him: " I, through whose word the world came into being, I bring men to Me and do not thrust them back. I permitted Jethro to approach Me, and did not push him from Me. So do thou, too, receive this man, who desires to betake himself under the wings of the Shekinah, let him approach, and do not repulse him." God herewith taught Moses that one should repulse with the left hand, and beckon with the right.[154]

Moses, Aaron, Nadab, and Abihu, together with the seventy elders of Israel, carrying with them the sacred Ark, hastened to welcome Jethro kindly; and Moses so honored his father-in-law as to make an obeisance before him and kiss him. Before Moses told his father-in-law of the great miracles God had wrought for Egypt, such as the exodus from Egypt, the cleaving of the sea, the rain of manna, and the rest, he offered him the greeting of peace; for great is peace, that precedes even the praise of God.[155] After the peace-greeting, Moses, to draw his father-in-law nearer to true faith in God and His revelation, began to relate to him the miracles that God had wrought for them at the exodus from Egypt, during the passing through the Red Sea, and during the war with Amalek. He said, moreover, "In the manna that God gives us we perceive the taste of bread, of meat, of fish, in short, of all the dishes there are. Out of the well that God gives us we draw a drink that possesses the taste of old wine as well as new, of milk and of honey, in short, of all the beverages that exist." "We shall," Moses continued, "receive six other gifts from God, the land of Israel, the future world, the new world, the sovereignty of David, the institution of priests, and of Levites."

When Jethro heard all this, he determined to become a Jew and to believe in the only God, and although he felt a pang at heart upon hearing that the Egyptians had perished —for no one should scoff at a heathen before a proselyte who is not a Jew of ten generations' standing—still he burst into a song of praise to God for the deeds He had done for His people. In truth, it reflects shame upon Moses and the sixty myriads of Jews that they had not given thanks to God for the release from Egypt, until Jethro came and did so. He said: "Praised be God who delivered Moses and Aaron, as well as the whole nation of Israel, from the bondage of

Pharaoh, that great dragon, and of the Egyptians. Truly, great is the Lord before all gods, for whereas formerly not a single slave succeeded in escaping from Egypt, He led sixty myriads out of Egypt. There is no god whom I had not, at some time in my life, worshipped, but now I must admit that none is like the God of Israel. This God had not been unbeknown to me heretofore, but now I know Him better, for His fame will sound throughout the world, because He visited upon the Egyptians exactly what they had planned to undertake against Israel. They wanted to destroy Israel by water, and by water were they destroyed." [156]

With sacrifices and a feast was the arrival of Jethro celebrated, for after he had made the burnt offering not far from the bush of thorns that had been unscathed by fire, Jethro prepared a feast of rejoicing for the whole people,[157] at which Moses did not consider it below his dignity to wait on the guests in person. In this he followed the example of Abraham, who in person waited on the three angels, though they appeared in the guise of idolatrous Arabs.

Abraham like Moses sought to follow in the ways of the Lord, to provide for each according to his wants, and to grant to everybody what he lacks, whether he be a righteous man, or an idolater, who through his sins conjures up God's wrath.[158]

To this feast the people sat down according to their tribes. They ate, drank, and were merry, while Aaron and Jethro with their relatives sang songs of thanksgiving to God, and praised Him as the Creator and Donor of their lives and their liberty. At the same time they gave due appreciation to Moses, through whose courage everything had happily come to pass. In his words of gratitude to Moses, Jethro also gave expression to many glorious eulogies on the people of Israel, but he especially extolled Moses, who through difficulties and dangers had shown so much courage in the salvation of his friends.[159]

THE INSTALLATION OF ELDERS

Jethro, who had come to Moses shortly before the revelation on Mount Sinai, stayed with his son-in-law for more than a year. In the first months, however, he had no opportunity of observing Moses in the capacity of judge, for Moses spent the time from the day of the revelation to the tenth day of Tishri almost entirely in heaven. Hence Jethro could not be present at a court proceeding of his before the eleventh day of Tishri, the first day after Moses' return from heaven. Jethro now perceived how Moses sat like a king upon his throne, while the people, who brought their lawsuits before him, stood around him. This so displeased him that he said to his son-in-law: " Why sittest thou thyself alone, and all the people stand by thee from morning until even?" Moses answered: " Because the people come unto me to enquire of God. It is not in my honor that they stand, but in honor of God, whose judgment they would know. When they are in doubt over a case of clean or unclean, or when there is a dispute between two parties, which they desire to have settled exactly according to the law, or in conformity with a compromise, they come to me; and when the parties at dispute leave me, they part as friends and no longer as enemies. I expound to the poeple, besides, the words of God and His decisions."

On the day that Moses again took up his activity as a judge, and Jethro had for the first time the chance of observing him, came the mixed multitude with the plea that they, like the other Israelites, wanted their share in the Egyptian booty. Moses' method, first seen by him in practice,[180] struck Jethro as most absurd, and he therefore said: " The thing that thou doest is not good," through delicacy softening his real opinion, " It is bad " to " It is not good." [181] " The people," he continued, " will surely upbraid thee and Aaron, his two sons Nadab and Abihu, and the seventy elders, if thou continuest in this fashion. But if thou hearkenest now to my voice, thou wilt fare well, provided God approves of my plan. This is, that thou shalt be ' the vessel of the revelations of God,' and shalt lay the revelations of God before the people, as often as thou receivest them; so that they may understand the exposition of the Torah, as well as its decisions. And thou shalt instruct them how to pray in the synagogues, how to tend the sick, how to bury their dead, how to render the services of friendship to one another, how to practice justice, and how, in some cases, not to insist on strict justice. But as for trying the people as a judge, thou shouldst, in accordance with thy prophetic insight, choose men that are possessed of wisdom, fear of God, modesty, hate of covetousness, love of truth, love of humanity, and a good name, and these shall devote all their time to trials, and to the study of the Torah. If God approve my plan, then wilt thou and Aaron, his sons and the seventy elders, and all the people dwell in peace." [182]

This counsel of Jethro's found great favor in Moses' eyes, for he had been only too well aware of the difficulties and annoyances with which he had had to contend. The people were very disputatious, being willing to spend seventy silverlings in litigation costs for the sake of gaining one silverling, and did their utmost to lengthen their disputes at law. When one saw that Moses was about to cast a decision against him, he demanded that his lawsuit be adjourned, declaring that he had witnesses and other proofs, which he would bring forward on the next occasion. But they were not merely litigious and disputatious, they were also spiteful, and vented their temper on Moses. If Moses went out early, they would say: "Behold the son of Amram, who betakes himself early to the gathering of manna, that he may get the largest grains." If he went out late, they would say: "Behold the son of Amram, he ate and drank, and hence slept so long, that he had to get up late." If he went through the thick of the multitude, they said: "Behold the son of Amram, he goes through the multitude, to gather in marks of honor." But if he chose a path aside from the crowd, they said: "Behold the son of Amram, who makes it impossible for us to follow the simple commandment, to honor a sage." Then Moses said: "If I did this you were not content, and if I did that you were not content! I can no longer bear you alone. ' The Eternal, your God, hath multiplied you, and behold, ye are this day as the stars of heaven for multitude. The Lord, God of your fathers, make you a thousand times so many as ye are, and bless you, as he hath promised you!' "

The Israelites were not content with this blessing of Moses, and said to him: "O our teacher Moses, we do not desire thee to bless us, we have had much greater blessings

given to us. God spoke to our father Abraham: 'I will
bless thee and in multiplying I will multiply thy seed as the
stars of the heaven, and as the sand which is upon the sea
shore,' and thou dost limit our blessing." Moses cried:
"I am only a creature of flesh and blood, limited in my
powers, hence is my blessing limited. I give you my blessing, but the blessing of God remains preserved for ye, and
He will bless you unlimitedly, and multiply you as the fish of
the sea and the sands on the seashore, as the stars in the
sky and the plants on the earth." [168]

After he had bestowed his blessing upon them, he asked
them to propose capable and pious men, that he might appoint them as judges and leaders over them. He said: "If
a man were to present himself to me as a candidate for this
position of honor, I alone should not be able to decide to what
tribe he belonged, and whence he came; but you know them,
and hence it is advisable for you to propose them. Do not
think, however, that I feel I must abide by your choice, for it
depends solely upon me, whether or not I shall appoint
them."

The people were very eager to carry this plan of Moses
into execution, and requested him to settle the matter as
quickly as possible. But their motive was self-interested,
for every one among them said: "Moses will now appoint
about eighty thousand officials. If I myself should not be
among them, surely my son will be, and if not he, my grandson, and with a gift of some kind it will be an easy matter to
induce such a judge to look after my interests at court."
Moses, of course, was not deceived about their true sentiments; still, he paid no further attention to them, and picked

out the best men among the people, though they were not possessed of nearly all the good qualities Jethro had thought essential for judges and leaders of the people. With kindly words he invited them to assume their offices, and said: " Blessed are ye that are judged worthy of being leaders of the children of Abraham, Isaac, and Jacob, of a people whom God called His friends, His brothers, His flock, and other titles of love." He impressed upon them that they must possess much patience, and must not become impatient if a lawsuit is brought before them more than once. " Heretofore," he said," you belonged to yourselves, but from now you belong to the people; for you judge between every man, and his brother and his neighbor. If ye are to appoint judges, do so without respect of persons. Do not say, ' I will appoint that man because he is a handsome man or a strong man, because he is my kinsman, or because he is a linguist.' Such judges will declare the innocent guilty and the guilty innocent, not through wickedness, but through ignorance; and God will reckon the appointment of such judges against you, as a perversion of justice, on account of your respect of persons. If a wealthy man and a poor man come before you to court, do not say: ' Why should I insult a rich man for so small a matter? I will rather give judgment in his favor, and then, outside the court, tell him to give the poor man what he demands, as he is in the right.' But do not, on the other hand, if the poor man is in the wrong, say: ' The rich man is obliged to assist the poor anyhow, I will now decide in favor of the poor, that in a decent way he may, without begging, obtain money from his rich fellow-man.' Do not, moreover, say: ' I fear to pronounce judgment, lest that man kill my son, burn my barn, or destroy my plants,' for the judgment is God's."

After these admonitions, Moses instructed the new judges in legal procedure, in both civil and criminal cases, and at the same time urged the people not to deny the judges the veneration due them.[164] For great is the importance of justice. For him who hates it, there is no remedy; but the judge who decides conscientiously is the true peacemaker, for the weal of Israel, of the commonwealth, and indeed of all living creatures.[165]

JETHRO REWARDED

Although the installation of elders on Moses' part came to pass in accordance with the command of God, still it was Jethro upon whose advice Moses besought God to lighten his burden, and to permit him partly to transfer the leadership of the people to others.[166] Hence he did not conceal the name of this adviser, but announced it to all the people, and immortalized him as such in the Holy Scriptures; for he deemed it praiseworthy to appreciate duly the merits of others.[167] It had, however, been part of God's scheme to reward Jethro for the love he bore the Torah; and for this reason did He allow it to come to pass that Moses had to have his attention called to the plan of installing the elders through his father-in-law, that the Holy Scriptures might devote a whole chapter to the plan of Jethro.[168]

This, however, is not the only reward for Jethro's piety, who, in his love for the Torah, excelled all proselytes. A miracle occurred on the very first day of his arrival in camp, for manna in his honor descended at the noon hour, the hour

of his arrival; and, moreover, in as great quantities as was
wont to rain down for sixty myriads of Israelites. He did
not have to exert himself to gather the food, for it came over
his body, so all he had to do was to carry his hand to his
mouth to partake of it.[169] Jethro, nevertheless, did not remain with Moses, but returned to his native land. Moses,
of course, tried to persuade his father-in-law to stay. He
said to him: "Do not think that we shall continue to move
thus slowly through the desert, nay, we shall now move
directly to the promised land." Only to urge Jethro to stay
longer with them did Moses use the words "*we* move," so
that his father-in-law might believe that Moses too would
enter the promised land, for otherwise he would hardly have
allowed himself to be persuaded to join the march to Palestine. Moses continued: "I do not want to mislead thee,
hence I will tell thee that the land will be divided only among
the twelve tribes, and that thou hast no claim to possession
of lands; but God bade us be kind to the proselytes, and to
thee we shall be kinder than to all other proselytes." Jethro,
however, was not to be persuaded by his son-in-law, considering himself in duty bound to return to his native land.
For the inhabitants of his city had for many years made a
habit of having him store their valuables, as none possessed
their confidence in such a measure as he. If he had stayed
still longer with Moses, people would have declared that he
had absconded with all these things and fled to Moses to
share it with him, and that would have been a blot on his
fair name and that of Moses. Jethro had furthermore made
many debts during the year in which he came to Moses, for,
owing to the hail God had sent upon Egypt before the

exodus of Israel, a great famine had arisen in Jethro's home too, and he had found himself obliged to lend money for the support of the poor. If he were not now to return to his home, people would say that he had run away in order to evade his creditors, and such talk concerning a man of piety would have been desecration of the Divine Name. So he said to Moses: " There are people who have a fatherland, but no property there ; there are also property-holders who have no family ; but I have a fatherland, and have property there as well as a family ; hence I desire to return to my fatherland, my property, and my family." But Moses would not yield so soon, and said to his father-in-law : " If thou dost not accompany us as a favor, I will command thee to do so, that the Israelites might not say thou hadst been converted to our religion only in the expectation of receiving a share in the promised land, but hadst returned to thy home when thou didst discover that proselytes have no claim on property in the Holy Land. Through thy refusal to move with us, thou wilt give the heathens an opportunity to say that the Jews do not accept proselytes, since they did not accept even their own king's father-in-law, but allowed him to return to his own land. Thy refusal will injure the glory of God, for the heathens will keep away from the true faith. But if thou wilt wander with us, I assure thee that thy seed shall share with us the Temple, the Torah, and the future reward of the pious. How canst thou, moreover, who hast seen all the miracles God wrought for us during the march through the desert; who wert a witness of the way in which even the Egyptians became fond of us—how canst thou now depart from us? It is a sufficient motive for thee to remain with us, in order to officiate as a member of the Sanhedrin, and teach the Torah. We, on our part, want to retain thee, only that thou mightest in difficult cases enlighten our eyes; for thou wert the man who gave us good and fair counsel, to which God Himself could not refuse His assent." Jethro replied: " A candle may glow in the dark, but not when the sun and the moon shed their rays. Thou art the sun, and Aaron the moon; of what avail would my candle-light be? I had, therefore, better return to my home city that I may make proselytes of its inhabitants, instruct them in the Torah, and lead them under the wings of the Shekinah." Amid great marks of honor, and provided with rich gifts, Jethro returned to his home, where he converted his kinsmen and his compatriots to the belief in the true God, as he had intended.[170]

The descendants of Jethro later settled in Palestine, where the fruitful land of Jericho was allotted to them as a dwelling place. After the capture of Palestine, the tribes, by mutual consent, agreed that the fertile strip of land at Jericho should fall to the share of the tribe on whose land the Temple was to be erected. But when its erection was postponed for a long time, they agreed to allot this piece of land to Jethro's sons, because they, being proselytes, had no other possession in the Holy Land. Four hundred and eighty years did the descendants of Jethro dwell in Jericho, when, upon the erection of the Temple at Jerusalem, they relinquished it to the tribe of Judah, who claimed it as an indemnity for the site of the Temple.[171]

Jethro's descendants inherited his devotion to the Torah, like him dedicating their lives entirely to its study. So long as Joshua lived, they sat at this master's feet, but when he

died, they said: "We left our fatherland and came here
only for the sake of studying the Torah; if we were now to
spend our time in cultivating the soil, when should we study
the Torah?" They therefore gave up their dwelling-place
in Jericho, and moved to the cold and barren wilderness, to
Jabez, who there had his house of instruction. But when
they there beheld the priests, the Levites, and the noblest of
the Jews, they said, "How can we, proselytes, presume to
sit beside these?" Instead of sitting within the house of
instruction, they remained at the entrance of it, where they
listened to the lectures, and in this manner made further
progress in the study of the Torah."² They were rewarded
for their piety, their prayer was heard by God, and their
good deeds served as a protection to Israel; and on account
of their pious actions they were called "the families of the
scribes," the Tirathites, the Shimeathites, and the Sucha-
thites, names designating their piety and devotion to the
Torah.

One of the descendants of Jethro was Jonadab, son of
Rechab, who, when he heard from a prophet that God would
destroy the Temple, bade all his children, as a token of
mourning, to drink no wine, use no oil for anointing themselves, nor cut their hair, nor dwell in houses. The Rechabites obeyed this command of their sire, and as a reward for
this, God made a covenant with them that their descendants
should always be members of the Sanhedrin, and teachers of
Israel. The covenant with the Rechabites was even stronger
than that with David, for to the house of the latter God
promised to keep the covenant only if his descendants were
pious, but He made an unconditional covenant with the

Rechabites. God rewarded them for their devotion to Him in this way, although they did not belong to the Jewish nation. From this one can gather how great would have been their reward if they had been Israelites.[112]

The Time Is at Hand

Moses sent his father-in-law Jethro back to his home, shortly before the revelation on Mount Sinai. He thought: "When God gave us a single commandment of the Torah in Egypt, the Passover, He said, 'There shall no stranger eat thereof.' Surely Jethro may not look on when God bestows on us the whole Torah." Moses was right: God did not want Jethro to be present at the revelation. He said: "Israel was in Egypt, bound to work with clay and bricks, at the same time as Jethro was sitting at home in peace and quiet. He who suffers with the community shall share their future joys, but he who does not share the sufferings of the community shall not take part in their rejoicing."[114]

God had not only good cause to delay the giving of the Torah until after the departure of Jethro, but the time He chose for bestowing it was also chosen for a good reason. Just as a female proselyte, or a woman freed from captivity, or an emancipated slave, may not enter wedlock before she has for three months lived as a free Jewess, so God also waited three months after the deliverance of Israel from the bondage and the slavery of Egypt, before His union with Israel on Mount Sinai.[115] God furthermore treated His bride as did that king who went to the marriage ceremony only after he had overwhelmed his chosen bride with many gifts. So did Israel first receive manna, the well, and the quails,

and not till then was the Torah granted them. Moses, who
had received this promise when God had first appeared to
him, viz., " When thou hast brought forth the people out of
Egypt, ye shall serve God upon this mountain "—waited
most longingly for the promised time, saying, " When will
this time come to pass? " When the time drew near, God
said to Moses, " The time is at hand when I shall bring
about something entirely new."

This new miracle of which God spoke was the healing of
all the sick among the Jews. God had wanted to give the
Torah to the Jews immediately after the exodus from Egypt,
but among them were found many that were lame, halt, or
deaf; wherefore God said: " The Torah is without a blemish,
hence would I not bestow it on a nation that has in it
such as are burdened with defects. Nor do I want to wait
until their children shall have grown to manhood, for I do
not desire any longer to delay the delight of the Torah."
For these reasons nothing was left Him to do, but to heal
those afflicted with disease. In the time between the exodus
from Egypt and the revelation on Mount Sinai, all the blind
among the Israelites regained their sight, all the halt became
whole, so that the Torah might be given to a sound and
healthy people. God wrought for that generation the same
miracle which He will hereafter bring about in the future
world, when " the eyes of the blind shall be opened, the ears
of the deaf shall be unstopped, the lame man leap as an hart,
and the tongues of the dumb sing." [176] Not only physically
was this generation free from blemishes, but spiritually, too,
it stood on a high plane, and it was the combined merits of
such a people that made them worthy of their high calling.

Never before or after lived a generation as worthy as this of receiving the Torah. Had there been but one missing, God would not have given them the Torah: " for He layeth up wisdom for the righteous; He is a buckler to them that walk uprightly." [177]

For one other reason did God delay the revelation of the Torah. He had intended giving them the Torah immediately after their exodus from Egypt, but at the beginning of the march through the desert, great discord reigned among them. Nor was harmony established until the new moon of the third month, when they arrived at Mount Sinai; whereupon God said: " The ways of the Torah are ways of loveliness, and all its paths are paths of peace; I will yield the Torah to a nation that dwells in peace and amity." [178] This decision of God, now to give them the Torah, also shows how mighty is the influence of penance. For they had been sinful upon their arrival at Mount Sinai, continuing to tempt God and doubting His omnipotence. After a short time, however, they changed in spirit; and hardly had they reformed, when God found them worthy of revealing to them the Torah.

The third month was chosen for the revelation, because everything that is closely connected with the Torah and with Israel is triple in number. The Torah consists of three parts, the Pentateuch, the Prophets, and the Hagiographa; similarly the oral law consists of Midrash, Halakah, and Haggadah. The communications between God and Israel were carried on by three, Moses, Aaron, and Miriam. Israel also is divided into three divisions, priests, Levites, and laymen; and they are, furthermore, the descendants of the three Patriarchs, Abraham, Isaac, and Jacob. For God has a preference for " the third ": It was the third of Adam's sons, Seth, who became the ancestor of humanity, and so too it was the third among Noah's sons, Shem, who attained high station. Among the Jewish kings, too, it was the third, Solomon, whom God distinguished before all others. The number three plays a particularly important part in the life of Moses. He belonged to the tribe of Levi, which is not only the third of the tribes, but has a name consisting of three letters. He himself was the third of the children of the family; his own name consists of three letters; in his infancy he had been concealed by his mother throughout three months; and in the third month of the year, after a preparation of three days, did he receive the Torah on a mountain, the name of which consists of three letters.[179]

THE GENTILES REFUSE THE TORAH

The mountain on which God made his revelation bears six names: It is called the Desert Sin, because God there announced His commandments; it is called the Desert Kadesh, because Israel was sanctified there; the Desert Kadmut because the pre-existing Torah was there revealed; the Desert Paran because Israel there was greatly multiplied; the Desert Sinai because the hatred of God against the heathens began there, for the reason that they would not accept the Torah; and for this same reason is it called Horeb, because the annihilation of the heathens was there decreed by God.[180] For the wrath of God against the heathens dates from their refusal to accept the Torah offered them.

Before God gave Israel the Torah, He approached every

tribe and nation, and offered them the Torah, that hereafter
they might have no excuse to say, " Had the Holy One,
blessed be He, desired to give us the Torah, we should have
accepted it." He went to the children of Esau and said,
" Will ye accept the Torah? " They answered Him, saying,
" What is written therein? " He answered them, " Thou
shalt not kill." Then they all said : " Wilt Thou perchance
take from us the blessing with which our father Esau was
blessed? For he was blessed with the words, ' By thy sword
shalt thou live.' We do not want to accept the Torah."
Thereupon He went to the children of Lot and said to them,
" Will ye accept the Torah? " They said, " What is written therein? " He answered, " Thou shalt not commit
unchastity." They said : " From unchastity do we spring ;
we do not want to accept the Torah." Then He went to the
children of Ishmael and said to them, " Do ye want to
accept the Torah? " They said to Him, " What is written
therein? " He answered, " Thou shalt not steal." They
said : " Wilt Thou take from us the blessing with which our
father was blessed? God promised him : ' His hand will
be against every man.' We do not want to accept Thy
Torah." Thence He went to all the other nations, who likewise rejected the Torah, saying : " We cannot give up the
law of our fathers, we do not want Thy Torah, give it to
Thy people Israel." Upon this He came to Israel and spoke
to them, " Will ye accept the Torah? " They said to Him,
" What is written therein? " He answered, " Six hundred
and thirteen commandments." They said : " All that the
Lord has spoken will we do and be obedient." [111] " O Lord
of the world ! " [2] they continued, " We acted in accordance with

Thy commandments before they were revealed to us. Jacob fulfilled the first of the Ten Commandments by bidding his sons put away the strange gods that were among them. Abraham obeyed the commandment not to take the name of the Lord in vain, for he said: 'I have lifted up mine hand unto the Lord, the most high God.' Joseph fulfilled the commandment to remember the Sabbath and keep it holy; and when his brothers came to him, he had everything for their welcome prepared on Friday. Isaac observed the law to honor his father and his mother, when he allowed Abraham to bind him on the altar as a sacrifice. Judah observed the commandment not to kill when he said to his brothers, 'What profit is it if we slay our brother and conceal his blood?' Joseph observed the law: 'Thou shalt not commit adultery,' when he repulsed the desire of the wife of Potiphar. The other sons of Jacob observed the commandment: 'Thou shalt not steal,' saying: 'How then should we steal out of thy lord's house silver and gold?' Abraham observed the commandment: 'Thou shalt not bear false witness,' for he was a true witness, and bore witness before all the world that Thou art the Lord of all creation. It was Abraham, also, who observed the last of the Ten Commandments: 'Thou shalt not covet,' saying: 'I will not take from a thread even to a shoe-latchet.'" [182]

THE CONTEST OF THE MOUNTAINS

While the nations and peoples were refusing to accept the Torah, the mountains among themselves were fighting for the honor of being chosen as the spot for the revelation. One said: "Upon me shall the Shekinah of God rest, and mine shall be this glory," whereupon the other mountain replied: "Upon me shall the Shekinah rest, and mine shall be this glory." The mountain Tabor said to the mountain Hermon: "Upon me shall the Shekinah rest, mine shall be this glory, for in times of old, when in the days of Noah the flood came over the earth, all the mountains that are under the heavens were covered with water, whereas it did not reach my head, nay, not even my shoulder. All the earth was sunk under water, but I, the highest of the mountains, towered high above the waters, hence I am called upon to bear the Shekinah." Mount Hermon replied to Mount Tabor: "Upon me shall the Shekinah rest, I am the destined one, for when Israel wished to pass through the Red Sea, it was I who enabled them to do so, for I settled down between the two shores of the sea, and they moved from one side to the other, through my aid, so that not even their clothes became wet." Mount Carmel was quite silent, but settled down on the shore of the sea, thinking: "If the Shekinah is to repose on the sea, it will rest upon me, and if it is to repose on the mainland, it will rest upon me." Then a voice out of the high heavens rang out and said: "The Shekinah shall not rest upon these high mountains that are so proud, for it is not God's will that the Shekinah should rest upon high mountains that quarrel among themselves and look upon one another with disdain. He prefers the low mountains, and Sinai among these, because it is the smallest and most insignificant of all. Upon it will He let the Shekinah rest." [188] The other mountains hereupon said to God, "Is it possible that Thou art partial, and wilt give us no reward for our good intention?" God replied: "Because ye have striven in My honor will I reward ye. Upon Tabor will I grant aid to Israel at the time of Deborah, and upon Carmel will I give aid to Elijah." [184]

Mount Sinai was given the preference not for its humility alone, but also because upon it there had been no worshipping of idols; whereas the other mountains, owing to their height, had been employed as sanctuaries by the idolaters. [185] Mount Sinai has a further significance, too, for it had been originally a part of Mount Moriah, on which Isaac was to have been sacrificed; but Sinai separated itself from it, and came to the desert. Then God said: " Because their father Isaac lay upon this mountain, bound as a sacrifice, it is fitting that upon it his children receive the Torah." Hence God now chose this mountain for a brief stay during the revelation, for after the Torah had been bestowed, He withdrew again to heaven. In the future world, Sinai will return to its original place, Mount Moriah, when " the mountain of the Lord's house shall be established in the top of the mountains, and shall be exalted above the hills." [186]

Just as Sinai was chosen as the spot for the revelation, owing to its humility, so likewise was Moses. When God said to Moses, " Go, deliver Israel," he in his great humility, said: " Who am I that I should go to Pharaoh and lead the children of Israel out of Egypt? There are nobler and wealthier than I." But God replied: " Thou art a great man, thee have I chosen out of all Israel. Of thee shall the prophet of the future say, ' I have laid help upon one that is mighty; I have exalted one chosen out of the people.' " Moses in his humility, however, still stood apart and would not accept the office offered him, until God said to him:

"Why dost thou stand apart? If they are not to be delivered by thee, by none other will they be delivered." When, likewise, at God's command Moses had erected the Tabernacle, he did not enter it, out of great humility, until God said to him, "Why dost thou stand outside? Thou art worthy to serve Me." [187]

THE TORAH OFFERED TO ISRAEL

On the second day of the third month, Moses received word from God to betake himself to Mount Sinai, for without this direct summons he would not have gone there. This time, as at all times, when God desired to speak with Moses, He twice called him by name, and after he had answered, "Here I am," God's revelation to him followed. [188] When Moses had been carried to God in a cloud, which was always ready to bear him to God and then restore him to men, God said to him: "Go and acquaint the women of Israel with the principles of Judaism, and try with kindly words to persuade them to accept the Torah; but expound the full contents of the Torah to the men, and with them speak solemn words concerning it."

There were several reasons for his going to the women first. God said: "When I created the world, I gave My commandment concerning the forbidden fruit to Adam only, and not to his wife Eve, and this omission had the effect that she tempted Adam to sin. Hence it appears advisable that the women first hear My commandments, and the men will then follow their counsel." [189] God, furthermore, knew that women are more scrupulous in their observance of religious precepts, and hence He first addressed Himself to them. Then, too, God expected the women to instruct their children in the ways of the Torah, wherefore He sent His messenger first to them.[190]

The words that Moses was to address to the women as well as to the men, to the Sanhedrin as well as to the people, were as follows: " You yourselves have seen—for it is not from writings, or through tradition, or from the mouths of others that ye learn it—what I did for you in Egypt; for although they were idolaters, slayers of men, and men of lewd living, still I punished them not for these sins, but only for the wrong done to you. But ye will I carry on the wings of eagles, on the day of the revelation at Sinai, and ye will I bring to Me when the Temple shall be erected. Since I have wrought for you so many miracles, even before you had received the Torah and observed the laws, how many more miracles will I work for you, when you will have received the Torah and observed the laws! The beginning of all things is hard, but as soon as you will have grown accustomed to obedience, all else will be easy for you. If you will now observe the Abrahamic covenant, the Sabbath, and the commandment against idolatry, then will you be My possession; for although everything belongs to Me, Israel will be My especial possession, because I led them out of Egypt, and freed them from bondage. With respect to Israel, God is like one who received many fields as an heritage, but one he purchased himself, and the one he earned was dearest to his heart. I will reign alone over you, as My possession, I and none other, so long as you keep yourselves aloof from other peoples. If not, other peoples shall reign over you. But if you obey Me, you shall be a nation, not only free from care, but also a nation of priests, and a holy nation."

If Israel had not sinned through worshipping the Golden Calf, there would be among them no caste of priests, the nation would have been a nation of priests, and it was only after their sin that the greater part of the people lost the right to priesthood.

God now instructed Moses to transmit to the people His words without adding to them or diminishing from them, in the precise order and in the same tongue, the Hebrew. Moses hereupon betook himself to the people to deliver his message, without first seeing his family. He first addressed the word of God to the elders, for he never forgot the honor due the elders. Then, in simple and well arranged form, he repeated it to all the people, including the women. Joyfully and of his own impulse, every Israelite declared himself willing to accept the Torah, whereupon Moses returned to God to inform Him of the decision of the people. For although God, being omniscient, had no need of hearing from Moses the answer of the people, still propriety demands that one who is sent on a message return to make a report of his success to him who sent him. God hereupon said to Moses: " I will come to thee in a thick cloud and repeat to thee the commandments that I gave thee on Marah, so that what thou tellest them may seem to the people as important as what they hear from Me. But not only in thee shall they have faith, but also in the prophets and sages that will come after thee."

Moses then returned to the people once more, and explained to them the serious effects that disregard of the law

would have upon them. The first time he spoke to them
about the Torah, he expounded its excellencies to them, so
as to induce them to accept it; but now he spoke to them of
the terrible punishments they would bring upon themselves,
if they did not observe the laws. The people did not, however, alter their resolution, but were full of joy in the expectation of receiving the Torah. They only wished Moses
to voice to God their desire to hear Him impart His words
directly to them, so they said to Moses, " We want to hear
the words of our King from Himself." They were not even
content with this, but wanted to see the Divine presence, for
" hearing is not like seeing." God granted both their wishes,
and commanded Moses to tell them to prepare themselves
during the next two days for receiving the Torah.[191]

ISRAEL PREPARES FOR THE REVELATION

Just as one who is to be admitted to Judaism must first
submit to the three ceremonies of circumcision, baptism, and
sacrifice, so Israel did not receive the Torah until they had
performed these three ceremonies. They had already under-
gone circumcision in Egypt. Baptism was imposed upon
them two days before the revelation on Mount Sinai. On
the day preceding the revelation Moses recorded in a book
the covenant between Israel and their God, and on the morning of the day of the revelation, sacrifices were offered as a
strengthening of the covenant.[192]

As there were no priests at that time, the service was performed by the elders of Israel, who in spite of their age
performed their duty with youthful vigor.[193] Moses erected
an altar on Mount Sinai, as well as twelve memorial pillars,

one for each tribe, and then bade them bring bulls, as a
burnt offering and a peace offering.¹⁹⁴ The blood of these
animals was then separated exactly into two halves. This
was attended to by the angel Michael, who guided Moses'
hand, and so conducted the separation of the blood that there
might be not a drop more in one half than in the other. God
upon this said to Moses: " Sprinkle the one half of the blood
upon the people, as a token that they will not barter My
glory for the idols of other peoples; and sprinkle the other
half on the altar, as a token that I will not exchange them
for any other nation." Moses did as he was bidden, and lo!
the miracle came to pass that the blood of a few animals
sufficed to sprinkle every single Israelite.

Before this covenant between God and Israel had been
made, Moses read aloud to the people all of the Torah, that
they might know exactly what they were taking upon themselves. This covenant was made a second time in the desert
of Moab by Moses, and a third time by Joshua after the
entrance into the promised land, on the mountains of Gerizim
and Ebal.¹⁹⁵

Although the people had now clearly expressed their desire to accept the Torah, still God hesitated to give it to them,
saying: " Shall I without further ado give you the Torah?
Nay, bring Me bondsmen, that you will observe it, and I will
give you the Torah." Israel: " O Lord of the world! Our
fathers are bondsmen for us." God: " Your fathers are
My debtors, and therefore not good bondsmen. Abraham
said, ' Whereby shall I know it? ' and thus proved himself
lacking in faith. Isaac loved Esau, whom I hated, and Jacob
did not immediately upon his return from Padan-Aram keep

his vow that he had made upon his way there. Bring Me good bondsmen and I will give you the Torah." Israel: " Our prophets shall be our bondsmen." God: " I have claims against them, for 'like foxes in the deserts became your prophets.' Bring Me good bondsmen and I will give you the Torah." Israel: " We will give Thee our children as bondsmen." God: " Well, then, these are good bondsmen, on whose bond I will give you the Torah." Hereupon the Israelites brought their wives with their babes at their breasts, and their pregnant wives, and God made the bodies of the pregnant women transparent as glass, and He addressed the children in the womb with these words: " Behold, I will give your fathers the Torah. Will you be surety for them that they will observe it?" They answered: " Yea." He furthermore said: " I am your God." They answered: " Yea." " Ye shall have no other gods." They said: " Nay." In this wise the children in the womb answered every commandment with " Yea," and every prohibition with " Nay." As it was the little children upon whose bond God gave His people the Torah, it comes to pass that many little children die when Israel does not observe the Torah.[190]

The Revelation on Mount Sinai

From the first day of the third month, the day on which Israel arrived at Mount Sinai, a heavy cloud rested upon them, and every one except Moses was forbidden to ascend the mountain, yea, they durst not even stay near it, lest God smite those who pushed forward, with hail or fiery arrows.[191] The day of the revelation announced itself as an ominous day even in the morning, for diverse rumblings sounded from Mount Sinai. Flashes of lightning, accompanied by an ever swelling peal of horns, moved the people with mighty fear and trembling. God bent the heavens, moved the earth, and shook the bounds of the world, so that the depths trembled, and the heavens grew frightened. His splendor passed through the four portals of fire, earthquake, storm, and hail. The kings of the earth trembled in their palaces, and they all came to the villain Balaam, and asked him if God intended the same fate for them as for the generation of the flood. But Balaam said to them: "O ye fools! The Holy One, blessed be He, has long since promised Noah never again to punish the world with a flood." The kings of the heathen, however, were not quieted, and furthermore said: "God has indeed promised never again to bring a flood upon the world, but perhaps He now means to destroy it by means of fire." Balaam said: "Nay, God will not destroy the world either through fire or through water. The commotion throughout nature was caused through this only, that He is now about to bestow the Torah upon His people. 'The Eternal will give strength unto His people.'" At this all the kings shouted, "May the Eternal bless His people with peace," and each one, quieted in spirit, went to his house.[198]

Just as the inhabitants of the earth were alarmed at the revelation, and believed the end of all time had arrived, so too did the earth. She thought the resurrection of the dead was about to take place, and she would have to account for the blood of the slain that she had absorbed, and for the bodies of the murdered whom she covered. The earth was not calmed until she heard the first words of the Decalogue.[199]

Although phenomena were perceptible on Mount Sinai in the morning, still God did not reveal Himself to the people until noon. For owing to the brevity of the summer nights, and the pleasantness of the morning sleep in summer, the people were still asleep when God had descended upon Mount Sinai. Moses betook himself to the encampment and awakened them with these words: "Arise from your sleep, the bridegroom is at hand, and is waiting to lead his bride under the marriage-canopy." Moses, at the head of the procession, hereupon brought the nation to its bridegroom, God, to Sinai, himself going up the mountain.[200] He said to God: "Announce Thy words, Thy children are ready to obey them." These words of Moses rang out near and far, for on this occasion, his voice, when he repeated the words of God to the people, had as much power as the Divine voice that he heard.[201]

It was not indeed quite of their own free will that Israel declared themselves ready to accept the Torah, for when the whole nation, in two divisions, men and women, approached Sinai, God lifted up this mountain and held it over the heads of the people like a basket, saying to them: "If you accept the Torah, it is well, otherwise you will find your grave under this mountain." They all burst into tears and poured out their heart in contrition before God, and then said: "All that the Lord hath said, will we do, and be obedient."[202] Hardly had they uttered these words of submission to God, when a hundred and twenty myriads of angels descended, and provided every Israelite with a crown and a girdle of glory—Divine gifts, which they did not lose until they worshipped the Golden Calf, when the angels came and took

the gifts away from them.[203] At the same time with these
crowns and girdles of glory, a heavenly radiance was shed
over their faces, but this also they later lost through their
sins. Only Moses retained it, whose face shone so brightly,
that if even to-day a crack were made in his tomb, the light
emanating from his corpse would be so powerful that it could
not but destroy all the world.[204]

After God had bestowed upon Israel these wonderful gifts,
He wanted to proceed to the announcement of the Torah, but
did not desire to do so while Moses was with Him, that the
people might not say it was Moses who had spoken out of
the cloud. Hence He sought an excuse to be rid of him.
He therefore said to Moses: "Go down, warn the people,
that they shall not press forward to see, for if even one of
them were to be destroyed, the loss to Me would be as great
as if all creation had been destroyed. Bid Nadab and Abihu
also, as well as the first born that are to perform priestly
duties, beware that they do not press forward." Moses,
however, desirous of remaining with God, replied: "I have
already warned the people and set the bounds beyond which
they may not venture." God hereupon said to Moses: "Go,
descend and call upon Aaron to come up with thee, but let
him keep behind thee, while the people do not move beyond
the positions thou hadst assigned them." Hardly had Moses
left the mountain, when God revealed the Torah to the
people.[205]

This was the sixth revelation of God upon earth since the
creation of the world. The tenth and last is to take place
on the Day of Judgment.

The heavens opened and Mount Sinai, freed from the

earth, rose into the air, so that its summit towered into the heavens, while a thick cloud covered the sides of it, and touched the feet of the Divine Throne.[206] Accompanying God on one side, appeared twenty-two thousand angels with crowns for the Levites, the only tribe that remained true to God while the rest worshipped the Golden Calf. On the second side were sixty myriads, three thousand five hundred and fifty angels, each bearing a crown of fire for each individual Israelite. Double this number of angels was on the third side, whereas on the fourth side they were simply innumerable. For God did not appear from one direction, but from all four simultaneously, which, however, did not prevent His glory from filling the heaven as well as all the earth.[207]

In spite of these innumerable hosts of angels there was no crowding on Mount Sinai, no mob, there was room for all the angels that had appeared in honor of Israel and the Torah. They had, however, at the same time received the order to destroy Israel in case they intended to reject the Torah.[208]

THE FIRST COMMANDMENT

The first word of God on Sinai was Anoki, " It is I." It was not a Hebrew word, but an Egyptian word that Israel first heard from God. He treated them as did that king his home-coming son, whom, returning from a long stay over sea, he addressed in the language the son had acquired in a foreign land. So God addressed Israel in Egyptian, because it was the language they spoke. At the same time Israel recognized in this word " Anoki," that it was God who addressed them. For when Jacob had assembled his children around his death-bed, he warned them to be mindful of the glory of God, and confided to them the secrets that God would hereafter reveal to them with the word " Anoki." He said: " With the word ' Anoki ' He addressed my grandfather Abraham; with the word ' Anoki ' He addressed my father Isaac, and with the word ' Anoki ' He addressed me. Know, then, that when He will come to you, and will so address you, it will be He, but not otherwise." [209]

When the first commandment had come out of the mouth of God, thunder and lightning proceeded from His mouth, a torch was at His right, and a torch at His left, and His voice flew through the air, saying: " My people, My people, House of Israel! I am the Eternal, your God, who brought you out of the land of Egypt." When Israel heard the awful voice, they flew back in their horror twelve miles, until their souls fled from them. Upon this the Torah turned to God, saying: " Lord of the world! Hast Thou given me to the living, or to the dead? " God said: " To the living." The Torah: " But they are all dead." God: " For thy sake will I restore them to life." Hereupon He let fall upon them the dew that will hereafter revive the dead, and they returned to life.

The trembling of heaven and earth that set in upon the perception of the Divine voice, alarmed Israel so greatly that they could hardly stand on their feet. God hereupon sent to every one of them two angels; one to lay his hand upon the heart of each, that his soul might not depart, and one to lift the head of each, that he might behold his Maker's splendor. They beheld the glory of God as well as the otherwise

invisible word when it emanated from the Divine vision, and
rolled forward to their ears, whereupon they perceived these
words: "Wilt thou accept the Torah, which contains two
hundred and forty-eight commandments, corresponding to
the number of the members of thy body?" They answered:
"Yea, yea." Then the word passed from the ear to the mouth;
it kissed the mouth, then rolled again to the ear, and called
to it: "Wilt thou accept the Torah, which contains three
hundred and sixty-five prohibitions, corresponding to the
days of the year?" And when they replied, "Yea, yea,"
again the word turned from the ear to the mouth and kissed
it. After the Israelites had in this wise taken upon themselves the commandments and the prohibitions, God opened
the seven heavens and the seven earths, and said: "Behold,
these are My witnesses that there is none like Me in the
heights or on earth! See that I am the Only One, and that
I have revealed Myself in My splendor and My radiance!
If anyone should say to you, 'Go, serve other gods,' then
say: 'Can one who has seen his Maker, face to face, in His
splendor, in His glory and His strength, leave Him and become an idolater?' See, it is I that have delivered you out
of the house of bondage; it is I that cleaved the seas before
you and led you on dry land, while I submerged your
enemies in the depths.[110] I am the God of the dry land as
well as of the sea, of the past as well as of the future, the
God of this world as well as of the future world.[111] I am the
God of all nations, but only with Israel is My name allied.
If they fulfil My wishes, I, the Eternal, am merciful,
gracious and long suffering, and abundant in goodness and
truth; but if you are disobedient, then will I be a stern judge.

If you had not accepted the Torah, no punishment could have fallen upon you were you not to fulfil it, but now that you have accepted it, you must obey it." [212]

In order to convince Israel of the unity and uniqueness of God, He bade all nature stand still, that all might see that there is nothing beside Him. When God bestowed the Torah, no bird sang, no ox lowed, the Ofannim did not fly, the Seraphim uttered not their " Holy, holy, holy," the sea did not roar, no creature uttered a sound—all listened in breathless silence to the words announced by an echoless voice, " I am the Lord your God." [213]

These words as well as the others, made known by God on Mount Sinai, were not heard by Israel alone, but by the inhabitants of all the earth. The Divine voice divided itself into the seventy tongues of men, so that all might understand it; but whereas Israel could listen to the voice without suffering harm, the souls of the heathens almost fled from them when they heard it. [214] When the Divine voice sounded, all the dead in Sheol were revived, and betook themselves to Sinai; for the revelation took place in the presence of the living as well as of the dead, yea, even the souls of those who were not yet born were present. Every prophet, every sage, received at Sinai his share of the revelation, which in the course of history was announced by them to mankind. [215] All heard indeed the same words, but the same voice, corresponding to the individuality of each, was God's way of speaking with them. And as the same voice sounded differently to each one, so did the Divine vision appear differently to each, wherefore God warned them not to ascribe the various forms to various beings, saying: " Do not believe that because you have seen Me in various forms, there are various gods, I am the same that appeared to you at the Red Sea as a God of war, and at Sinai as a teacher." [216]

THE OTHER COMMANDMENTS REVEALED ON SINAI

After Israel had accepted the first commandment with a "Yea," God said: "As you have now acknowledged Me as your sovereign, I can now give you commands: Thou shalt not acknowledge the gods of other nations as such, for they bring no advantage to those who adore them; this thou shalt not do while I exist. I have given you My Torah in order to lend sovereignty to you, hence you must not kindle My wrath by breaking My covenant through idolatry. You shall not worship dead idols, but Him who kills and restores to life, and in whose hand are all living things. Do not learn the works of other nations, for their works are vanity. I, the Eternal, your God, rule over zeal and am not ruled by it; I wait until the fourth generation to visit punishment upon the offenders, but if these generations are one after the other sinful, I will wait no longer with punishment. But those who love Me, or fear Me, will I reward even unto the thousandth generation."

When Moses heard these words, according to which God would visit upon the descendants the sins of their fathers only if the consecutive generations were one after another sinful, he cast himself upon the ground and thanked God for it; for he knew it never occurred among Israel that three consecutive generations were sinful. [217]

The third commandment read: "O My people Israel, none among you shall call the name of the Lord in vain, for he who swears falsely by the name of the Lord shall not go unpunished on the great Judgment Day." [218] Swearing falsely has terrible consequences not only for the one who does it, but it endangers all the world. For when God created the world, He laid over the abyss a shard, on which is engraved the Ineffable Name, that the abyss may not burst forth and destroy the world. But as often as one swears falsely in God's name, the letters of the Ineffable Name fly away, and as there is then nothing to restrain the abyss, the waters burst forth from it to destroy the world. This would surely come to pass, if God did not send the angel Ya'asriel, who has charge of the seventy pencils, to engrave anew the Ineffable Name on the shard. [219]

God said then to Israel, " If you accept My Torah and observe My laws, I will give you for all eternity a thing most precious that I have in My possession." " And what," replied Israel, " is that precious thing which Thou wilt give us if we obey Thy Torah?" God: " The future world." Israel: " But even in this world should we have a fore-taste of that other." God: " The Sabbath will give you this foretaste. [220] Be mindful of the Sabbath, to make it holy; be mindful of the promise I made to the Sabbath on the seventh day of the creation of the world." For when the world was created, the seventh day came before God, and said to Him: "All that Thou hast created is in couples, why not I?" Whereupon God replied, " The community of Israel shall be thy spouse." Of this promise that God had made to the seventh day, He reminded the people on Mount Sinai, when He gave them the fourth commandment, to keep the Sabbath holy. [221]

When the nations of the earth heard the first commandment, they said: " There is no king that does not like to see
himself acknowledged as sovereign, and just so does God
desire His people to pledge unto Him their allegiance." At
the second commandment they said: " No king suffers a
king beside himself, nor does the God of Israel." At the
third commandment they said: " Is there a king that would
like to have people swear false oaths by his name?" At the
fourth commandment they said: " No king dislikes to see
his birthday celebrated." But when the people heard the
fifth commandment, " Honor thy father and thy mother,"
they said: " According to our laws, if a man enrolls himself as a servant of the king, he thereby disowns his parents.
God, however, makes it a duty to honor father and mother;
truly, for this is honor due to Him." [122]

It was with these words that the fifth commandment was
emphasized: " Honor thy parents to whom thou owest existence, as thou honorest Me. Honor the body that bore thee,
and the breasts that gave thee suck, maintain thy parents,
for thy parents took part in thy creation." [123] For man owes
his existence to God, to his father, and to his mother, in that
he receives from each of his parents five of the parts of his
body, and ten from God. The bones, the veins, the nails, the
brain, and the white of the eye come from the father. The
mother gives him skin, flesh, blood, hair, and the pupil of the
eye. God gives him the following: breath, soul, light of
countenance, sight, hearing, speech, touch, sense, insight, and
understanding. [124] When a human being honors his parents,
God says: " I consider it as if I had dwelled among men and
they had honored Me," but if people do not honor their

parents, God says: "It is good that I do not dwell among men, or they would have treated Me superciliously, too." [225]

God not only commanded to love and fear parents as Himself, but in some respects He places the honor due to parents even higher than that due Him. A man is only then obliged to support the poor or to perform certain religious ceremonies, if he has the wherewithal, but it is the duty of each one even to go begging at men's doors, if he cannot otherwise maintain his parents. [226]

The sixth commandment said: "O My people Israel, be no slayers of men, do not associate with murderers, and shun their companionship, that your children may not learn the craft of murder." As a penalty for deeds of murder, God will send a devastating war over mankind. [227] There are two divisions in Sheol, an inner and an outer. In the latter are all those who were slain before their time. There they stay until the course of the time predestined them is run; and every time a murder has been committed, God says: "Who has slain this person and has forced Me to keep him in the outer Sheol, so that I must appear unmerciful to have removed him from earth before his time?" [228] On the Judgment Day the slain will appear before God, and will implore Him: "O Lord of the world! Thou hast formed me, Thou hast developed me, Thou hast been gracious unto me while I was in the womb, so that I left it unharmed. Thou in Thy great mercy hast provided for me. O Lord of all worlds! Grant me satisfaction from this villain that knew no pity for me." Then God's wrath will be kindled against the murderer, into Gehenna will He throw him and damn him for all eternity, while the slain will see satisfaction given him, and be glad. [229]

The seventh commandment says: "O My people Israel, be not adulterers, nor the accomplices or companions of adulterers, that your children after you may not be adulterers. Commit no unchaste deeds, with your hands, feet, eyes, or ears, for as a punishment therefor the plague will come over the world." [230]

This is the eighth commandment: "Be no thief, nor the accomplice or companion of thieves, that your children may not become thieves." As a penalty for robbery and theft famine will come upon the world. [231] God may forgive idolatry, but never theft, and He is always ready to listen to complaints against forgers and robbers. [232]

The ninth commandment reads: "O My people Israel, bear not false witness against your companions, for in punishment for this the clouds will scatter, so that there may be no rain, and famine will ensue owing to drought." God is particularly severe with a false witness because falsehood is the one quality that God did not create, but is something that men themselves produced. [233]

The content of the tenth commandment is: "O My people Israel, covet not the possessions of your neighbors, for owing to this sin will the government take their possessions from the people, so that even the wealthiest will become poor and will have to go into exile." [234] The tenth commandment is directed against a sin that sometimes leads to a trespassing of all the Ten Commandments. If a man covets his neighbor's wife and commits adultery, he neglects the first commandment: "I am the Eternal, thy God," for he commits his crime in the dark and thinks that none sees him, not even the Lord, whose eyes float over all the world, and see good as well as evil. He oversteps the second commandment: "Thou shalt not have strange gods beside Me . . ., I am a jealous God," who is wroth against faithlessness, whether toward Me, or toward men. He breaks the third commandment: "Thou shalt not take the name of the Lord in vain," for he swears he has not committed adultery, but he did so. He is the cause of profanation of the Sabbath, the consecration of which God commands in the fourth commandment, because in his illegal relation he generates descendants who will perform priestly duties in the Temple on the Sabbath, which, being bastards, they have no right to do. The fifth commandment will be broken by the children of the adulterer, who will honor as a father a strange man, and will not even know their true father. He breaks the sixth commandment: "Thou shalt not kill," if he is surprised by the rightful husband; for every time a man goes to a strange woman, he does so with the consciousness that this may lead to his death or to the death of his neighbor. The trespassing of the seventh commandment: "Thou shalt not commit adultery," is the direct outcome of a forbidden coveting. The eighth commandment: "Thou shalt not steal," is broken by the adulterer, for he steals another man's fountain of happiness. The ninth commandment: "Thou shalt not bear false witness," is broken by the adulterous woman, who pretends that the fruit of her criminal relations is the child of her husband. In this way, the breaking of the tenth commandment has not only led to all the other sins, but has also the evil effect that the deceived husband leaves his whole property to one who is not his son, so that the adulterer robs him of his possessions as well as of his wife.[235]

The Unity of the Ten Commandments

The Ten Commandments are so closely interwoven, that the breaking of one leads to the breaking of another. But there is a particularly strong bond of union between the first five commandments, which were written on one table, and the last five, which were on the other table. The first commandment: " I am the Lord, thy God," corresponds to the sixth: " Thou shalt not kill," for the murderer slays the image of God. The second: " Thou shalt have no strange gods before me," corresponds to the seventh: " Thou shalt not commit adultery," for conjugal faithlessness is as grave a sin as idolatry, which is faithlessness to God. The third commandment: " Thou shalt not take the name of the Lord in vain," corresponds to the eighth: " Thou shalt not steal," for theft leads to a false oath. The fourth commandment: " Remember the Sabbath day, to keep it holy," corresponds to the ninth: " Thou shalt not bear false witness against thy neighbor," for he who bears false witness against his neighbor commits as grave a sin as if he had borne false witness against God, saying that He had not created the world in six days and rested on the seventh, the Sabbath. The fifth commandment: " Honor thy father and thy mother," corresponds to the tenth: " Covet not thy neighbor's wife," for one who indulges this lust produces children who will not honor their true father, but will consider a stranger their father.[236]

The Ten Commandments, which God first revealed on Mount Sinai, correspond in their character to the ten words of which He had made use at the creation of the world. The first commandment: " I am the Lord, thy God," corresponds to the first word at the creation: "Let there be light," for God is the eternal light. The second commandment: "Thou shalt have no strange gods before me," corresponds to the second word: "Let there be a firmament in the midst of the waters, and let it divide the waters from the waters." For God said: "Choose between Me and the idols; between Me, the fountain of living waters, and the idols, the stagnant waters." The third commandment: "Thou shalt not take the name of thy God in vain," corresponds to the word: "Let the waters be gathered together," for as little as water can be gathered in a cracked vessel, so can a man maintain his possessions which he has obtained through false oaths. The fourth commandment: "Remember to keep the Sabbath holy," corresponds to the word: "Let the earth bring forth grass," for he who truly observes the Sabbath will receive good things from God without having to labor for them, just as the earth produces grass that need not be sown. For at the creation of man it was God's intention that he be free from sin, immortal, and capable of supporting himself by the products of the soil without toil. The fifth commandment: "Honor thy father and thy mother," corresponds to the word: "Let there be lights in the firmament of the heaven," for God said to man: "I gave thee two lights, thy father and thy mother, treat them with care." The sixth commandment: "Thou shalt not kill," corresponds to the word: "Let the waters bring forth abundantly the moving creature," for God said: "Be not like the fish, among whom the great swallow the small." The seventh commandment: "Thou shalt not commit adultery," corresponds to the word: "Let the earth bring forth the living

creature after his kind," for God said: " I chose for thee a
spouse, abide with her." The eighth commandment: " Thou
shalt not steal," corresponds to the word: " Behold, I have
given you every herb-bearing seed," for none, said God,
should touch his neighbor's goods, but only that which grows
free as the grass, which is the common property of all. The
ninth commandment: " Thou shalt not bear false witness
against thy neighbor," corresponds to the word: " Let us
make man in our image." Thou, like thy neighbor, art
made in My image, hence bear not false witness against thy
neighbor. The tenth commandment: " Thou shalt not covet
the wife of thy neighbor," corresponds to the tenth word of
the creation: " It is not good for man to be alone," for God
said: " I created thee a spouse, let each keep to his spouse,
and let not one among ye covet his neighbor's wife." [337]

MOSES CHOSEN AS INTERMEDIATOR

After Israel had heard the Ten Commandments, they supposed that God would on this occasion reveal to them all the
rest of the Torah. But the awful vision on Mount Sinai,
where they heard the visible and saw the audible—the privilege was granted them that even the slave women among
them saw more than the greatest prophet of later times—this
vision had so exhausted them that they would surely have
perished, had they heard another word from God. They
therefore went to Moses and implored him to be the intermediator between them and God. God found their wish
right, so that He not only employed Moses as His intermediator, but determined in all future times to send prophets to
Israel as messengers of His words. Turning to Moses, God

said: "All that they have spoken is good. If it were possible, I would even now dismiss the Angel of Death, but death against humanity has already been decreed by Me, hence it must remain.[238] Go, say unto them: 'Return to your tents,' but stay thou with Me." In these words God indicated to Israel that they might again enter upon conjugal relations, from which they had abstained throughout three days, while Moses should forever have to deny himself all earthly indulgences.[239]

Moses in his great wisdom now knew how, in a few words, to calm the great excitement of the myriads of men, saying to them: "God gave you the Torah and wrought marvels for you, in order, through this and through the observance of the laws which He imposed upon you, to distinguish you before all other nations on earth. Consider, however, that whereas up to this time you have been ignorant, and your ignorance served as your excuse, you now know exactly what to do and what not to do. Until now you did not know that the righteous are to be rewarded and the godless to be punished in the future world, but now you know it. But as long as you will have a feeling of shame, you will not lightly commit sins." Hereupon the people withdrew twelve miles from Mount Sinai, while Moses stepped quite close before the Lord.[240]

In the immediate proximity of God are the souls of the pious, a little farther Mercy and Justice, and close to these was the position Moses was allowed to occupy.[241] The vision of Moses, owing to his nearness to God, was clear and distinct, unlike that of the other prophets, who saw but dimly. He is furthermore distinguished from all the other prophets, that he was conscious of his prophetic revelations, while they were unconscious in the moments of prophecy. A third distinction of Moses, which he indeed shared with Aaron and Samuel, was that God revealed Himself to him in a pillar of cloud.[242]

In spite of these great marks of favor to Moses, the people still perceived the difference between the first two commandments, which they heard directly from God, and those that they learned through Moses' intercession. For when they heard the words, "I am the Eternal, thy Lord," the understanding of the Torah became deep-rooted in their hearts, so that they never forgot what they thus learned. But they forgot some of the things Moses taught, for as man is a being of flesh and blood, and hence ephemeral, so are his teachings ephemeral. They hereupon came to Moses, saying: "O, if He would only reveal Himself once more! O that once more He would kiss us with the kisses of His mouth! O that understanding of the Torah might remain firm in our hearts as before!" Moses answered: "It is no longer possible now, but it will come to pass in the future world, when He will put His law in their inward parts, and write it in their hearts."

Israel had another reason for regretting the choice of an intermediator between themselves and God. When they heard the second commandment: "Thou shalt have no strange gods beside Me," the evil impulse was torn out from their hearts. But as soon as they requested Moses to intercede for them, the evil impulse set in once more in its old place. In vain, however, did they plead with Moses to restore the former direct communication between them and

God, so that the evil impulse might be taken from them. For he said: "It is no longer possible now, but in the future world He will 'take out of your flesh the stony heart.'" [242]

Although Israel had now heard only the first two commandments directly from God, still the Divine apparition had an enormous influence upon this generation. Never in the course of their lives was any physical impurity heard of among them, nor did any vermin succeed in infesting their bodies, and when they died, their corpses remained free from worms and insects. [244]

Moses and the Angels Strive for the Torah

The day on which God revealed Himself on Mount Sinai was twice as long as ordinary days. For on that day the sun did not set, a miracle that was four times more repeated for Moses' sake. [245] When this long day had drawn to its close, Moses ascended the holy mountain, where he spent a week to rid himself of all mortal impurity, so that he might betake himself to God into heaven. At the end of his preparations, God called him to come to Him. [246] Then a cloud appeared and lay down before him, but he knew not whether to ride upon it or merely to hold fast to it. Then suddenly the mouth of the cloud flew open, and he entered into it, and walked about on the firmament as a man walks about on earth. Then he met Ḳemuel, the porter, the angel who is in charge of twelve thousand angels of destruction, who are posted at the portals of the firmament. He spoke harshly to Moses, saying: "What dost thou here, son of Amram, on this spot, belonging to the angels of fire?" Moses answered: "Not of my own impulse do I come here, but with the permission of the Holy One, to receive the Torah and bear it down to Israel." As Ķemuel did not want to let him pass, Moses struck him and destroyed him out of the world, whereupon he went on his way until the angel Hadarniel came along.

This angel is sixty myriads of parasangs taller than his fellows, and at every word that passes out of his mouth, issue twelve thousand fiery lightning flashes. When he beheld Moses he roared at him: "What dost thou here, son of Amram, here on the spot of the Holy and High?" When Moses heard his voice, he grew exceedingly frightened, his eyes shed tears, and soon he would have fallen from the cloud. But instantly the pity of God for Moses was awakened, and He said to Hadarniel: "You angels have been quarrelsome since the day I created you. In the beginning, when I wanted to create Adam, you raised a complaint before Me and said, 'What is man that Thou art mindful of him!' and My wrath was kindled against you and I burned scores of you with My little finger. Now again ye commence strife with the faithful one of My house, whom I have bidden to come up here to receive the Torah and carry it down to My chosen children Israel, although you know that if Israel did not receive the Torah, you would no longer be permitted to dwell in heaven." When Hadarniel heard this, he said quickly to the Lord: "O Lord of the world! It is manifest and clear to Thee, that I was not aware he came hither with Thy permission, but since I now know it, I will be his messenger and go before him as a disciple before his master." Hadarniel hereupon, in a humble attitude, ran before Moses as a disciple before his master, until he reached the fire of

Sandalfon, when he spoke to Moses, saying: "Go, turn about, for I may not stay in this spot, or the fire of Sandalfon will scorch me."

This angel towers above his fellows by so great a height, that it would take five hundred years to cross over it. He stands behind the Divine Throne and binds garlands for his Lord. Sandalfon does not know the abiding spot of the Lord either, so that he might set the crown on His head, but he charms the crown, so that it rises of its own accord until it reposes on the head of the Lord. As soon as Sandalfon bids the crown rise, the hosts on high tremble and shake, the holy animals burst into pæans, the holy Seraphim roar like lions and say: "Holy, holy, holy is the Lord of hosts, the whole earth is full of His glory." When the crown has reached the Throne of Glory, the wheels of the Throne are instantly set in motion, the foundations of its footstool tremble, and all the heavens are seized with trembling and horror. As soon as the crown now passes the Throne of Glory, to settle upon its place, all the heavenly hosts open their mouths, saying: "Praised be the glory of the Eternal from His place." And when the crown has reached its destination, all the holy animals, the Seraphim, the wheels of the Throne, and the hosts on high, the Cherubim and the Hashmalim speak with one accord: "The Eternal is King, the Eternal was King, the Eternal will be King in all eternity."

Now when Moses beheld Sandalfon, he was frightened, and in his alarm came near to falling out of the cloud. In tears he imploringly begged God for mercy, and was answered. In His bountiful love for Israel, He Himself descended from the Throne of His glory and stood before Moses, until he had passed the flames of Sandalfon.

After Moses had passed Sandalfon, he ran across Rigyon, the stream of fire, the coals of which burn the angels, who dip into them every morning, are burned, and then arise anew. This stream with the coals of fire is generated beneath the Throne of Glory out of the perspiration of the holy Ḥayyot, who perspire fire out of fear of God. God, however, quickly drew Moses past Rigyon without his suffering any injury.

As he passed on he met the angel Gallizur, also called Raziel. He it is who reveals the teachings of his Maker, and makes known in the world what is decreed by God. For he stands behind the curtains that are drawn before the Throne of God, and sees and hears everything. Elijah on Horeb hears that which Raziel calls down into the world, and passes his knowledge on. This angel performs other functions in heaven. He stands before the Throne with outspread wings, and in this way arrests the breath of the Ḥayyot, the heat of which would otherwise scorch all the angels. He furthermore puts the coals of Rigyon into a glowing brazier, which he holds up to kings, lords, and princes, and from which their faces receive a radiance that makes men fear them. When Moses beheld him, he trembled, but God led him past unhurt.

He then came to a host of Angels of Terror that surround the Throne of Glory, and are the strongest and mightiest among the angels. These now wished to scorch Moses with their fiery breath, but God spread His radiance of splendor over Moses, and said to him: " Hold on tight to the Throne

of My Glory, and answer them." ᵗᵗ For as soon as the angels
became aware of Moses in heaven, they said to God:
" What does he who is born of woman here?" And God's
answer was as follows: " He has come to receive the Torah."
They furthermore said: " O Lord, content Thyself with the
celestial beings, let them have the Torah, what wouldst Thou
with the dwellers of the dust?" Moses hereupon answered
the angels: " It is written in the Torah: ' I am the Eternal,
thy Lord, that have led thee out of the land of Egypt and out
of the house of bondage.' Were ye perchance enslaved in
Egypt and then delivered, that ye are in need of the Torah?
It is further written in the Torah: ' Thou shalt have no
other gods.' Are there perchance idolaters among ye, that
ye are in need of the Torah? It is written: ' Thou shalt not
utter the name of the Eternal, thy God, in vain.' Are there
perchance business negotiations among ye, that ye are in
need of the Torah to teach you the proper form of invocation? It is written: ' Remember to keep the Sabbath holy.'
Is there perchance any work among you, that ye are in need
of the Torah? It is written: ' Honor thy father and thy
mother.' Have ye perchance parents, that ye are in need of
the Torah? It is written: ' Thou shalt not kill.' Are there
perchance murderers among ye, that ye are in need of the
Torah? It is written: ' Thou shalt not commit adultery.'
Are there perchance women among ye, that ye are in need of
the Torah? It is written: ' Thou shalt not steal.' Is there
perchance money in heaven, that ye are in need of the Torah?
It is written: ' Thou shalt not bear false witness against thy
neighbor.' Is there perchance any false witness among ye,
that ye are in need of the Torah? It is written: ' Covet not

the house of thy neighbor.' Are there perchance houses, fields, or vineyards among ye, that ye are in need of the Torah?" The angels hereupon relinquished their opposition to the delivering of the Torah into the hands of Israel, and acknowledged that God was right to reveal it to mankind, saying: "Eternal, our Lord, how excellent is Thy name in all the earth! Who hast set Thy glory upon the heavens."

Moses now stayed forty days in heaven to learn the Torah from God. But when he started to descend and beheld the hosts of the angels of terror, angels of trembling, angels of quaking, and angels of horror, then through his fear he forgot all he had learned. For this reason God called the angel Yefefiyah, the prince of the Torah, who handed over to Moses the Torah, "ordered in all things and sure." All the other angels, too, became his friends, and each bestowed upon him a remedy as well as the secret of the Holy Names, as they are contained in the Torah, and as they are applied. Even the Angel of Death gave him a remedy against death. The applications of the Holy Names, which the angels through Yefefiyah, the prince of the Torah, and Metatron, the prince of the Face, taught him, Moses passed on to the high-priest Eleazar, who passed them to his son Phinehas, also known as Elijah.[248]

MOSES RECEIVES THE TORAH

When Moses reached heaven, he found God occupied ornamenting the letters in which the Torah was written, with little crown-like decorations, and he looked on without saying a word. God then said to him: "In thy home, do not people know the greeting of peace?" Moses: "Does it behoove a servant to address his Master?" God: "Thou mightest at least have wished Me success in My labors." Moses hereupon said: "Let the power of my Lord be great according as Thou hast spoken."[249] Then Moses inquired as to the significance of the crowns upon the letters, and was answered: "Hereafter there shall live a man called Akiba, son of Joseph, who will base in interpretation a gigantic mountain of Halakot upon every dot of these letters." Moses said to God: "Show me this man." God: "Go back eighteen ranks." Moses went where he was bidden, and could hear the discussions of the teacher sitting with his disciples in the eighteenth rank, but was not able to follow these discussions, which greatly grieved him. But just then he heard the disciples questioning their master in regard to a certain subject: "Whence dost thou know this?" And he answered, "This is a Halakah given to Moses on Mount Sinai," and now Moses was content. Moses returned to God and said to Him: "Thou hast a man like Akiba, and yet dost Thou give the Torah to Israel through me!" But God answered: "Be silent, so has it been decreed by Me." Moses then said: "O Lord of the world! Thou hast permitted me to behold this man's learning, let me see also the reward which will be meted out to him." God said: "Go, return and see." Moses saw them sell the flesh of the martyr Akiba at the meat market. He said to God: "Is this the reward for such erudition?" But God replied: "Be silent, thus have I decreed."[250]

Moses then saw how God wrote the word "long-suffering" in the Torah, and asked: "Does this mean that Thou hast patience with the pious?" But God answered: "Nay, with sinners also am I long-suffering." "What!" exclaimed Moses, "Let the sinners perish!" God said no more, but when Moses implored God's mercy, begging Him to forgive the sin of the people of Israel, God answered him: "Thou thyself didst advise Me to have no patience with sinners and to destroy them." "Yea," said Moses, "but Thou didst declare that Thou art long-suffering with sinners also, let now the patience of the Lord be great according as Thou hast spoken." [251]

The forty days that Moses spent in heaven were entirely devoted to the study of the Torah, he learned the written as well as the oral teaching, yea, even the doctrines that an able scholar would some day propound were revealed to him. [252] He took an especial delight in hearing the teachings of the Tanna Rabbi Eliezer, and received the joyful message that this great scholar would be one of his descendants. [253]

The study of Moses was so planned for the forty days, that by day God studied with him the written teachings, and by night the oral. In this way was he enabled to distinguish between night and day, for in heaven "the night shineth as the day." There were other signs also by which he could distinguish night from day; for if he heard the angels praise God with "Holy, holy, holy is the Lord of hosts," he knew that it was day; but if they praised Him with "Blessed be the Lord to whom blessing is due," he knew that it was night. Then, too, if he saw the sun appear before God and cast itself down before Him, he knew that it was night; if, however, the moon and the stars cast themselves at His feet, he knew that it was day. He could also tell time by the occupation of the angels, for by day they prepared manna for Israel, and by night they sent it down to earth. The prayers he heard in heaven served him as another token whereby he might know the time, for if he heard the recitation of the Shema' precede prayer, he knew that it was day, but if the prayer preceded the recitation of the Shema', then it was night.[354]

During his stay with Him, God showed Moses all the seven heavens, and the celestial temple, and the four colors that he was to employ to fit up the tabernacle. Moses found it difficult to retain the colors, whereupon God said to him: "Turn to the right," and as he turned, he saw a host of angels in garments that had the color of the sea. "This," said God, "is violet." Then He bade Moses turn to the left, and there he saw angels dressed in red, and God said: "This is royal purple." Moses hereupon turned around to the rear, and saw angels robed in a color that was neither purple nor violet, and God said to him: "This color is crimson." Moses then turned about and saw angels robed in white, and God said to him: "This is the color of twisted linen."[255]

Although Moses now devoted both night and day to the study of the Torah, he still learned nothing, for hardly had he learned something from God when he forgot it again. Moses thereupon said to God: "O Lord of the world! Forty days have I devoted to studying the Torah, without having profited anything by it." God therefore bestowed the Torah upon Moses, and now he could descend to Israel, for now he remembered all that he had learned.[256]

Hardly had Moses descended from heaven with the Torah, when Satan appeared before the Lord and said: "Where, forsooth, is the place where the Torah is kept?"

For Satan knew nothing of the revelation of God on Sinai, as God had employed him elsewhere on purpose, that he might not appear before Him as an accuser, saying: " Wilt Thou give the Torah to a people that forty days later will worship the Golden Calf?" In answer to Satan's question regarding the whereabouts of the Torah, God said: " I gave the Torah to Earth." To earth, then, Satan betook himself with his query: "Where is the Torah?" Earth said: " God knows of its course, He knoweth its abiding-place, for ' He looketh to the ends of the earth, and seeth under the whole heaven.' " Satan now passed on to the sea to seek for the Torah, but the sea also said: " It is not with me," and the abyss said: " It is not in me." Destruction and death said: " We have heard the fame thereof with our ears." Satan now returned to God and said: " O Lord of the world! Everywhere have I sought the Torah, but I found it not." God replied: " Go, seek the son of Amram." Satan now hastened to Moses and asked him: " Where is the Torah that God hath given thee?" Whereupon Moses answered: " Who am I, that the Holy One, blessed be He, should have given me the Torah?" God hereupon spoke to Moses: " O Moses, thou utterest a falsehood." But Moses answered: " O Lord of the world! Thou hast in Thy possession a hidden treasure that daily delights Thee. Dare I presume to declare it my possession?" Then God said: " As a reward for thy humility, the Torah shall be named for thee, and it shall henceforth be known as the Torah of Moses." [257]

Moses departed from the heavens with the two tables on which the Ten Commandments were engraved, and just as the words of it are by nature Divine, so too are the tables on which they are engraved. These were created by God's own hand in the dusk of the first Sabbath at the close of the creation, and were made of a sapphire-like stone. On each of the two tables are the Ten Commandments, four times repeated, and in such wise were they engraved that the letters were legible on both sides, for, like the tables, the writing and the pencils for inscription, too, were of heavenly origin. Between the separate commandments were noted down all the precepts of the Torah in all their particulars, although the tables were not more than six hands in length and as much in width.[258] It is another of the attributes of the tables, that although they are fashioned out of the hardest stone, they can still be rolled up like a scroll.[259] When God handed the tables to Moses, He seized them by the top third, whereas Moses took hold of the bottom third, but one third remained open, and it was in this way that the Divine radiance was shed upon Moses' face.[260]

THE GOLDEN CALF

When God revealed Himself upon Mount Sinai, all Israel sang a song of jubilation to the Lord, for their faith in God was on this occasion without bounds and unexampled, except possibly at the time of the Messiah, when they likewise will cherish this firm faith. The angels, too, rejoiced with Israel, only God was down-cast on this day and sent His voice " out of thickest darkness," in token of His sorrow. The angels hereupon said to God: " Is not the joy that Thou hast created Thine?" But God replied: "You do not know what the future will bring." He knew that forty days later

Israel would give the lie to the words of God: " Thou shalt
have no other gods before Me," and would adore the
Golden Calf.[261]   And truly, God had sufficient cause to grow
sad at this thought, for the worship of the Golden Calf had
more disastrous consequences for Israel than any other of
their sins.   God had resolved to give life everlasting to the
nation that would accept the Torah, hence Israel upon accept-
ing the Torah gained supremacy over the Angel of Death.
But they lost this power when they worshipped the Golden
Calf. As a punishment for this, their sin, they were doomed
to study the Torah in suffering and bondage, in exile and
unrest, amid cares of life and burdens, until, in the Messianic time and in the future world, God will compensate
them for all their sufferings.[262]   But until that time there is
no sorrow that falls to Israel's lot that is not in part a punishment for their worship of the Golden Calf.[263]

Strange as it may seem that Israel should set out to worship this idol at the very time when God was busied with
the preparation of the two tables of the law, still the following circumstances are to be considered.   When Moses departed from the people to hasten to God to receive the Torah,
he said to them: " Forty days from to-day I will bring you
the Torah."   But at noon on the fortieth day Satan came,
and with a wizard's trick conjured up for the people a vision
of Moses lying stretched out dead on a bier that floated mid-
way between earth and heaven.   Pointing to it with their
fingers, they cried: " This is the man Moses that brought
us up out of the land of Egypt." [264]   Under the leadership of
the magicians Jannes and Jambres, they appeared before
Aaron, saying: " The Egyptians were wont to carry their

gods about with them, to dance and play before them, that each might be able to behold his gods; and now we desire that thou shouldst make us a god such as the Egyptians had." When Hur, the son of Miriam, whom Moses during his absence had appointed joint leader of the people with Aaron, owing to his birth which placed him among the notables of highest rank, beheld this, he said to them: "O ye frivolous ones, you are no longer mindful of the many miracles God wrought for you." In their wrath, the people slew this pious and noble man; and, pointing out his dead body to Aaron, they said to him threateningly: "If thou wilt make us a god, it is well, if not we will dispose of thee as of him." Aaron had no fear for his life, but he thought: "If Israel were to commit so terrible a sin as to slay their priest and prophet, God would never forgive them." He was willing rather to take a sin upon himself than to cast the burden of so wicked a deed upon the people. He therefore granted them their wish to make them a god, but he did it in such a way that he still cherished the hope that this thing might not come to pass. Hence he demanded from them not their own ornaments for the fashioning of the idol, but the ornaments of their wives, their sons, and their daughters, thinking: "If I were to tell them to bring me gold and silver, they would immediately do so, hence I will demand the earrings of their wives, their sons, and their daughters, that through their refusal to give up their ornaments, the matter might come to nought." But Aaron's assumption was only in part true; the women indeed did firmly refuse to give up their jewels for the making of a monster that is of no assistance to his worshippers. As a reward for this, God gave the new moons as holidays to women, and in the future world too they will be rewarded for their firm faith in God, in that, like the new moons, they too, may monthly be rejuvenated. But when the men saw that no gold or silver for the idol was forthcoming from the women, they drew off their own earrings that they wore in Arab fashion, and brought these to Aaron.[265]

No living calf would have shaped itself out of the gold of these earrings, if a disaster had not occurred through an oversight of Aaron. For when Moses at the exodus of Israel from Egypt set himself to lifting the coffin of Joseph out of the depths of the Nile, he employed the following means: He took four leaves of silver, and engraved on each the image of one of the beings represented at the Celestial Throne,—the lion, the man, the eagle, and the bull. He then cast on the river the leaf with the image of the lion, and the waters of the river became tumultuous, and roared like a lion. He then threw down the leaf with the image of man, and the scattered bones of Joseph united themselves into an entire body; and when he cast in the third leaf with the image of the eagle, the coffin floated up to the top. As he had no use for the fourth leaf of silver with the image of the bull, he asked a woman to store it away for him, while he was occupied with the transportation of the coffin, and later forgot to reclaim the leaf of silver. This was now among the ornaments that the people brought to Aaron, and it was exclusively owing to this bull's image of magical virtues, that a golden bull arose out of the fire into which Aaron put the gold and silver.[266]

When the mixed multitude that had joined Israel in their

exodus from Egypt saw this idol conducting itself like a living being, they said to Israel: "This is thy God, O Israel." [267] The people then betook themselves to the seventy members of the Sanhedrin and demanded that they worship the bull that had led Israel out of Egypt. "God," said they, "has not delivered *us* out of Egypt, but only Himself, who had in Egypt been in captivity." The members of the Sanhedrin remained loyal to their God, and were hence cut down by the rabble. [268] The twelve heads of the tribes did not answer the summons of the people any more than the members of the Sanhedrin, and were therefore rewarded by being found worthy of beholding the Divine vision. [269]

But the people worshipped not only the Golden Calf, they made thirteen such idols, one each for the twelve tribes, and one for all Israel. More than this, they employed manna, which God in His kindness did not deny them even on this day, as an offering to their idols. [270] The devotion of Israel to this worship of the bull is in part explained by the circumstance that while passing through the Red Sea, they beheld the Celestial Throne, and most distinctly of the four creatures about the Throne, they saw the ox. It was for this reason that they hit upon the notion that the ox had helped God in the exodus from Egypt, and for this reason did they wish to worship the ox beside God. [271]

The people then wanted to erect an altar for their idol, but Aaron tried to prevent this by saying to the people: "It will be more reverential to your god if I build the altar in person," for he hoped that Moses might appear in the meantime. His expectation, however, was disappointed, for on the morning of the following day, when Aaron had at length completed the altar, Moses was not yet at hand, and the people began to offer sacrifices to their idol, and to indulge in lewdness.[272]

Moses Blamed for Israel's Sin

When the people turned from their God, He said to Moses, who was still in heaven: "' Go, get thee down; for thy people, which thou broughtest out of the land of Egypt, have corrupted themselves.'" Moses, who until then had been superior to the angels, now, owing to the sins of Israel, feared them greatly. The angels, hearing that God meant to send him from His presence, wanted to kill him, and only by clinging to the Throne of God, who covered him with His mantle, did he escape from the hands of the angels, that they might do him no harm.[273] He had a particularly hard struggle with the five Angels of Destruction: Kezef, Af, Ḥemah, Mashhit, and Ḥaron, whom God had sent to annihilate Israel. Moses then hastened to the three Patriarchs, Abraham, Isaac, and Jacob, and said to them: "If ye are men who are participators of the future life, stand by me in this hour, for your children are as a sheep that is led to the slaughter." The three Patriarchs united their prayers with those of Moses, who said to God: "Hast Thou not made a vow to these three to multiply their seed as the stars, and are they now to be destroyed?" In recognition of the merits of these three pious men, God called away three of the Angels of Destruction, leaving only two; whereupon Moses further importuned God: "For the vow Thou madest to Israel, take from them the angel Mashhit;" and God granted his prayer. Moses continued: "For the vow Thou madest me, take from them also the angel Haron." God now stood by Moses, so that he was able to conquer this angel, and he thrust him down deep into the earth in a spot that is a possession of the tribe of Gad, and there held him captive.

So long as Moses lived this angel was held in check by him, and if he tried, even when Israel sinned, to rise out of the depths, open wide his mouth, and destroy Israel with his panting, all Moses had to do was to utter the name of God, and Haron, or as he is sometimes called, Peor, was drawn once more into the depths of the earth. At Moses' death, God buried him opposite the spot where Peor is bound. For should Peor, if Israel sinned, reach the upper world and open his mouth to destroy Israel with his panting, he would, upon seeing Moses' grave, be so terror-stricken, that he would fall back into the depths once more.[274]

Moses did indeed manage the Angels of Destruction, but it was a more difficult matter to appease God in His wrath. He addressed Moses harshly, crying: " The grievous sins of men had once caused Me to go down from heaven to see their doings. Do thou likewise go down from heaven now. It is fitting that the servant be treated as his master. Do thou now go down. Only for Israel's sake have I caused this honor to fall to thy lot, but now that Israel has become disloyal to Me, I have no further reason thus to distinguish thee." Moses hereupon answered: " O Lord of the world! Not long since didst Thou say to me: ' Come now, therefore, and I will send thee that thou mayest bring forth My people out of Egypt;' and now Thou callest them *my* people. Nay, whether pious or sinful, they are Thy people still." Moses continued: " What wilt Thou now do with them?" God answered: " I will consume them, and I will make of thee a great nation." " O Lord of the world! " replied Moses, " If the three-legged bench has no stability, how then shall the one-legged stand? Fulfil not, I implore Thee, the prophecies of the Egyptian magicians, who predicted to their king that the star 'Ra'ah' would move as a harbinger of blood and death before the Israelites." [275] Then he began to implore mercy for Israel: " Consider their readiness to accept the Torah, whereas the sons of Esau rejected it." God: " But they transgressed the precepts of the Torah; one day were they loyal to Me, then instantly set to work to make themselves the Golden Calf." Moses: " Consider that when in Thy name I came to Egypt and announced to them Thy name, they at once believed in me, and bowed down their heads and worshipped Thee." God: " But they now bow down their heads before their idol." Moses: " Consider that they sent Thee their young men to offer Thee burnt offerings." God: " They now offered sacrifices to the Golden Calf." Moses: " Consider that on Sinai they acknowledged that Thou art their God." God: " They now acknowledge that the idol is their god."

All these arguments with God did not help Moses; he even had to put up with having the blame for the Golden Calf laid on his shoulders. " Moses," said God, " when Israel was still in Egypt, I gave thee the commission to lead them out of that land, but not to take with thee the mixed multitude that wanted to join them. But thou in thy clemency and humility didst persuade Me to accept the penitent that do penance, and didst take with thee the mixed multitude. I did as thou didst beg Me, although I knew what the consequences would be, and it is now these people, ' *thy* people,' that have seduced Israel to idolatry." Moses now thought it would be useless to try to secure God's forgiveness for Israel, and was ready to give up his intercession, when God, who in reality meant to preserve Israel, but only liked to hear Moses pray, now spoke kindly to Moses to let him see that He was not quite inaccessible to his exhortations, saying: " Even in Egypt did I foresee what this people would do after their deliverance. Thou foresawest only the receiving of the Torah on Sinai, but I foresaw the worship of the Calf as well." With these words, God let Moses perceive that the defection of Israel was no surprise to Him, as He had considered it even before the exodus from Egypt; hence Moses now gathered new courage to intercede for Israel. He said: " O Lord of the world! Israel has indeed created a rival for Thee in their idol, that Thou art angry with them. The Calf, I suppose, shall bid stars and moon to appear, while Thou makest the sun to rise; Thou shalt send the dew and he will cause the wind to blow; Thou shalt send down the rain, and he shall bid the plants to grow." God: " Moses, thou art mistaken, like them, and knowest not that the idol is absolutely nothing." " If so," said Moses, " why art Thou angry with Thy people for that which is nothing? " " Besides," he continued, " Thou didst say Thyself that it was chiefly *my* people, the mixed multitude, that was to blame for this sin, why then art Thou angry with *Thy* people? If Thou art angry with them only because they have not observed the Torah, then let me vouch for the observance of it on the part of my companions, such as Aaron and his sons, Joshua and Caleb, Jair and Machir, as well as many

pious men among them, and myself." But God said: "I
have vowed that ' He that sacrificeth unto any god, save unto
the Lord only, he shall be utterly destroyed,' and a vow that
has once passed My lips, I can not retract." Moses replied:
" O Lord of the world! Hast not Thou given us the law of
absolution from a vow, whereby power is given to a learned
man to absolve any one from his vows? But every judge
who desires to have his decisions accounted valid, must subject himself to the law, and Thou who hast prescribed the
law of absolution from vows through a learned man, must
subject Thyself to this law, and through me be absolved
from Thy vow." Moses thereupon wrapped his robe about
him, seated himself, and bade God let him absolve Him
from His vow, bidding Him say: ' I repent of the evil that
I had determined to bring upon My people." Moses then
cried out to Him: " Thou art absolved from Thine oath and
vow." [276]

THE PUNISHMENT OF THE SINNERS

When Moses descended from Sinai, he there found his
true servant Joshua, who had awaited him on the slope of the
mountain throughout all the forty days during which Moses
stayed in heaven,[277] and together they repaired to the encampment. On approaching it, they heard the cries of the people,
and Joshua remarked to Moses: " There is a noise of war in
the camp," but Moses replied: " Is it possible that thou,
Joshua, who art one day destined to be the leader of sixty
myriads of people, canst not distinguish among the different
kinds of dins? This is no cry of Israel conquering, nor of
their defeated foe, but their adoration of an idol." [278] When

Moses had now come close enough to the camp to see what was going on there, he thought to himself: " How now shall I give to them the tables and enjoin upon them the prohibition of idolatry, for the very trespassing of which, Heaven will inflict capital punishment upon them? " Hence, instead of delivering to them the tables, he tried to turn back, but the seventy elders pursued him and tried to wrest the tables from Moses. But his strength excelled that of the seventy others, and he kept the tables in his hands, although these were seventy Seah in weight. All at once, however, he saw the writing vanish from the tables, and at the same time became aware of their enormous weight; for while the celestial writing was upon them, they carried their own weight and did not burden Moses, but with the disappearance of the writing all this changed. Now all the more did Moses feel loath to give the tables without their contents to Israel, and besides he thought: " If God prohibited one idolatrous Israelite from partaking of the Passover feast, how much more would He be angry if I were now to give all the Torah to an idolatrous people? " Hence, without consulting God, he broke the tables. God, however, thanked Moses for breaking the tables. [279]

Hardly had Moses broken the tables, when the ocean wanted to leave its bed to flood the world. Moses now " took the Calf which they had made, and burnt it in the fire, and ground it to powder, and strewed it upon the water," saying to the waters: " What would ye upon the dry land? " And the waters said: " The world stands only through the observance of the Torah, but Israel has not been faithful to it." Moses hereupon said to the waters: " All that have com-

mitted idolatry shall be yours. Are you now satisfied with
these thousands?" But the waters were not to be appeased
by the sinners that Moses cast into them, and the ocean
would not retreat to its bed until Moses made the children
of Israel drink of it.[280]

The drinking of these waters was one of the forms of
capital punishment that he inflicted upon the sinners. When,
in answer to Moses' call: "Who is on the Lord's side?
Let him come unto me," all the sons of Levi gathered themselves together unto him—they who had not taken part in
the adoration of the Golden Calf,—Moses appointed these
Levites as judges, whose immediate duty it was to inflict the
lawful punishment of decapitation upon all those who had
been seen by witnesses to be seduced to idolatry after they
had been warned not to do so. Moses gave this command
as though he had been commissioned to do so by God. This
was not actually so, but he did it in order to enable the judges
appointed by him to punish all the guilty in the course of
one day, which otherwise, owing to the procedure of Jewish
jurisprudence, could not well have been possible. Those who,
according to the testimony of witnesses, had been seduced
to idolatry, but who could not be proven to have been warned
beforehand, were not punished by temporal justice, they died
of the water that Moses forced them to drink; for this water
had upon them the same effect as the curse-bringing water
upon the adulterous woman. But those sinners, too, against
whom no witnesses appeared, did not escape their fate, for
upon them God sent the plague to carry them off.[281]

MOSES INTERCEDES FOR THE PEOPLE

Those who were executed by these judgments numbered three thousand, so that Moses said to God: "O Lord of the world! Just and merciful art Thou, and all Thy deeds are deeds of integrity. Shall six hundred thousand people—not to mention all who are below twenty years of age, and all the many proselytes and slaves—perish for the sake of three thousand sinners?" God could no longer withhold His mercy, and determined to forgive Israel their sins.[282] It was only after long and fervent prayers that Moses succeeded in quite propitiating God, and hardly had he returned from heaven, when he again repaired thither to advance before God his intercession for Israel. He was ready to sacrifice himself for the sake of Israel, and as soon as punishment had been visited on the sinners, he turned to God with the words: "O Lord of the world! I have now destroyed both the Golden Calf and its idolaters, what cause for ill feeling against Israel can now remain? The sins these committed came to pass because Thou hadst heaped gold and silver upon them, so that the blame is not wholly theirs. ' Yet now, if Thou wilt, forgive their sin; and if not, blot me, I pray Thee, out of Thy book which Thou hast written.' "[283]

These bold words of Moses were not without consequences for him, for although God thereupon replied: " Whosoever hath sinned against Me, him will I blot out of My book," still it was on account of this that his name was omitted from one section of the Pentateuch.[284] But for Israel his words created an instant revulsion of feeling in God, who now addressed him kindly, and promised that He would send His angel, who would lead the people into the promised land.

These words indicated to Moses that God was not yet entirely appeased, and he could further see this in the punishment that fell upon Israel on that day. Their weapons, which every man among them had received at the revelation on Sinai, and which had miraculous virtues, having the name of God engraved upon them, were taken from them by the angels, and their robes of purple likewise. When Moses saw from this that God's wrath was still upon Israel, and that He desired to have nothing further to do with them, he removed his tent a mile away from the camp, saying to himself: "The disciple may not have intercourse with people whom the master has excommunicated."

Not only the people went out to this tent whenever they sought the Lord, but the angels also, the Seraphim, and the heavenly hosts repaired thither, the sun, the moon, and the other heavenly bodies, all of whom knew that God was to be found there, and that the tent of Moses was the spot where they were to appear before their Creator. God, however, was not at all pleased to see Moses keep himself aloof from the people, and said to him: "According to our agreement, I was to propitiate thee every time thou wert angry with the people, and thou wert to propitiate Me when My wrath was kindled against them. What is now to become of these poor people, if we be both angry with them? Return, therefore, into the camp to the people. But if thou wilt not obey, remember that Joshua is in the camp at the sanctuary, and he can well fill thy place." Moses replied: "It is for Thy sake that I am angry with them, and now I see that still Thou canst not forsake them." "I have," said God, "already told thee, that I shall send an angel before them."

But Moses, by no means content with this assurance, continued to importune God not to entrust Israel to an angel,
but to conduct and guide them in person.[285]

Forty days and forty nights, from the eighteenth day of
Tammuz to the twenty-eighth day of Ab, did Moses stay in
heaven,[286] beseeching and imploring God to restore Israel
once more entirely into His favor. But all his prayers and
exhortations were in vain, until at the end of forty days he
implored God to set the pious deeds of the three Patriarchs
and of the twelve sons of Jacob to the account of their descendants; and only then was his prayer answered. He said:
" If Thou art angry with Israel because they transgressed
the Ten Commandments, be mindful for their sake of the
ten tests to which Thou didst subject Abraham, and through
which he nobly passed. If Israel deserves at Thy hands punishment by fire for their sin, remember the fire of the lime-
kiln into which Abraham let himself be cast for the glory of
Thy name. If Israel deserves death by sword, remember the
readiness with which Isaac laid down his neck upon the altar
to be sacrificed to Thee. If they deserve punishment by
exile, remember for their sake how their father Jacob wandered into exile from his paternal home to Haran." Moses
furthermore said to God: " Will the dead ever be restored
to life? " God in surprise retorted: " Hast thou become a
heretic, Moses, that thou dost doubt the resurrection? "
" If," said Moses, " the dead never awaken to life, then truly
Thou art right to wreak vengeance upon Israel; but if the
dead are to be restored to life hereafter, what wilt Thou
then say to the fathers of this nation, if they ask Thee what
has become of the promise Thou hadst made to them? I

demand nothing more for Israel," Moses continued, " than what Thou wert willing to grant Abraham when he pleaded for Sodom. Thou wert willing to let Sodom survive if there were only ten just men therein, and I am now about to enumerate to Thee ten just men among the Israelites: myself, Aaron, Eleazar, Ithamar, Phinehas, Joshua, and Caleb." " But that is only seven," objected God. Moses, not at all abashed, replied: " But Thou hast said that the dead will hereafter be restored to life, so count with these the three Patriarchs to make the number ten complete." Moses' mention of the names of the three Patriarchs was of more avail than all else, and God granted his prayer, forgave Israel their transgression, and promised to lead the people in person.[287]

THE INSCRUTABLE WAYS OF THE LORD

Moses still cherished three other wishes: that the Shekinah might dwell with Israel; that the Shekinah might not dwell with other nations; and lastly, that he might learn to know the ways of the Lord whereby He ordained good and evil in the world, sometimes causing suffering to the just and letting the unjust enjoy happiness, whereas at other times both were happy, or both were destined to suffer. Moses laid these wishes before God in the moment of His wrath, hence God bade Moses wait until His wrath should have blown over, and then He granted him his first two wishes in full, but his third in part only.[288] God showed him the great treasure troves in which are stored up the various rewards for the pious and the just, explaining each separate one to him in detail: in this one were the rewards of those who give alms; in that one, of those who bring up orphans. In this way He showed him the destination of each one of the treasures, until at length they came to one of gigantic size. "For whom is this treasure?" asked Moses, and God answered: "Out of the treasures that I have shown thee I give rewards to those who have deserved them by their deeds; but out of this treasure do I give to those who are not deserving, for I am gracious to those also who may lay no claim to My graciousness, and I am bountiful to those also who are not deserving of My bounty."

Moses now had to content himself with the certainty that the pious were sure of their deserts; without, however, learning from God, how it sometimes comes to pass that evil doers, too, are happy. For God merely stated that He also shows Himself kind to those who do not deserve it, but without further assigning the why and the wherefore. But the reward of the pious, too, was only in part revealed to him, for he beheld the joys of Paradise of which they were to partake, but not the real reward that is to follow the feast in Paradise; for truly "eye hath not seen, beside the Lord, what He hath prepared for him that waiteth for Him." [289]

By means of the following incident God showed Moses how little man is able to fathom the inscrutable ways of the Lord. When Moses was on Sinai, he saw from that station a man who betook himself to a river, stooped down to drink, lost his purse, and without noticing it went his way. Shortly after, another man came, found the money, pocketed it, and took to his heels. When the owner of the purse became aware of his loss, he returned to the river, where he did not find his money, but saw a man, who came there by chance

to fetch water. To him he said: " Restore to me the money
that a little while ago I left here, for none can have taken it
if not thou." When the man declared that he had found
none of the money nor seen any of it, the owner slew him.
Looking with horror and amazement on this injustice on
earth, Moses said to God: " I beseech Thee, show me Thy
ways. Why has this man, who was quite innocent, been
slain, and why hath the true thief gone unpunished?" God
replied: " The man who found the money and kept it merely
recovered his own possession, for he who had lost the purse
by the river, had formerly stolen it from him; but the one
who seemed to be innocently slain is only making atonement
for having at one time murdered the father of his slayer." [290]
In this way, God granted the request of Moses, " to show
him His ways," in part only. He let him look into the future,
and let him see every generation and its sages, every generation and its prophets, every generation and its expounders of
the Scriptures, every generation and its leaders, every generation and its pious men. But when Moses said: " O Lord
of the world! Let me see by what law Thou dost govern the
world; for I see that many a just man is lucky, but many a
one is not; many a wicked man is lucky, but many a one is
not; many a rich man is happy, but many a one is not; many
a poor man is happy, but many a one is not; " then God answered: " Thou canst not grasp all the principles which I
apply to the government of the world, but some of them
shall I impart to thee. When I see human beings who have
no claim to expectations from Me either for their own deeds
or for those of their fathers, but who pray to Me and implore
Me, then do I grant their prayers and give them what they
require for subsistence." [291]

Although God had now granted all of his wishes, still Moses received the following answer to his prayer, " I beseech Thee, show me Thy glory ": " Thou mayest not behold My glory, or else thou wouldst perish, but in consideration of My vow to grant thee all thy wishes, and in view of the fact that thou art in possession of the secret of My name, I will meet thee so far as to satisfy thy desire in part. Lift the opening of the cave, and I will bid all the angels that serve Me pass in review before thee; but as soon as thou hearest the Name, which I have revealed to thee, know then that I am there, and bear thyself bravely and without fear." [202]

God had a reason for not showing His glory to Moses. He said to him: " When I revealed Myself to thee in the burning bush, thou didst not want to look upon Me; now thou art willing, but I am not." [203]

THE THIRTEEN ATTRIBUTES OF GOD

The cave in which Moses concealed himself while God passed in review before him with His celestial retinue, was the same in which Elijah lodged when God revealed Himself to him on Horeb. If there had been in it an opening even as tiny as a needle's point, both Moses and Elijah would have been consumed by the passing Divine light,[204] which was of an intensity so great that Moses, although quite shut off in the cave, nevertheless caught the reflection of it, so that from its radiance his face began to shine.[205] Not without great danger, however, did Moses earn this distinction; for as soon as the angels heard Moses request God to show him His glory. they were greatly incensed against him, and said to God: " We, who serve Thee night and day, may not see Thy glory, and he, who is born of woman, asks to see it!" In their anger they made ready to kill Moses, who would certainly have perished, had not God's hand protected him from the angels. Then God appeared in the cloud.

It was the seventh time that He appeared on earth,[295] and taking the guise of a precentor of a congregation, He said to Moses: "Whenever Israel hath sinned, and calleth Me by the following thirteen attributes, I will forgive them their sins. I am one and the same Merciful God before men have sinned, and after they have sinned and repented their sins. I am the Almighty God who provides for all creatures. I am the Merciful One who restrains evil from human kind. I am the Gracious One who helps in time of need. I am the Long-Suffering to the upright as well as to the wicked. I am Bountiful to those whose own deeds do not entitle them to lay claim to rewards. I am Faithful to those who have a right to expect good from Me; and preserve graciousness unto the two-thousandth generation. I forgive misdeeds and even atrocious actions, in forgiving those who repent."[297] When Moses heard this, and particularly that God is long-suffering with sinners,[298] he prayed: "O forgive, then, Israel's sin which they committed in worshipping the Golden Calf." Had Moses now prayed, "Forgive the sins of Israel unto the end of all time," God would have granted that too, as it was a time of mercy; but as Moses asked forgiveness for this one sin only, this one only was pardoned, and God said: "I have pardoned according to thy word."[299]

The day on which God showed Himself merciful to Moses and to His people, was the tenth day of Tishri, the day on

which Moses was to receive the tables of the law from God
for the second time, and all Israel spent it amid prayer and
fasting, that the evil spirit might not again lead them astray.
Their ardent tears and exhortations, joined with those of
Moses, reached heaven, so that God took pity upon them and
said to them: "My children, I swear by My lofty Name
that these your tears shall be tears of rejoicing for you; that
this day shall be a day of pardon, of forgiveness, and of the
cancelling of sins for you, for your children, and your children's children to the end of all generations." [300]

This day was now set for the annual Day of Atonement,
without which the world could not exist, and which will
continue even in the future world when all other holy days
will cease to be. The Day of Atonement, however, is not
only a reminiscence of the day on which God was reconciled
to Israel and forgave them their sins, but it is also the day
on which Israel finally received the Torah. [301] For after
Moses had spent forty days in prayer, until God finally forgave Israel their sins, he began to reproach himself for having broken the tables of the law, saying: "Israel asked me
to intercede for them before God, but who will, on account of
my sin, intercede before God for my sake?" Then God said
to him: "Grieve not for the loss of the first two tables.
which contained only the Ten Commandments. The second
tables that I am now ready to give thee, shall contain
Halakot, Midrash, and Haggadot." [302]

At the new moon of the month Elul, Moses had the
trumpet sounded throughout the camp, announcing to the
people that he would once more betake himself to God for
forty days to receive the second tables from Him, so that

they might not be alarmed by his absence; and he stayed in heaven until the tenth day of Tishri, on which day he returned with the Torah and delivered it to Israel.[808]

THE SECOND TABLES

Whereas the first tables had been given on Mount Sinai amid great ceremonies, the presentation of the second tables took place quietly, for God said: " There is nothing lovelier than quiet humility. The great ceremonies on the occasion of presenting the first tables had the evil effect of directing an evil eye toward them, so that they were finally broken." [804] In this also were the second tables differentiated from the first, that the former were the work of God, and the latter, the work of man. God dealt with Israel like the king who took to himself a wife and drew up the marriage contract with his own hand. One day the king noticed his wife engaged in very intimate conversation with a slave; and, enraged at her unworthy conduct, he turned her out of his house. Then he who had given the bride away at the wedding came before the king and said to him: " O sire, dost thou not know whence thou didst take thy bride? She had been brought up among the slaves, and hence is intimate with them." The king allowed himself to be appeased, saying to the other: " Take paper and let a scribe draw up a new marriage contract, and here take my authorization, signed in my own hand." Just so did Israel fare with their God when Moses offered the following excuse for their worship of the Golden Calf: " O Lord, dost Thou not know whence Thou hast brought Israel, out of a land of idolaters? " God replied: " Thou desirest Me to forgive them. Well, then, I

shall do so, now fetch Me hither tables on which I may
write the words that were written on the first. But to reward thee for offering up thy life for their sake, I shall in
the future send thee along with Elijah, that both of you
together may prepare Israel for the final deliverance." [305]

Moses fetched the tables out of a diamond quarry which
God pointed out to him, and the chips that fell, during the
hewing, from the precious stone made a rich man of Moses,
so that he now possessed all the qualifications of a prophet—
wealth, strength, humility, and wisdom. In regard to the
last-named be it said, that God had given in Moses' charge
all the fifty gates of wisdom except one.

As the chips falling from the precious stone were designed
for Moses alone, so too had originally the Torah, written on
these tables, been intended only for Moses and his descendants; but he was benevolent of spirit, and imparted the
Torah to Israel. [306] The wealth that Moses procured for himself in fashioning the Torah, was a reward for having taken
charge of the corpse of Joseph while all the people were
appropriating to themselves the treasures of the Egyptians.
God now said: "Moses deserves the chips from the tables.
Israel, who did not occupy themselves with labors of piety,
carried off the best of Egypt at the time of their exodus.
Shall Moses, who saw to the corpse of Joseph, remain poor?
Therefore will I make him rich through these chips." [307]

During the forty days he spent in heaven, Moses received
beside the two tables all the Torah—the Bible, Mishnah,
Talmud, and Haggadah, yea, even all that ever clever
scholars would ask their teacher was revealed to him. When
he now received the command from God to teach all this to

Israel, he requested God to write down all the Torah and to
give it to Israel in that way. But God said: " Gladly would
I give them the whole in writing, but it is revealed before Me
that the nations of the world will hereafter read the Torah
translated into Greek, and will say: ' We are the true
Israel, we are the children of God.' Then I shall say to the
nations: ' Ye claim to be My children, do ye not know that
those only are My children to whom I have confided My
secret, the oral teaching ? ' " This was the reason why the
Pentateuch only was given to Moses in writing, and the other
parts of the Torah by word of mouth. Hence the covenant
God made with Israel reads: " I gave ye a written and an oral
Torah. My covenant with you says that ye shall study the
written Torah as a written thing, and the oral as an oral ; but
in case you confound the one with the other you will not be
rewarded. For the Torah's sake alone have I made a covenant with you ; had ye not accepted the Torah, I should not
have acknowledged you before all other nations. Before you
accepted the Torah, you were just like all other nations, and
for the Torah's sake alone have I lifted you above the others.
Even your king, Moses, owes the distinction he enjoys in
this world and in the world hereafter to the Torah alone.
Had you not accepted the Torah, then should I have dissolved the upper and the under worlds into chaos." [305]

Forty days and forty nights Moses now devoted to the
study of the Torah, and in all that time he ate no bread and
drank no water, acting in accordance with the proverb, " If
thou enterest a city, observe its laws." The angels followed
this maxim when they visited Abraham, for they there ate
like men ; and so did Moses, who being among angels,

like the angels partook of no food. He received nourishment from the radiance of the Shekinah, which also sustains the holy Ḥayyot that bear the Throne. Moses spent the day in learning the Torah from God, and the night in repeating what he had learned. In this way he set an example for Israel, that they might occupy themselves with the Torah by night and by day.

During this time Moses also wrote down the Torah, although the angels found it strange that God should have given him the commission to write down the Torah, and gave expression to their astonishment in the following words, that they addressed to God: "How is it that Thou givest Moses permission to write, so that he may write whatever he will, and say to Israel, ' I gave you the Torah, I myself wrote it, and then gave it to you? ' " But God answered: " Far be it from Moses to do such a thing, he is a faithful servant! "

When Moses had completed the writing of the Torah, he wiped his pen on the hair of his forehead, and from this heavenly ink that cleaved to his forehead originated the beams of light that radiated from it.[309] In this way God fulfilled to Moses the promise: "Before all thy people I will do marvels, such as have not been done in all the earth, nor in any nation." [310] On Moses' return from heaven, the people were greatly amazed to see his face shining, and there was fear, too, in their amazement. This fear was a consequence of their sin, for formerly they had been able to bear without fear the sight of " the glory of the Lord that was like devouring fire," although it consisted of seven sheaths of fire, laid one over another; but after their transgression they could not even bear to look upon the countenance of the man who had been the intermediator between themselves and God.[111] But Moses quieted them, and instantly set about imparting to the people the Torah he had received from God.

His method of instruction was as follows: first came Aaron, to whom he imparted the word of God, and as soon as he had finished with Aaron, came the sons of Aaron, Eleazar and Ithamar, and he instructed them, while Aaron sat at his right hand, listening. When he had finished with the sons of Aaron, the elders appeared to receive instruction, while Eleazar sat at the right hand of his father, and Ithamar at the left hand of Moses, and listened; and when he had finished with the elders, the people came and received instruction, whereupon Moses withdrew. Then Aaron went over what had been taught, and his sons likewise, and the elders, until every one, from Aaron down to every man out of the people, had four times repeated what he had learned, for in this way had God bidden Moses impress the Torah four times upon Israel.[112]

The Census of the People

At sight of the rays that emanated from Moses' face, the people said to him: "We were humbled by God owing to that sin we had committed. God, thou sayest, has forgiven us, and is reconciled to us. Thou, Moses, wert included in our humiliation, and we see that He has once more exalted thee, whereas, in spite of the reconciliation with God, we remain humbled." Hereupon Moses betook himself to God and said: "When Thou didst humble them, Thou didst humble me also, hence shouldst Thou now raise them too, if Thou hast raised me." God replied: "Truly, as I have exalted thee, so will I exalt them also; record their numbers, and through this show the world how near to My heart is the nation that before all others acknowledged Me as their king, singing by the Red Sea: 'This is my God, and I will exalt Him.'" Moses then said to God: "O Lord of the world! Thou hast so many nations in Thy world, but Thou carest nothing about recording their numbers, and only Israel dost Thou bid me count." God replied: "All these multitudes do not belong to Me, they are doomed to the destruction of Gehenna, but Israel is My possession, and as a man most prizes the possession he paid for most dearly, so is Israel most dear to Me, because I have with great exertions made it My own." [113] Moses further said to God: "O Lord of the world! To our father Abraham Thou madest the following promises: 'And I will make thy seed in number as the dust of the earth; and I will make thy seed as the stars in the heavens,' but now Thou biddest me number Israel. If their forefather Abraham could not count them, how, then, should I?" But God quieted Moses, saying: "Thou needest not actually count them, but if thou wouldst determine their number, add together the numerical value of the names of the tribes, and the result will be their number." And truly in this way did Moses procure the sum total of the Jews, which amounted to sixty myriads less three thousand, the three thousand having been swept away by the plague in punishment for their worship of the Golden Calf. Hence the difference between the number at the exodus from Egypt, when Moses had counted them for the first time, and the number at the second census, after the losses incurred by the plague. God treated Israel as did that king his herd, who ordered the shepherds tell the tale of the sheep when he heard that wolves had been among them and had killed some, having this reckoning made in order to determine the amount of his loss.

The occasions on which, in the course of history, Israel were numbered, are as follows: Jacob counted his household upon entering Egypt; Moses counted Israel upon the exodus from Egypt; after the worship of the Golden Calf; at the arrangement into camp divisions; and at the distribution of the promised land. Saul twice instituted a census of the people, the first time when he set out against Nahash, the Ammonite, and the second time when he set out in war upon Amalek. It is significant of the enormous turn in the prosperity of the Jews during Saul's reign, that at the first census every man put down a pebble, so that the pebbles might be counted, but at the second census the people were so prosperous that instead of putting down a pebble, every man brought a lamb. There was a census in the reign of David, which, however, not having been ordered by God, had unfortunate consequences both for the king and for the people. Ezra instituted the last census when the people returned from Babylon to the Holy Land. Apart from these nine censuses, God will Himself count His people in the future time when their number will be so great that no mortal will be able to count them.[214]

There was an offering to the sanctuary connected with the second census in Moses' time, when every one above twenty years of age had to offer up half a shekel. For God said to Moses: "They indeed deserve death for having made the

Golden Calf, but let each one offer up to the Eternal atonement money for his soul, and in this way redeem himself from capital punishment." When the people heard this, they grieved greatly, for they thought: "In vain did we exert ourselves in taking booty from the Egyptians, if we are now to yield up our hard-earned possessions as atonement money. The law prescribes that a man must pay fifty shekels of silver for dishonoring a woman, and we who have dishonored the word of God, should have to pay at least an equal amount. The law furthermore decrees that if an ox kill a servant, his owner shall pay thirty shekels of silver, hence every Israelite should have to discharge such a sum, for 'we changed our glory into the similitude of an ox that eateth grass.' But these two fines would not suffice, for we slandered God, Him who brought us out of Egypt, by calling out to the Calf, 'This is thy God, that brought thee up out of Egypt,' and slander is punishable by law with one hundred shekels of silver." God who knew their thoughts, said to Moses: "Ask them why they are afraid. I do not ask of them to pay as high a fine as he who dishonors or seduces a woman, nor the penalty of a slanderer, nor that of the owner of a goring ox, all that I ask of them is this," and hereupon he showed Moses at the fire a small coin that represented the value of half a shekel. This coin each one of those who had passed through the Red Sea was to give as an offering.

There were several reasons why God asked particularly for the value of half a shekel as a penalty. As they committed their sin, the worship of the Golden Calf, in the middle, that is the half of the day, so they were to pay half of a shekel; and, furthermore, as they committed their sin in the sixth hour of the day, so were they to pay half a shekel, which is six grains of silver. This half shekel, furthermore, contains ten gerahs, and is hence the corresponding fine for those who trespassed the Ten Commandments. The half shekel was also to be an atonement for the sin committed by the ten sons of Jacob, who sold their brother Joseph as a slave, for whom each had received half a shekel as his share.[315]

THE ERECTION OF THE TABERNACLE COMMANDED

When, on that memorable Day of Atonement, God indicated His forgiveness to Israel with the words, " I have forgiven them according as I have spoken," Moses said: " I now feel convinced that Thou hast forgiven Israel, but I wish Thou wouldst show the nations also that Thou art reconciled with Israel." For these were saying: " How can a nation that heard God's word on Sinai, ' Thou shalt have no other gods before Me,' and that forty days later called out to the Calf, ' This is thy god, O Israel,' expect that God would ever be reconciled to them?" God therefore said to Moses: " As truly as thou livest, I will let My Shekinah dwell among them, so that all may know that I have forgiven Israel. My sanctuary in their midst will be a testimony of My forgiveness of their sins, and hence it may well be called a ' Tabernacle of Testimony.' "[316]

The erection of a sanctuary among Israel was begun in answer to a direct appeal from the people, who said to God: " O Lord of the world! The kings of the nations have palaces in which are set a table, candlesticks, and other royal insignia, that their king may be recognized as such. Shalt not Thou, too, our King, Redeemer, and Helper, employ royal insignia, that all the dwellers of the earth may recognize that Thou art their King?" God replied: "My children, the kings of flesh and blood need all these things, but I do not, for I need neither food nor drink; nor is light necessary to Me, as can well be seen by this, that My servants, the sun and the moon, illuminate all the world with the light they receive from Me; hence ye need do none of these things for Me, for without these signs of honor will I let all good things fall to your lot in recognition of the merits of your fathers." But Israel answered: "O Lord of the world! We do not want to depend on our fathers. 'Doubtless Thou art our Father, though Abraham be ignorant of us, and Israel acknowledge us not.'" God hereupon said: "If you now insist upon carrying out your wish, do so, but do it in the way I command you. It is customary in the world that whosoever has a little son, cares for him, anoints him, washes him, feeds him, and carries him, but as soon as the son is come of age, he provides for his father a beautiful dwelling, a table, and a candlestick. So long as you were young, did I provide for you, washed you, fed you with bread and meat, gave you water to drink, and bore ycu on eagles' wings; but now that you are come of age, I wish you to build a house for Me, set therein a table and a candlestick, and make an altar of incense within it." [317] God then gave them detailed instruction for furnishing the Tabernacle, saying to Moses: "Tell Israel that I order them to build Me a tabernacle not because I lack a dwelling, for, even before the world had been created, I had erected My temple in the heavens; but only as a token of My affection for you will I leave My heavenly temple and dwell among you, 'they shall make Me a sanctuary, that I may dwell among them.'"

At these last words Moses was seized by a great fear, such as had taken possession of him only on two other occasions. Once, when God said to him, " Let each give a ransom for his soul," when, much alarmed, he said: " If a man were to give all that he hath for his soul, it would not suffice." God quieted him with the words, " I do not ask what is due Me, but only what they can fulfil, half a shekel will suffice." Then again, fear stirred Moses when God said to him: " Speak to Israel concerning My offering, and My bread for My sacrifices made by fire," and he said trembling, " Who can bring sufficient offerings to Thee? ' Lebanon is not sufficient to burn, nor the beasts thereof sufficient for a burnt offering.' " Then again God quieted him with the words, " I demand not according to what is due Me, but only that which they can fulfil, one sheep as a morning sacrifice, and one sheep as an evening sacrifice." The third time, God was in the midst of giving Moses instructions concerning the building of the sanctuary, when Moses exclaimed in fear: " Behold, the heaven and heaven of heavens cannot contain Thee, how much less this sanctuary that we are to build Thee?" And this time also God quieted him with the words, " I do not ask what is due Me, but only that which they can fulfil; twenty boards to the north, as many to the south, eight in the west, and I shall then so draw My Shekinah together that it may find room under them." [818] God was indeed anxious to have a sanctuary erected to Him, it was the condition on which He led them out of Egypt,[819] yea, in a certain sense the existence of all the world depended on the construction of the sanctuary, for when the sanctuary had been erected, the world stood firmly founded, whereas until then it had always been swaying hither and thither.[120] Hence the Tabernacle in its separate parts also corresponded to the creations of the six days. The two tables in the Ark corresponded to the heaven and the earth, that had been created on the first day. As the firmament had been created on the second day to divide the waters which were under the firmament from the waters which were above, so there was a curtain in the Tabernacle to divide between the holy and the most holy. As God created the great sea on the third day, so did He appoint the laver in the sanctuary to symbolize it, and as He had on that day destined the plant kingdom as nourishment for man, so did He now require a table with bread in the Tabernacle. The candlestick in the Tabernacle corresponded to the two luminous bodies, the sun and the moon, created on the fourth day; and the seven branches of the candlestick corresponded to the seven planets, the Sun, Venus, Mercury, the Moon, Saturn, Jupiter, and Mars. Corresponding to the birds created on the fifth day, the Tabernacle contained the Cherubim, that had wings like birds. On the sixth, the last day of creation, man had been created in the image of God to glorify his Creator, and likewise was the high priest anointed to minister in the Tabernacle before his Lord and Creator.[121]

THE MATERIALS FOR THE CONSTRUCTION OF THE TABERNACLE

When, on the Day of Atonement, God said to Moses, " Let them make Me a sanctuary, that I may dwell among them," that the nations of the world might see that He had forgiven Israel their sin, the worship of the Golden Calf, it was gold He bade them bring for the adornment of the sanctuary. God said: "The gold of the Tabernacle shall serve as an expiation for the gold they employed in the construction of the Golden Calf. Besides gold, let them bring Me twelve other materials for the construction of the Tabernacle: 'silver, brass, and blue, and purple, and scarlet, fine linen, and goats' hair, and rams' skins dyed red, and badgers' skins, and shittim wood, oil for the light, spices for anointing-oil, and for sweet incense, onyx stones and stones to be set in the ephod and in the breatsplate.'" To these instructions, God added these words: "But do not suppose that you are giving Me these thirteen objects as gifts, for thirteen deeds did I perform for you in Egypt, which these thirteen objects now repay. For 'I clothed you with broidered work, and shod you with badgers' skins, and girded you about with fine linen, and I covered you with silk. I decked you also with ornaments, and I put bracelets upon your arms, and chains about your necks. And I put jewels on your foreheads, and earrings in your ears, and a beautiful crown upon your heads.' But in the future world, in return for these thirteen offerings to the Tabernacle, you shall receive thirteen gifts from Me, when 'I shall create upon every dwelling place of Mount Zion, and upon her assemblies, a cloud and smoke by day, and the shining of a flaming fire by night, for upon all the glory shall be a defence. And there shall be a tabernacle for a shadow in the daytime from the heat, and for a place of refuge, and for a covert, from storm and from rain.'" God continued: "Give your contributions to the sanctuary with a willing heart. Do not think that you need give anything out of your pockets, for all you have belongs to Me, through whom you received it in your passage through the Red Sea, when you took their wealth from the Egyptians.[322] I demand nothing from the other nations, but from you I do so, because it was I that led you out of Egypt. But you shall erect a sanctuary to Me not in this world only, but in the future world also. At first the Torah dwelt with Me, but now that it is in your possession, you must let Me dwell among you with the Torah."

Through the various objects God bade them dedicate to the sanctuary, the course of their history was indicated. The gold signified their yoke under Babylon, " the head of gold ; " the silver pointed toward the sovereignty of Persia and Media, who through silver tried to bring about the destruction of Israel; brass stood for the Greek Empire, that like this metal is of inferior quality, its rule also was less significant than that of its predecessors in the sovereignty over the world ; the rams' skins dyed red indicate the sovereignty of " red Rome." God now said to Israel: " Although you now behold the four nations that will hold sway over you, still shall I send you help out of your bondage, ' oil for the light,' the Messiah, who will enlighten the eyes of Israel, and who will make use of ' spices for anointing-oil,' for he will anoint the high priest, that once again ' I may accept you with your sweet savour.' " [323]

When Moses was in heaven, God showed him the Tabernacle, as well as models for all the holy vessels therein, hence Moses naturally supposed that he was destined to be the builder of the Tabernacle. But he was mistaken, for when he was about to leave heaven, God said to Moses: " Thee have I appointed king, and it does not behoove a king to execute works in person, but to give people directions. Therefore thou art not to execute the building of the Tabernacle in person, but thou art to give them thy directions to be executed." Moses now asked God whom he should select as the man to carry out his orders, whereupon God fetched out the book of Adam and laid it before Moses. In this book he found recorded all the generations, from the creation of the world to the resurrection of the dead, and the kings, leaders, and prophets set down beside every generation. Then God said to Moses: "In that hour did I decree every man's calling, and Bezalel was then appointed to his task." [324]

Bezalel

Bezalel was, first of all, of a noble line. His father Hur was a son of Caleb from his union with Miriam, Moses' sister, that Hur who gave his life to restrain Israel from the worship of the Golden Calf. As a reward for his martyrdom, his son Bezalel was to build the Tabernacle, and one of his later descendants, King Solomon, was to build the Temple at Jerusalem. Bezalel was not only of a distinguished family, he was himself a man of distinction, possessed of wisdom, insight and understanding. By means of these three God created the world; Bezalel erected the Tabernacle. Through their aid was the Temple completed, and even in the future world will it be wisdom, insight, and understanding, these three, that God will employ to set up the new Temple. Bezalel, furthermore, had wisdom in the Torah, insight into the Halakah, and understanding in the Talmud, [325] but more than this, he was well versed in secret lore, knowing as he did the combination of letters by means of which God created heaven and earth. The name Bezalel, "in the shadow of God," was most appropriate for this man whose wisdom made clear to him what none could know save one who dwelt "in the shadow of God."

Moses had an instant opportunity of testing the wisdom of this builder appointed by God. God had bidden Moses first to erect the Tabernacle, then the Holy Ark, and lastly to prepare the furnishings of the Tabernacle; but Moses, to put Bezalel's wisdom to the test, ordered him to construct first the Holy Ark, then the furnishings of the Tabernacle, and only then the sanctuary. Hereupon wise Bezalel said to Moses: "O our teacher Moses, it is the way of man first to build his house, and only then to provide its furnishings. Thou biddest me first provide furnishings and then build a sanctuary. What shall I do with the furnishings when there is no sanctuary ready to receive them?" Moses, delighted with Bezalel's wisdom, replied: "Now truly, the command was given just as thou sayest. Wert thou, perchance, 'in the shadow of God,' that thou knewest it?"

Although God knew that Bezalel was the right man for the erection of the Tabernacle, still He asked Moses, "Dost thou consider Bezalel suited to this task?" Moses replied: "O Lord of the world! If Thou considerest him suitable, then surely do I!" But God said: "Go, nevertheless, and ask Israel if they approve My choice of Bezalel." Moses did as he was bidden, and the people assented in these words: "If Bezalel is judged good enough by God and by thee, assuredly he is approved by us." [326] As the builder of the Tabernacle, God gave Bezalel five other names to bear. He called him Reaiah, "to behold," for Bezalel was beheld by God, by

Moses, and by Israel, as the one who had been decreed for his activity since the beginning of the world. He called him "the son of Shobal," because he had erected the Tabernacle that towered high, like a dove-cote. He called him Jahath, "the Trembler," because he made the sanctuary, the seat of the fear of God. He called him Ahumai, because, through his work, the sanctuary, Israel, and God were united; and finally Lahad, as the one who brought splendor and loftiness to Israel, for the sanctuary is the pride and splendor of Israel.

At the side of Bezalel, the noble Judean, worked Oholiab, of the insignificant tribe of Dan, to show that "before God, the great and the lowly are equal." And as the Tabernacle rose, thanks to the combined efforts of a Judean and a Danite, so too did the Temple of Jerusalem, which was built at the command of the Judean Solomon by the Danite Hiram.[327] As the head-workers of the Tabernacle were filled with the holy spirit of God in order to accomplish their task aright, so too were all who aided in its construction, yes, even the beasts that were employed on this occasion possessed wisdom, insight, and understanding.[328]

THE ARK WITH THE CHERUBIM

The very first thing that Bezalel constructed was the Ark of the Covenant, contrary to Moses' order, first to erect the Tabernacle and then to supply its separate furnishings. He succeeded in convincing Moses that it was the proper thing to begin with the Ark, saying: "What is the purpose of this Tabernacle?" Moses: "That God may let His Shekinah rest therein, and so teach the Torah to His people Israel."

Bezalel: "And where dost thou keep the Torah?" Moses: "As soon as the Tabernacle shall have been completed, we shall make the Ark for keeping the Torah." Bezalel: "O our teacher Moses, it does not become the dignity of the Torah that in the meanwhile it should lie around like this, let us rather first make the Ark, put the Torah into it, and then continue with the erection of the Tabernacle, for the Tabernacle exists only for the sake of the Torah." Moses saw the justice of this argument, and Bezalel began his work with the construction of the Ark. In this he followed the example of God, who created light before all the rest of the creation. So Bezalel first constructed the Ark that contains the Torah, the light that illuminates this world and the other world; and only then followed the rest.[329]

The Ark consisted of three caskets, a gold one, the length of ten spans and a fractional part; within this a wooden one, nine spans long, and within this wooden one, one of gold, eight spans long, so that within and without the wooden was overlaid with the golden caskets. The Ark contained the two tables of the Ten Commandments as well as the Ineffable Name, and all His other epithets. The Ark was an image of the celestial Throne, and was therefore the most essential part of the Tabernacle, so that even during the march it was spread over with a cloth wholly of blue, because this color is similar to the color of the celestial Throne. It was through the Ark, also, that all the miracles on the way through the desert had been wrought. Two sparks issued from the Cherubim that shaded the Ark, and these killed all the serpents and scorpions that crossed the path of the Israelites, and furthermore burned all thorns that threatened to injure the wanderers on their march through the desert. The smoke rising from these scorched thorns, moreover, rose straight as a column, and shed a fragrance that perfumed all the world, so that the nations exclaimed: " Who is this that cometh out of the wilderness like pillars of smoke, perfumed with myrrh and frankincense, with all powders of the merchant ? " [330]

Apart from this Ark, which was kept in the Tabernacle, they had another ark, in which were contained the tables broken by Moses, which they carried with them whenever they went to war.[331] The Ark that Bezalel constructed was also used again in Solomon's Temple, for he retained the Ark used by Moses in the Tabernacle, even though all the other furnishings of the Temple were fashioned anew. It remained there up to the time of the destruction of the Temple by Nebuchadnezzar, when it was concealed under the pavement of the wood-house, that it might not fall into the hands of the enemy. This place remained a secret for all time. Once a priest, noticing about the wood-house that something lay hidden under it, called out to his colleagues, but was suddenly stricken dead before divulging the secret.[332]

On the Ark were the Cherubim with their faces of boys and their wings. Their number was two, corresponding to the two tables, and to the two sacred names of God, Adonai and Elohim, which characterized Him as benevolent and as powerful. The face of each Cherub measured one span, and the wings extended each ten spans, making twenty-two spans in all, corresponding to the twenty-two letters of the Hebrew alphabet.[333] It was " from between the two Cherubim " that God communed with Moses, for the Shekinah never wholly descended to earth any more than any mortal ever quite mounted into the heaven, even Moses and Elijah stood a slight distance from heaven; for, " The heaven, even the heavens, are the Lord's: but the earth hath He given to the children of men." Therefore God chose the Cherubim that were ten spans above the earth as the place where the Shekinah betook itself to commune with Moses.[334] The heads of the Cherubim were slightly turned back, like that of a scholar bidding his master farewell; but as a token of God's delight in His people Israel, the faces of the Cherubim, by a miracle, " looked one to another " whenever Israel were devoted to their Lord, yea, even clasped one another like a loving couple. During the festivals of the pilgrimage the priests used to raise the curtain from the Holy of Holies to show the pilgrims how much their God loved them as they could see in the embrace of the two Cherubim.[335]

A two-fold miracle came to pass when the Cherubim were brought into the Temple by Solomon: the two staves that were attached to the Ark extended until they touched the curtain, so that two protuberances like a woman's breasts became visible at the back of it, and the wings of the Cherubim furthermore extended until they reached the ceiling of the Holy of Holies.[336]

THE TABLE AND THE CANDLESTICK

While the number of Cherubim was the same in the Temple as in the Tabernacle, Solomon had, on the other hand, ten tables set up in the Temple in place of the one fashioned by Moses. This was because the one table sufficed to bring sustenance to Israel so long as they were maintained by manna in the desert; but as the demand for food was greater after they settled in the promised land, Solomon had ten tables set up. But in the Temple also did the table of Moses retain its ancient significance, for only upon it was the shewbread placed, and it stood in the centre, whereas the tables fashioned by Solomon stood five to the south and five to the north. For from the south come "the dews of blessing and the rains of plenty," while all evil comes from the north; hence Solomon said: "The tables on the south side shall cause the rains of plenty and the dews of blessing to come upon the earth, while the tables on the north side shall keep off all evil from Israel." [337]

Moses had great difficulty with the construction of the candlestick, for although God had given him instructions about it, he completely forgot these when he descended from heaven. He thereupon betook himself to God once more to be shown, but in vain, for hardly had he reached earth, when he again forgot. When he betook himself to God the third time, God took a candlestick of fire and plainly showed him every single detail of it, that he might now be able to reconstruct the candlestick for the Tabernacle. When he found it still hard to form a clear conception of the nature of the candlestick, God quieted him with these words: "Go to Bezalel, he will do it aright." And indeed, Bezalel had no difficulty in doing so, and instantly executed Moses' commission. Moses cried in amazement: "God showed me repeatedly how to make the candlestick, yet I could not properly seize the idea; but thou, without having had it shown thee by God, couldst fashion it out of thy own fund of knowledge. Truly dost thou deserve thy name Bezalel, 'in the shadow of God,' for thou dost act as if thou hadst been ' in the shadow of God ' while He was showing me the candle-stick." [338]

This candlestick was later set up in the Temple of Solomon, and although he set up ten other candlesticks, still this one was the first to be lighted. Solomon chose the number ten because it corresponds to the number of Words revealed on Sinai; and each of these candlesticks had seven lamps, seventy in all, to correspond to the seventy nations. For while these lamps burned the power of these nations was held in check, but on the day on which these lamps are extinguished the power of the nations is increased. [339] The candlestick stood toward the south, and the table to the north of the sanctuary, the table to indicate the delights of which the pious would partake in Paradise, which lies to the north; the light of the candestick to symbolize the light of the Shekinah, for in the future world there will be but one delight, to gaze at the light of the Shekinah. [340] On account of its sacredness the candlestick was one of the five sacred objects that God concealed at the destruction of the Temple by Nebuchadnezzar, and that He will restore when in His loving-kindness He will erect His house and Temple. These sacred objects are: the Ark, the candlestick, the fire of the altar, the Holy Spirit of prophecy, and the Cherubim. [341]

THE ALTAR

One of the most miraculous parts of the Tabernacle was the altar. For when God bade Moses make an altar of shiṭṭim wood and overlay it with brass, Moses said to God: " O Lord of the world! Thou badest me make the altar of wood and overlay it with brass, but Thou didst also bid me have ' a fire kept burning upon the altar continually.' Will not the fire destroy the overlay of brass, and then consume the wood of the altar?" God replied: " Moses, thou judgest by the laws that apply to men, but will these also apply to Me? Behold, the angels that are of burning flame. Beside them are My store-houses of snow and My store-houses of hail. Doth the water quench their fire, or doth their fire consume the water? Behold, also, the Ḥayyot that are of fire. Above their heads extends a terrible sea of ice that no mortal can traverse in less than five hundred years. Yet doth the water quench their fire, or doth their fire consume the water? For, ' I am the Lord who maketh peace between these elements in My high places.' But thou, because I have bidden thee to have ' a fire kept burning upon the altar continually,' art afraid that the wood might be consumed by the fire. Dead things come before Me, and leave Me imbued with life, and thou art afraid the wood of the altar might be consumed! Thine own experience should by now have taught thee better; thou didst pierce the fiery chambers of heaven, thou didst enter among the fiery hosts on high, yea, thou didst even approach Me, that ' am a consuming fire.' Surely thou shouldst then have been consumed by fire, but thou wert unscathed because thou didst go into the fire at My command; no more shall the brass overlay of the altar be injured by fire, even though it be no thicker than a denarium."

In the words, " Dead things come before Me and leave Me imbued with life," God alluded to the three following incidents. The rod of Aaron, after it had lain for a night in the sanctuary, " brought forth buds, and bloomed blossoms, and even yielded almonds." The cedars that Hiram, king of Tyre, sent to Solomon for the building of the Temple, as soon as the incense of the sanctuary reached them, thrilled green anew, and throughout centuries bore fruits, by means of which the young priests sustained themselves. Not until Manasseh brought the idol into the Holy of Holies, did these cedars wither and cease to bear fruit. The third incident to which God alluded was the stretching of the staves of the Ark when Solomon set them in the Holy of Holies, and the staves, after having been part of the Ark for four hundred and eighty years, suddenly extended until they touched the curtain.

Solomon erected a new altar for offerings, but knowing how dear to God was the altar erected by Moses, the brazen altar, he at least retained the same name for his altar. But in the following words it is evident how much God prized the altar erected by Moses, for He said: "To reward Israel for having had 'a fire kept burning upon the altar continually,' I shall punish 'the kingdom laden with crime' by fire 'that shall not be quenched night or day; the smoke thereof shall go up forever.' "[342]

Beside the brazen altar there was also one of gold, which corresponded to the human soul, while the former corresponded to the body; and as gold is more valuable than brass, so also is the soul greater than the body. But both altars were used daily, as man must also serve his Maker with both body and soul. On the brazen altar sacrifices were offered, as the body of man, likewise, is nourished by food; but on the golden altar, spices and sweet incense, for the soul takes delight in perfumes only.[343]

The materials employed for the construction of the Tabernacle, the skins and the wood, were not of the common order.
God created the animal Taḥash exclusively for the needs of
the Tabernacle, for it was so enormous that out of one skin
could be made a curtain, thirty cubits long. This species of
animal disappeared as soon as the demands of the Tabernacle
for skins were satisfied. The cedars for the Tabernacle, also,
were obtained in no common way, for whence should they
have gotten cedars in the desert? They owed these to their
ancestor Jacob. When he reached Egypt, he planted a cedar-
grove and admonished his sons to do the same, saying:
" You will in the future be released from bondage in Egypt,
and God will then demand that you erect Him a sanctuary to
thank Him for having delivered you. Plant cedar trees, then,
that when God will bid you build Him a sanctuary, you may
have in your possession the cedars required for its construction." His sons acted in accordance with the bidding of their
father, and upon leaving Egypt took along the cedars for
the anticipated erection of the sanctuary. Among these
cedars was also that wonderful cedar out of which was
wrought " the middle bar in the midst of the boards, that
reached from end to end," and which Jacob took with him
from Palestine when he emigrated to Egypt, and then left to
remain among his descendants. When the cedars were
selected for the construction of the Tabernacle, they intoned
a song of praise to God for this distinction.

But not all the twenty-four species of cedar might be used
for the Tabernacle, nay, not even the seven most excellent
among them were found worthy, but only the species
shittim might be used. For God, who foresees all, knew

that Israel would in the future commit a great sin at Shittim, and therefore ordained that shittim wood be used for the Tabernacle to serve as atonement for the sin committed at Shittim. Shittim furthermore signifies " follies," hence Israel were to construct the place of penance for their folly in adoring the Golden Calf, out of shittim wood, to atone for this " folly." And finally, the letters of which the word " Shittim " is composed, stand for Shalom, " peace," Tobah, " good," Yesh'uah, " salvation," and Mehillah, " forgiveness." [344] The boards that were made for the Tabernacle out of shittim wood never decayed, but endure in all eternity. [345]

The Symbolical Significance of the Tabernacle

The separate parts of the Tabernacle had each a symbolical significance, for to all that is above there is something corresponding below. There are stars above, but likewise below, where " a star shall come out of Jacob; " God has His hosts above, and likewise below, His people Israel, " the hosts of the Lord; " above there are Ofannim, and on earth likewise there is an Ofan; above, God has Cherubim, and likewise below in the sanctuary of Israel; God hath His dwelling above, but likewise below; and, lastly, God hath stretched out the heavens above like a curtain, and below, in the sanctuary, were curtains of goats' hair. [346]

The number of curtains, also, corresponds to those in heaven, for just as there are eleven upper heavens, so also were there eleven curtains of goats' hair. [347] The size of the Tabernacle was seventy cubits, corresponding to the seventy holy days celebrated annually by the Jews, to wit: fifty-two Sabbaths, seven days of Passover, eight of Tabernacles, and a day each for Pentecost, the Day of Atonement, and New Year's Day. The number of vessels amounted to seventy also; as likewise God, Israel, and Jerusalem bear seventy names; and as, correspondingly, in the time between the building of the first and of the second Temple, there were seventy consecutive Sanhedrin.[848]

Like the Tabernacle, so the altar, too, had its symbolical significance. Its length and its breadth were five cubits each, corresponding respectively to the five Commandments on the two tables of the law. Its height was three cubits, corresponding to the three deliverers God sent to deliver Israel from Egypt,—Moses, Aaron, and Miriam. It had four horns in the four corners thereof, to atone for the sins of the people that on Sinai received four horns, " the horn of the Torah," " the horn of the Shekinah," " the horn of Priesthood," and " the horn of the Kingdom."[849]

In the Tabernacle, as later in the Temple, gold, silver, and brass were employed, but not iron. God meant to indicate by the exclusion of iron that " in the future time," " the golden Babylon, the silver Media, and the brazen Greece," would be permitted to bestow gifts on the new Temple, but not " the iron Rome." It is true that Babylon also destroyed the sanctuary of God, like Rome, but not with such fury and such thorough-going wrath as Rome, whose sons cried: " Raze it, raze it, even to the foundations thereof," and for this reason Rome may not contribute to the Messianic Temple. And as God will reject the gifts of Rome, so also will the Messiah, to whom all the nations of the earth will have to offer gifts. Egypt will come with her gifts, and although the Messiah will at first refuse to accept anything from the former taskmaster of Israel, God will say to him: "The Egyptians granted My children an abode in their land, do not repulse them." Then the Messiah will accept their gift. After Egypt will follow her neighbor, Ethiopia, with her gifts, thinking that if the Messiah accepted gifts from the former taskmaster of Israel, he will also accept gifts from her. Then the Messiah will also accept Ethiopia's gifts. After these two kingdoms will follow all others with their gifts, and all will be accepted save those from Rome. This kingdom will be sorely disappointed, for, depending upon their kinship with Israel, they will expect kind treatment from the Messiah, who had graciously received the other nations not connected with Israel. But God will call out to the Messiah: "Roar at this monster that devours the fat of the nations, that justifies its claims for recognition through being a descendant of Abraham by his grandson Esau, the nation that forgives all for the sake of money, that kept Israel back from the study of the Torah, and tempted them to deeds that are in accord with the wishes of Satan." [350]

The Priestly Robes

Simultaneously with the construction of the Tabernacle and its vessels, were fashioned the priestly robes for Aaron and his sons. It was at this time that God made known Aaron's appointment to the office of high priest, saying: "Go and appoint a high priest." Moses: "Out of which tribe?" God: "Of the tribe of Levi." Moses was most happy upon hearing that the high priest was to be chosen out of his tribe, and his joy was increased when God added:

" Appoint thy brother Aaron as high priest." This choice of
Aaron was, of course, also a disappointment to Moses, who
had hoped God would appoint him as His high priest, but
God had designed this dignity for Aaron to reward him for
his pious deeds when Israel worshipped the Golden Calf.
For when Moses returned from Sinai and saw the Calf
fashioned by Aaron, he thought his brother was no better
than the rest of the people, and had, like them, devoted himself to idolatry. But God knew that Aaron's participation in
the construction of the Calf was merely due to the pious
motive of delaying the people until Moses should return,
hence He even then said to Aaron : " I am fully aware of thy
motive, and, as truly as thou livest, I shall appoint thee as
warden over the sacrifices that My children offer Me." In
consideration of Moses' feelings, God gave into his hands the
appointment of Aaron, saying to him : " I might have installed thy brother as high priest without having informed
thee of it, but I relinquish his appointment to thee, that thou
mayest have an opportunity of showing the people thy
humility, in that thou dost not seek this high office for thyself." [351] At God's bidding, Aaron and his two sons were now
chosen as priests, and, moreover, not for a limited period,
but Aaron and his house were invested with the priesthood
for all eternity. As soon as these were installed as priests,
Moses set to work to instruct them thoroughly in the priestly
laws. [352]

God ordered the following eight garments as Aaron's
garb : coat, breeches, mitre, girdle, breastplate, ephod, robe,
and golden plate ; but his sons needed only the first four garments. All these garments had expiatory virtues, and each

expiated a definite sin. The coat atoned for murder, the breeches for unchastity, the mitre for pride, the girdle for theft, the breastplate for partial verdicts, the ephod for idolatry, the bells on the robe for slander, and the golden plate for effrontery.[353]

The breastplate and the ephod were set with precious stones, which were the gifts of the noble to the sanctuary, though, to be exact, they were in reality a gift from God. For precious stones and pearls had rained down with the manna, which the noble among Israel had gathered up and laid away until the Tabernacle was erected, when they offered them as gifts.[354]

The ephod had only two precious stones, one on each shoulder, and on each of these stones were engraved the names of six tribes in the following order: Reuben, Levi, Issachar, Naphtali, Gad, Jehoseph, on the right shoulder-piece; Simeon, Judah, Zebulun, Dan, Asher, Benjamin, on the left shoulder. The name Joseph was spelled Jehoseph, a device by which the two stones had exactly the same number of letters engraved upon them.[355] On the breastplate were twelve precious stones, on which the names of the three Patriarchs preceded those of the twelve tribes, and at the end were engraved the words, "All these are the twelve tribes of Israel." [356]

THE STONES IN THE BREASTPLATE

The twelve stones differed not only in color, but also in certain qualities peculiar to each, and both quality and color had especial reference to the tribe whose name it bore. Reuben's stone was the ruby, that has the property, when grated by a woman and tasted by her, of promoting pregnancy, for it was Reuben who found the mandrakes which induce pregnancy.

Simeon's stone was the smaragd, that has the property of breaking as soon as an unchaste woman looks at it, a fitting stone for the tribe whose sire, Simeon, was kindled to wrath by the unchaste action of Shechem. It was at the same time a warning to the tribe of Simeon, that committed whoredom at Shiṭṭim with the daughters of Moab, to be mindful of chastity, and like its stone, to suffer no prostitution.

Levi's stone was the carbuncle, that beams like lightning, as, likewise, the faces of that tribe beamed with piety and erudition. This stone has the virtue of making him who wears it wise; but true wisdom is the fear of God, and it was this tribe alone that did not join in the worship of the Golden Calf.

Judah's stone was the green emerald, that has the power of making its owner victorious in battle, a fitting stone for this tribe from which springs the Jewish dynasty of kings, that routed its enemies. The color green alludes to the shame that turned Judah's countenance green when he publicly confessed his crime with Tamar.

Issachar's stone was the sapphire, for this tribe devoted themselves completely to the study of the Torah, and it is this very stone, the sapphire, out of which the two tables of the law were hewn. This stone increases strength of vision and heals many diseases, as the Torah, likewise, to which this tribe was so devoted, enlightens the eye and makes the body well.

The white pearl is the stone of Zebulun, for with his merchant ships he sailed the sea and drew his sustenance from the ocean from which the pearl, too, is drawn. The pearl has also the quality of bringing its owner sleep, and it is all the more to the credit of this tribe that they nevertheless spent their nights on commercial ventures to maintain their brother-tribe Issachar, that lived only for the study of the Torah. The pearl is, furthermore, round, like the fortune of the rich, that turns like a wheel, and in this way the wealthy tribe of Zebulun were kept in mind of the fickleness of fortune.

Dan's stone was a species of topaz, in which was visible the inverted face of a man, for the Danites were sinful, turning good to evil, hence the inverted face in their stone.

The turquoise was Naphtali's stone, for it gives its owner speed in riding, and Naphtali was "a hind let loose."

Gad's stone was the crystal, that endows its owner with courage in battle, and hence served this warlike tribe that battled for the Lord as an admonition to fear none and build on God.

The chrysolite was Asher's stone, and as this stone aids digestion and makes its owner sturdy and fat, so were the agricultural products of Asher's tribe of such excellent quality that they made fat those who ate of them.

Joseph's stone was the onyx, that has the virtue of endowing him who wears it with grace, and truly, by his grace, did Joseph find favor in the eyes of all.

Jasper was Benjamin's stone, and as this stone turns color, being now red, now green, now even black, so did Benjamin's feelings vary to his brothers. Sometimes he was angry with them for having sold into slavery Joseph, the only other brother by his mother Rachel, and in this mood he came near betraying their deed to his father; but, that he might not disgrace his brothers, he did not divulge their secret. To this discretion on his part alludes the Hebrew name of his stone, Yashpeh, which signifies, " There is a mouth," for Benjamin, though he had a mouth, did not utter the words that would have covered his brothers with disgrace.[857]

The twelve stones in the breastplate, with their bright colors, were of great importance in the oracular sentences of the high priest, who by means of these stones made the Urim and Tummim exercise their functions. For whenever the king or the head of the Sanhedrin wished to get directions from the Urim and Tummim he betook himself to the high priest. The latter, robed in his breastplate and ephod, bade him look into his face and submit his inquiry. The high priest, looking down on his breastplate, then looked to see which of the letters engraved on the stones shone out most brightly, and then constructed the answer out of these letters. Thus, for example, when David inquired of the Urim and Tummim if Saul would pursue him, the high priest Abiathar beheld gleaming forth the letter Yod in Judah's name, Resh in Reuben's name, and Dalet in Dan's name, hence the answer read as follows: Yered, " He will pursue."

The information of this oracle was always trustworthy, for the meaning of the name Urim and Tummim is in the fact that " these answers spread light and truth," but not every high priest succeeded in obtaining them. Only a high priest who was permeated with the Holy Spirit, and over whom rested the Shekinah, might obtain an answer, for in other cases the stones withheld their power. But if the high priest was worthy, he received an answer to every inquiry, for on these stones were engraved all the letters of the alphabet, so that all conceivable words could be constructed from them.[858]

THE COMPLETION OF THE TABERNACLE

On the eleventh day of Tishri Moses assembled the people, and informed them that it was God's wish to have a sanctuary among them, and each man was bidden to bring to the sanctuary any offering he pleased. At the same time he impressed upon them that, however pious a deed participation in the construction of the Tabernacle might be, still they might under no circumstances break the Sabbath to hasten the building of the sanctuary. Moses thereupon expounded to them the kind of work that was permissible on the Sabbath, and the kind that was prohibited, for there were not less than thirty-nine occupations the pursuit of which on the Sabbath was punishable by death.[859] Owing to the importance of keeping the Sabbath, Moses imparted the precepts concerning it directly to the great masses of the people that he had gathered together, and not to the elders alone. In this he acted according to God's command, who said to him: " Go, Moses, call together great assemblages and announce the Sabbath laws to them, that the future generations may follow thy example, and on Sabbath days assemble the people in the synagogues and instruct them in the Torah, that they may know what is prohibited and what is permitted, that My name may be glorified among My children." In the spirit of this command did Moses institute that on every holy day there might be preaching in the synagogues, and instruction concerning the significance of the special holy day. He summoned the people to these teachings with the words: "If you will follow my example, God will count it for you as if you had acknowledged God as your king throughout the world." [360]

The stress laid on the observance of the Sabbath laws was quite necessary, for the people were so eager to deliver up their contributions, that on the Sabbath Moses had to have an announcement proclaimed that they were to take nothing out of their houses, as the carrying of things on the Sabbath is prohibited.[361] For Israel is a peculiar people, that answered the summons to fetch gold for the Golden Calf, and with no less zeal answered the summons of Moses to give contributions for the Tabernacle. They were not content to bring things out of their houses and treasuries, but forcibly snatched ornaments from their wives, their daughters, and their sons, and brought them to Moses for the construction of the Tabernacle. In this way they thought they could cancel their sin in having fashioned the Golden Calf; then had they used their ornaments in the construction of the idol, and now they employed them for the sanctuary of God.[362]

The women, however, were no less eager to contribute their mite, and were especially active in producing the woolen hangings. They did this in so miraculous a way, that they spun the wool while it was still upon the goats.[363] Moses did not at first want to accept contributions from the women, but these brought their cloaks and their mirrors, saying: "Why dost thou reject our gifts? If thou doest so because thou wantest in the sanctuary nothing that women use to enhance their charms, behold, here are our cloaks that we use to conceal ourselves from the eyes of the men. But if thou art afraid to accept from us anything that might be not our property, but our husbands', behold, here are our mirrors that belong to us alone, and not to our husbands." When Moses beheld the mirrors, he waxed very angry, and bade the women to be driven from him, exclaiming: " What right in the sanctuary have these mirrors that exist only to arouse sensual desires?" But God said to Moses: " Truly dearer to Me than all other gifts are these mirrors, for it was these mirrors that yielded Me My hosts. When in Egypt the men were exhausted from their heavy labors, the women were wont to come to them with food and drink, take out their mirrors, and caressingly say to their husbands: ' Look into the mirror, I am much more beautiful than thou,' and in this way passion seized the men so that they forgot their cares and united themselves with their wives, who thereupon brought many children into the world. Take now these mirrors and fashion out of them the laver that contains the water for the sanctifying of the priests." Furthermore out of this laver was fetched the water that a woman suspected of adultery had to drink to prove her innocence. As formerly the mirrors had been used to kindle conjugal affection, so out of them was made the vessel for the water that was to restore broken peace between husband and wife.

When Moses upon God's command made known to the people that whosoever was of a willing heart, man or woman, might bring an offering, the zeal of the women was so great, that they thrust away the men and crowded forward with their gifts,[364] so that in two days all that was needful for the construction of the Tabernacle was in Moses' hands. The princes of the tribes came almost too late with their contribu-

tions, and at the last moment they brought the precious
stones for the garments of Aaron, that they might not be
entirely unrepresented in the sanctuary. But God took their
delay amiss, and for this reason they later sought to be the
first to offer up sacrifices in the sanctuary.[365]

After everything had been provided for the construction of
the Tabernacle, Bezalel set to work with the devotion of his
whole soul, and as a reward for this, the Holy Scriptures
speak of him only as the constructor of the sanctuary, although many others stood by him in this labor. He began
his work by fashioning the boards, then attended to the over-
laying of them, and when he had completed these things,
he set to work to prepare the curtains, then completed the
Ark with the penance-cover belonging to it, and finally the
table for the shewbread, and the candlestick.[366]

THE SETTING UP OF THE TABERNACLE

The work on the Tabernacle progressed rapidly, for everything was ready in the month of Kislew, but it was not set
up until three months later. The people were indeed eager
to set up the sanctuary at once and to dedicate it, but God
bade Moses wait until the first day of the month of Nisan,
because that was Isaac's birthday, and God wished the joy of
dedication to take place on this day of joy. The mockers
among Israel, of course, to whom this was not known, made
fun of Moses, saying: " Of course, is it possible that the
Shekinah should rest over the work of Amram's sons? " [367]

In regard to the Tabernacle, Moses had to suffer much besides from the fault-finders and wicked tongues. If he
showed himself upon the street, they called out to one

another: " See what a well-fed neck, what sturdy legs the son of Amram has, who eats and drinks from our money!" The other would answer: " Dost thou believe that one who has the construction of the Tabernacle in his hands will remain a poor man?" Moses said nothing, but resolved, as soon as the Tabernacle should have been completed, to lay an exact account before the people, which he did. But when it came to giving his account, he forgot one item of seven hundred seventy-five shekels which he had expended for hooks upon which to hang the curtains of the Tabernacle. Then, as he suddenly raised his eyes, he saw the Shekinah resting on the hooks and was reminded of his omission of this expenditure. Thereafter all Israel became convinced that Moses was a faithful and reliable administrator.[368]

As the people had brought much more material than was necessary for the Tabernacle, Moses erected a second Tabernacle outside the encampment on the spot where God had been accustomed to reveal Himself to him, and this " Tabernacle of revelation " was in all details like the original sanctuary in the camp.[369]

When everything was ready, the people were very much disappointed that the Shekinah did not rest upon their work, and they betook themselves to the wise men who had worked on the erection of the Tabernacle, and said to them: " Why do ye sit thus idle, set up the Tabernacle, that the Shekinah may dwell among us." These now attempted to put up the Tabernacle, but did not succeed, for hardly did they believe it was up, when it fell down again. Now all went to Bezalel and his assistant Oholiab, saying to them: " Do you now set up the Tabernacle, you who constructed it, and perhaps it

12

will then stand." But when even these two master-builders did not succeed in setting up the Tabernacle, the people began to find fault, and say: "See now what the son of Amram has brought upon us. We spent our money and went through a great deal of trouble, all because he assured us that the Holy One, blessed be He, would descend from His place with the angels and dwell among us under 'the hangings of goats' hair,' but it has all been in vain." The people now went to Moses, saying: "O our teacher Moses, we have done all thou hast bidden us do, we gave all thou didst ask of us. Look now upon this completed work, and tell us if we have omitted aught, or have done aught we should have refrained from doing, examine it with care and answer us." Moses had to admit that all had been done according to his instructions. "But if it be so," continued the people, "why then cannot the Tabernacle stand? Bezalel and Oholiab failed to set it up, and all the wise men as well!" This communication sorely grieved Moses, who could not understand why the Tabernacle could not be set up. But God said to him: "Thou wert sorry to have had no share in the erection of the Tabernacle, which the people supplied with material, and on which Bezalel, Oholiab, and the other wise men labored with the work of their hands. For this reason did it come to pass that none could set up the Tabernacle, for I want all Israel to see that it cannot stand if thou dost not set it up." Moses replied: "O Lord of the world! I do not know how to put it up." But God answered: "Go, get busy with its setting-up, and while thou art busy at it, it will rise of its own accord." And so it came to pass. Hardly had Moses put his hand upon the Tabernacle, when it stood erect, and the rumors among the people that Moses had arbitrarily put up the Tabernacle without the command of God ceased forevermore.[170]

THE CONSECRATION OF THE PRIESTS

Before the sanctuary and its vessels were dedicated for service, they were anointed with holy oil. On this occasion the miracle came to pass that twelve lugs of oil sufficed not only to anoint the sanctuary and its vessels, and Aaron and his two sons throughout the seven days of their consecration, but with this same oil were anointed all the successors of Aaron in the office of high priest, and several kings until the days of Josiah.

An especial miracle occurred when Aaron was anointed and on his pointed beard two drops of holy oil hung pendant like two pearls. These drops did not even disappear when he trimmed his beard, but rose to the roots of the hair. Moses at first feared that the useless waste of these drops of holy oil on Aaron's beard might be considered sacrilege, but a Divine voice quieted him. A Divine voice quieted Aaron, also, who likewise feared the accident that had turned the holy oil to his personal use.[171]

The anointing of Aaron and his two sons was not the only ceremony that consecrated them as priests, for during a whole week did they have to live near the Tabernacle, secluded from the outer world. During this time Moses performed all priestly duties, even bringing sacrifices for Aaron and his sons, and sprinkling them with the blood of these sacrifices.[172] It was on the twenty-third day of Adar that God bade Moses consecrate Aaron and his sons as priests, saying to him: "Go, persuade Aaron to accept his priestly office, for he is a man who shuns distinctions. But effect his appointment before all Israel, that he may be honored in this way, and at the same time warn the people that after the choice of Aaron none may assume priestly rights. Gather thou all the congregation together unto the door of the Tabernacle." At these last words Moses exclaimed: "O Lord of the world! How shall I be able to assemble before the door of the Tabernacle, a space that measures only two seah, sixty myriads of adult men and as many youths?" But God answered: "Dost thou marvel at this? Greater miracles than this have I accomplished. The heaven was originally as thin and as small as the retina of the eye, still I caused it to stretch over all the world from one end to the other. In the future world, too, when all men from Adam to the time of the Resurrection will be assembled in Zion, and the multitude will be so great that one shall call to the other, ' The place is too strait for me, give place to me that I may dwell,' on that day will I so extend the holy city that all will conveniently find room there." [878]

Moses did as he was bidden, and in presence of all the people took place the election of Aaron and his sons as priests, whereupon these retired for a week to the door of the Tabernacle. During this week, in preparing the burnt offering and the sin offering, Moses showed his brother Aaron and Aaron's sons how to perform the different priestly functions in the sanctuary. Moses made a sin offering because he feared that among the gifts out of which the sanctuary had been constructed, there might have been ill-gotten gains, and as God loves justice and hates loot as an

offering, Moses through a sin offering sought to obtain forgiveness for a possible wrong. During this week, however,
the sanctuary was only temporarily used. Moses would set
it up mornings and evenings, then fold it together again, and
it was not until this week had passed that the sanctuary was
committed to the general use. After that it was not folded
together except when they moved from one encampment to
another.[374]

These seven days of retirement were assigned to Aaron
and his sons not only as a preparation for their regular service, they had another significance also. God, before bringing the flood upon the earth, observed the seven days preceding as a week of mourning, and in the same way He bade
Aaron and his sons live in absolute retirement for a week, as
is the duty of mourners, for a heavy loss awaited them—the
death of Nadab and Abihu, which took place on the joyous
day of their dedication.[375]

THE DAY OF THE TEN CROWNS

The first day of Nisan was an eventful day, " a day that
was distinguished by ten crowns." It was the day on which
the princes of the tribes began to bring their offerings; it was
the first day on which the Shekinah came to dwell among
Israel; the first day on which sacrifice on any but the
appointed place was forbidden; the first day on which priests
performed sacrificial rites; the first day on which the priests
bestowed their blessing upon Israel; the first day for regular
sacrificial service; the first day on which the priests partook
of certain portions of the offering; the first day on which the
heavenly fire was seen on the altar; it was besides the first

day of the week, a Sunday, the first day of the first month of
the year.[376]

It was on this day after " the week of training " for Aaron
and his sons that God said to Moses: " Thinkest thou that
thou art to be high priest because thou hast been attending to
priestly duties during this week? Not so, call Aaron and
announce to him that he has been appointed high priest, and
at the same time call the elders and in their presence announce his elevation to this dignity, that none may say
Aaron himself assumed this dignity." [377]   Following the
example of God, who on Sinai distinguished Aaron before
all others, saying, " And thou shalt come up, thou and Aaron
with thee, but let not the priests and the people break
through," Moses went first to Aaron, then to Aaron's sons,
and only then to the elders, to discuss with them the preparations for the installation of Aaron into office.[378]

When Moses approached Aaron with the news of God's
commission to appoint him as high priest, Aaron said:
" What! Thou hadst all the labor of erecting the Tabernacle,
and I am now to be its high priest! " But Moses replied:
" As truly as thou livest, although thou art to be high priest,
I am as happy as if I had been chosen myself. As thou didst
rejoice in my elevation, so do I now rejoice in thine." [379]
Moses continued: " My brother Aaron, although God has
become reconciled to Israel and has forgiven them their sin,
still, through thy offering must thou close the mouth of
Satan, that he may not hate thee when thou enterest the
sanctuary. Take then a young calf as a sin-offering, for as
thou didst nearly lose thy claim to the dignity of high priest
through a calf, so shalt thou now through the sacrifice of a

calf be established in thy dignity." Then Moses turned to
the people, saying: "You have two sins to atone for: the
selling of Joseph, whose coat your fathers smeared with the
blood of a kid to convince their father that its owner had
been torn to pieces by a wild beast, and the sin you committed through the worship of the Golden Calf. Take, then,
a kid to atone for the guilt you brought upon yourselves with
a kid, and take a calf to atone for the sin you committed
through a calf. But to make sure that God has become
reconciled to you, offer up a bull also, and thereby acknowledge that you are slaughtering before God your idol, the bull
that you had erstwhile worshipped." The people, however,
said to Moses: "What avails it this nation to do homage to
its king, who is invisible?" Moses replied: "For this very
reason did God command you to offer these sacrifices, so
that He may show Himself to you." At these words they
rejoiced greatly, for through them they knew that God was
now completely reconciled to them, and they hastened to bring
the offerings to the sanctuary. Moses admonished them with
the words: "See to it now that you drive evil impulse from
your hearts, that you now have but one thought and one resolution, to serve God; and that your undivided services are
devoted singly and solely to the one God, for He is the God
of gods and the Lord of lords. If you will act according to
my words, 'the glory of the Lord shall appear unto you.'"

But Aaron in his humility still did not dare to enter on his
priestly activities. The aspect of the horned altar filled him
with fear, for it reminded him of the worship of the bull by
Israel, an incident in which he felt he had not been altogether
without blame. Moses had to encourage him to step up to

the altar and offer the sacrifices. After Aaron had offered up the prescribed sacrifices, he bestowed his blessing upon the people with lifted hands, saying: " The Eternal bless thee and keep thee: The Eternal make His face shine upon thee and be gracious unto thee: The Eternal lift up His countenance upon thee and give thee peace."

In spite of the offerings and the blessing, there was still no sign of the Shekinah, so that Aaron, with a heavy heart, thought, " God is angry with me, and it is my fault that the Shekinah has not descended among Israel, I merely owe it to my brother Moses that to my confusion I entered the sanctuary, for my service did not suffice to bring down the Shekinah." Upon this Moses went with his brother into the sanctuary a second time, and their united prayers had the desired effect, there came " a fire out from before the Lord, and consumed upon the altar the burnt offering and the fat," and stayed upon the altar well-nigh one hundred and sixteen years, and neither was the wood of the altar consumed, nor its brazen overlay molten.

When the people saw the heavenly fire, the evident token of God's grace and His reconciliation with them, they shouted, and fell on their faces, and praised God, intoning in His honor a song of praise. Joy reigned not only on earth, but in heaven also, for on this day God's joy over the erection of the sanctuary was as great as had been His joy on the first day of creation over His works, heaven and earth.[380] For, in a certain sense, the erection of the Tabernacle was the finishing touch to the creation of the world. For the world exists for the sake of three things, the Torah, Divine service, and works of love. From the creation of the world to the revelation on Sinai the world owed its existence to the love and grace of God; from the revelation to the erection of the sanctuary, the world owed its existence to the Torah and to love, but only with the erection of the Tabernacle did the world secure its firm basis, for now it had three feet whereupon to rest, the Torah, Divine service, and love. From another point of view, too, is the day of the consecration of the sanctuary to be reckoned with the days of creation, for at the creation of the world God dwelt with mortals and withdrew the Shekinah to heaven only on account of the sin of the first two human beings. But on the day of the consecration of the Tabernacle the Shekinah returned to its former abode, the earth. The angels therefore lamented on this day, saying: " Now God will leave the celestial hosts and will dwell among mortals." God indeed quieted them with the words, " As truly as ye live, My true dwelling will remain on high," but He was not quite in earnest when He said so, for truly the earth is His chief abode. Only after the Tabernacle on earth had been erected did God command the angels to build one like it in heaven, and it is this Tabernacle in which Metatron offers the souls of the pious before God as an expiation for Israel, at the time of the exile when His earthly sanctuary is destroyed.

This day marks an important change in the intercourse between God and Moses. Before this, the voice of God would strike Moses' ear as if conducted through a tube, and on such an occasion the outer world recognized only through Moses' reddened face that he was receiving a revelation; now, at the consecration of the sanctuary, this was changed. For when, on this day, he entered the sanctuary, a sweet, pleasant and

lovely voice rang out toward him, whereupon he said: " I
will hear what God the Lord will speak." Then he heard
the words: " Formerly there reigned enmity between Me and
My children, formerly there reigned anger between Me and
My children, formerly there reigned hatred between Me and
My children; but now love reigns between Me and My children, friendship reigns between Me and My children, peace
reigns between Me and My children."

It was evident that peace reigned, for on this day the undisturbed freedom of movement over the world, which had
until then been accorded the demons, was taken from them.
Until then these were so frequently met with, that Moses
regularly recited a special prayer whenever going to Mount
Sinai, entreating God to protect him from the demons. But
as soon as the Tabernacle had been erected, they vanished.
Not entirely, it is true, for even now these pernicious
creatures may kill a person, especially within the period from
the seventeenth day of Tammuz to the ninth day of Ab, when
the demons exercise their power. The most dangerous one
among them is Ķeṭeb, the sight of whom kills men as well as
animals. He rolls like a ball and has the head of a calf with
a single horn on his forehead.

Just as God destroyed the power of these demons through
the Tabernacle, so too, through the priestly blessing that
He bestowed upon His people before the consecration of the
sanctuary, did He break the spell of the evil eye, which
might otherwise have harmed them now as it had done at
the revelation on Sinai. The great ceremonies on that occasion had turned the eyes of all the world upon Israel, and
the evil eye of the nations brought about the circumstance of

the breaking of the two tables. As God blessed His people on this occasion, so too did Moses, who upon the completion of the Tabernacle blessed Israel with the words: " The Eternal God of your fathers make you a thousand times so many more as ye are, and bless you, as He hath promised you! " The people made answer to this blessing, saying: " Let the beauty of the Lord our God be upon us: and establish Thou the work of our hands upon us; yea the work of our hands establish Thou it." [381]

THE INTERRUPTED JOY

The happiest of women on this day was Elisheba, daughter of Amminadab, for beside the general rejoicing at the dedication of the sanctuary, five particular joys fell to her lot: her husband, Aaron, was high priest; her brother-in-law, Moses, king; her son, Eleazar, head of the priests; her grandson, Phinehas, priest of war; and her brother, Nahshon, prince of his tribe. But how soon was her joy turned to grief! Her two sons, Nadab and Abihu, carried away by the universal rejoicing at the heavenly fire, approached the sanctuary with the censers in their hands, to increase God's love for Israel through this act of sacrifice, but paid with their lives for this offering. From the Holy of Holies issued two flames of fire, as thin as threads, then parted into four, and two each pierced the nostrils of Nadab and Abihu, whose souls were burnt, although no external injury was visible. [382]

The death of these priests was not, however, unmerited, for in spite of their piety they had committed many a sin. Even at Sinai they had not conducted themselves properly,

for instead of following the example of Moses, who had
turned his face away from the Divine vision in the burning
bush, they basked in the Divine vision on Mount Sinai.
Their fate had even then been decreed, but God did not want
to darken the joy of the Torah by their death, hence He
waited for the dedication of the Tabernacle. On this occasion God acted like the king who, discovering on the day of
his daughter's wedding that the best-man was guilty of a
deadly sin, said: "If I cause the best-man to be executed
on the spot, I shall cast a shadow on my daughter's joy. I
will rather have him executed on my day of gladness than
on hers." God inflicted the penalty upon Nadab and Abihu
"in the day of the gladness of His heart," and not on the
day on which the Torah espoused Israel.

Among the sins for which they had to atone was their
great pride, which was expressed in several ways. They did
not marry, because they considered no woman good enough
for them, saying: "Our father's brother is king, our father
is high priest, our mother's brother is prince of his tribe, and
we are heads of the priests. What woman is worthy of us?"
And many a woman remained unwed, waiting for these
youths to woo her. In their pride they even went so far in
sinful thoughts as to wish for the time when Moses and
Aaron should die and they would have the guidance of the
people in their hands. But God said: "'Boast not thyself
of to-morrow;' many a colt has died and his hide has
been used as a cover for his mother's back." Even in the
performance of the act that brought death upon them, did
they show their pride, for they asked permission of neither
Moses nor Aaron whether they might take part in the sacri-

ficial service. What is more, Nadab and Abihu did not even consult with each other before starting out on this fatal deed, they performed it independently of each other. Had they previously taken counsel together, or had they asked their father or their uncle, very likely they would never have offered the disastrous sacrifice. For they were neither in a proper condition for making an offering, nor was their offering appropriate. They partook of wine before entering the sanctuary, which is forbidden to priests; they did not wear the prescribed priestly robes, and, furthermore, they had not sanctified themselves with water out of the laver for washing. They made their offering, moreover, in the Holy of Holies, to which admittance had been prohibited, and used " strange fire," and the offering was all in all out of place because they had had no command from God to offer up incense at that time. Apart from this list of sins, however, they were very pious men, and their death grieved God more than their father Aaron, not alone because it grieves God to see a pious father lose his sons, but because they actually were worthy and pious youths.[383]

When Aaron heard of the death of his sons, he said: " All Israel saw Thee at the Red Sea as well as at Sinai without suffering injury thereafter; but my sons, whom Thou didst order to dwell in the Tabernacle, a place that a layman may not enter without being punished by death— my sons entered the Tabernacle to behold Thy strength and Thy might, and they died!" God hereupon said to Moses: " Tell Aaron the following: ' I have shown thee great favor and have granted thee great honor through this, that thy sons have been burnt. I assigned to thee and thy sons a place nearer to the sanctuary, before all others, even before thy brother Moses. But I have also decreed that whosoever enters the Tabernacle without having been commanded, he shall be stricken with leprosy. Wouldst thou have wished thy sons, to whom the innermost places had been assigned, to sit as lepers outside the encampment as a penalty for having entered the Holy of Holies?" When Moses imparted these words to his brother, Aaron said: "I thank Thee, O God, for that which Thou hast done for me, for the kindness Thou hast shown me in causing my sons to die rather than having them waste their lives as lepers. It behooves me to thank Thee and praise Thee, 'because Thy lovingkindness is better than life, my lips shall praise Thee.'" [384]

Moses endeavored to comfort his brother in still another way, saying: "Thy sons died to glorify the name of the Lord, blessed be His name, for on Sinai God said to me: 'And there will I meet with the children of Israel, the Tabernacle shall be sanctified by those that glorify Me.' I knew that this sanctuary of God was to be sanctified by the death of those that stood near it, but I thought either thou or I was destined for this, but now I perceive that thy sons were nearer to God than we." These last words sufficed to induce Aaron to control his grief over the loss of his sons, and like the true wise man he silently bore the heavy blow of fate without murmur or lament. God rewarded him for his silence by addressing him directly, and imparting an important priestly law to him.

Aaron could not take part in the burial of Nadab and Abihu, for a high priest is not permitted to take part in a funeral procession, even if the deceased be a near kinsman.

Eleazar and Ithamar, also, the surviving sons of Aaron, were not permitted to mourn or attend the funeral on the day of their dedication as priests, so that Aaron's cousins, the Levites Mishael and Elzaphan, the next of kin after these. had to attend to the funeral. These two Levites were the sons of a very worthy father, who was not only by descent a near kinsman of Aaron, but who was also closely akin to Aaron in character. As Aaron pursued peace, so too did his uncle Uzziel, father to Mishael and Elzaphan. Being Levites they might not enter the place where the heavenly fire had met their cousins, hence an angel had thrust Nadab and Abihu out of the priestly room, and they did not die until they were outside it, so that Mishael and Elzaphan might approach them.[335]

Whereas the whole house of Israel was bidden to bewail the death of Nadab and Abihu, for " the death of a pious man is a greater misfortune to Israel than the Temple's burning to ashes," [336]—Aaron and his sons, on the other hand, were permitted to take no share in the mourning, and Moses bade them eat of the parts of the offering due them, as if nothing had happened. Now when Moses saw that Aaron had burnt to ashes one of the three sin offerings that were offered on that day, without himself or his sons having partaken of it, his wrath was kindled against his brother, but in consideration of Aaron's age and his office Moses addressed his violent words not to Aaron himself, but to his sons. He reproached them with having offended against God's commandment in burning one sin offering and eating of the other two. He asked them, besides, if they were not wise enough to profit by the example of their deceased brothers, who paid for their arbitrary actions with their lives, particularly since they also had been doomed to death, and owed their lives only to his prayer, which had power to preserve for their father half the number of sons. Moses' reproof, however, was unjustified, for Aaron and his sons had done what the statutes required, but Moses had on this occasion, as on two others, owing to his wrath, forgotten the laws which he himself had taught Israel. Hence Aaron opposed him decidedly and pointed out his error to him. Moses, far from taking Aaron's reprimand amiss, caused a herald to make an announcement throughout the camp: " I have falsely interpreted the law, and Aaron, my brother, has corrected me. Eleazar and Ithamar also knew the law, but were silent out of consideration for me." As a reward for their considerateness, God thereupon revealed important laws to Moses with a special injunction to tell them to Aaron as well as to Eleazar and Ithamar.[387]

THE GIFTS OF THE PRINCES

When Moses called on the people to make their offerings for the erection of the sanctuary, it sorely vexed the princes of the tribes that he had not summoned them particularly. Hence they withheld their contributions, waiting for the people to give according to their powers, so that they might step in and make up the deficiency, and all should observe that without them the Tabernacle could not have been completed. But they were mistaken, for in their ready devotion the people provided all needful things for the sanctuary, and when the princes of the tribes perceived their mistake and brought their contributions, it was too late. All that they could do was to provide the jewels for the robes of the high priest, but they could no longer take a hand in the erection of the Tabernacle. On the day of the dedication they tried to make partial amends for letting slip their opportunity, by following the advice of the tribe of Issachar, renowned for wisdom and erudition, to bring wagons for the transportation of the Tabernacle. These princes of the tribes were no upstarts or men newly risen to honor, they were men who even in Egypt had been in office and exposed to the anger of the Egyptians; they had also stood at Moses' side when he undertook the census of the people. They now brought as an offering to Moses six covered wagons, fully equipped, and even painted blue, the color of the sky, and also twelve oxen to draw the wagons. The number of wagons as well as of oxen had been set with a purpose. The six wagons corresponded to the six days of creation; to the six Mothers, Sarah, Rebekah, Rachel, Leah, Bilhah, and Zilpah; to the six laws that the Torah prescribes exclusively for the king; to the six orders of the Mishnah, and to the six heavens. The number of the oxen corresponded to the twelve constellations, and to the twelve tribes. Moses did not at first want to accept the teams, but God not only bade him accept them, He also ordered him to address the princes kindly, and to thank them for their gifts. Moses now even thought the Shekinah had deserted him and would rest on the princes of the tribes, assuming that they had received direct communication from God to make this offering to the sanctuary. But God said to Moses: "If it had been a direct command from Me, then I should have ordered thee to tell them, but they did this on their own initiative, which indeed meets with My wish." Moses now accepted the gifts, not without misgivings, fearing lest a wagon should break, or an ox die, leaving this tribe or that unrepresented by a gift. But God assured him that no accident should occur to either wagon or ox,—yes, a great miracle came to pass in regard to these wagons and oxen, for the animals live forever without ailing or growing old, and the wagons likewise endure to all eternity.

Moses then distributed the wagons among the Levites so that the division of the sons of Gershon received two wagons, and the sons of Merari four, because the latter were entrusted with the transportation of the heavy portions of the Tabernacle, boards, bars, and similar things, whereas the former, having the lighter portions, had enough with two wagons. The third division of the Levites, the sons of Kohath, received no wagons, for they were entrusted with the transportation of the Holy Ark, which might not be lifted upon a wagon, but was to be borne upon their shoulders. David, who forgot to observe this law and had the Ark lifted upon a wagon, paid heavily for his negligence, for the priests who tried to carry the Ark to the wagon were flung down upon the ground. Ahithophel then called David's attention to the need of following the example of Kohath's sons, who bore the Ark on their shoulders through the desert, and David ordered them to do the same.

But the princes of the tribes were not content with having provided the means for transporting the sanctuary, they wanted to be the first, on the day of the dedication, to present offerings. As with the wagons, Moses was doubtful whether or not to permit them to bring their offerings, for these were of an unusual kind that were not ordinarily permissible.

But God bade him accept the dedication offerings of the princes, though Moses was still in doubt whether to let all the twelve princes make their offerings on the same day, or to set a special day for each, and if so, in what order they should make their offerings. God thereupon revealed to him that each one of the princes of the tribes was to sacrifice on a special day, and that Nahshon, the prince of Judah, was to make the start. He was rewarded in this way for the devotion he had shown God during the passage through the Red Sea. When Israel, beset by the Egyptians, reached the sea, the tribes among themselves started quarreling who should first go into the sea. Then suddenly Nahshon, the prince of Judah, plunged into the sea, firmly trusting that God would stand by Israel in their need.[338]

Nahshon's offering was one silver charger that had been fashioned for the sanctuary, the weight whereof was an hundred and thirty shekels; one bowl of equal size, but of lighter weight, of seventy shekels; both of them full of fine flour mingled with oil for a meat offering. Furthermore, one spoon of ten shekels of gold, full of incense; one young bullock, the picked of his herd; one excellent ram, and one lamb a year old, these three for a burnt offering; and a kid of the goats for a sin offering, to atone for a possible uncleanness in the sanctuary. These sacrifices and gifts Nahshon offered out of his own possessions, not out of those of his tribe. God's acceptance of the offerings of the princes of the tribes shows how dear they were to God; for at no other time was an individual allowed to offer up incense, as Nahshon and his fellows did. They also brought sin offerings, which is ordinarily not permitted unless one is conscious of having committed a sin. Finally the prince of the tribe of Ephraim brought his offering on the seventh day of the dedication, which was on a Sabbath, though ordinarily none but the daily sacrifices may be offered on the Sabbath.[380]

The offerings of all the princes of the tribes were identical, but they had a different significance for each tribe. From the time of Jacob, who foretold it to them, every tribe knew his future history to the time of the Messiah, hence at the dedication every prince brought such offerings as symbolized the history of his tribe.

Nahshon, the prince of Judah, brought a silver charger and a silver bowl, the one to stand for the sea, the other for the mainland, indicating that out of his tribe would spring such men as Solomon and the Messiah, who would rule over all the world, both land and sea. The golden spoon of ten shekels signified the ten generations from Perez, son of Judah, to David, first of Judean kings, all whose actions were sweet as the incense contained in the spoon. The three burnt offerings, the bullock, the ram, and the lamb, corresponded to the three Patriarchs, Abraham, Isaac, and Jacob, whereas the kid of the goats was to atone for the sin of Judah, who sought to deceive his father with the blood of a kid. The two oxen of the peace offering pointed to David and Solomon, and the three small cattle of the peace offering, the rams, the goats, and the lambs, corresponded to the descendants and successors of these two Judean kings, who may also be classified in three groups, the very pious, the very wicked, and those who were neither pious nor wicked.

On the second day of the dedication appeared the prince of the tribe of Reuben and wanted to present his offering, say-

ing: " 'Tis enough that Judah was permitted to offer sacrifice before me, surely it is now time for our tribe to present
our offerings." But Moses informed him that God had or-
dained·that the tribes should present offerings in the order in
which they moved through the desert, so that the tribe Issachar followed Judah. This tribe had altogether good claims
to be among the first to offer sacrifices, for, in the first place,
this tribe devoted itself completely to the study of the Torah,
so that the great scholars in Israel were among them; and
then, too, it was this tribe that had proposed to the others the
bringing of the dedication offerings. As this was the tribe of
erudition, its gifts symbolized things appertaining to the
Torah. The silver charger and the silver bowl corresponded
to the written and to the oral Torah; and both vessels alike
are filled with fine flour, for the two laws are not antago-
nistic, but form a unity and contain the loftiest teachings.
The fine flour was mingled with oil, just as knowledge of the
Torah should be added to good deeds; for he who occupies
himself with the Torah, who works good deeds, and keeps
himself aloof from sin, fills his Creator with delight. The
golden spoon of ten shekels symbolizes the two tables on
which God with His palm wrote the Ten Commandments, and
which contained between the commandments all the particulars of the Torah, just as the spoon was filled with incense.
The three burnt offerings, the bullock, the ram, and the lamb
corresponded to the three groups of priests, Levites, and
Israelites, whereas the kid of the goats alluded to the proselytes, for the Torah was revealed not only for Israel but for
all the world; and " a proselyte who studies the Torah is no
less than a high priest." The two oxen of the peace offering

corresponded to the oral and the written Torah, the study of which brings peace on earth and peace in heaven.[390]

After Nahshon, the temporal king, and Nethanel the spiritual king, came the turn of Eliab, the prince of the tribe of Zebulun. This tribe owed its distinction to the circumstance that it followed commerce and through the profits thereof was enabled to maintain the tribe of Issachar, which, entirely devoted to study, could not support itself. The charger and bowl that he presented to the sanctuary symbolize the food and drink with which Zebulun provided the scholar-tribe Issachar. The spoon indicated the border of the sea, which Jacob in his blessing had bestowed on Zebulun as his possession, and the ten shekels of its weight corresponded to the ten words of which this blessing consisted. The two oxen point to the two blessings which Moses bestowed upon Zebulun, as the three small cattle, the ram, the goat, and the lamb, correspond to the three things which gave Zebulun's possessions distinction before all others, the tunny, the purple snail, and white glass.[391]

After the tribes that belonged to Judah's camp division had brought their offerings, followed Reuben and the tribes belonging to his division. The gifts of the tribe of Reuben symbolized the events in the life of their forefather Reuben. The silver charger recalled Reuben's words when he saved Joseph's life, whom the other brothers wanted to kill, for " the tongue of the just is as choice silver." The silver bowl, from which was sprinkled the sacrificial blood, recalled the same incident, for it was Reuben who advised his brothers to throw Joseph into the pit rather than to kill him. The spoon of ten shekels of gold symbolizes the deed of Reuben, who restrained Jacob's sons from bloodshed, hence the gold out of which the spoon was fashioned had a blood-red color. The spoon was filled with incense, and so too did Reuben fill his days with fasting and prayer until God forgave his sin with Bilhah, and " his prayer was set forth before God as incense." As penance for this crime, Reuben offered the kid of the goats as a sin offering, whereas the two oxen of the peace offering corresponded to the two great deeds of Reuben, the deliverance of Joseph, and the long penance for his sin.[392]

Just as Reuben interceded to save his brother Joseph's life so did Simeon rise up for his sister Dinah when he took vengeance upon the inhabitants of Shechem for the wrong they had done her. Hence the prince of the tribe of Simeon followed the prince of the tribe of Reuben. As the sanctuary was destined to punish unchastity among Israel, so were the gifts of the tribe whose sire figured as the avenger of unchastity symbolical of the different parts of the Tabernacle. The charger corresponded to the court that surrounded the Tabernacle, and therefore weighed one hundred and thirty shekels, to correspond to the size of the court that measured one hundred cubits, of which the Tabernacle occupied thirty. The bowl of seventy shekels corresponded to the empty space of the Tabernacle. These two, the charger and the bowl, were filled with fine flour mingled with oil, because in the court of the Tabernacle were offered up meat offerings, mingled with oil, whereas in the Tabernacle was the shewbread of fine flour, and the candlestick filled with oil. The spoon of ten shekels of gold corresponded to the scroll of the Torah and the tables with the Ten Commandments that rested in the Ark. The sacrificial animals, the bullock, the ram, the lamb, and the kid corresponded to the four different kinds of curtains and hangings that were used in the sanctuary, and that were fashioned out of the hides of these animals. The two oxen of the peace offering pointed to the two curtains, the one in front of the Tabernacle, the other in front of the court, whereas the three kinds of small cattle that were used as offerings corresponded to the three curtains of the court, one to the north, one to the south, one to the west of it; and as each of these was five cubits long, so were five of each kind presented as offerings.[393]

As Simeon, sword in hand, battled for his sister, so, by force of arms, did the tribe Gad set out to gain the land beyond the Jordan for their brethren. Therefore did their prince follow Shelumiel, prince of Simeon, with his offerings. This tribe, so active in gaining the promised land, symbolized in its gifts the exodus from Egypt, which alone made possible the march to Palestine. The charger of the weight of a hundred and thirty shekels alluded to Jochebed, who at the age of one hundred and thirty years bore Moses, who had a symbolical connection with the bowl, for he was thrown into the Nile. This bowl weighed seventy shekels, as Moses extended his prophetic spirit over the seventy elders; and as the bowl was filled with fine flour, so did Moses' prophetic spirit in no way diminish because the seventy elders shared in prophecy. The three burnt offerings recalled the three virtues Israel possessed in Egypt, which were instrumental in their deliverance—they did not alter their Hebrew names, they did not alter their Hebrew language, and they lived a life of chastity. The sin offerings were to atone for the idolatry to which they were addicted in Egypt, so that God did not permit their deliverance until they had renounced idolatry. The two oxen of the peace offering corresponded to Jacob and Joseph, for whose sake God had delivered Israel out of Egypt. They brought, besides, fifteen heads of small cattle as a sacrifice, because God was mindful of His vow to the three Patriarchs and the twelve fathers of the tribes, and released Israel out of bondage.[394]

A special distinction was granted to the tribe of Ephraim, for God allowed their prince to make his offering on the Sabbath, a day on which otherwise none but the daily offerings were allowed to be offered. This distinction the tribe of Ephraim owed to its ancestor Joseph in recognition of his strict observance of the Sabbath as governor of Egypt. The gifts of this tribe represent the history of Jacob and of Joseph, for the descendants of the latter owed much to Jacob's love for his son Joseph. The charger alluded to Jacob, the bowl to Joseph, and as both these vessels were filled with fine flour mingled with oil, so too were both Jacob and Joseph very pious men, and the course of their lives ran evenly. The spoon symbolized Jacob's right hand, which he laid on the head of Ephraim to bless him; the spoon was filled with incense; Jacob laid his right hand upon Ephraim and not upon his elder brother Manasseh because he knew that the former was worthy of the distinction. The three burnt offerings corresponded to the three Patriarchs, whereas the kid of the goats stood for Joseph, whose coat had been smeared with a kid's blood. The two oxen of the peace offering indicated the two blessings that the sons of Joseph had received from their grandfather, Jacob, and the

three kinds of small cattle that were offered as peace offerings corresponded to the three generations of Ephraim that
Joseph was permitted to see before his death.⁸⁹⁵

Joseph not only observed the Sabbath, he was also chaste,
not to be tempted by Potiphar's wife, and he was faithful in the
service of his master. God therefore said to Joseph : " Thou
hast kept the seventh commandment, ' Thou shalt not commit adultery,' and hast not committed adultery with Potiphar's wife; and thou hast also kept the following commandment, the eighth, ' Thou shalt not steal,' for thou didst steal
neither Potiphar's money nor his conjugal happiness, hence
there will come a time when I shall give thee the reward due
thee. When, hereafter, the princes of the tribes will offer
their offerings at the dedication of the altar, the two princes
among thy descendants shall one after the other offer their
offerings, the one on the seventh, the other on the eighth day
of the dedication, as a reward because thou didst observe the
seventh and the eighth commandments." The prince of the
tribe of Manasseh now followed that of Ephraim, trying like
the preceding, symbolically to represent Jacob's and Joseph's
lives. The charger, one hundred and thirty shekels in
weight, indicated that Jacob at the age of one hundred and
thirty years migrated to Egypt for the sake of Joseph. The
bowl of seventy shekels corresponded to Joseph who caused
seventy souls of the Hebrews to migrate to Egypt. The
spoon of ten shekels of gold indicated the ten portions of
land that fell to Manasseh. The three burnt offerings corresponded to the three generations of Manasseh that Joseph
was permitted to see before his death, whereas the kid of
the goats recalled Jair, son of Manasseh, who died childless.

The two oxen of the peace offering indicated that the possessions of the tribe of Manasseh were to be divided into two parts, one on this side the Jordan, and one beyond it. The three kinds of small cattle for peace offerings corresponded to the triple attempt of Joseph to influence his father in favor of Manasseh, whereas the five heads of each indicated the five daughters of Zelophehad, the only women who, like men, received their shares in the distribution of the promised land.[396]

As the sanctuary stood first in Shiloh, Joseph's possession, then in Jerusalem, Benjamin's possession, so did this tribe with its sacrifices follow Joseph's tribes. The charger signified Rachel, the mother of Benjamin, who bore him to Jacob when he was a hundred years old, and in memory of this, as well as of Benjamin's attainment of thirty years when he came to Egypt, the weight of the charger amounted to one hundred and thirty shekels. The bowl indicated the cup Joseph employed to discover his brothers' sentiments toward Benjamin, and both vessels, charger and cup, were filled with fine flour, for both Joseph's and Benjamin's lands were found worthy of being sites for God's sanctuary. The spoon of ten shekels of gold full of incense corresponded to the ten sons of Benjamin, all of whom were pious men. The three burnt offerings corresponded to the three temples erected in Jerusalem, Benjamin's property, the Temple of Solomon, the Temple of the exiles returned from Babylon, and the Temple to be erected by the Messiah. The sin offering, the kid of the goats, points to the building of the Temple by the wicked king Herod, who atoned for his execution of the learned men by the erection of the sanctuary. The two

oxen of the peace offering corresponded to the two deliverers
of the Jews that sprang from the tribe of Benjamin, Mordecai and Esther. The five heads each of the three kinds of
small cattle for a peace offering symbolized the triple distinction of Benjamin and his tribe by five gifts. The gift of
honor that Joseph gave his brother Benjamin five times exceeded that of all his other brothers; when Joseph made himself known to his brothers, he gave Benjamin five changes of
raiment, and so too did the Benjamite Mordecai receive
from Ahasuerus five garments of state.[397]

In his blessing Jacob likened Dan to Judah, hence the
tribe of Dan stood at the head of the fourth camp of
Israel, and their prince offered his gifts before those of
Asher and Naphtali. Jacob in his blessing to Dan thought
principally of the great hero, Samson, hence the gifts of this
tribe allude chiefly to the history of this Danite judge. Samson was a Nazirite, and to this alluded the silver charger for
storing bread, for it is the duty of a Nazirite, at the expira-
tion of the period of his vow, to present bread as an offering.
To Samson, too, alluded the bowl, in Hebrew called Mizrak,
"creeping," for he was lame of both feet, and hence could
only creep and crawl. The spoon of ten shekels of gold recalled the ten laws that are imposed upon Nazirites, and that
Samson had to obey. The three burnt offerings had a similar significance, for Samson's mother received three injunc-
tions from the angel, who said to her husband, Manoah:
"She may not eat of anything that cometh of the vine,
neither let her drink wine or strong drink, nor eat any unclean thing." The sin offering, which consisted of a kid,
called in Hebrew Sa'ir, corresponded to the admonition given

to Samson's mother, not to shave his hair, in Hebrew Se'ar.
The two oxen corresponded to the two pillars of which Samson took hold to demolish the house of the Philistines;
whereas the three kinds of small cattle that were presented as
offerings symbolized the three battles that Samson undertook against the Philistines.[398]

The judge must pronounce judgment before it be executed, hence, too, the tribe of Asher, " the executors of justice," followed Dan, the judges. The name Asher also signifies " good fortune," referring to the good fortune of
Israel that was chosen to be God's people, and in accordance
with this name also do the gifts of the prince of the tribe of
Asher allude to the distinction of Israel. The charger, one
hundred and thirty shekels of silver in weight, corresponds
to the nations of the world, whom, however, God repudiated,
choosing Israel in their stead. The bowl of seventy shekels
corresponds to the seventy pious souls of whom Israel consisted when they moved to Egypt. Both vessels were filled
with fine flour. God sent His prophets to the other nations
as well as to Israel, but Israel alone declared itself willing
to accept the Torah. This nation accepted " the spoon of ten
shekels of gold filled with incense," every man among them
being willing to accept the Ten Commandments and the
Torah. The three burnt offerings corresponded to the three
crowns that Israel received from their God, the crown of the
Torah, the crown of the Priesthood, and the crown of the
Kingdom, for which reason also golden crowns were fashioned on the Ark in which the Torah was kept, on the altar
on which the priests offered sacrifices, and on the table that
symbolized the kingdom. But the highest of all is the crown

of a good name, which a man earns through dood deeds, for
the crucial test is not the study of the Torah, but the life
conforming to it.   For this reason also there was a sin offering among the offerings, corresponding to the crown of good
deeds, for these alone can serve men as an expiation.   The
two oxen indicate the two Torot that God gave His people,
the written and the oral, whereas the fifteen peace offerings
of small cattle correspond to the three Patriarchs and the
twelve fathers of the tribes, for these fifteen God had
chosen.[309]

As Jacob blessed first Asher and then Naphtali, so too did
these two tribes succeed each other in the offerings at the
dedication of the Tabernacle.   Naphtali, Jacob's son, was a
very affectionate son, who was ever ready to execute his
father's every command.   The prince of the tribe of
Naphtali followed his ancestor's example, and by his gifts to
the sanctuary sought to recall the three Patriarchs and their
wives.   "One silver charger, the weight whereof was an
hundred and thirty shekels," symbolized Sarah, who was
unique among her sex in her piety, and who almost attained
the age of a hundred and thirty years.   A silver bowl for
sprinkling blood recalled Abraham, who was thrown far
away from his home.   The weight of the bowl was seventy
shekels, as Abraham also was seventy years old when God
made with him the covenant between the pieces.   The
charger and the bowl were both filled with fine flour mingled
with oil, as also Abraham and Sarah were imbued with a
love for good and pious deeds.   The spoon of ten shekels of
gold alludes to Abraham as well, for Abraham conquered
the evil inclination and resisted the ten temptations, whereas

the three burnt offerings and the sin offering corresponded
to the offerings made by Abraham at the covenant between
the pieces. The two oxen for the peace offering indicate
Isaac and Rebekah, whereas the three kinds of small cattle
allude to Jacob, Leah, and Rachel, but the sum total of the
offerings of these three species was fifteen, corresponding
to these three and the twelve fathers of the tribes.[400]

Apart from the significance that the offerings of the
tribal princes had for each individual tribe respectively, they
also symbolized the history of the world from the time of
Adam to the erection of the Tabernacle. The silver charger
indicated Adam, who lived nine hundred and thirty years, and
the numerical equivalent of the letters of Ḳaarat Kesef, " silver charger," amounts to the same. Corresponding to the
weight of " an hundred and thirty shekels," Adam begat his
son Seth, the actual father of the future generations, at the
age of a hundred and thirty years. The silver bowl alludes to
Noah, for, as it weighed seventy shekels, so too did seventy
nations spring from Noah. Both these vessels were filled
with fine flour, as Adam and Noah were both full of good
deeds. The spoon " of ten shekels of gold " corresponds to
the ten words of God by which the world was created, to
the ten Sefirot, to the ten lists of generations in the Scriptures, to the ten essential constituent parts of the human
body, to the ten miracles God wrought for Israel in Egypt,
to the ten miracles Israel experienced by the Red Sea. The
three burnt offerings were meant to recall the three
Patriarchs. The kid of the goats indicated Joseph; the two
oxen corresponded to Moses and Aaron; the five rams to the
five distinguished sons of Zerah: Zimri, Ethan, Heman,

Calcol, and Dara; whereas the five gcats and the five lambs symbolized the five senses of mankind by means of which the existence of things is determined.

The sum total of the gifts of the twelve princes of the tribes had also a symbolical significance. The twelve chargers correspond to the twelve constellations; the twelve bowls to the twelve months; the twelve spoons to the twelve guides of men, which are: the heart, that bestows under-standing and insight; the kidneys, that give counsels, good as well as evil; the mouth, that cuts all kinds of food; the tongue, that renders speech possible; the palate, that tastes the flavors of food; the windpipe, that renders possible breathing and the utterance of sounds; the esophagus, that swallows food and drink; the lungs, that absorb fluids; the liver, that promotes irritation; the spleen, that promotes laughter; the crop, that grinds all food; and the stomach, that affords pleasant sleep. " All the silver of the vessels that weighed two thousand and four hundred shekels " corre-sponded to the years that had passed from the creation of the world to the advent of Moses in the fortieth year of his life. All the gold of the spoons, the weight of which was an hun-dred and twenty shekels, corresponded to the years of Moses' life, for he died at the age of a hundred and twenty.[401]

The different species of animals offered as sacrifices cor-responded to the different ranks of the leaders of Israel. The twelve bullocks to the kings, the twelve rams to the princes of the tribes, the twelve kids of the goats to the governors, and the twelve sheep to the government officials. The twenty-four oxen for a peace offering corresponded to the books of the Scriptures, and the divisions of the priests.

and were also meant to serve as atonement for the twenty-four thousand men, who, owing to their worship of Peor, died of the plague. The sixty rams of the peace offering corresponded to the sixty myriads of Israel's fighting hosts; the sixty he-goats to the sixty empires; and the sixty he-lambs to the building of the second Temple that measured sixty cubits in height and sixty in width.[402]

The gifts of the twelve princes of the tribes were not only equal in number, but also in the size and width of the objects bestowed, every tribe making exactly the same offering to the sanctuary. None among them wished to outrival the others, but such harmony reigned among them and such unity of spirit that God valued the service of each as if he had brought not only his own gifts but also those of his companions. As a reward for this mutual regard and friendship, God granted them the distinction of permitting them to present their offerings even on the Sabbath day.[403]

The Revelations in the Tabernacle

" Honor pursues him who tries to escape it." Moses in his humility felt that his mission as leader of the people ended with the erection of the Tabernacle, as Israel could now satisfy all their spiritual needs without his aid. But God said: " As truly as thou livest, I have for thee a far greater task than any thou hast yet accomplished, for thou shalt instruct My children about ' clean and unclean,' and shalt teach them how to offer up offerings to Me." God hereupon called Moses to the Tabernacle, to reveal to him there the laws and teachings.[404] Moses in his humility did

14

not dare to enter the Tabernacle, so that God had to sum-
mon him to enter. Moses, however, could not enter the
sanctuary while a cloud was upon it, this being a sign " that
the demons held sway," but waited until the cloud had moved
on. The voice that called Moses came from heaven in the
form of a tube of fire and rested over the two Cherubim,
whence Moses perceived its sound. This voice was as powerful as at the revelation at Sinai when the souls of all Israel
escaped in terror, still it was audible to none but Moses.
Not even the angels heard it, for the words of God were
destined exclusively for Moses. Aaron, too, with the exception of three cases in which God revealed Himself to him,
never received His commands except through the communications of Moses. God would call Moses twice caressingly
by name, and when he had answered, " Here am I," God's
words were revealed to him, and every commandment as a
special revelation. God always allowed a pause to take
place between the different laws to be imparted, that Moses
might have time rightly to grasp what was told him.⁴⁰⁵

On the first day of the dedication of the Tabernacle, not
less than eight important sections of laws were communicated to Moses by God.⁴⁰⁶ As a reward for his piety, Aaron
and his descendants to all eternity received the laws of
sanctity, which are a special distinction of the priests,⁴⁰⁷ and
these laws were revealed on this day. It was on this day,
also, that Aaron and his sons received the gifts of the priests,
for although even at the revelation on Sinai Israel had set
them aside, still they were not given to Aaron and his sons
until this day when the sanctuary was anointed.⁴⁰⁸

The second law revealed on this day was the separation of

the Levites from among the children of Israel, that they
might be dedicated to the sanctuary. " For God elevates no
man to an office unless He has tried him and found him
worthy of his calling." He did not say, " and the Levites
shall be Mine," before He had tried this tribe, and found
them worthy. In Egypt none but the tribe of Levi observed
the Torah and clung to the token of the Abrahamic covenant,
while the other tribes, abandoning both Torah and token of
covenant, like the Egyptians, practiced idolatry. In the
desert, also, it was this tribe alone that did not take part
in the worship of the Golden Calf. Justly, therefore, did
God's choice fall upon this godly tribe, who on this day
were consecrated as the servants of God and His sanctuary.[400]

The ceremonies connected with the consecration of the
Levites had much in common with the regulations for the
cleansing of lepers. Originally, the firstborn had been the
servants of the sanctuary, but, owing to the worship of the
Golden Calf, they lost this prerogative, and the Levites replaced them. It was for this reason that the Levites were
obliged to observe regulations similar to those for the
cleansing of lepers, because they took the place of men who
by their sins had defiled themselves. The offerings that the
Levites brought on this occasion consisted of two bullocks,
one for a burnt offering and one for a sin offering; for the
law prescribes that a bullock be offered as a burnt offering
whenever the congregation, seduced by others, commits
idolatry; and Israel would not have worshipped the Golden
Calf had not the mixed multitude misled them. " But whosoever worships an idol, by this act renounces the whole
Torah," hence did the Levites have to offer up another

bullock for a sin offering, in accordance with the law that " if the whole congregation of Israel have done somewhat against any of the commandments of the Lord concerning things which should not be done, and are guilty, then they shall offer up a young bullock for the sin." As the Levites had been chosen " to do the service of the children of Israel in the Tabernacle of the congregation, and to make an atonement for the children of Israel," God ordered all the congregation of Israel to be present at the consecration of the Levites, for whosoever had a sin offering offered up for himself must in person bring it to the Tabernacle. Therefore, too, did the elders of Israel have to put their hands upon the Levites, according to the prescription that the elders must put their hands upon the sin offering that was to make atonement for the sin of the congregation. Aaron, like the elders, participated in the ceremony of the consecration, lifting up every single Levite as a token that he was now dedicated to the sanctuary.[410] Aaron's extraordinary strength is proven by the fact that he was able to lift up twenty-twc thousand men in one day.[411]

The Cleansing of the Camp

The third law revealed on this day was the command that the children of Israel put out of the camp every leper and every unclean person. When Israel moved out of Egypt, the majority of the people were afflicted with physical defects and diseases, contracted during their work on the structures they had been compelled to erect in Egypt. One had his hand crushed by a falling stone, another's eye was blinded by splashings of loam. It was a battered and crippled host

that reached Sinai, eager to receive the Torah, but God said:
" Does it become the glory of the Torah that I should bestow
it on a race of cripples? Nor do I want to await the coming
of another, sound generation, for I desire no further delay of
the revelation of the Torah." Hereupon God sent angels to
heal all among Israel that were diseased or afflicted with
defects, so that all the children of Israel were sound and
whole when they received the Torah. They remained in this
condition until they worshipped the Golden Calf, when all
their diseases returned as a punishment for their defection
from God. Only the women, during their stay in the desert,
were exempt from the customary ailments to which women
are subject, as a reward for being the first who declared
themselves ready to accept the Torah. When the Tabernacle had been consecrated, God now said to Moses: " So
long as you had not yet erected the Tabernacle, I did not
object to having the unclean and the lepers mingle with the
rest of the people, but now that the sanctuary is erected, and
that My Shekinah dwells among you, I insist upon your
separating all these from among you, that they may not
defile the camp in the midst of which I dwell."

The law in regard to lepers was particularly severe, for
they were denied the right of staying within the camp,
whereas the unclean were prohibited merely from staying
near the sanctuary.[412] The lepers were the very ones who
had worshipped the Golden Calf, and had as a consequence
been smitten with this disease, and it was for this reason
that God separated them from the community. Thirteen sins
are punished with leprosy by God: blasphemy, unchastity,
murder, false suspicion, pride, illegal appropriation of the

rights of others, slander, theft, perjury, profanation of the
Divine Name, idolatry, envy, and contempt of the Torah.
Goliath was stricken with leprosy because he reviled God;
the daughters of Zion became leprous in punishment of their
unchastity; leprosy was Cain's punishment for the murder of
Abel. When Moses said to God, " But behold, they will not
believe me," God replied: " O Moses, art thou sure that they
will not believe thee? They are believers and the sons of believers. Thou who didst suspect them wrongly, put now thy
hand into thy bosom, ... and he put his hand into his
bosom: and when he took it out, behold, his hand was leprous
as snow." Uzziah presumed upon the rights of the priesthood, and went into the Temple to burn incense upon the
altar of incense. He was just about to commit the offence,
when " the leprosy brake forth in his forehead." Leprosy
fell upon Naaman, who had grown arrogant because of his
heroic deeds. For slandering Moses Miriam became
leprous as snow; and Gehazi was punished by leprosy because he frustrated the purpose of Elisha, who desired to
accept nothing from Naaman in order that the cure might
redound to the glory of God.⁴¹³

Another important law revealed on this day referred to
the celebration of " the second Passover feast." Mishael and
Elzaphan, who had attended to the burial of Nadab and
Abihu, were godly men, anxious to fulfil the commandments
of God, hence they went to the house where Moses and
Aaron instructed the people, and said to them: " We are
defiled by the dead body of a man; wherefore are we kept
back that we may not offer an offering of the Lord in His
appointed season among the children of Israel?" Moses at

first answered that they might not keep the Passover owing to their condition of uncleanness, but they argued with him, asking that even if, owing to their condition, they might not partake of the sacrificial meat, they might, at least, be permitted to participate in the offering of the paschal lamb by having the blood of the offering sprinkled for them. Moses admitted that he could not pass judgment on this case before receiving instruction concerning it from God. For Moses had the rare privilege of being certain of receiving revelations from God whenever he applied to Him. He therefore bade Mishael and Elzaphan await God's judgment concerning their case, and sentence was indeed revealed immediately.[414]

It was on this day also that God said to Moses: "A heavy blow of fate has fallen upon Aaron to-day, but instead of murmuring he thanked Me for the death that robbed him of his two sons, which proves his trust in My justice toward them, who had deserved punishment more severe. Go then, and comfort him; and at the same time tell him 'that he come not at all times into the holy place within the vail before the mercy seat, which is upon the Ark.'" These last words greatly aggrieved Moses, who now thought: "Woe is me! For it seems as if Aaron had lost his rank, since he may not at all times enter the sanctuary. The statement of the periods for his admission into the sanctuary is also so indeterminate that I am not at all sure whether they are to recur hourly, or daily, or annually, every twelve years, perhaps even seventy, or not at all." But God replied: "Thou art mistaken, I was not thinking of fixing a certain time, whether hour, or day, or year, for Aaron may enter the sanctuary at any time, but when he does so, he must observe certain ceremonies." The ceremonies that Aaron, as well as every other high priest, had to perform on the Day of Atonement before his entrance into the Holy of Holies were symbolical of the three Patriarchs, of the four wives of the Patriarchs, and of the twelve tribes. Only by depending upon the merits of these pious men and women might the high priest venture to enter the Holy of Holies without having to fear the angels that filled this space. These were obliged to retreat upon the entrance of the high priest, and even Satan had to flee whenever he beheld the high priest, and did not dare to accuse Israel before God.[415]

Aaron's grief about the death of his sons was turned to joy when God, on the day of their death, granted him the distinction of receiving a direct revelation from the Lord, which prohibited both him and his sons from drinking wine or strong drink when they went into the Tabernacle.[416]

On this day, also, Moses received the revelation concerning the red heifer, whose significance was never vouchsafed to any other human being beside himself. On the following day, under the supervision of Eleazar, Aaron's son, it was slaughtered and burned. Although, beside this one, a number of other red heifers were provided in future generations, this one was distinguished by having its ashes kept forever, which, mingled with the ashes of other red heifers, were always used for the purification of Israel. But it is in this world alone that the priest can purify the unclean by sprinkling with this water of purification, whereas in the future world God will sprinkle clean water upon Israel, " that they may be cleansed from all their filthiness, and from all their idols." [417]

The Lighting of the Candlestick

The eighth law revealed on this day was the lighting of the candlestick. After all the princes of the tribes had brought their gifts to the sanctuary, and God had bidden Moses to let them offer each his offering, one a day, throughout twelve days, Aaron, profoundly agitated, thought: "Woe is me! It seems as if, owing to my sin, my tribe has been excluded by God from participating in the dedication of the sanctuary." Hereupon God said to Moses: "Go to Aaron and say to him, 'Do not fear that thou art slighted, and art deemed inferior to the other princes of the tribes. Thou, on the contrary, shalt enjoy a greater glory than all of these, for thou art to light the lamps of the candlestick in the sanctuary.'" When Israel heard God's command that the lights of the sanctuary be lighted, they said: "O Lord of the world! Thou biddest us make a light for Thee that art the light of the world, and with whom light dwelleth." But God replied: "Not because I need your light do I bid you burn lamps before Me, but only that I might thereby distinguish you in the eyes of the nations that will say, 'Behold the people of Israel, that hold up a light before Him who bestoweth light upon all the world.' By your own eye-sight can you see how little need I have of your light. You have the white of the eye and the black of the eye, and it is by means of this dark part of the eye that you are enabled to see, and not through the light part of the white of the eye. How should I, that am all light, have need of your light!" God furthermore said: "A mortal of flesh and blood lights one light by means of another that is burning, I have brought forth light out of darkness: 'In the beginning darkness was upon the face of the deep,' whereupon I spake, 'Let there be light: and there was light.' Shall I now be in need of your illumination? Nay, I commanded you to light the candles in the sanctuary that I might distinguish you and give you another opportunity of doing a pious deed, the execution of which I will reward in the future world by letting a great light shine before you; and, furthermore, if you will let the candles shine before Me in My sanctuary, I shall protect from all evil your spirit, ' the candle of the Lord.' " [413]

Simultaneously with the command to light the sanctuary, Moses received the instruction to celebrate the Sabbath by the lighting of candles, for God said to him: " Speak unto the children of Israel; if you will observe My command to light the Sabbath candles, I shall permit you to live to see Zion illuminated, when you will no longer require the light of the sun, but My glory will shine before you so that the nations will follow your light." [419]

Aaron was distinguished not only by being selected to dedicate the sanctuary through the lighting of the candles, God ordered Moses to communicate to his brother the following revelation: " The sanctuary will on another occasion also be dedicated by the lighting of candles, and then it will be done by thy descendants, the Hasmoneans, for whom I will perform miracles and to whom I will grant grace. Hence there is greater glory destined for thee than for all the other princes of the tribes, for their offerings to the sanctuary shall be employed only so long as it endures, but the lights of the Ḥanukkah festival will shine forever; and, moreover, thy descendants shall bestow the priestly blessing upon Israel even after the destruction of the Temple." [420]

The candlestick that Aaron lighted in the sanctuary, was not the common work of mortal hands, but was wrought by a miracle. When God bade Moses fashion a candlestick, he found it difficult to execute the command, not knowing how to set to work to construct it in all its complicated details. God therefore said to Moses: "I shall show thee a model." He then took white fire, red fire, green fire, and black fire, and out of these four kinds of fires He fashioned a candlestick with its bowls, its knops, and its flowers. Even then Moses was not able to copy the candlestick, whereupon God drew its design upon his palm, saying to him: "Look at this, and imitate the design I have drawn on thy palm." But even that did not suffice to teach Moses how to execute the commission, whereupon God bade him cast a talent of gold into the fire. Moses did as he was bidden, and the candlestick shaped itself out of the fire. As on this occasion, so upon other occasions also did God have to present the things tangibly before Moses in order to make certain laws intelligible to him. In this way, for example, at the revelation concerning clean and unclean animals, God showed one specimen of each to Moses, saying: "This ye shall eat, and this ye shall not eat." [421]

THE TWELVE PRINCES OF THE TRIBES

God in His love for Israel had frequent censuses taken of them, so that He might accurately estimate His possession. In scarcely half a year they were twice counted, once shortly before the erection of the Tabernacle, and the second time a month after its dedication. [422] On the first day of the month of Iyyar, Moses received instructions to take a census of all men over twenty who were physically fit to go to war. He was ordered to take Aaron as his assistant, so that in case he should overlook some of the men Aaron might remind him of them, for "two are better than one." They were also to take as their subordinate assistants Eleazar and Ithamar, Aaron's sons, and a man each from the several tribes. These twelve men were appointed not only to conduct the census, but also to look after the spiritual welfare of their respective tribes, the sins of which would be upon their heads unless, with all their powers, they strove to prevent them. Moses and Aaron nevertheless adjured the princes of the tribes, in spite of their high rank, not to tyrannize over the people, whereas, on the other hand, they admonished the people to pay all due respect to their superiors.[423]

The names of these twelve princes of the tribes indicated the history of the tribes they represented. The prince of the tribe of Reuben was called Elizur, "my God is a rock," referring to the ancestor of this tribe, Reuben, Jacob's son, who sinned, but, owing to his penance, was forgiven by God, who bore his sin as a rock bears the house built upon it. The name of Elizur's father was Shedeur, "cast into the fire," because Reuben was converted to repentance and atonement through Judah, who confessed his sin when his daughter-in-law Tamar was about to be cast into the fire.

The prince of the tribe of Simeon was named Shelumiel, "my God is peace," to indicate that in spite of the sin of Zimri, head of this tribe, through whom four and twenty thousand men among Israel died, God nevertheless made peace with this tribe.

The prince of the tribe of Judah bore the name Nahshon,

" wave of the sea," the son of Amminadab, " prince of My people," because the prince received this dignity as a reward for having plunged into the waves of the Red Sea to glorify God's name.

The tribe of Issachar had for its prince Nethanel, " God gave," for this tribe devoted its life to the Torah given by God to Moses. Accordingly Nethanel was called the son of Zuar, " burden," for Issachar assumed the burden of passing judgment on the lawsuits of the other tribes.

Corresponding to the occupation of the tribe of Zebulun, its prince was called Eliab, " the ship," son of Helon, " the sand," for this tribe spent its life on ships, seeking " treasures hidden in the sand."

Elishama, son of Ammihud, the name of the prince of the tribe of Ephraim, points to the history of Joseph, their forefather. God said: " Elishama, ' he obeyed Me,' who bade him be chaste and not covet his master's wife that wanted to tempt him to sin, and Ammihud, ' Me he honored,' and none other."

The other tribe of Joseph, Manasseh, also named their prince in reference to their forefather, calling him Gamaliel, son of Pedahzur, which signifies, " God rewarded Joseph for his piety by releasing him from bondage and making him ruler over Egypt."

The prince of the tribe of Benjamin was named Abidan, " my father decreed," son of Gideoni, " mighty hosts," referring to the following incident. When Rachel perceived that she would die at the birth of her son, she called him " son of faintness," supposing that a similar fate would overtake him, and that he was doomed through weakness to die young. But Jacob, the child's father, decreed otherwise, and called him Benjamin, " son of might and of many years."

The prince of the tribe of Dan bore the name Ahiezer, " brother of help," son of Ammishaddai, " My people's judge," because he was allied with the helpful tribe of Judah at the erection of the Tabernacle, and like this ruling tribe brought forth a mighty judge in the person of Samson.

The tribe of Asher was distinguished by the beauty of its women, which was so excellent that even the old among them were fairer and stronger than the young girls of the other tribes. For this reason kings chose the daughters of this tribe to be their wives, and these, through their intercession before the kings, saved the lives of many who had been doomed to death. Hence the name of the prince of the tribe of Asher, Pagiel, " the interceder," son of Ochran, " the afflicted," for the women of the tribe of Asher, through their intercession, obtained grace for the afflicted.

The prince of the tribe of Gad bore the name Eliasaph, " God multiplied ;" son of Deuel, " God is a witness." To reward them for passing over the Jordan and not returning to their property on this side of the river until the promised land was won, their wealth was multiplied by God ; for when, upon returning, they found the enemy at home, God aided them and they gained all their enemy's possessions. God was furthermore witness that this tribe had no wicked motive when they erected an altar on their land.

The prince of the tribe of Naphtali was called Ahira, " desirable meadow," son of Enan, " clouds ; " for the land of this tribe was distinguished by its extraordinary excellence. Its products were exactly what their owners " desired," and all this owing to the plenty of water, for the "clouds" poured plentiful rain over their land.

At the census of the people the tribes were set down in the order in which they put up their camp and moved in their marches. The tribes of Judah, Issachar, and Zebulun formed the first group, the royal tribe of Judah being associated with the tribe of learned men, Issachar, and with Zebulun, which through its generosity enabled Issachar to devote itself to the study of the Torah. The second group consisted of Reuben, Simeon, and Gad. The sinful tribe of Simeon was supported on the right by the penance of Reuben and on the left by the strength of Gad. The tribes of Ephraim, Manasseh, and Benjamin formed a group by themselves, for these before all the other tribes were destined to appear gloriously against Amalek. The Ephraimite Joshua was the first who was victorious against Amalek, the Benjamite Saul followed his example in his war against Agag, king of Amalek, and, under the leadership of men out of the tribe of Manasseh, the tribe of Simeon at the time of king Jehoshaphat succeeded in destroying the rest of the Amalekites, and to take possession of their lands. The tribes of Dan, Asher, and Naphtali formed the last group, and for the following reason were united in this way. The tribe of Dan had already at the time of the exodus from Egypt been possessed of the sinful thought to fashion an idol. To counteract this "dark thought" Asher was made its comrade, from whose soil came "the oil for lighting;" and that Dan might participate in the blessing, Naphtali, "full with the blessing of the Lord," became its second companion.[424]

At this third census the number of men who were able to

go to war proved to be exactly the same as at the second census, taken in the same year. Not one among Israel had died during this period, from the beginning of the erection of the Tabernacle to its dedication, when the third census took place.[425] But no conclusive evidence concerning the sum total of the separate tribes can be drawn from this number of men able to go to war, because the ratio of the two sexes varied among the different tribes, as, for example, the female sex in the tribe of Naphtali greatly outnumbered the male.[426]

THE CENSUS OF THE LEVITES

Moses at the census did not take into consideration the tribe of Levi, because God had not commanded him to select a prince for this tribe as for all others, hence he drew the conclusion that they were not to be counted. Naturally he was not sure of his decision in this matter, and wavered whether or not to include the Levites in the number, when God said to him: " Do not muster the tribe of Levi, nor number them among the children of Israel." At these words Moses was frightened, for he feared that his tribe was considered unworthy of being counted with the rest, and was therefore excluded by God. But God quieted him, saying: " Do not number the Levites among the children of Israel, number them separately." There were several reasons for numbering the Levites separately. God foresaw that, owing to the sin of the spies who were sent to search the land, all men who were able to go to war would perish in the wilderness, " all that were numbered of them, according to their whole number, from twenty years old and upward." Now had the Levites been included in the sum total of Israel, the

Angel of Death would have held sway over them also, wherefore God excluded them from the census of all the tribes, that
they might in the future be exempt from the punishment
visited upon the others, and might enter the promised land.
The Levites were, furthermore, the body-guard of God, to
whose care the sanctuary was entrusted—another reason for
counting them separately. God in this instance conducted
Himself like the king who ordered one of his officers to number his legions, but added: "Number all the legions excepting only the legion that is about me." [427]

The extent of God's love for Levi is evident through the
command given to Moses, to number in the tribe of Levi "all
males from a month old and upward," whereas in the other
tribes none were numbered save men able to go to war, from
twenty years and upward. Upon other occasions God had
even the embryos among the Levites numbered. This occurred upon Jacob's entrance into Egypt, when the number
seventy for his family was attained only by including
Jochebed who was still in the womb; and similarly at a future
time upon the return of the exiles from Babylon. For at that
time only twenty-three of the priestly sections returned,
hence to complete their number they had to include Bigvai,
who belonged to the missing section, even though he was still
in the womb. [428]

When Moses was ordered to number among the Levites
all children from a month old and upward, he said to God:
"Thou biddest me count them from a month old and upward. Shall I now wander about in their courts and houses
and count each child, seeing that Thou givest me such a
command?" But God replied: "Do thou what thou canst

do, and I will do what I can do." It now came to pass that whenever Moses betook himself to a Levite tent he found the Shekinah awaiting him, telling him exactly the number of children without his having to count them.[429]

In the choice of this tribe God showed His preference for the seventh, for Levi was the seventh pious man, starting from Adam, to wit: Adam, Noah, Enoch, Abraham, Isaac, Jacob, and Levi. As in this instance, so in many others did God indicate His love for the seventh. He sits enthroned in the seventh heaven; of the seven worlds the seventh alone is inhabited by human beings; of the early generations the seventh was the most excellent, for it produced Enoch. Moses, seventh among the Patriarchs, was judged worthy of receiving the Torah. David, seventh son of Jesse, was chosen as king. In periods of time, also, the seventh was the favorite. The seventh day is the Sabbath; the seventh month, Tishri, is the month of the holy days; the seventh year is the Sabbatical year of rest, and every seventh Sabbatical year of rest is the year of jubilee.[430]

Another reason for numbering even the youngest boys among the Levites was that the tribe of Levi as a whole had the responsibility of atoning for the sin of the first-born among the children of Israel. For it was these who until the time of the worship of the Golden Calf performed the services of the priesthood, and their privilege was taken from them owing to this, their sin. This prerogative was then conferred upon the tribe of Levi, who, moreover, dedicating themselves, man for man, to the service of the Lord, served as an atonement for the first-born of Israel, that they might not be destroyed as they deserved.[431]

The exchange of Levites in place of the first-born did, however, present a difficulty. For God had communicated the number of Levites to Moses in the following way: "Their number amounts to as many as the number of My legion." For, when God came down upon Sinai, twenty-two thousand angels surrounded Him, and just as many men did the Levites number. Outside of these there were three hundred first-born among the Levites that could not well be offered in exchange for the first-born among the other tribes, because their standing was the same as theirs. As the number of first-born among the other tribes exceeded the number of Levites by two hundred seventy-three, this surplus remained without actual atonement. Hence God ordered Moses to take from them five shekels apiece by the poll as redemption money, and give it to the priests. This sum was fixed upon by God, who said: "Ye sold the first-born of Rachel for five shekels, and for this reason shall ye give as redemption money for every first-born among ye five shekels."

To avoid quarrels among the first-born, as otherwise each one would try to lay the payment of redemption money upon his neighbor, Moses wrote upon twenty-two thousand slips of paper the word "Levi," and upon two hundred seventy-three the words "five shekels," all of which were then thrown into an urn and mixed. Then every first-born had to draw one of the slips. If he drew a slip with "Levi" he was not obliged to remit any payment, but if he drew "five shekels," he had to pay that sum to the priests.[482]

THE FOUR DIVISIONS OF THE LEVITES

Apart from the census of all male Levites, Moses now took another census of the men from the ages of thirty to fifty, for only at this age were the Levites permitted to perform service in the Tabernacle throughout their march through the desert, a law that indeed ceased to hold good when Israel settled in the Holy Land.[83] These officiating Levites, as well as the priests, were divided by Moses into eight sections, a number that was not doubled until the prophet Samuel increased it to sixteen, to which David again added eight, so that there were later twenty-four divisions among the Levites and priests.[84]

The most distinguished among the Levites were the sons of Kohath, whose charge during the march through the desert was the Holy of Holies, and among the vessels particularly the Holy Ark. This latter was a dangerous trust, for out of the staves attached to it would issue sparks that consumed Israel's enemies, but now and then this fire wrought havoc among the bearers of the Ark. It therefore became a customary thing, when the camp was about to be moved, for Kohath's sons to hasten into the sanctuary and seek to pack up the different portions of it, each one planning cautiously to shift the carrying of the Ark upon another. But this even more kindled God's anger against them, and He slew many of the Kohathites because they ministered to the Ark with an unwilling heart. To avert the danger that threatened them, God ordered Aaron and his sons to enter first into the sanctuary, and "to appoint to the Kohathites, every one, his service and his burden, that they might not go in to see when the holy things are covered, lest they die."

This was done because previous to this command the sons of Kohath had been accustomed to feast their eyes on the sight of the Ark, which brought them instantaneous death. But, according to this order, Aaron and his sons first took apart the different portions of the sanctuary, covered the Ark, and not till then called the sons of Kohath to bear the burden.

During the march the Levites might wear no shoes, but had to walk barefoot because they carried and ministered to holy objects. The Kohathites had, moreover, to walk backwards, for they might not turn their backs to the Holy Ark. They were, furthermore, owing to their office as bearers of the Ark, distinguished by being the first of the Levites to be numbered in the census, although in other respects the sons of Gershon led, for Gershon was the first-born of Levi.[435]

When giving the commission to count the sons of Kohath, God explicitly mentioned that Moses should undertake the census with Aaron, but He did not do so when He ordered the numbering of the sons of Gershon. Moses now thought that God had done this intentionally because the former were directly under Aaron's supervision while the Gershonites were not. Nevertheless, out of respect to his brother, he bade his brother, as well as, out of courtesy, the princes of the tribes, to be present at the numbering of the Levites, but he did not tell Aaron that he did so in the name of God. In this Moses erred, for God wished Aaron to be present at the numbering of the Levites. For this reason, when He ordered the census of the third division, Merari's sons, to be taken, He expressly mentioned Aaron's name. At the apportionment of the service among the individual Levites, however, Aaron paid attention only to the sons of Kohath, each of

whom had his special task allotted to him, whereas Moses
appointed their tasks to the sons of Gershon and Merari.[486]
The highest chief of the Levites, however, was Eleazar, who
was " to have the oversight of them that keep the charge of
the sanctuary.' But despite his high position, Eleazar was
modest enough to participate in the service in person. During their marches from place to place, he himself would carry
all needful things for the daily offering. In his right hand
he carried the oil for the candlestick, in his left hand the
incense, on his arm the things that were made in the pans,
and, attached to his girdle, the phial with the oil for oint-
ment.[487] Ithamar, Eleazar's brother, also had a duty in the
sanctuary, for it was he to whom the guidance of the service
of Gershon's and Merari's sons was assigned. For these
must perform none but the service God had specially assigned
to them, as no Gershonite might perform the duty of a
Merarite, and vice versa, and each individual, too, had his
special duty, that no quarrel might arise among them.[488]

The Four Standards

When God appeared upon Sinai, He was surrounded by
twenty-two thousand angels, all in full array and divided into
groups, each of which had its own standard. Looking upon
these angel hosts, Israel wished like them to be divided into
groups with standards, and God fulfilled their wish. After
Moses had completed the census of the people, God said to
him: " Fulfil their wish and provide them with standards
as they desire. ' Every man of the children of Israel shall
pitch by his own standard, with the ensign of their father's
house; far off about the Tabernacle of the congregation shall

they pitch.'" This commission greatly agitated Moses, who thought: "Now will there be much strife among the tribes. If I bid the tribe of Judah pitch in the East, it will surely state its preference for the South, and every tribe will likewise choose any direction but the one assigned to it." But God said to Moses: "Do not concern thyself with the position of the standards of the tribes, for they have no need of thy direction. Their father Jacob before his death ordered them to group themselves about the Tabernacle just as his sons were to be grouped about his bier at the funeral procession." When Moses now told the people to divide themselves in groups round about the Tabernacle, they did it in the manner Jacob had bidden them.[49]

"The Lord by wisdom hath founded the earth; by understanding hath He established the heavens." The division of the tribes of Israel according to four standards, as well as their subdivision at each standard, is not arbitrary and accidental, it corresponds to the same plan and direction as that of which God made use in heaven. The celestial Throne is surrounded by four angels: to the right Michael, in front Gabriel, to the left Uriel, and to the rear Raphael. To these four angels corresponded the four tribes of Reuben, Judah, Dan, and Ephraim, the standard bearers. Michael earned his name, "Who is like unto God," by exclaiming during the passage of Israel through the Red Sea, "Who is like unto Thee, O Lord, among the gods?" and he made a similar statement when Moses completed the Torah, saying: "There is none like unto the God of Jeshurun." In the same way Reuben bore upon his standard the words, "Hear, O Israel: the Lord our God is one Lord," hence Reuben's position with his standard to the right of the sanctuary corresponded exactly to Michael's post at the right of the celestial Throne. Gabriel, " God is mighty," stands in front of the Throne, as Judah, " mightiest among his brethren," was the standard bearer in front of the camp. Dan, the tribe " from which emanated dark sin," stood at the left side of the camp with his standard, corresponding to the angel Uriel, " God is my light," for God illuminated the darkness of sin by the revelation of the Torah, in the study of which this angel instructed Moses, and devotion to which is penance for sin. The tribe of Ephraim was the standard bearer to the rear of the camp, occupying the same position as Raphael, " God heals," holds at the celestial Throne; for this tribe, from which sprang Jeroboam, was in need of God's healing for the wound that this wicked king dealt Israel.⁴⁴⁰

God had other reasons for the divisions of the tribes that He decreed, for He said to Moses: " In the East whence comes the light shall the tribe of Judah, whence arises the light of sovereignty, pitch its camp, and with them the tribe of Issachar, with whom dwells the light of the Torah, and Zebulun, shining through its wealth. From the South come the dews of blessing and the rains of plenty, hence shall Reuben pitch on this side, for this tribe owes its existence to the penitent deeds of its forefather, penance being that which causes God to send His blessing upon the world. Beside Reuben shall stand the warlike tribe of Gad, and between these two Simeon, in order that this tribe, made weak by its sins, might be protected on either side by the piety of Reuben and the heroism of Gad. In the West are the storehouses of snow, the storehouses of hail, of cold, and of heat, and as

powerless as are mortals against these forces of nature, so
ineffectual shall be the enemies of the tribes of Ephraim,
Manasseh, and Benjamin, for which reason their post was to
the West of the camp. From the North comes the darkness,
and so from the tribe of Dan will come the darkness of sin,
for this tribe alone will declare itself willing to accept the
idols of Jeroboam, hence its place is to the North of the
camp. To illuminate its darkness, put beside it shining
Asher, and Naphtali, filled with God's plenty." [41]

The four standards were distinguished from one another
by their different colors, and by the inscriptions and figures
worked upon each. The color of Judah's standard corresponded to the color of the three stones in the breastplate of
the high priest, on which were engraved the names of Judah,
Issachar, and Zebulun, and was composed of red, green, and
fiery red. Judah's name, as well as Issachar's and Zebulun's,
was inscribed on the banner, and beside the names was this
inscription: " Rise up, Lord, and let Thine enemies be scattered; and let them that hate Thee flee before Thee." The
standard of Reuben, about which gathered also the tribes of
Simeon and Gad, was the color of the emerald, the sapphire,
and the sabhalom, for on these three stones were the names
of these tribes engraved on the breastplate of the high priest.
Beside the names of Reuben, Simeon, and Gad the following
device was wrought on the second standard, " Hear, O
Israel: the Lord our God is one Lord." The third standard, around which rallied the tribes of Ephraim, Manasseh,
and Benjamin, bore the color of the diamond, the turquoise,
and the amethyst, for on these three stones in the high
priest's breastplate were engraved the names of these three

tribes. On this standard beside the names of these three tribes was the motto, " And the cloud of the Lord was upon them by day, when they went out of the camp." As on the breastplate of the high priest the stones chrysolite, beryl and panther-stone bore the names of Dan, Asher, and Naphtali, so too did the fourth standard, round which these three tribes gathered, bear a color resembling these three stones. This standard contained the names of Dan, Asher, and Naphtali, and the device: " Return, O Lord, unto the many thousands of Israel." [442]

The standards had also other distinguishing characteristics. Judah's standard bore in its upper part the figure of a lion, for its forefather had been characterized by Jacob as " a lion's whelp," and also sword-like hooks of gold. On these hooks God permitted a strip of the seventh cloud of glory to rest, in which were visible the initials of the names of the three Patriarchs, Abraham, Isaac, and Jacob, the letters being radiations from the Shekinah. Reuben's standard had in its upper part the figure of a man, corresponding to the mandrakes that Reuben, forefather of this tribe, found, for this plant had the form of a manikin. The hooks on this standard were like those on the standard of Judah, but the second letters of the names of the three Patriarchs, Bet, Zade, and 'Ayyin were seen above them in the cloud. In the standard of Ephraim was fashioned the form of a fish, for Jacob had blessed the forefather of this tribe by telling him to multiply like a fish; in all other respects it was like the other two standards, save that above the sword-like hooks of gold were seen the third letters in the names of the Patriarchs, Resh, Het, and Kof. Dan's standard contained the form of a serpent, for "Dan shall be a serpent by the way," was Jacob's blessing for this tribe; and the gleaming letters over the hooks were: Mem for Abraham, Ḳof for Isaac, and Bet for Jacob. The letter He of Abraham's name was not indeed visible over the standards, but was reserved by God for a still greater honor. For, over the Holy Ark, God let a pillar of cloud rest, and in this were visible the letters Yod and He, spelling the name Yah, by means of which God had created the world. This pillar of cloud shed sunlight by day and moonlight by night, so that Israel, who were surrounded by clouds, might distinguish between night and day. These two sacred letters, Yod, He, would on week-days fly about in the air over the four standards, hovering now upon this, now upon that. But as soon as Friday was over and the Sabbath began, these letters stood immovable on the spot where they chanced to be at that moment, and remained in this rigid position from the first moment of the Sabbath to the last.

Whenever God wanted Israel to break up camp and move on, He would send on from its place over the Ark the cloud in which beamed the two sacred letters Yod and He in the direction in which Israel was to march, and the four strips of cloud over the standards would follow. As soon as the priests saw these clouds in motion, they blew the trumpets as a signal for starting, and the winds thereupon from all sides breathed myrrh and frankincense.[443]

Although it was the clouds that gave the signal for taking down and pitching tents, still they always awaited the word of Moses. Before starting the pillar of cloud would contract and stand still before Moses, waiting for him to say: "Rise up, Lord, and let Thine enemies be scattered; and let them that hate Thee flee before Thee," whereupon the pillar of cloud would be set in motion. It was the same when they pitched camp. The pillar of cloud would contract and stand still before Moses, waiting for him to say : " Return, O Lord, unto the many thousands of Israel," whereupon it would expand first over the tribes that belonged to the standard of Judah, and then over the sanctuary, within and without.⁴⁴

The Camp

The camp was in the form of a square, twelve thousand cubits on each side, and in the middle was the space, four thousand cubits in size, for the sanctuary, and the dwelling place of priests and Levites. In the East of the sanctuary lived Moses, Aaron, and Aaron's sons ; the Levites of the family of Kohath lived in the South, the sons of Gershon in the West, and the sons of Merari in the North. Each of these divisions had for its dwelling place a space of a hundred cubits, while each group of three tribes that joined under one standard had a space of four thousand cubits. This was only for the dwelling place of the people, the cattle were outside the encampment, and the cloud of glory separated the dwelling places of the human beings from those of the animals. Rivers surrounded the camp from without, and so also were the different groups separated one from the other by rivers. But in order that on the Sabbath, when riding was prohibited, intercourse among the different parts of the camp might not be rendered impossible, there were bridges of boards over the rivers. The purple color of the cloud of glory was reflected in the waters of the rivers, so that it spread afar a radiance like that of the sun and the stars.

The heathens, whenever they beheld these wondrous radiant waters, were frightened and feared Israel, but at the same time praised God for the miracles He wrought for Israel.[446]

These were miracles that were visible to the outer world as well, but there were others that were known to Israel alone. During their forty years' march they had no need of change of raiment. The robe of purple with which the angels clothed each one among them at their exodus from Egypt remained ever new; and as a snail's shell grows with it, so did their garments grow with them. Fire could not injure these garments, and though they wore the same things throughout forty years, still they were not annoyed by vermin, yes, even the corpses of this generation were spared by worms.[446]

During their marches, as well as in their stay at a certain place, they had not only the four standards that divided them into four groups of three tribes each, each individual tribe had furthermore its own special spot and its special ensign. Reuben's flag was red, and on it were pictured mandrakes. Simeon's flag was green, with a picture of the city of Shechem upon it, for the forefather of the tribe had conquered this city. Judah's flag was azure, and bore the form of a lion. Issachar's flag was black, and had two figures, the sun and the moon, for from this tribe sprung the learned men who busied themselves with astronomy and the science of the calendar. Zebulun's flag was white, with the form of a ship, for this tribe was devoted to navigation. Dan's flag had a color like a sapphire, with the figure of a serpent. Naphtali's flag was a dull red, the color of wine, and on it was the figure of a hind, in memory of its forefather, who was like " a hind let loose." Asher's flag was red like fire, and had the token of an olive tree, because this tribe had much olive oil of excellent quality. The two tribes descended from Joseph,—Ephraim, and Manasseh—both had flags of the same deep black color with a representation of Egypt, but they had other forms besides. Ephraim's had the picture of a bull, to symbolize Joshua, sprung of this tribe, whose glory was like "the firstling of his bullock, that pusheth the people together to the ends of the earth;" whereas Manasseh's was that of a unicorn, symbolizing the judge Gideon that sprang from this tribe, "who with his horns of unicorns pushed the people." Benjamin's flag had a color composed of all the other eleven colors, and a wolf for his token, Jacob having described this tribe as "a wolf that ravineth." The different colors of the flags corresponded to the colors of the stones set in the breastplate of the high priest, on which were engraved the names of the twelve tribes. Reuben's stone had a red color like his flag, Simeon's flag was green like the color of his stone, and in this way with all the tribes the color of stones and of flags harmonized.⁴⁴⁷

THE BLASPHEMER AND THE SABBATH-BREAKER

When Israel received the Torah from God, all the other nations envied them and said: "Why were these chosen by God out of all the nations?" But God stopped their mouths, replying: "Bring Me your family records, and My children shall bring their family records." The nations could not prove the purity of their families, but Israel stood without a blemish, every man among them ready to prove his pure descent, so that the nations burst into praise at Israel's family purity, which was rewarded by God with the Torah for this its excellence.[448]

How truly chastity and purity reigned among Israel was shown by the division of the people into groups and tribes. Among all these thousands was found only a single man who was not of pure descent, and who therefore at the pitching of the standards could attach himself to none of the groups. This man was the son of Shelomith, a Danite woman, and the Egyptian,[449] whom Moses, when a youth of eighteen, had slain for having offered violence to Shelomith, the incident that had necessitated Moses' flight from Egypt. It had happened as follows: When Moses came to Goshen to visit his parents, he witnessed how an Egyptian struck an Israelite, and the latter, knowing that Moses was in high favor at Pharaoh's court, sought his assistance, appealing to him with these words: " O, my lord, this Egyptian by night forced his way into my house, bound me with chains, and in my presence offered violence to my wife. Now he wants to kill me besides." Indignant at this infamous action of the Egyptian, Moses slew him, so that the tormented Israelite might go home. The latter, on reaching his house, informed his wife that he intended getting a divorce from her, as it was not proper for a member of the house of Jacob to live together with a woman that had been defiled. When the wife told her brothers of her husband's intentions, they wanted to kill their brother-in-law, who eluded them only by timely flight.[450]

The Egyptian's violence was not without issue, for Shelomith gave birth to a son whom she reared as a Jew, even though his father had been an Egyptian. When the division

of the people according to the four standards took place, this
son of Shelomith appeared among the Danites into whose
division he meant to be admitted, pointing out to them that
his mother was a woman of the tribe of Dan. The Danites,
however, rejected him, saying: "The commandment of God
says, ' each man by his own standard, with the ensign of his
father's house.' Paternal, not maternal descent decides a
man's admission to a tribe." As this man was not content
with this answer, his case was brought to Moses' court, who
also passed judgment against him. This so embittered him
that he blasphemed the Ineffable Name which he had heard
on Mount Sinai, and cursed Moses. He at the same time
ridiculed the recently announced law concerning the shewbread that was to be set on the table in the sanctuary every
Sabbath, saying: "It behooves a king to eat fresh bread
daily, and no stale bread." [451]

At the same time as the crime of blasphemy was committed
by the son of Shelomith, Zelophehad committed another
capital crime. On a Sabbath day he tore trees out of the
ground although he had been warned by witnesses not to
break the Sabbath. The overseers whom Moses had appointed to enforce the observance of the Sabbath rest seized
him and brought him to the school, where Moses, Aaron, and
other leaders of the people studied the Torah.

In both these cases Moses was uncertain how to pass judgment, for, although he knew that capital punishment must
follow the breaking of the Sabbath, still the manner of capital
punishment in this case had not yet been revealed to him.
Zelophehad was in the meantime kept in prison until Moses
should learn the details of the case, for the law says that a

man accused of a capital charge may not be given liberty of person. The sentence that Moses received from God was to execute Zelophehad in the presence of all the community by stoning him. This was accordingly done, and after the execution his corpse was for a short time suspended from the gallows.[452]

The sin of the Sabbath-breaker was the occasion that gave rise to God's commandment of Ẓiẓit to Israel. For He said to Moses, " Dost thou know how it came to pass that this man broke the Sabbath? " Moses: " I do not know." God: " On week days he wore phylacteries on his head and phylacteries on his arm to remind him of his duties, but on the Sabbath day, on which no phylacteries may be worn, he had nothing to call his duties to his mind, and he broke the Sabbath. Go now, Moses, and find for Israel a commandment the observance of which is not limited to week days only, but which will influence them on Sabbath days and on holy days as well." Moses selected the commandment of Ẓiẓit, the sight of which will recall to the Israelites all the other commandments of God.[453]

Whereas in the case of the Sabbath breaker Moses had been certain that the sin was punishable by death, and had been in doubt only concerning the manner of execution, in the case of the blasphemer matters were different. Here Moses was in doubt concerning the nature of the crime, for he was not even sure if it was at all a capital offence. Hence he did not have these two men imprisoned together, because one of them was clearly a criminal, whereas the status of the other was undetermined. But God instructed Moses that the blasphemer was also to be stoned to death, and that this was to be the punishment for blasphemers in the future.[454]

There were two other cases beside these two in Moses' career on which he could not pass judgment without appealing to God. These were the claims of Zelophehad's daughters to the inheritance of their father, and the case of the unclean that might not participate in the offering of the paschal lamb. Moses hastened in his appeal to God concerning the two last mentioned cases, but took his time with the two former, for on these depended human lives. In this Moses set the precedent to the judges among Israel to despatch civil cases with all celerity, but to proceed slowly in criminal cases. In all these cases, however, he openly confessed that he did not at the time know the proper decision, thereby teaching the judges of Israel to consider it no disgrace, when necessary, to consult others in cases when they were not sure of true judgment.[455]

THE UNGRATEFUL MULTITUDE

When God commanded Israel to set out from Sinai and continue their march, the Israelites were glad, for during their stay in that place they had throughout eleven days received new laws daily, and they hoped that after having departed from the holy mountain they would receive no further laws. Hence, instead of making a day's march from Sinai, as God had commanded them, they marched incessantly for three days, in order to be as far as possible from the holy spot. They behaved like a boy who runs quickly away after dismissal from school, that his teacher might not call him back. Although this antipathy to His laws vexed God, He

did not therefore forsake them, but let the Ark move before
them as long as they desired to continue the march. For
it was by this token that the Israelites knew that the
Shekinah was among them, as God had promised them. As
often as they broke camp or pitched camp Moses would say
to them: "Do what the Shekinah within the Ark bids you
do." But they would not believe Moses that the Shekinah
dwelt among them unless he spoke the words: "Rise up,
Lord, and let Thine enemies be scattered; and let them that
hate Thee flee before Thee," whereupon the Ark would begin to move, and they were convinced of the presence of the
Shekinah. The Ark furthermore gave the signal for breaking camp by soaring up high,[456] and then swiftly moving
before the camp at a distance of three days' march, until it
found a suitable spot upon which Israel might encamp.[457]

Hardly had they departed from Sinai when they once more
began to lead the wicked course of life that they had for a
time abandoned. They began to seek a pretext to renounce
God and again to be addicted to idolatry.[458] They complained about the forced marches which at God's command
they had been obliged to make after their departure from
Sinai, and in this way showed their ingratitude to God who
wanted them as quickly as possible to reach the Holy Land,
and for this reason allowed them to cover an eleven days'
distance in three days.[459] Their murmurs and complaints,
however, were not silent, but quite loud, for they were
anxious that God should hear their wicked words. In punishment for their defamation of the Divine glory, God sent
upon them a fire emanating from that very glory.[460]

Upon twelve occasions did God send a Divine fire upon

earth, six times as a token of honor and distinction, but as
many times as a punishment. To the first class belong the
fire at the consecration of the Tabernacle, at the offering of
Gideon as at that of Manoah and of David; at the dedication
of Solomon's Temple, and at the offering of Elijah upon
Mount Carmel. The six fatal fires are the following: the
fire that consumed Nadab and Abihu; that which wrought
havoc among the murmuring and complaining multitude;
the fire that consumed the company of Korah; the fire that
destroyed Job's sheep, and the two fires that burned the first
and the second troops which Ahaziah sent against Elijah.[461]

This celestial fire wrought the greatest havoc among the
idolatrous tribe of Dan, and among the mixed multitude
that had joined the Israelites upon their exodus from
Egypt.[462] The elders of the people turned to Moses, saying:
" Rather deliver us as a sheep to the slaughter, but not to
a celestial fire that consumes earthly fire." [463] They should
by right have prayed to God themselves, but in this instance they were like the king's son who had kindled his
father's anger against him, and who now hastened to his
father's friend, begging him to intercede for him. So did
Israel say to Moses: " Go thou to God and pray for us."
Moses instantly granted their wish, and God without delay heard Moses' prayer and halted the destroying fire.[464]
But God did not simply take the fire away from Israel
and put it elsewhere, for it was of such a nature that it
would gradually have spread on all sides and finally have destroyed everything. It had in this way caused the destruction in Israel, for, beginning at one end of the camp, it
spread so rapidly that one could at no time tell how far it had

gone. That the presence of this Divine fire might continue to restrain Israel from sin, God did not allow it to rise back to heaven, but it found its place on the altar of the Tabernacle, where it consumed all the offerings that were brought during Israel's stay in Egypt. This is the same fire that destroyed Aaron's sons as well as Korah's company, and it is the Divine fire that every mortal beholds in the moment of his death.[465]

On this occasion also it was evident that pious men are greater than the angels, for Moses took bundles of wool and laid them upon the Divine fire, which thereupon went out.[466] He then said to the people: " If you repent of your sin, then the fire will go out, but otherwise it will burst forth and consume you." [467]

THE FLESH-POTS OF EGYPT

Not mindful of the punishment by fire, Israel still did not mend their ways, but soon again began to murmur against God. As so often before, it was again the mixed multitude that rebelled against God and Moses, saying: " Who shall give us flesh to eat? We remember the fish that we did eat in Egypt freely; the cucumbers, and the melons, and the leeks, and the onions, and the garlick. But now our soul is dried away: there is nothing at all, beside this manna before our eyes " But all this murmuring and these complaints were only a pretext to sever themselves from God, for first of all, they actually possessed many herds and much cattle, enough plentifully to satisfy their lusting after flesh if they had really felt it; and manna, furthermore, had the flavor of every conceivable kind of food, so all they had to do while

eating it was to wish for a certain dish and they instantly
perceived in manna the taste of the desired food. It is true
that manna never gave them the flavor of the five vegetables
they mentioned, but they should have been grateful to God
for sparing them the taste of these vegetables injurious to
health. Here they showed their perversity in being dissatis-
fied with measures for which they should have been grateful
to God. Manna displeased them because it did not contain
the flavor injurious to health, and they also objected to it
because it remained in their bodies, wherefore they said:
"The manna will swell in our stomachs, for can there be a
human being that takes food without excreting it!" God
had, as a special mark of distinction, given them this food
of the angels, which is completely dissolved in the body, and
of which they could always partake without injury to their
health. It is a clear proof of the excellent taste of manna
that at a later time, when the last manna fell on the day of
Moses' death, they ate of it for forty days, and would not
make use of other food until the manna had been exhausted
to the last grain, clearly showing that the taking of any
different food was disagreeable. But while manna was at
hand in abundance, they complained about seeing before
them, morning and evening, no other food than manna.[468]

The true state of affairs was that they had a lurking dissatisfaction with the yoke of the law. It is certain that they
had not had in Egypt better food for which they now longed,
for their taskmasters, far from giving them dainties, gave
them not even straw for making bricks. But in Egypt they
had lived undisturbed by laws, and it was this unrestrained
life that they desired back. Especially hard for them were

the new laws on marriage, for in Egypt they had been accustomed to marry those closely related by blood, from whom they were now obliged to separate. They now trooped together in families, and awaiting the moment when Moses, about to leave the house of study, would have to pass them, they began to murmur publicly,[469] accusing him of being to blame for all the sufferings they had been obliged to bear. Upon his advice, they said, had they abandoned a most fruitful land, and instead of enjoying the great fortune promised to them, they were now wandering about in misery, suffering thirst from lack of water, and were apprehensive of dying of starvation in case the supply of manna should cease. When these and similar abuses were uttered against Moses, one out of the people stepped forth and exhorted them not so soon to forget the many benefactions they had known from Moses, and not to despair of God's aid and support. But the multitude upon this became even more excited, and raged and shouted more violently than ever against Moses.[470] This conduct of Israel called forth God's wrath, but Moses, instead of interceding for the people, began to complain of their treatment of him, and announced to God that he could not now execute the commission he had undertaken in Egypt, namely, to lead Israel in spite of all reverses, until he had reached the promised land. He now begged God to relieve him of the leadership of the people in some way, and at the same time to stand by him in his present predicament, that he might satisfy the people's desire for flesh.[471]

THE APPOINTMENT OF THE SEVENTY ELDERS

The sad predicament of Moses on this occasion is partly
traceable to the fact that he had to face alone the murmurs
and complaints of the people without the accustomed assistance of the seventy elders.   Since the exodus from Egypt
the seventy elders of the people had always been at his side,
but these had recently been killed by the fire from heaven at
Taberah, so that he now stood all alone.   This death overtook
the elders because like Nadab and Abihu they had not shown
sufficient reverence in ascending Mount Sinai on the day of
the revelation, when, in view of the Divine vision, they conducted themselves in an unseemly manner.   Like Nadab and
Abihu the elders would have received instantaneous punishment for their offense, had not God been unwilling to spoil
the joyful day of the revelation by their death.   But they
had to pay the penalty nevertheless: Nadab and Abihu, by
being burned at the consecration of the Tabernacle, and the
elders similarly, at Taberah.[412]

As Moses now utterly refused to bear the burden of the
people alone, God said to him: "I gave thee sufficient understanding and wisdom to guide My children alone, that thou
mightest be distinguished by this honor.   Thou, however,
wishest to share this guidance with others.   Go, then, and
expect no help from Me, 'but I will take of the spirit that is
upon thee and will put it upon them; and they shall bear the
burden of the people with thee, that thou bear it not thyself alone.' " [413]

God bade Moses choose as his helpers in the guidance of
the people such men as had already been active leaders and
officers in Egypt.   In the days of Egyptian bondage it

frequently happened that the officers of the children of Israel were beaten if the people had not fulfilled their task in making bricks, but " he that is willing to sacrifice himself for the benefit of Israel shall be rewarded with honor, dignity, and the gift of the Holy Spirit." The officers suffered in Egypt for Israel, and were now found worthy of having the Holy Spirit come upon them.[474] God moreover said to Moses : " With kindly words welcome the elders to their new dignity, saying, ' Hail to you that are deemed worthy by God of being fit for this office.' At the same time, however, speak seriously with them also, saying, ' Know ye that the Israelites are a troublesome and stiffnecked people, and that you must ever be prepared to have them curse you or cast stones at you.' "

God commanded the selection of the elders to take place at the Tabernacle, that Israel might reverence them, saying, " Surely these are worthy men," but they were not permitted with Moses to enter the Tabernacle and hear God's word. The people were however mistaken in assuming that God's word reached the ears of the elders, for He spoke with Moses alone, even though the prophetic spirit came upon them also.[475]

Now when Moses wished to proceed to the selection of the seventy elders, he was in a sore predicament because he could not evenly divide the number seventy among the twelve tribes, and was anxious to show no partiality to one tribe over another, which would lead to dissatisfaction among Israel. Bezalel, son of Uri, however, gave Moses good advice. He took seventy slips of paper on which was written " elder," and with them two blank slips, and mixed all these in an urn. Seventy-two elders, six to each tribe, now advanced and each drew a slip. Those whose slips were marked " elder " were elected, while those who had drawn blank slips were rejected, but in such a wise that they could not well accuse Moses of partiality.[476]

By this method of appointment, it came to pass that there were six elders for each tribe except the tribe of Levi. The names of those chosen were: from the tribe of Reuben,— Hanoch, Carmi, Pallu, Zaccur, Eliab, Nemuel; from the tribe of Simeon,—Jamin, Jachin, Zohar, Ohad, Shaul, Zimri; from the tribe of Levi,—Amram, Hananiah, Nethanel, Sithri; from the tribe of Judah,—Zerah, Dan, Jonadab, Bezalel, Shephatiah, Nahshon; from the tribe of Issachar,— Zuar, Uzza, Igal, Palti, Othniel, Haggi; from the tribe of Zebulun,—Sered, Elon, Sodi, Oholiab, Elijah, Nimshi; from the tribe of Benjamin,—Senaah, Kislon, Elidad, Ahitub, Jediael, Mattaniah; from the tribe of Joseph,—Jair, Joezer, Malchiel, Adoniram, Abiram, Sethur; from the tribe of Dan, —Gedaliah, Jogli, Ahinoam, Ahiezer, Daniel, Seraiah; from the tribe of Naphtali,—Elhanan, Eliakim, Elishama, Sem- achiah, Zabdi, Johanan; from the tribe of Gad,—Haggai, Zarhi, Keni, Mattathiah, Zechariah, Shuni; from the tribe of Asher,—Pashhur, Shelomi, Samuel, Shalom, Shecaniah, Abihu.[477]

Moses gathered these seventy elders of noble extraction and of lofty and pious character round about the tent in which God used to reveal Himself, bidding thirty of them take their stand on the south side, thirty on the northern, and ten on the eastern, whereas he himself stood on the western side. For this tent was thirty cubits long and ten cubits wide, so that a cubit each was apportioned to the elders.[478]

God was so pleased with the appointment of the elders that, just as on the day of the revelation, He descended from heaven and permitted the spirit of prophecy to come upon the elders, so that they received the prophetic gift to the end of their days, as God had put upon them of the spirit of Moses. But Moses' spirit was not diminished by this, he was like a burning candle from which many others are lighted, but which is not therefore diminished; and so likewise was the wisdom of Moses unimpaired. Even after the appointment of the elders did Moses remain the leader of the people, for he was the head of this Sanhedrin of seventy members which he guided and directed.[479]

The position of the elders was not of the same rank as that of Moses, for he was the king of Israel, and it was for this reason that God had bidden him to secure trumpets, to use them for the calling of the assembly, that this instrument might be blown before him as before a king. Hence shortly before Moses' death these trumpets were recalled from use, for his successor Joshua did not inherit from him either his kingly dignity or these royal insignia. Not until David's time were the trumpets used again which Moses had fashioned in the desert.[480]

ELDAD AND MEDAD

When Moses had completed the appointment of the elders and had asked them to accompany him to the Tabernacle, there to receive the Holy Spirit, Eldad and Medad, two of these elders, in their humility, did not obey his summons, but hid themselves, deeming themselves unworthy of this distinction. God rewarded them for their humility by dis-

tinguishing them five-fold above the other elders. These
prophesied what would take place on the following day, announcing the appearance of the quails, but Eldad and Medad
prophesied what was still veiled in the distant future. The
elders prophesied only on this one day, but Eldad and Medad
retained the gift for life. The elders died in the desert,
whereas Eldad and Medad were the leaders of the people
after the death of Joshua. The elders are not mentioned by
name in the Scriptures, whereas these two are called by
name. The elders, furthermore, had received the prophetic
gift from Moses, whereas Eldad and Medad received it
directly from God.[481]

Eldad now began to make prophecies, saying: " Moses
will die, and Joshua the son of Nun will be his successor as
leader of the people, whom he will lead into the land of
Canaan, and to whom he will give it as a possession."
Medad's prophecy was as follows: " Quails will come from
the sea and will cover the camp of Israel, but they will
bring evil to the people." Beside these prophecies, both
together announced the following revelation: " At the end
of days there will come up out of the land of Magog a
king to whom all nations will do homage. Crowned kings,
princes, and warriors with shields will gather to make war
upon those returned from exile in the land of Israel. But
God, the Lord, will stand by Israel in their need and will
slay all their enemies by hurling a flame from under His
glorious Throne. This will consume the souls in the hosts
of the king of Magog, so that their bodies will drop lifeless
upon the mountains of the land of Israel, and will become a
prey to the beasts of the field and the fowls of the air.

Then will all the dead among Israel arise and rejoice in the good that at the beginning of the world was laid up for them, and will receive the reward for their good deeds." [452]

When Gershon, Moses' son, heard these prophecies of Eldad and Medad, he hurried to his father and told him of them. Joshua was now greatly agitated about the prophecy that Moses was to die in the desert and that he was to be his successor, and said to Moses: " O lord, destroy these people that prophesy such evil news!" But Moses replied: " O Joshua, canst thou believe that I begrudge thee thy splendid future? It is my wish that thou mayest be honored as much as I have been and that all Israel be honored like thee." [453]

Eldad and Medad were distinguished not only by their prophetic gift, but also by their noble birth, being half-brothers of Moses and Aaron. When the marriage laws were revealed, all those who had been married to relatives by blood had to be divorced from them, so that Amram, too, had to be separated from his wife Jochebed, who was his aunt, and he married another woman. From this union sprang Eldad, " not of an aunt," and Medad, " in place of an aunt," so called by Amram to explain by these names why he had divorced his first wife, his aunt. [454]

THE QUAILS

The prophecy of these men concerning the quails turned out as they had predicted, the quails being, as God had foretold to Moses, no blessing for the people. For God said to Moses: " Tell the people to be prepared for impending punishment, they shall eat flesh to satiety, but then they shall loathe it more than they now lust for it. I know, however, how they came to have such desires. Because My Shekinah is among them they believe that they may presume anything. Had I removed My Shekinah from their midst they would never have cherished so foolish a desire." Moses, knowing that the granting of the people's wish would be disastrous to them, said to God: "O Lord, why, pray, dost Thou first give them flesh, and then, in punishment for their sin, slay them? Who ever heard any one say to an ass, ' Here is a measure of wheat; eat it, for we want to cut off thy head?' Or to a man, ' Here is a loaf of bread for thee; take it, and go to hell with it?'" God replied: "Well, then, what wouldst thou do?" Moses: "I will go to them and reason with them that they may desist from their lusting after flesh." God: "I can tell thee beforehand that thy endeavors in this matter will be fruitless." Moses betook himself to the people, saying to them: "Is the Lord's hand waxed short? Behold, He smote the rock, that the waters gushed out, and the streams overflowed; He can give bread also; can He not provide flesh for His people?" The people, however, said: "Thou art only trying to soothe us; God cannot grant our wish." [485] But they erred vastly, for hardly had the pious among them retired to their tents, when upon the godless, who had remained in the open, came down quails in masses as thick as snowflakes, so that many more were killed by the descent of the quails than later by the tasting of them. The quails came in such masses that they completely filled the space between heaven and earth, so that they even covered the sun's disk, and settled down on the north side and the south side of the camp, as it were a day's journey, lying, however, not directly upon the ground but two cubits above it, that people might not have to stoop to gather them up. Considering this abundance, it is not surprising that even the halt that could not go far, and the lazy that would not, gathered each a hundred kor. These vast quantities of flesh did not, however, benefit them, for hardly had they tasted of it, when they gave up the ghost. This was the punishment for the grave sinners, while the better ones among them enjoyed the taste of the flesh for a month before they died, whereas the pious without suffering harm caught the quails, slaughtered them, and ate of them. This was the heaviest blow that had fallen upon Israel since their exodus from Egypt, and in memory of the many men who had died because of their forbidden lusting after flesh, they changed the name of the place where this misfortune occurred to Kibroth-hattaavah, " Graves of those who lusted." [486] The wind that went forth to bring the quails was so powerful a storm that it could have destroyed the world, so great was God's anger against the ungrateful people, and it was only due to the merits of Moses and Aaron that this wind finally left the world upon its hinges.[487]

Aaron and Miriam Slander Moses

When the seventy elders were appointed, and the spirit of the Lord came upon them, all the women lighted the candles of joy, to celebrate by this illumination the elevation of these men to the dignity of prophets. Zipporah, Moses' wife, saw the illumination, and asked Miriam to explain it. She told her the reason, and added, " Blessed are the women who behold with their eyes how their husbands are raised to dignity." Zipporah answered, " It would be more proper to

say, ' Woe to the wives of these men who must now abstain
from all conjugal happiness!' " Miriam: " How dost thou
know this?" Zipporah: " I judge so from the conduct of
thy brother, for ever since he was chosen to receive Divine
revelations, he no longer knows his wife." *** Miriam hereupon went to Aaron, and said to him: " I also received
Divine revelations, but without being obliged to separate myself from my husband," whereupon Aaron agreed, saying:
" I, too, received Divine revelations, without, however, being
obliged to separate myself from my wife." Then both said:
" Our fathers also received revelations, but without discon-
tinuing their conjugal life. Moses abstains from conjugal
joys only out of pride, to show how holy a man he is." Not
only did they speak evil of Moses to each other, but hastened
to him and told him to his face their opinion of his conduct.***
But he, who could be self-assured and stern when it touched
a matter concerning God's glory, was silent to the unde-
served reproaches they heaped upon him, knowing that upon
God's bidding he had foresworn earthly pleasures. God
therefore said: " Moses is very meek and pays no attention
to the injustice meted out to him, as he did when My glory
was detracted from, and boldly stepped forth and exclaimed,
' Who is on the Lord's side? Let him come unto me.' I will
therefore now stand by him."

It is quite true that this was not the only occasion on
which Moses proved himself humble and gentle, for it was
part of his character. Never among mortals, counting even
the three Patriarchs, was there more meek a man than he.
The angels alone excelled him in humility, but no human
being; for the angels are so humble and meek, that when

they assemble to praise God, each angel calls to the other
and asks him to precede him, saying among themselves:
" Be thou the first, thou art worthier than I." [400]

God carried out His intention to uphold Moses' honor, for
just as Aaron was with his wife and Miriam with her husband, a Divine call suddenly reached Amram's three children, one voice that simultaneously called, " Aaron! "
"Moses! " and "Miriam! "—a miracle that God's voice alone
can perform. The call went to Moses also, that the people
might not think that Aaron and Miriam had been chosen
to take Moses' place. He was ready to hearken to God's
words, but not so his brother and his sister, who had been
surprised in the state of uncleanness, and who therefore,
upon hearing God's call, cried, " Water, water," that they
might purify themselves before appearing before God. [401]
They then left their tents and followed the voice until
God appeared in a pillar of cloud, a distinction that was
conferred also upon Samuel. The pillar of cloud did not,
however, appear in the Tabernacle, where it always rested
whenever God revealed Himself to Moses, and this was due
to the following reasons. First of all, God did not want to
create the impression of having removed Moses from his
dignity, and of giving it to his brother and sister, hence He
did not appear to them in the holy place. At the same time,
moreover, Aaron was spared the disgrace of being reproached by God in his brother's presence, for Moses did not
follow his brother and sister, but awaited God's word in the
sanctuary. But there was still another reason why God did
not want Moses to be present during His conference with
Aaron and Miriam—" Never praise a man to his face." As

God wanted to praise Moses before Aaron and Miriam, He preferred to do so in his absence.[402]

Hardly had God addressed Aaron and Miriam, when they began to interrupt Him, whereupon He said to them: "Pray, contain yourselves until I have spoken." In these words He taught people the rule of politeness, never to interrupt. He then said: "Since the creation of the world hath the word of God ever appeared to any prophet otherwise than in a dream? Not so with Moses, to whom I have shown what is above and what is below; what is before and what is behind; what was and what will be. To him have I revealed all that is in the water and all that is upon the dry land; to him did I confide the sanctuary and set him above the angels. I Myself ordered him to abstain from conjugal life, and the word he received was revealed to him clearly and not in dark speeches, he saw the Divine presence from behind when It passed by him. Wherefore then were ye not afraid to speak against a man like Moses, who is, moreover, My servant? Your censure is directed to Me, rather than to him, for 'the receiver is no better than the thief,' and if Moses is not worthy of his calling, I, his Master, deserve censure."[408]

MIRIAM'S PUNISHMENT

God now gently rebuked Aaron and Miriam for their transgression, and did not give vent to His wrath until He had shown them their sin. This was an example to man never to show anger to his neighbor before giving his reason for his anger. The effects of God's wrath were shown as soon as He had departed from them, for while He was with them, His mercy exceeded His anger, and nothing happened

to them, but when He was no longer with them, punishment
set in. Both Aaron and Miriam became leprous, for this is
the punishment ordained for those who speak ill of their
neighbors.[494] Aaron's leprosy, however, lasted for a moment
only, for his sin had not been as great as that of his sister,
who started the talk against Moses. His disease vanished as
soon as he looked upon his leprosy. Not so with Miriam.
Aaron in vain tried to direct his eyes upon her leprosy and
in this way to heal her, for in her case the effect was the
reverse; as soon as he looked upon her the leprosy increased,
and nothing remained but to call for Moses' assistance, who
was ready to give it before being called upon.[495] Aaron thereupon turned to his brother with the following words: "Think
not that the leprosy is on Miriam's body only, it is as if it
were on the body of our father Amram, of whose flesh and
blood she is." Aaron did not, however, try to extenuate their
sin, saying to Moses: "Have we, Miriam and I, ever
done harm to a human being?" Moses: "No." Aaron:
"If we have done evil to no strange people, how then
canst thou believe that we wished to harm thee? For
a moment only did we forget ourselves and acted in an unnatural way toward our brother. Shall we therefore lose
our sister? If Miriam's leprosy doth not now vanish, she
must pass all her life as a leper, for only a priest who is not
a relative by blood of the leper may under certain conditions declare her clean, but all the priests, my sons and I,
are her relatives by blood. The life of a leper is as of one
dead, for as a corpse makes unclean all that comes in contact with it, so too the leper. Alas!" so Aaron closed his
intercession, "Shall our sister, who was with us in Egypt,

who with us intoned the song at the Red Sea, who took upon
herself the instruction of the women while we instructed the
men, shall she now, while we are about to leave the desert
and enter the promised land, sit shut out from the camp?"

These words of Aaron, however, were quite superfluous,
for Moses had determined, as soon as his sister became
diseased, to intercede for her with God, saying to himself:
"It is not right that my sister should suffer and I dwell in
contentment." [496] He now drew a circle about himself, stood
up, and said a short prayer to God, which he closed with the
words: "I will not go from this spot until Thou shalt have
healed my sister. But if Thou do not heal her, I myself
shall do so, for Thou hast already revealed to me, how
leprosy arises and how it disappears." This prayer was fervent, spoken with his whole heart and soul, though very
brief. Had he spoken long, some would have said: "His
sister is suffering terribly and he, without heeding her,
spends his time in prayer." Others again would have said:
"He prayeth long for his sister, but for us he prayeth
briefly." God said to Moses: "Why dost thou shout so?"
Moses: "I know what suffering my sister is enduring. I
remember the chain to which my hand was chained, for I
myself once suffered from this disease." God: "If a king,
or if her father had but spit in her face, should she not be
ashamed seven days? I, the King of kings, have spit
in her face, and she should be ashamed at least twice seven
days. For thy sake shall seven days be pardoned her, but
the other seven days let her be shut out from the camp."
For want of a priest who, according to the tenets of the law,
must declare a leper clean after the healing, God Himself

assumed this part, declaring Miriam unclean for a week, and clean after the passing of that period.[407]

Although leprosy came to Miriam as a punishment for her sin, still this occasion served to show how eminent a personage she was. For the people were breaking camp and starting on the march when, after having saddled their beasts of burden for the march, upon turning to see the pillar of cloud moving before them, they missed the sight of it. They looked again to see if Moses and Aaron were in the line of procession, but they were missing, nor was there anywhere to be seen a trace of the well that accompanied them on their marches. Hence they were obliged to return again to camp, where they remained until Miriam was healed. The clouds and the well, the sanctuary and the sixty myriads of the people, all had to wait a week in this spot until Miriam recovered. Then the pillar of cloud moved on once more and the people knew that they had not been permitted to proceed on their march only because of this pious prophetess. This was a reward for the kind deed Miriam had done when the child Moses was thrown into the water. Then Miriam for some time walked up and down along the shore to wait the child's fate, and for this reason did the people wait for her, nor could they move on until she had recovered.[408]

THE SENDING OF THE SPIES

The punishment that God brought upon Miriam was meant as a lesson of the severity with which God punishes slander. For Miriam spoke no evil of Moses in the presence of any one except her brother Aaron. She had moreover no evil motive, but a kindly intention, wishing only to induce

Moses to resume his conjugal life. She did not even dare
to rebuke Moses to his face, and still, even in spite of her
great piety, Miriam was not spared this heavy punishment.[499]
Her experience, nevertheless, did not awe the wicked men
who, shortly after this incident, made an evil report of the
promised land, and by their wicked tongues stirred up the
whole people in rebellion against God, so that they desired
rather to return to Egypt than to enter Palestine. The
punishment that God inflicted upon the spies as well as upon
the people they had seduced was well deserved, for had they
not been warned of slander by Miriam's example, there
might still have been some excuse. In that case they might
have been ignorant of the gravity of the sin of slander, but
now they had no excuse to offer.[500]

When Israel approached the boundaries of Palestine, they
appeared before Moses, saying: " We will send men before
us, and they shall search out the land, and bring us word
again by what way we must go up, and into what cities we
shall come." This desire caused God to exclaim: " What!
When you went through a land of deserts and of pits, you
had no desire for scouts, but now that you are about to enter
a land full of good things, now you wish to send out scouts.
Not only was the desire in itself unseemly, but also the way
in which they presented their request to Moses; for instead
of approaching as they had been accustomed, letting the
older men be the spokesmen of the younger they appeared
on this occasion without guidance or order, the young
crowding out the old, and these pushing away their leaders.[501]
Their bad conscience after making this request—for they
knew that their true motive was lack of faith in God—

caused them to invent all sorts of pretexts for their plans. They said to Moses: "So long as we are in the wilderness, the clouds act as scouts for us, for they move before us and show us the way, but as these will not proceed with us into the promised land, we want men to search out the land for us." Another plea that they urged for their desire was this. They said: "The Canaanites fear an attack from us and therefore hide their treasures. This is the reason why we want to send spies there in time, to discover for us where they are hiding their treasures." They sought in other ways to give Moses the impression that their one wish was exactly to carry out the law. They said: "Hast not thou taught us that an idol to which homage is no longer paid may be used, but otherwise it must be destroyed? If we now enter Palestine and find idols, we shall not know which of them were adored by the Canaanites and must be destroyed, and which of them were no longer adored, so that we might use them." Finally they said the following to Moses: "Thou, our teacher, hast taught us that God 'would little by little drive the Canaanites before us.' If this be so, we must send out spies to find out which cities we must attack first."[502] Moses allowed himself to be influenced by their talk, and he also liked the idea of sending out spies, but not wishing to act arbitrarily he submitted to God the desire of the people. God answered: "It is not the first time that they disbelieve My promises. Even in Egypt they ridiculed Me, it is now become a habit with them, and I know what their motive in sending spies is. If thou wishest to send spies do so, but do not pretend that I have ordered thee."

Moses hereupon chose one man from every tribe with the

exception of Levi, and sent these men to spy out the land. These twelve men were the most distinguished and most pious of their respective tribes, so that even God gave His assent to the choice of every man among them.[503] But hardly had these men been appointed to their office when they made the wicked resolve to bring up an evil report of the land, and dissuade the people from moving to Palestine. Their motive was a purely personal one, for they thought to themselves that they would retain their offices at the head of the tribes so long as they remained in the wilderness, but would be deprived of them when they entered Palestine.[504]

SIGNIFICANT NAMES

Significant of the wickedness of these men are their names, all of which point to their godless action. The representative of the tribe of Reuben was called Shammua, the son of Zaccur, because he did not obey God, which was counted against him just as if he had pursued sorcery. Shaphat, the son of Hori, was Simeon's representative. His name signifies, " He did not conquer his evil inclination, and hence went out empty-handed, without having received a possession in the land of Israel." The tribe of Issachar was represented by Igal, the son of Joseph. He bore this name because he soiled the reputation of the Holy Land, and therefore died before his time. Benjamin's representative was Palti, the son of Raphu, so called because " he spat out the good qualities that had previously been his, and therefore wasted away." The name of Gaddiel, the son of Sodi, Zebulun's representative, signifies, " He spoke infamous things against God in executing the secret plan of the spies."

Manasseh's representative, Gaddi, the son of Susi, was so called because he blasphemed God and aroused His wrath; for it was he who said of the land, " it eateth up its inhabitants." But the worst one among them was Ammiel, the son of Gemalli, the representative of Dan, for it was he who said, " The land is so strong that not even God could go up against it," hence his name, which means, " He cast a shadow upon God's strength," and he was punished according to his wicked words, for he did not enter the promised land. Asher's representative was Sethur, the son of Michael, who had resolved to act against God and instead of saying, " Who is like unto God? " he said, " Who is God? " Naphtali's representative was named Nahbi, the son of Vophsi, for he suppressed the truth, and faith found no room in his mouth, for he brought forth lies against God. The last of these spies, Gad's representative, bore the name Geuel, the son of Machi, for he was humbled because he urged untruths against God.

As the ten sinners were named in accordance with their actions, so too did the names of the two pious spies among them correspond to their pious actions. Judah's representative was named Caleb, the son of Jephunneh, because " he spoke what he felt in his heart and turned aside from the advice of the rest of the spies." The pious representative of Ephraim was Hoshea, the son of Nun, a fitting name for him, for he was full of understanding and was not caught like a fish by the spies. Moses who perceived, even when he sent out the spies, the evil intentions they harbored, changed Hoshea's name to Joshua, saying: " May God stand by thee, that thou mayest not follow the counsel of the spies." [606]

This change of name that was brought about by the pre-fixing of the letter Yod at last silenced the lamentations of this letter. For ever since God had changed Sarai's name to Sarah, the letter Yod used to flit about the celestial Throne and lament: "Is it perchance because I am the smallest among the letters that Thou hast taken me away from the name of the pious Sarah?" God quieted this letter, saying: "Formerly thou wert in a woman's name, and, moreover, at the end. I will now affix thee to a man's name, and, more-over, at the beginning." This promise was redeemed when Hoshea's name was changed to Joshua.[506]

When the spies set out on their way, they received in-structions from Moses how to conduct themselves, and what, in particular, they were to note. He ordered them not to walk on the highways, but to go along private pathways, for although the Shekinah would follow them, they were still to incur no needless danger. If they entered a city, however, they were not to slink like thieves in alleyways, but to show themselves in public and answer those who asked what they wanted by saying: "We came only to buy some pome-granates and grapes." They were emphatically to deny that they had any intention of destroying the idols or of felling the sacred trees. Moses furthermore said: "Look about carefully what manner of land it is, for some lands produce strong people and some weak, some lands produce many people and some few. If you find the inhabitants dwelling in open places, then know that they are mighty warriors, and depending upon their strength have no fear of hostile at-tack. If, however, they live in a fortified place, they are weaklings, and in their fear of strangers seek shelter within their walls. Examine also the nature of the soil. If it be hard, know then that it is fat; but if it be soft, it is lean." [507] Finally he bade them inquire whether Job was still alive, for if he was dead, then they assuredly needed not to fear the Canaanites, as there was not a single pious man among them whose merits might be able to shield them. [508] And truly when the spies reached Palestine, Job died, and they found the inhabitants of the land at his grave, partaking of the funeral feast. [509]

The Spies in Palestine

On the twenty-seventh day of Siwan Moses sent out the spies from Kadesh-Barnea in the wilderness of Paran, [510] and following his directions they went first to the south of Palestine, the poorest part of the Holy Land. Moses did like the merchants, who first show the poorer wares, and then the better kind; so Moses wished the spies to see better parts of the land the farther they advanced into it. When they reached Hebron, they could judge what a blessed land this was that had been promised them, for although Hebron was the poorest tract in all Palestine, it was still much better than Zoan, the most excellent part of Egypt. When, therefore, the sons of Ham built cities in several lands, it was Hebron that they erected first, owing to its excellence, and not Zoan, which they built in Egypt fully seven years later.

Their progress through the land was on the whole easy, for God had wished it so, that as soon as the spies entered a city, the plague struck it, and the inhabitants, busied with the burial of their dead, had neither time nor inclination to concern themselves with the strangers. [511] Although they met

with no evil on the part of the inhabitants, still the sight of
the three giants, Ahiman, Sheshai, and Talmai inspired them
with terror. These were so immensely tall that the sun
reached only to their ankles, and they received their names
in accordance with their size and strength. The strongest
among them was Ahiman, beholding whom one fancied one-
self standing at the foot of a mountain that was about to fall,
and exclaimed involuntarily, "What is this that is coming
upon me?" Hence the name Ahiman. Strong as marble
was the second brother, wherefore he was called Sheshai,
"marble." The mighty strides of the third brother threw
up plots from the ground when he walked, hence he was
called Talmai, "plots." [512] Not only the sons of Anak were
of such strength and size, but his daughters also, whom
the spies chanced to see. For when these reached the city
inhabited by Anak, that was called Kiriath-Arba, "City of
Four," because the giant Anak and his three sons dwelt
there, they were struck with such terror by them that they
sought a hiding place. But what they had believed to be a
cave was only the rind of a huge pomegranate that the
giant's daughter had thrown away, as they later, to their
horror, discovered. For this girl, after having eaten the
fruit, remembered that she must not anger her father by
letting the rind lie there, so she picked it up with the twelve
men in it as one picks up an egg shell, and threw it into the
garden, never noticing that she had thrown with it twelve
men, each measuring sixty cubits in height. When they left
their hiding place, they said to one another: "Behold the
strength of these women and judge by their standard the
men!" [513]

They soon had an opportunity of testing the strength of the men, for as soon as the three giants heard of the pres ence of the Israelite men, they pursued them, but the Israel- ites found out with what manner of men they were dealing even before the giants had caught up with them. One of the giants shouted, and the spies fell down as men dead, so that it took a long time for the Canaanites to restore them to life by the aid of friction and fresh air. The Canaanites hereupon said to them: "Why do you come here? Is not the whole world your God's, and did not He parcel it out according to His wish? Came ye here with the purpose of felling the sacred trees?" The spies declared their inno- cence, whereupon the Canaanites permitted them to go their ways unmolested. As a reward for this kind deed, the nation to which these giants belonged has been preserved even to this day.[514]

They would certainly not have escaped from the hands of the giants, had not Moses given them two weapons against them, his staff and the secret of the Divine Name. These two brought them salvation whenever they felt they were in danger from the giants. For these were none other than the seed of the angels fallen in the antediluvian era. Sprung from their union with the daughters of men, and being half angels, half men, these giants were only half mortal. They lived very long, and then half their body withered away. Threatened by an eternal continuance of this condition, half life, and half death, they preferred either to plunge into the sea, or by a magic herb which they knew to put an end to their existence.[515] They were furthermore of such enormous size that the spies, listening one day while the giants discussed them, heard them say, pointing to the Israelites: "There are grasshoppers by the trees that have the semblance of men," for "so they were in their sight." [516]

The spies, with the exception of Joshua and Caleb, had resolved from the start to warn the people against Palestine, and so great was their influence that Caleb feared he would yield to it. He therefore hastened to Hebron where the three Patriarchs lie, and, standing at their graves, said: "Joshua is proof against the pernicious influence of the spies, for Moses had prayed to God for him. Send up prayers now, my fathers, for me, that God in His mercy may keep me far from the counsel of the spies." [517]

There had always been a clash between Caleb and his comrades during their crossing through Palestine. For whereas he insisted upon taking along the fruits of the land to show their excellence to the people, they strongly opposed this suggestion, wishing as they did to keep the people from gaining an impression of the excellence of the land. Hence they yielded only when Caleb drew his sword, saying: "If you will not take of the fruits, either I shall slay you, or you will slay me." They hereupon cut down a vine, which was so heavy that eight of them had to carry it, putting upon each the burden of one hundred and twenty seah. The ninth spy carried a pomegranate, and the tenth a fig, which they brought from a place that had once belonged to Eshcol, one of Abraham's friends, but Joshua and Caleb carried nothing at all, because it was not consistent with their dignity to carry a burden. [518] This vine was of such gigantic size that the wine pressed from its grapes sufficed for all the sacrificial libations of Israel during its forty years' march. [519]

After the lapse of forty days they returned to Moses and the people, after having crossed through Palestine from end to end. By natural means it would not, of course, have been possible to traverse all the land in so short a time, but God made it possible by "bidding the soil leap for them," and they covered a great distance in a short time. God knew that Israel would have to wander in the wilderness forty years, a year for every day the spies had spent in Palestine, hence He hastened their progress through the land, that Israel might not have to stay too long in the wilderness.[530]

THE SLANDEROUS REPORT

When Moses heard that the spies had returned from their enterprise, he went to his great house of study, where all Israel too assembled, for it was a square of twelve miles, affording room to all.[521] There too the spies betook themselves and were requested to give their report. Pursuing the tactics of slanderers, they began by extolling the land, so that they might not by too unfavorable a report arouse the suspicion of the community. They said: "We came unto the land whither thou sentest us, and surely it floweth with milk and honey." This was not an exaggeration, for honey flowed from the trees under which the goats grazed, out of whose udders poured milk, so that both milk and honey moistened the ground. But they used these words only as an introduction, and then passed on to their actual report, which they had elaborated during those forty days, and by means of which they hoped to be able to induce the people to desist from their plan of entering Palestine.[522] "Nevertheless," they continued, "the people be strong that dwell in the land,

and the cities are walled, and very great: and moreover we saw the children of Anak there." Concerning the latter they spoke an untruth with the intention of inspiring Israel with fear, for the sons of Anak dwelt in Hebron, whither Caleb alone had gone to pray at the graves of the Patriarchs,[523] at the same time as the Shekinah went there to announce to the Patriarchs that their children were now on the way to take possession of the land which had been promised to them of yore.[524] To intensify to the uttermost their fear of the inhabitants of Palestine, they furthermore said: " The Amalekites dwell in the land of the South." They threatened Israel with Amalek as one threatens a child with a strap that had once been employed to chastise him, for they had had bitter experiences with Amalek. The statement concerning Amalek was founded on fact, for although southern Palestine had not originally been their home, still they had recently settled there in obedience to the last wish of their forefather Esau, who had bidden them cut off Israel from their entrance into the promised land. " If, however," continued the spies in their report, " you are planning to enter the land from the mountain region in order to evade Amalek, let us inform you that the Hittites, and the Jebussites, and the Amorites dwell in the mountains; and if you plan to go there by sea, let us inform you that the Canaanites dwell by the sea, and along the Jordan." [525]

As soon as the spies had completed their report, Joshua arose to contradict them, but they gave him no chance to speak, calling out to him: " By what right dost thou, foolish man, presume to speak? Thou hast neither sons nor daughters, so what dost thou care if we perish in our attempt to

conquer the land? We, on the other hand, have to look out
for our children and wives." Joshua, therefore, very much
against his will, had to be silent. Caleb now considered in
what way he could manage to get a hearing without being
shouted down as Joshua had been.

Caleb had given his comrades an entirely false impression
concerning his sentiments, for when these formed the plan to
try to make Israel desist from entering Palestine, they drew
him into their council, and he pretended to agree with them,
whereas he even then resolved to intercede for Palestine.
Hence, when Caleb arose, the spies were silent, supposing he
would corroborate their statements, a supposition which his
introductory words tended to strengthen. He began: " Be
silent, I will reveal the truth. This is not all for which we
have to thank the son of Amram." But to the amazement of
the spies, his next words praised, not blamed, Moses. He
said: " Moses—it is he who drew us up out of Egypt, who
clove the sea for us, who gave us manna as food." In this
way he continued his eulogy on Moses, closing with the
words: " We should have to obey him even if he bade us
ascend to heaven upon ladders! " [129] These words of Caleb
were heard by all the people, for his words were so mighty
that they could be heard twelve miles off. It was this same
powerful voice that had saved the life of the spies. For
when the Canaanites first took note of them and suspected
them of being spies, the three giants, Ahiman, Sheshai, and
Talmai pursued them and caught up with them in the plain
of Judea. When Caleb, hidden behind a fence, saw that the
giants were at their heels, he uttered such a shout that the
giants fell down in a swoon because of the frightful din.

When they had recovered, the giants declared that they had pursued the Israelites not because of the fruits, but because they had suspected them of the wish to burn their cities.[527]

Caleb's mighty voice did not, however, in the least impress the people or the spies, for the latter, far from retracting their previous statements, went so far as to say: "We be not able to go up against the people; for they are stronger than we, they are so strong that even God can not get at them. The land through which we have gone to search it is a land that eateth up the inhabitants thereof through disease; and all the people that we saw in it are men of wicked traits. And here we saw men upon sight of whom we almost swooned of fright, the giants, the sons of Anak, which come of giants: and we were in our own sight as grasshoppers, and so we were in their sight."[528] At these last words, God said: "I have no objection to your saying, 'We were in our own sight as grasshoppers,' but I take it amiss if you say, 'And so we were in their sight,' for how can you tell how I made you appear in their sight? How do you know if you did not appear to them to be angels?"[529]

THE NIGHT OF TEARS

The words of the spies were heard by willing ears. The people believed them implicitly, and when called to task by Moses, replied: "O our teacher Moses, if there had been only two spies or three, we should have had to give credence to their words, for the law tells us to consider the testimony of even two as sufficient, whereas in this case there are fully ten![530] Our brethren have made us faint of heart. Because the Lord hated us, He hath brought us forth out of the land of Egypt, to deliver us into the hand of the Amorites, to destroy us." By these words the Israelites revealed that they hated God, and for this reason did they believe that they were hated by Him, for " whatever a man wisheth his neighbor, doth he believe that his neighbor wisheth him." They even tried to convince Moses that God hated them. They said: " If an earthly king has two sons and two fields, one watered by a river, and the other dependent upon rains, will he not give the one that is watered by the river to his favorite son, and give the other, less excellent field to his other son? God led us out of Egypt, a land that is not dependent upon rain, only to give us the land of Canaan, which produces abundantly only if the rains fall." [581]

Not only did the spies in the presence of Moses and Aaron voice their opinion that it was not advisable to attempt conquering Palestine, but they employed every means of inciting the people into rebellion against Moses and God. On the following evening every one of them betook himself to his house, donned his mourning clothes, and began to weep bitterly and to lament. Their housemates quickly ran toward them and in astonishment asked their reason for these tears and lamentations. Without interrupting their wailings, they answered: " Woe is me for ye, my sons, and woe is me for ye, my daughters and daughters-in-law, that are doomed to be dishonored by the uncircumcised and to be given as a prey to their lusts. These men that we have beheld are not like unto mortals. Strong and mighty as angels are they; one of them might well slay a thousand of us. How dare we look into the iron faces of men so powerful that a nail of theirs is sufficient to stop up a spring of water!" At these words all the household, sons, daughters, and daughters-in-law, burst into tears and loud lamentations. Their neighbors came running to them and joined in the wails and sobs until they spread throughout all the camp, and all the sixty myriads of people were weeping. When the sound of their weeping reached heaven, God said: " Ye weep to-day without a cause, I shall see to it that in the future ye shall have a cause to weep on this day." It was then that God decreed to destroy the Temple on the ninth day of Ab, the day on which Israel in the wilderness wept without cause, so that this day became forever a day of tears.[532]

The people were not, however, content with tears, they resolved to set up as leaders in place of Moses and Aaron, Dathan and Abiram, and under their guidance to return to Egypt.[533] But worse than this, not only did they renounce their leader, but also their God, for they denied Him and wished to set up an idol for their God.[534] Not only the wicked ones among them such as the mixed multitude demurred against Moses and Aaron, but those also who had heretofore been pious, saying: " Would to God that we had died in the land of Egypt! Or would to God we had died in this wilderness!"

When Joshua and Caleb heard these speeches of the people teeming with blasphemy, they rent their garments and tried to restrain the people from their sinful enterprise, exhorting them particularly to have no fear of the Canaanites, because the time was at hand when God had promised Abraham to give the land of Canaan to his descendants, and because there were no pious men among the inhabitants of the land for whose sake God would have been willing to leave it longer in their possession. They also assured the people that God had hurled from heaven the guardian angel of the inhabitants of Palestine, so that they were now impotent.[585] The people, however, replied: " We do not believe you; the other spies have our weal and woe more at heart than you." [586] Nor were the admonitions of Moses of more avail, even though he brought them a direct message from God to have no fear of the Canaanites. In vain did he say to them, " He who wrought all those miracles for you in Egypt and during your stay in the wilderness will work miracles for you as well when you will enter the promised land. Truly the past ought to inspire you with trust in the future." The only answer the people had to this was, " Had we heard this report of the land from strangers, we should not have given it credit, but we have heard it from men whose sons are our sons, and whose daughters are our daughters." [587] In their bitterness against their leaders they wanted to lay hands upon Moses and Aaron, whereupon God sent His cloud of glory as a protection to them, under which they sought refuge. But far from being brought to a realization of their wicked enterprise by this Divine apparition, they cast stones at the cloud, hoping in this way to kill Moses and Aaron. This outrage on their part completely wore out God's patience, and He determined upon the destruction of the spies, and a severe punishment of the people misled by them.[588]

INGRATITUDE PUNISHED

God now appeared to Moses, bidding him convey the following words to the people: "You kindle My anger on account of the very benefits I conferred upon you. When I clove the sea for you that you might pass through, while the Egyptians stuck in the loam at its bottom, you said to one another, 'In Egypt we trod loam, and He led us out of Egypt, only that we might again tread it.' I gave you manna as food, which made you strong and fat, but you, perceiving that you felt no need of easing yourselves after partaking of it, said: 'How comes it to pass that twenty days have gone by and we have not eased ourselves? Ordinarily a human being dies if after four or five days he does not excrete the food he has taken. Surely we are doomed to die.' When the spies came to Palestine, I arranged it so that as soon as they entered a city its king or governor died, in order that the inhabitants, occupied with the burial of their ruler, might not take account of the spies' presence and kill them. Instead of being thankful for this, the spies returned and reported, 'The land through which we have gone to search it, is a land that eateth up the inhabitants thereof.' To you I gave the Torah; for your sake I said to the Angel of Death, 'Continue to hold sway over the rest of the world, but not over this nation that I have chosen as My people.' Truly I had hopes that after all this you would sin no more, and like Myself and the angels would live eternally, without ever tasting death. You, however, in spite of the great opportunity that I offered you, conducted yourselves like Adam. Upon him also did I lay a commandment, promising him life eternal on condition he observed it, but he brought ruin upon himself by trespassing My commandment and eating of the tree. To him I said, 'Dust thou art, and unto dust shalt thou return.' Similar was My experience with you. I said, 'You are angels,' but you conducted yourselves like Adam in your sins, and hence like Adam you must die. I had thought and hoped you would follow the example of the Patriarchs, but you act like the inhabitants of Sodom, who in punishment for their sins were consumed by fire." [589] "If," continued God, turning to Moses, " they suppose that I have need of swords or spears to destroy them, they are mistaken. As through the word I created the world, so can I destroy the world by it, which would be a proper punishment for them. As through their words and their talk they angered Me, so shall the word kill them, and thou shalt be their heir, for ' I will make of thee a greater nation and mightier than they.' " [590]

Moses said: " If the chair with three legs could not withstand the moment of Thy wrath, how then shall a chair that hath but one leg endure? Thou art about to destroy the seed of the three Patriarchs; how then may I hope that my seed is to fare better? This is not the only reason for which Thou shouldst preserve Israel, as there are other considerations why Thou shouldst do so. Wert Thou to destroy Israel, the Edomites, Moabites, and all the inhabitants of Canaan would say [591] that Thou hadst done this only because Thou wert not able to maintain Thy people, and therefore Thou didst destroy them. These will furthermore declare that the gods of Canaan are mightier than those of Egypt, that Thou hadst indeed triumphed over the river gods of Egypt, but that Thou wert not the peer of the rain gods of Canaan. Worse even than this, the nations of the world will accuse Thee of continuous cruelty, saying, ' He destroyed the generation of the flood through water; He rased to the ground the builders of the tower, as well as the inhabitants of Sodom; and no better than theirs was the fate of the Egyptians, whom He drowned in the sea. Now He hath also ruined Israel whom He had called, ' My firstborn son,' like Lilith who, when she can find no strange children, slays her own. So did He slay His own son." [542] Moses furthermore said: " Every pious man makes a point of cultivating a special virtue. Do Thou also in this instance bring Thy special virtue to bear." God: " And what is My special virtue? " Moses: " Long-suffering, love, and mercy, for Thou art wont to be long-suffering with them that kindle Thy wrath, and to have mercy for them. In Thy very mercy is Thy strength best shown. Mete out to Thy children, then, justice in small measure only, but mercy in great measure." [543]

Moses well knew that mercy was God's chief virtue. He remembered that he had asked God, when he interceded for Israel after their sin of the Golden Calf, " Pray tell me by what attribute of Thine Thou rulest the world. " God answered: " I rule the world with loving-kindness, mercy, and long-suffering." " Can it be," said Moses, " that Thy long-suffering lets sinners off with impunity? " To this question Moses had received no answer, hence he felt he might now say to God: " Act now as Thou didst then assent. [544] Justice, that demands the destruction of Israel, is on one side of the scales, but it is exactly balanced by my prayer on the other side. Let us now see how the scales will balance." God replied: " As truly as thou livest, Moses, thy prayer shall dip the scales to the side of mercy. For thy sake must I cancel My decision to annihilate the children of Israel, so that the Egyptians will exclaim, ' Happy the servant to whose wish his master defers.' I shall, however, collect My debt, for although I shall not annihilate Israel all at once, they shall make partial annual payments during the following forty years. Say to them, ' Your carcases shall fall in this wilderness; and all that were numbered of you, according to your whole number, from twenty years old and upward, which have murmured against Me. And your children shall be wanderers in the wilderness forty years, and shall bear your whoredoms, until your carcases be consumed in the wilderness.' " [54b]

This punishment was not, however, as severe as it might appear, for none among them died below the age of sixty, whereas those who had at the time of the exodus from Egypt been either below twenty or above sixty were entirely exempt from this punishment. Besides only such were smitten as had followed the counsel of the spies, whereas the others, and the Levites and the women were exempt. [55] Death, moreover, visited the transgressors in such fashion that they were aware it was meant as punishment for their sins. Throughout all the year not one among them died. On the eighth day of the month Ab, Moses would have a herald proclaim throughout the camp, " Let each prepare his grave." They dug their graves, and spent there the following night, the same night on which, following the counsel of the spies, they had revolted against God and Moses. In the morning a herald would once more appear and cry: " Let the living separate themselves from the

---

dead." Those that were still alive arose, but about fifteen thousand of them remained dead in their graves. After forty years, however, when the herald repeated his customary call on the ninth day of Ab, all arose, and there was not a single dead man among them. At first they thought they had made a miscalculation in their observation of the moon, that it was not the ninth day of Ab at all, and that this was the reason why their lives had been spared. Hence they repeated their preparations for death until the fifteenth day of Ab. Then the sight of the full moon convinced them that the ninth day of Ab had gone by, and that their punishment had been done away with. In commemoration of the relief from this punishment, they appointed the fifteenth day of Ab to be a holy day.[547]

The Years of Disfavor

Although God had now cancelled His resolution to annihilate Israel, He was not yet quite reconciled with them, and they were out of favor during the following years of their march through the desert, as was made evident by several circumstances. During these years of disfavor the north wind did not blow, with the result that the boys who were born in the desert could not be circumcised, as the absence of this wind produced an excessively high temperature, a condition that made it very dangerous for the young boys to have this operation performed upon them.[548] As the law, however, prohibits the offering of the paschal lamb unless the boys have been circumcised, Israel could not properly observe the feast of Passover after the incident of the spies.[549] Moses also felt the effects of the disfavor, for

during this time he received from God none but the absolutely essential directions, and no other revelations. This was because Moses, like all other prophets, received this distinction only for the sake of Israel, and when Israel was in disgrace, God did not communicate with him affectionately.[550] Indeed Moses' fate, to die in the desert without entering the promised land, had been decreed simultaneously with the fate of the generation led by him out of Egypt.[551]

But the most terrible punishment of all fell upon the spies who, with their wicked tongues, had brought about the whole disaster. God repaid them measure for measure. Their tongues stretched to so great a length that they touched the navel; and worms crawled out of their tongues, and pierced the navel; in this horrible fashion these men died.[552] Joshua and Caleb, however, who had remained true to God and had not followed the wicked counsel of their colleagues, were not only exempted from death, but were furthermore rewarded by God, by receiving in the Holy Land the property that had been allotted to the other spies.[553] Caleb was forty years of age at the time when he was sent out as a spy. He had married early, and at the age of ten had begot a son, still at the age of eighty-five he was sturdy enough to enjoy his possession in the Holy Land.[554]

God's mercy is also extended to sinners, hence He bade Moses say to the people: "The Amalekites and the Canaanites are now dwelling in the valley, to-morrow turn you, and get you into the wilderness by the way of the Red Sea." God did this because He had firmly resolved, in the event of a war between Israel and the inhabitants of Palestine, not to aid the former. Knowing that in this case their annihilation was sure, He commanded them to make no attempt to enter the land by force.[555] "It had been My intention," said God, "to exalt you, but now if you were to attempt to make war upon the inhabitants of Palestine, you would suffer humiliation." The people did not, however, hearken to the words of God that Moses communicated to them, and all at once formed in battle array in order to advance against the Amorites. They thought that after they had confessed their sin of having been misled by the spies, God would stand by them in their battles, so they said to Moses: "Surely these few drops have not filled the bucket." Their transgression against God seemed to them only a peccadillo that had long since been forgiven. They were, however, mistaken. Like bees the enemies swarmed down upon them, and whereas these had in former times fallen dead of fright upon hearing the names of the Israelites, now a blow from them sufficed to kill the Israelites. Their attempt to wage war without the Holy Ark in their midst proved a miserable failure. Many of them, and Zelophehad among these, met their death, and as many others returned to camp covered with wounds. The wailing and weeping of the people was of no avail, God persisted in His resolve, and they brought upon themselves grave punishment for this new proof of disobedience, for God said to Moses: "If I were to deal with them now in accordance with strict justice, they should never enter the land. After a while, however, I shall let them 'possess the land, which I sware unto their fathers to give unto them.' " [556]

In order to comfort and encourage Israel in their dejection, Moses received directions to announce the law of sacrifices, and other precepts laid down for the life in the Holy Land, that the people might see that God did not mean to be angry with them forever. When Moses announced the laws to them, a dispute arose between the Israelites and the proselytes, because the former declared that they alone and not the others were to make offerings to God in His sanctuary. God hereupon called Moses, and said to him: "Why do these always quarrel one with another?" Moses replied: "Thou knowest why." God: "Have I not said to thee, 'One law and one ordinance shall be for you and for the stranger that sojourneth with you?'" [557]

Although the forty years' march through the desert was a punishment for the sin of Israel, still it had one advantage. At the time when Israel departed from Egypt, Palestine was in poor condition; the trees planted in the time of Noah were old and withered. Hence God said: "What! Shall I permit Israel to enter an uninhabitable land? I shall bid them wander in the desert for forty years, that the Canaanites may in the meantime fell the old trees and plant new ones, so that Israel, upon entering the land, may find it abounding in plenty." So did it come to pass, for when Israel conquered Palestine, they found the land not only newly cultivated,[558] but also filled to overflowing with treasures. The inhabitants of this land were such misers that they would not indulge in a drop of oil for their gruel; if an egg broke, they did not use it, but sold it for cash. The hoardings of these miserly Canaanites God later gave to Israel to enjoy and to use.[559]

The Rebellion of Korah

The Canaanites were not the only ones who did not enjoy
their wealth and money, for a similar fate was decreed for
Korah. He had been the treasurer of Pharaoh, and possessed treasures so vast that he employed three hundred
white mules to carry the keys of his treasures; but " let not
the rich man boast of his riches," for Korah through his sin
lost both life and property. Korah had obtained possession
of his riches in the following way: When Joseph, during
the lean years, through the sale of grain amassed great
treasures, he erected three great buildings, one hundred
cubits wide, one hundred cubits long, and one hundred
cubits high, filled them with money and delivered them to
Pharaoh, being too honest to leave even five silver shekels
of this money to his children. Korah discovered one of these
three treasuries. On account of his wealth he became proud,
and his pride brought about his fall.[560] He believed Moses had
slighted him by appointing his cousin Elizaphan as chief of
the Levite division of Kohathites. He said: " My grandfather had four sons, Amram, Izhar, Hebron, and Uzziel.
Amram, as the firstborn, had privileges of which his sons
availed themselves, for Aaron is high priest and Moses is
king; but have not I, the son of Izhar, the second son of
Kohath, the rightful claim to be prince of the Kohathites?
Moses, however, passed me by and appointed Elizaphan,
whose father was Uzziel, the youngest son of my grandfather. Therefore will I now stir up rebellion against
Moses, and overthrow all institutions founded by him."
Korah was far too wise a man to believe that God would
permit success to a rebellion against Moses, and stand by in-

differently, but the very insight that enabled him to look into the future became his doom. He saw with his prophetic eye that Samuel, a man as great as both Aaron and Moses together, would be one of his descendants; and furthermore that twenty-four descendants of his, inspired by the Holy Spirit, would compose psalms and sing them in the Temple. This brilliant future of his descendants inspired him with great confidence in his undertaking, for he thought to himself that God would not permit the father of such pious men to perish. His eye did not, however, look sharply enough into the future, or else he would also have known that his sons would repent of the rebellion against Moses, and would for this reason be deemed worthy of becoming the fathers of prophets and Temple singers, whereas he was to perish in this rebellion.[561]

The names of this unfortunate rebel corresponded to his deeds and to his end. He was called Korah, "baldness," for through the death of his horde he caused a baldness in Israel. He was the son of Izhar, "the heat of noon," because he caused the earth to be made to boil "like the heat of noon;" and furthermore he was designated as the son of Kohath, for Kohath signifies "bluntness," and through his sin he made "his children's teeth be set on edge." His description as the son of Levi, "conduct," points to his end, for he was conducted to hell.[562]

Korah, however, was not the only one who strove to overthrow Moses. With him were, first of all, the Reubenites Dathan and Abiram, who well deserve their names, for the one signifies, "transgressor of the Divine law," and the other, "the obdurate." There were, furthermore, two hundred fifty men, who by their rank and influence belonged to the most prominent people in Israel; among them even the princes of the tribes. In the union of the Reubenites with Korah was verified the proverb, " Woe to the wicked, woe to his neighbor." For Korah, one of the sons of Kohath, had his station to the south of the Tabernacle, and as the Reubenites were also encamped there, a friendship was struck up between them, so that they followed him in his undertaking against Moses.[563]

The hatred Korah felt against Moses was still more kindled by his wife. When, after the consecration of the Levites, Korah returned home, his wife noticed that the hairs of his head and of his body had been shaved, and asked him who had done all this to him. He answered, " Moses," whereupon his wife remarked: " Moses hates thee and did this to disgrace thee." Korah, however, replied: " Moses shaved all the hair of his own sons also." But she said: " What did the disgrace of his own sons matter to him if he only felt he could disgrace thee? He was quite ready to make that sacrifice." [564] As at home, so also did Korah fare with others, for, hairless as he was, no one at first recognized him, and when people at last discovered who was before them, they asked him in astonishment who had so disfigured him. In answer to their inquiries he said, " Moses did this, who besides took hold of my hands and feet to lift me, and after he had lifted me, said, ' Thou art clean.' But his brother Aaron he adorned like a bride, and bade him take his place in the Tabernacle." Embittered by what they considered an insult offered him by Moses, Korah and his people exclaimed: " Moses is king, his brother did he appoint as high priest, his nephews as heads of the priests, he allots to the priests the heave offering and many other tributes." [565] Then he tried to make Moses appear ridiculous in the eyes of the people. Shortly before this Moses had read to the people the law of the fringes in the borders of their garments. Korah now had garments of purple made for the two hundred fifty men that followed him, all of whom were chief justices. Arrayed thus, Korah and his company appeared before Moses and asked him if they were required to attach fringes to the corners of these garments. Moses answered, " Yea." Korah then began this argument. " If," said he, " one fringe of purple suffices to fulfil this commandment, should not a whole garment of purple answer the requirements of the law, even if there be no special fringe of purple in the corners? " He continued to lay before Moses similar artful questions: " Must a Mezuzah be attached to the doorpost of a house filled with the sacred Books? " Moses answered, " Yea." Then Korah said: " The two hundred and seventy sections of the Torah are not sufficient, whereas the two sections attached to the door-post suffice! " Korah put still another question: " If upon a man's skin there show a bright spot, the size of half a bean, is he clean or is he unclean? " Moses: " Unclean." " And," continued Korah, " if the spot spread and cover all the skin of him, is he then clean or unclean? " Moses: " Clean." " Laws so irrational," said Korah, " cannot possibly trace their origin from God. The Torah that thou didst teach to Israel is not therefore God's work, but thy work, hence art thou no prophet and Aaron is no high priest! " [566]

KORAH ABUSES MOSES AND THE TORAH

Then Korah betook himself to the people to incite them to rebellion against Moses, and particularly against the tributes to the priests imposed upon the people by him. That the people might now be in a position to form a proper conception of the oppressive burden of these tasks, Korah told them the following tale that he had invented: " There lived in my vicinity a widow with two daughters, who owned for their support a field whose yield was just sufficient for them to keep body and soul together. When this woman set out to plow her field, Moses appeared and said: ' Thou shalt not plow with an ox and an ass together.' When she began to sow, Moses appeared and said: ' Thou shalt not sow with divers seeds.' When the first fruits showed in the poor widow's field, Moses appeared and bade her bring it to the priests, for to them are due ' the first of all the fruit of the earth '; and when at length the time came for her to cut it down, Moses appeared and ordered her ' not wholly to reap the corners of the field, nor to gather the gleanings of the harvest, but to leave them for the poor.' When she had done all that Moses had bidden her, and was about to thrash the grain, Moses appeared once more, and said: ' Give me the heave offering, the first and the second tithes to the priests.' When at last the poor woman became aware of the fact that she could not now possibly maintain herself from the yield of the field after the deduction of all the tributes that Moses had imposed upon her, she sold the field and with the proceeds purchased ewes, in the hope that she might now undisturbed have the benefit of the wool as well as of the younglings of the sheep. She was, however, mistaken. When the firstling of the sheep was born, Aaron appeared and demanded it, for the firstborn belongs to the priest. She had a similar experience with the wool. At shearing time Aaron reappeared and demanded ' the first of the fleece of the sheep,' which, according to Moses' law, was his. But not content with this, he reappeared later and demanded one sheep out of every ten as a tithe, to which again, according to the law, he had a claim. This, however, was too much for the long-suffering woman, and she slaughtered the sheep, supposing that she might now feel herself secure, in full possession of the meat. But wide of the mark! Aaron appeared, and, basing his claim on the Torah, demanded the shoulder, the two cheeks, and the maw. ' Alas! ' exclaimed the woman, ' The slaughtering of the sheep did not deliver me out of thy hands! Let the meat then be consecrated to the sanctuary.' Aaron said, ' Everything devoted in Israel is mine. It shall then be all mine.' He departed, taking with him the meat of the sheep, and leaving behind him the widow and her daughters weeping bitterly. Such men," said Korah, concluding his tale, " are Moses and Aaron, who pass their cruel measures as Divine laws." [567]

Pricked on by speeches such as these, Korah's horde appeared before Moses and Aaron, saying: " Heavier is the burden that ye lay upon us than was that of the Egyptians; and moreover as, since the incident of the spies, we are forced annually to offer as a tribute to death fifteen thousand men, it would have been better for us had we stayed in Egypt." They also reproached Moses and Aaron with an unjustified love of power, saying: " Upon Sinai all Israel heard the words of God, ' I am thy Lord.' Wherefore then lift ye up yourselves above the congregation of the Lord?" [568]   They knew no bounds in their attacks upon Moses, they accused him of leading an immoral life and even warned their wives to keep far from him.[569]   They did not, moreover, stop short at words, but tried to stone Moses,[570] when at last he sought protection from God and called to Him for assistance.   He said: "I do not care if they insult me or Aaron, but I insist that the insult of the Torah be avenged.   'If these men die the common death of all men,' I shall myself become a disbeliever and declare the Torah was not given by God." [571]

MOSES PLEADS IN VAIN WITH KORAH

Moses took Korah's transgression much to heart, for he thought to himself that perhaps, after the many sins of Israel, he might not succeed in obtaining God's pardon for them. He did not therefore have this matter decided immediately, but admonished the people to wait until the following day, having a lingering hope that Korah's horde, given time for calm reflection, might themselves perceive their sin to which an excess of drink might have carried them away.   Hence he said to them: "I may not now appear before the Lord, for although He partakes of neither food nor drink, still He will not judge such actions of ours as we have committed after feasting and revelling.   But 'to-morrow the Lord will show who are His.'[572]   Know ye now that just as God has set definite bounds in nature between day and night, between light and darkness, so also has He separated Israel from the other nations, and so also has He separated Aaron from the rest of Israel.   If you can obliterate the boundary between

light and darkness, then only can you remove the boundary
of separation between Israel and the rest, but not otherwise.
Other nations have many religions, many priests, and worship in many temples, but we have one God, one Torah,
one law, one altar, and one high priest, whereas ye are two
hundred fifty men, each of whom is imbued with the desire
of becoming high priest, as I too should like to be high priest,
if such a thing were possible. But to prove Aaron's claim
to his dignity, ' this do; take you censers, Korah, and all his
company; and put fire therein, and put incense upon them
before the Lord to-morrow.' The offering of incense is the
most pleasant offering before the Lord, but for him who hath
not been called this offering holds a deadly poison, for it
consumed Nadab and Abihu. But I exhort ye not to burden
your souls with a deadly sin, for none but the man God will
choose as high priest out of the number of you will remain
alive, all others will pay with their lives at the offering of
incense." These last words of Moses, however, far from
restraining them, only strengthened Korah in his resolve to
accomplish his undertaking, for he felt sure that God would
choose him, and none other. He had a prophetic presentiment that he was destined to be the forefather of prophets
and Temple singers, and for this reason thought he was
specially favored by God.

When Moses perceived that Korah was irreclaimable, he
directed the rest of his warning to those other Levites, the
men of Korah's tribe, who, he feared, would join Korah in
his rebellion. He admonished them to be satisfied with the
honors God had granted them, and not to strive for priestly
dignity. He concluded his speech with a last appeal to

Korah to cause no schism in Israel, saying: "Had Aaron
arbitrarily assumed the priestly dignity, you would do right
to withstand his presumption, but it was God, whose attributes are sublimity, strength, and sovereignty, who clothed
Aaron with this dignity, so that those who are against
Aaron are in reality against God." Korah made no answer
to all these words, thinking that the best course for him to
follow would be to avoid picking an argument with so great
a sage as Moses, feeling sure that in such a dispute he
should be worsted and, contrary to his own conviction, be
forced to yield to Moses.

Moses, seeing that it was useless to reason with Korah,
sent a messenger to Dathan and Abiram,[573] summoning them
to appear before his court. He did this because the law re-
quires that the accused be summoned to appear before the
judge, before judgment may be passed upon him, and Moses
did not wish these men to be punished without a hearing.[574]
These, however, made answer to the messenger sent by
Moses, "We will not come up!" This shameless answer
held an unconscious prophecy. They went not up, but, as
their end showed, down, to hell. Not only, moreover, did
they refuse to comply with Moses' demand, they sent the
following message in answer to Moses: "Why dost thou
set thyself up as master over us? What benefit didst thou
bring to us? Thou didst lead us out of Egypt, a land ' like
the garden of the Lord,' but hast not brought us to Canaan,
leaving us in the wilderness where we are daily visited by
the plague. Even in Egypt didst thou try to assume the
leadership, just as thou doest now. Thou didst beguile the
people in their exodus from Egypt, when thou didst promise

to lead them to a land of milk and honey; in their delusion
they followed thee and were disappointed. Now dost thou
attempt to persuade us as thou didst persuade them, but thou
shalt not succeed, for we will not come and obey thy summons." [575]

The shamelessness of these two men, who declined even to
talk about their transgression with Moses, aroused his wrath
to the uttermost, for a man does get a certain amount of
satisfaction out of discussing the dispute with his opponents,
whereas he feels badly if he cannot discuss the matter. In
his anger he said to God: "O Lord of the world! I well
know that these sinners participated in the offerings of the
congregation that were offered for all Israel, but as they
have withdrawn themselves from the community, accept not
Thou their share of the offering and let it not be consumed
by the heavenly fire. It was I whom they treated so, I who
took no money from the people for my labors, even when
payment was my due. It is customary for anyone who works
for the sanctuary to receive pay for his work, but I travelled
to Egypt on my own ass, and took none of theirs, although
I undertook the journey in their interests. It is customary
for those that have a dispute to go before a judge,
but I did not wait for this, and went straight to them to
settle their disputes, never declaring the innocent guilty, or
the guilty innocent."

When he now perceived that his words had no effect upon
Korah and his horde, he concluded his words with a threat to
the ring leaders: "Be thou and all thy company before the
Lord, thou and they, and Aaron, to-morrow."

Korah spent the night before the judgment in trying to

win over the people to his side, and succeeded in so doing.
He went to all the other tribes, saying to them: "Do not
think I am seeking a position of honor for myself. No, I
wish only that this honor may fall to the lot of each in turn,
whereas Moses is now king, and his brother high priest."
On the following morning, all the people, and not Korah's
original company alone, appeared before the Tabernacle and
began to pick quarrels with Moses and Aaron. Moses now
feared that God would destroy all the people because they
had joined Korah, hence he said to God: "O Lord of the
world! If a nation rebels against a king of flesh and blood
because ten or twenty men have cursed the king or his
ambassadors, then he sends his hosts to massacre the inhabitants of the land, innocent as well as guilty, for he is
not able with certainty to tell which among them honored
the king and which among them cursed him. But Thou
knowest the thoughts of man, and what his heart and kidneys counsel him to do, the workings of Thy creatures' minds
lie open before Thee, so that Thou knowest who hath rebelled against Thee and who hath not, for Thou knowest the
spirit of each one. 'Shall one man sin, and wilt Thou be
wroth with all the congregation?'" God hereupon said to
Moses: [576] "I have heard thy prayer for the congregation.
Say then, to them, 'Get you up from about the Tabernacle
of Korah, Dathan, and Abiram.'" [577]

Moses did not immediately carry out these instructions,
for he tried once again to warn Dathan and Abiram of the
punishment impending upon them, but they refused to give
heed to Moses, and remained within their tents. "Now,"
said Moses, "I have done all I could, and can do nothing

more." Hence, turning to the congregation, he said: [577]
" Depart, I pray you, from the tents of these wicked men,
that even in their youth deserved death as a punishment for
their actions. In Egypt they betrayed the secret of my slaying an Egyptian; at the Red Sea it was they that angered
God by their desire to return to Egypt; in Alush they broke
the Sabbath, and now they trooped together to rebel against
God. They now well deserve excommunication, and the destruction of all their property. ' Touch, therefore, nothing
of theirs, lest ye be consumed in all their sins.' " [579]

The community obeyed the words of Moses and drew back
from the dwellings of Dathan and Abiram. These, not at all
cowed, were not restrained from their wicked intention, but
stood at the doors of their tents, abusing and calumniating
Moses. Moses hereupon said to God: " If these men die
upon their beds like all men, after physicians have attended
to them and acquaintances have visited them, then shall I
publicly avow ' that the Lord hath not sent me ' to do all
these works, but that I have done them of mine own mind."
God replied: " What wilt thou have Me do?" Moses: " If
the Lord hath already provided the earth with a mouth to
swallow them, it is well, if not, I pray Thee, do so now."
God said: " Thou shalt decree a thing, and it shall be established unto thee." [580]

Moses was not the only one to insist upon exemplary punishment of the horde of Korah. Sun and Moon appeared before God, saying: " If Thou givest satisfaction to the son
of Amram, we shall set out on our course around the world,
but not otherwise." God, however, hurled lightnings after
them, that they might go about their duties, saying to them:

" You have never championed My cause, but now you stand up for a creature of flesh and blood." Since that time Sun and Moon have always to be driven to duty, never doing it voluntarily because they do not wish to look upon the sins of man upon earth.

KORAH AND HIS HORDE PUNISHED

God did not gainsay satisfaction to His faithful servant. The mouth of hell approached the spot upon which Dathan, Abiram, and their families stood,[581] and the ground under their feet grew so precipitous that they were not able to stand upright, but rolled to the opening and went quickly into the pit. Not these wicked people alone were swallowed by the earth, but their possessions also. Even their linen that was at the launderer's or a pin belonging to them rolled toward the mouth of the earth and vanished therein.[582] Nowhere upon earth remained a trace of them or of their possessions, and even their names disappeared from the documents upon which they were written.[583] They did not, however, meet an immediate death, but sank gradually into the earth, the opening of which adjusted itself to the girth of each individual. The lower extremities disappeared first, then the opening widened, and the abdomen followed, until in this way the entire body was swallowed. While they were sinking thus slowly and painfully, they continued to cry: " Moses is truth, and his Torah is truth. We acknowledge that Moses is rightful king and true prophet, that Aaron is legitimate high priest, and that the Torah has been given by God. Now deliver us, O our teacher Moses!" These words were audible throughout the

entire camp, so that all might be convinced of the wickedness of Korah's undertaking.[584]

Without regard to these followers of Korah, who were
swallowed up by the earth, the two hundred and fifty men
who had offered incense with Aaron found their death in
the heavenly fire that came down upon their offering
and consumed them. But he who met with the most
terrible form of death was Korah. Consumed at the incense offering, he then rolled in the shape of a ball of fire to
the opening in the earth, and vanished. There was a reason
for this double punishment of Korah. Had he received
punishment by burning alone, then those who had been swallowed by the earth, and who had failed to see Korah smitten
by the same punishment, would have complained about God's
injustice, saying: " It was Korah who plunged us into destruction, yet he himself escaped it." Had he, on the other
hand, been swallowed by the earth without meeting death by
fire, then those whom the fire had consumed would have
complained about God's injustice that permitted the author
of their destruction to go unpunished. Now, however, both
those who perished by fire and those who were swallowed up
by the earth witnessed their leader share their punishment.[585]

This terrible death did not, however, suffice to atone for
the sins of Korah and his company, for their punishment
continues in hell. They are tortured in hell, and at the end
of thirty days, hell again casts them up near to the surface
of the earth, on the spot where they had been swallowed.
Whosoever on that day puts his ear to the ground upon that
spot hears the cry: " Moses is truth, and his Torah is
truth, but we are liars." Not until after the Resurrection

will their punishment cease, for even in spite of their grave sin they were not given over to eternal damnation.

For a time Korah and his company believed that they should never know relief from these tortures of hell, but Hannah's words encouraged them not to despair. In reference to them she announced the prophecy, " The Lord bringeth low, to Sheol, and lifteth up." At first they had no real faith in this prophecy, but when God destroyed the Temple, and sank its portals deep into the earth until they reached hell, Korah and his company clung to the portals, saying: " If these portals return again upward, then through them shall we also return upward." God hereupon appointed them as keepers of these portals over which they will have to stand guard until they return to the upper world.[586]

On and the Three Sons of Korah Saved

God punishes discord severely, for although the decree of Heaven does not otherwise punish any one below twenty years of age, at Korah's rebellion the earth swallowed alive even children that were only a day old—men, women, and children, all together.[587] Out of all the company of Korah and their families only four persons escaped ruin, to wit: On, the son of Peleth, and Korah's three sons. As it was Korah's wife who through her inciting words plunged her husband into destruction, so to his wife does On owe his salvation. Truly to these two women applies the proverb: " Every wise woman buildeth her house: but the foolish plucketh it down with her own hands." On, whose abilities had won him distinction far beyond that of his father, had

originally joined Korah's rebellion. When he arrived home
and spoke of it to his wife, she said to him: "What benefit
shalt thou reap from it? Either Moses remains master and
thou art his disciple, or Korah becomes master and thou art
his disciple." On saw the truth of this argument, but declared that he felt it incumbent upon himself to adhere to
Korah because he had given him his oath, which he could
not now take back. His wife quieted him, however, entreating him to stay at home. To be quite sure of him, however, she gave him wine to drink, whereupon he fell into a
deep sleep of intoxication. His wife now carried out her
work of salvation, saying to herself: "All the congregation are holy, and being such, they will approach no woman
whose hair is uncovered." She now showed herself at the
door of the tent with streaming hair, and whenever one out
of the company of Korah, about to go to On, saw the woman
in this condition, he started back, and owing to this scheme
her husband had no part in the rebellion. When the earth
opened to swallow Korah's company, the bed on which On
still slept began to rock, and to roll to the opening in the
earth. On's wife, however, seized it, saying: "O Lord of
the world! My husband made a solemn vow never again to
take part in dissensions. Thou that livest and endurest to
all eternity canst punish him hereafter if ever he prove false
to his vow." God heard her plea, and On was saved. She
now requested On to go to Moses, but he refused, for he was
ashamed to look into Moses' face after he had rebelled
against him. His wife then went to Moses in his stead.
Moses at first evaded her, for he wished to have nothing to
do with women, but as she wept and lamented bitterly, she

was admitted and told Moses of all that had occurred. He
now accompanied her to her house, at the entrance of which
he cried: " On, the son of Peleth, step forth, God will forgive
thee thy sins." It is with reference to this miraculous deliverance and to his life spent in doing penance that this
former follower of Korah was called On, " the penitent,"
son of Peleth, " miracle." His true name was Nemuel, the
son of Eliab, a brother of Dathan and Abiram.[588]

More marvellous still than that of On was the salvation of
Korah's three sons. For when the earth yawned to swallow
Korah and his company, these cried: " Help us, Moses! "
The Shekinah hereupon said: " If these men were to repent,
they should be saved; repentance do I desire, and naught
else." Korah's three sons now simultaneously determined to
repent their sin, but they could not open their mouths, for
round about them burned the fire, and below them gaped
hell.[589] God was, however, satisfied with their good thought,
and in the sight of all Israel, for their salvation, a pillar arose
in hell, upon which they seated themselves. There did they
sit and sing praises and songs to the Lord sweeter than ever
mortal ear had heard, so that Moses and all Israel hearkened to them eagerly. They were furthermore distinguished
by God in receiving from Him the prophetic gift, and they
then announced in their songs events that were to occur in
the future world. They said: " Fear not the day on which
the Lord will ' take hold of the ends of the earth, and the
wicked be shaken out of it,' for the pious will cling to the
Throne of Glory and will find protection under the wings of
the Shekinah. Fear not, ye pious men, the Day of Judgment, for the judgment of sinners will have as little power

over you as it had over us when all the others perished and we were saved." [590]

Israel Convinced of Aaron's Priesthood

After the death of the two hundred and fifty followers of Korah, who perished at the offering of incense, Eleazar, the son of Aaron, was ordered " to take up the censers out of the burning," in which the souls, not the bodies of the sinners were burned,[591] that out of these brasen plates be made a covering for the altar. Eleazar, and not his father, the high priest, received this commission, for God said: " The censer brought death upon two of Aaron's sons, therefore let the third now fetch forth the censer and effect expiation for the sinners." [592] The covering of the altar fashioned out of the brass of these censers was " to be a memorial unto the children of Israel, to the end that no stranger, which is not of the seed of Aaron, come near to burn incense before the Lord." Such a one was not, however, to be punished like Korah and his company, but in the same way as Moses had once been punished by God, with leprosy. This punishment was visited upon king Uzziah, who tried to burn incense in the Temple, asserting that it was the king's task to perform the service before the King of all. The heavens hastened to the scene to consume him, just as the celestial fire had once consumed the two hundred and fifty men, who had wrongfully assumed the rights of priesthood; the earth strove to swallow him as it had once swallowed Korah and his company. But a celestial voice announced: " Upon none save Korah and his company came punishments like these, upon no others. This man's punishment shall be leprosy." Hence Uzziah became a leper.[593]

Peace was not, however, established with the destruction
of Korah and his company, for on the very day that followed
the terrible catastrophe, there arose a rebellion against Moses,
that was even more violent than the preceding one. For although the people were now convinced that nothing came to
pass without the will of God, still they thought God was doing all this for Moses' sake. Hence they laid at his door
God's violent anger against them, blaming not the wickedness of those who had been punished, but Moses, who, they
said, had excited God's revengefulness against them. They
accused Moses of having brought about the death of so many
of the noblest among them as a punishment for the people,
only that they might not again venture to call him to account,
and that he might thereby ensure his brother's possession of
the priestly office, since no one would hereafter covet it, seeing that on its account the noblest among them had met so
terrible a fate. The kinsmen of those who had perished
stirred the flame of resentment and spurred on the people to
set a limit to Moses' love of power, insisting that the public
welfare and the safety of Israel demanded such measures.[594]
These unseemly speeches and their unceasing, incorrigible
perverseness brought upon them God's wrath to such a degree that He wanted to destroy them all, and bade Moses and
Aaron go away from the congregation that He might instantly set about their ruin.

When Moses saw that "there was wrath gone out from
the Lord, and that the plague was begun," he called Aaron
to him, saying: "Take thy censer, and put fire therein
from off the altar, and lay incense thereon, and carry it
quickly unto the congregation, and make atonement for

them." This remedy against death Moses had learned from
the Angel of Death himself at the time he was staying in
heaven to receive the Torah. At that time he had received a
gift from each one of the angels, and that of the Angel of
Death had been the revelation of the secret that incense can
hold him at bay.[595] Moses, in applying this remedy, had in
mind also the purpose of showing the people the injustice of
their superstition concerning the offering of incense. They
called it death-bearing because it had brought death upon
Nadab and Abihu, as well as upon the two hundred and fifty
followers of Korah. He now wished to convince them that
it was this very incense that prevented the plague, and to
teach them that it is sin that brings death.[596] Aaron, however, did not know why he employed incense, and therefore
said to Moses: "O my lord Moses, hast thou perchance my
death in view? My sons were burned because they put
strange fires into the censers. Shall I now fetch holy fire
from the altar and carry it outside? Surely I shall meet
death through this fire!" Moses replied: "Go quickly and
do as I have bidden thee, for while thou dost stand and talk,
they die." Aaron hastened to carry out the command given
to him, saying: "Even if it be my death, I obey gladly if I
can only serve Israel thereby."[597]

The Angel of Death had meanwhile wrought terrible
havoc among the people, like a reaper mowing down line
after line of them, allowing not one of the line he touched to
escape, whereas, on the other hand, not a single man died before he reached the row in which the man stood. Aaron,
censer in hand, now appeared, and stood up between the
ranks of the living and those of the dead, holding the Angel

of Death at bay. The latter now addressed Aaron, saying:
" Leave me to my work, for I have been sent to do it by God,
whereas thou dost bid me stop in the name of a creature that
is only of flesh and blood." Aaron did not, however, yield,
but said: " Moses acts only as God commands him, and if
thou wilt not trust him, behold, God and Moses are both in
the Tabernacle, let us both betake ourselves thither." The
Angel of Death refused to obey his call, whereupon Aaron
seized him by force and, thrusting the censer under his face,
dragged him to the Tabernacle where he locked him in, so
that death ceased.[598]

In this way Aaron paid off a debt to Moses. After the
worship of the Golden Calf, that came to pass not without
some guilt on Aaron's part, God had decreed that all four of
Aaron's sons were to die, but Moses stood up between the
living and the dead, and through his prayer succeeded in
saving two out of the four. In the same way Aaron now
stood up between the living and the dead to ward off from
Israel the Angel of Death.[599]

God in His kindness now desired the people once and for
all to be convinced of the truth that Aaron was the elect, and
his house the house of priesthood, hence He bade Moses convince them in the following fashion. Upon God's command,
he took a beam of wood, divided it into twelve rods, bade
every prince of a tribe in his own hand write his name on
one of the rods respectively, and laid up the rods over night
before the sanctuary. Then the miracle came to pass that
the rod of Aaron, the prince of the tribe of Levi, bore the
Ineffable Name which caused the rod to bloom blossoms over
night and to yield ripe almonds. When the people, who all

night had been pondering which tribe should on the mor-
row be proven by the rod of its prince to be the chosen one,
betook themselves early in the morning to the sanctuary, and
saw the blossoms and almonds upon the rod of Aaron, they
were at last convinced that God had destined the priesthood
for his house. The almonds, which ripen more quickly than
any other fruit, at the same time informed them that God
would quickly bring punishment upon those who should
venture to usurp the powers of priesthood. Aaron's rod was
then laid up before the Holy Ark by Moses. It was this rod,
which never lost its blossoms or almonds, that the Judean
kings used until the time of the destruction of the Temple,
when, in miraculous fashion, it disappeared. Elijah will in
the future fetch it forth and hand it over to the Messiah.[600]

The Waters of Meribah

Korah's rebellion took place during Israel's sojourn in
Kadesh-Barnea, whence, a short time before, the spies had
been sent out. They remained in this place during nineteen
years, and then for as long a time wandered ceaselessly from
place to place through the desert.[601] When at last the time
decreed by God for their stay in the wilderness was over,
and the generation that God had said must die in the desert
had paid its penalty for its sin, they returned again to Kadesh-Barnea. They took delight in this place endeared to
them by long years of habitation, and settled down in the
expectation of a cheerful and agreeable time. But the prophetess Miriam now died, and the loss of this woman, who
occupied a place as high as that of her brothers, Moses and
Aaron, at once became evident in a way that was perceived

by the pious as well as by the godless. She was the only
woman who died during the march through the desert, and
this occurred for the following reasons. She was a leader of
the people together with her brothers, and as these two were
not permitted to lead the people into the promised land, she
had to share their fate. The well, furthermore, that had
provided Israel with water during the march through the
desert, had been a gift of God to the people as a reward for
the good deeds of this prophetess, and as this gift had been
limited to the time of the march through the desert, she had
to die shortly before the entrance into the promised land.

Hardly had Miriam died, when the well also disappeared
and a dearth of water set in, that all Israel might know that
only owing to the merits of the pious prophetess had they
been spared a lack of water during the forty years of the
march.[602] While Moses and Aaron were now plunged in
deep grief for their sister's death, a mob of the people col-
lected to wrangle with them on account of the dearth of
water. Moses, seeing the multitudes of people approaching
from the distance, said to his brother Aaron: "What may
all these multitudes desire?" The other replied: "Are not
the children of Abraham, Isaac, and Jacob kind-hearted people and the descendants of kind-hearted people? They come
to express their sympathy." Moses, however, said: "Thou
art not able to distinguish between a well-ordered procession
and this motley multitude; were these people assembled in
an orderly procession, they would move under the leadership
of the rulers of thousands and the rulers of hundreds, but behold, they move in disorderly troops. How then can their
intentions be to condole with us!"[603]

The two brothers were not long to remain in doubt concerning the purpose of the multitude, for they stepped up to them and began to pick a quarrel with Moses, saying: " It was a heavy blow for us when fourteen thousand and seven hundred of our men died of the plague; harder still to bear was the death of those who were swallowed up by the earth, and lost their lives in an unnatural way; the heaviest blow of all, however, was the death of those who were consumed at the offering of incense, whose terrible end is constantly recalled to us by the covering of the altar, fashioned out of the brasen plates that came of the censers used by those unfortunate ones. But we bore all these blows, and even wish we had all perished simultaneously with them instead of becoming victims to the tortures of death by thirst." [604]

At first they directed their reproaches against Moses alone, since Aaron, on account of his extraordinary love of peace and his kind-heartedness, was the favorite of the people, but once carried away by suffering and rage, they started to hurl their accusations against both of the brothers, saying: " Formerly your answer to us had always been that sorrows came upon us and that God did not stand by us because there were sinful and godless men among us. Now that we are ' a congregation of the Lord,' why have ye nevertheless led us to this poor place where there is not water, without which neither man nor beast can live? Why do not ye exhort God to have pity upon us since the well of Miriam has vanished with her death? " [605]

" A righteous man regardeth the life of his beast," and the fact that these people, so near to death, still considered the sufferings of their beasts shows that they were, notwithstanding their attitude toward Moses and Aaron, really pious men. And, in truth, God did not take amiss their words against Moses and Aaron, "for God holds no man accountable for that which he utters in distress." For the same reason neither Moses nor Aaron made reply to the accusations hurled against them, but hastened to the sanctuary to implore God's mercy for His people. They also considered that the holy place would shelter them in case the people meant to lay hands upon them. God actually did appear at once, and said to them: "Hasten from this place; My children die of thirst, and ye have nothing better to do than to mourn the death of an old woman!" [606] He then bade Moses "to speak unto the rock that it may give forth water," but impressed upon them the command to bring forth neither honey nor oil out of the rock, but water only. This was to prove God's power, who can pour out of the rock not only such liquids as are contained in it, but water too, that never otherwise issues from a rock. He also ordered Moses to speak to the rock, but not to smite it with his rod. "For," said God, "the merits of them that sleep in the Cave of Machpelah suffice to cause their children to receive water out of the rock." [607]

Moses then fetched out of the Tabernacle the holy rod on which was the Ineffable Name of God, and, accompanied by Aaron, betook himself to the rock to bring water out of it. [608] On the way to the rock all Israel followed him, halting at any rock by the way, fancying that they might fetch water out of it. The grumblers now went about inciting the people against Moses, saying: "Don't you know that the son of Amram had once been Jethro's shepherd, and all shepherds have knowledge of the places in the wilderness that are rich in water? Moses will now try to lead us to such a place where there is water, and then he will cheat us and declare he had caused the water to flow out of a rock. If he actually is able to bring forth water out of rocks, then let him fetch it out of any one of the rocks upon which we fix." Moses could easily have done this, for God said to him: "Let them see the water flow out of the rock they have chosen," but when, on the way to the rock, he turned around and perceived that instead of following him they stood about in groups around different rocks, each group around some rock favored by it, he commanded them to follow him to the rock upon which he had fixed. They, however, said: "We demand that thou bring us water out of the rock we have chosen, and if thou wilt not, we do not care to fetch water out of another rock." [608]

MOSES' ANGER CAUSES HIS DOOM

Throughout forty years Moses had striven to refrain from harshly addressing the people, knowing that if but a single time he lost patience, God would cause him to die in the desert. On this occasion, however, he was mastered by his rage, and shouted at Israel the words: "O ye madmen, ye stiffnecked ones, that desire to teach their teacher, ye that shoot upon your leaders with your arrows, do ye think that out of this rock that ye have chosen, we shall be able to bring forth water? [610] I vow that I shall let water flow out of that rock only that I have chosen." He addressed these harsh words not to a few among Israel, but to all the people, for God had brought the miracle to pass that the small space in

front of the rock held all Israel. Carried away by anger,
Moses still further forgot himself, and instead of speaking
to the rock as God had commanded him, he struck a rock
chosen by himself.[611] As Moses had not acted according to
God's command, the rock did not at once obey, and sent forth
only a few drops of water, so that the mockers cried: "Son
of Amram, is this for the sucklings and for them that are
weaned from the milk?" Moses now waxed angrier still,
and for a second time smote the rock, from which gushed
streams so mighty that many of his enemies met their death
in the currents, and at the same time water poured out of all
the stones and rocks of the desert.[612] God hereupon said
to Moses: "Thou and Aaron believed Me not, I forbade
you to smite the rock, but thou didst smite it; ye sanctified
Me not in the eyes of the children of Israel because ye
did not fetch water out of any one of the rocks, as the people
wished; ye trespassed against Me when ye said, 'Shall
we bring forth water out of this rock?' and ye acted contrary to My command because ye did not speak to the
rock as I had bidden ye. I vow, therefore, that 'ye shall
not bring this assembly into the land which I have given
them,' and not until the Messianic time shall ye two lead
Israel to the Holy Land."[613] God furthermore said to
Moses: "Thou shouldst have learned from the life of
Ishmael to have greater faith in Me; I bade the well to
spring up for him, even though he was only a single human
being, on account of the merits of his father Abraham. How
much more then hadst thou a right to expect, thou who
couldst refer to the merits of the three Patriarchs as well as
to the people's own, for they accepted the Torah and obeyed

many commandments. Yea, even from thine own experience shouldst thou have drawn greater faith in My will to aid Israel. When in Rephidim thou didst say to Me, ' They be almost ready to stone me,' did not I reply to thee, ' Why dost thou accuse My children? Go with thy rod before the people, and thou shalt smite the rock, and there shall come water out of it.' If I wrought for them miracles such as these when they had not yet accepted the Torah, and did not yet have faith in Me, shouldst thou not have known how much more I would do for them now? " [614]

God " taketh the wise in their own craftiness." He had long before this decreed that Moses die in the desert, and Moses' offense in Kadesh was only a pretext God employed that He might not seem to be unjust. But He gave to Moses himself the true reason why He did not permit him to enter the promised land, saying: " Would it perchance redound to thy glory if thou wert to lead into the land a new generation after thou hadst led out of Egypt the sixty myriads and buried them in the desert? People would declare that the generation of the desert has no share in the future world, therefore stay with them, that at their head thou mayest after the Resurrection enter the promised land." [615] Moses now said to God: " Thou hast decreed that I die in the desert like the generation of the desert that angered Thee. I implore Thee, write in Thy Torah wherefore I have been thus punished, that future generations may not say I had been like the generation of the desert." God granted this wish, and in several passages of the Scriptures set forth what had really been the offense on account of which Moses had been prohibited from entering the promised land. [616] It was

due only to the transgression at the rock in Kadesh, where
Moses failed to sanctify God in the eyes of the children of
Israel; and God was sanctified by allowing justice to take its
course without respect of persons, and punishing Moses.
Hence this place was called Kadesh, "sanctity," and En
Mishpat, "fountain of justice," because on this spot judg-
ment was passed upon Moses, and by this sentence God's
name was sanctified.[617]

As water had been the occasion for the punishment of
Moses, God did not say that that which He had created on
the second day of the creation "was good," for on that day
He had created water, and that which brought about Moses'
death was not good.[618]

If the death doomed for Moses upon this occasion was a
very severe punishment, entirely out of proportion to his
offense, then still more so was the death destined for Aaron
at the same time. For he had been guilty of no other offense
than that of joining Moses at his transgression, and "whoso
joins a transgressor, is as bad as the transgressor himself."
On this occasion, as usual, Aaron showed his absolute devotion and his faith in God's justice. He might have said, "I
have not sinned; why am I to be punished?" but he conquered himself and put up no defense, wherefore Moses
greatly praised him.[619]

EDOM'S UNBROTHERLY ATTITUDE TOWARD ISRAEL

From Kadesh Moses sent ambassadors to the king of
Edom, requesting him to permit Israel to travel through his
territory. "For," thought Moses, "When our father Jacob
with only a small troop of men planned to return to his

father's house, which was not situated in Esau's possessions, he previously sent a messenger to him to ask his permission. How much more then does it behoove us, a people of great numbers, to refrain from entering Edom's territory before receiving his sanction to do so!"

Moses' ambassadors had been commissioned to bear the following message to the king of Edom: "From the time of our grandfather Abraham, there was a promissory note to be redeemed, for God had imposed it upon him that in Egypt his seed should be enslaved and tortured. It had been thy duty, as well as ours, to redeem this note, and thou knowest that we have done our duty whereas thou wert not willing. God had, as thou knowest, promised Abraham that those who had been in bondage in Egypt should receive Canaan for their possession as a reward. That land, therefore, is ours, who were in Egypt, and thou who didst shirk the redemption of the debt, hast now no claim to our land. Let us then pass through thy land until we reach ours.[620] Know also that the Patriarchs in their grave sympathized with our sufferings in Egypt, and whenever we called out to God He heard us, and sent us one of His ministering angels to lead us out of Egypt. Consider, then, that all thy weapons will avail thee naught if we implore God's aid, who will then at once overthrow thee and thy hosts, for this is our inheritance, and ' the voice of Jacob ' never proves ineffectual.[621] That thou mayest not, however, plead that our passage through thy land will bring thee only annoyances and no gain, I promise thee that although we draw drink out of the well that accompanies us on our travels, and are provided with food through the manna, we shall, nevertheless, buy water and food from thy people, that ye may profit by our passage."

This was no idle promise, for Moses had actually asked
the people to be liberal with their money, that the Edomites
might not take them to be poor slaves, but might be convinced that in spite of their stay in Egypt, Israel was a
wealthy nation. Moses also pledged himself to provide the
cattle with muzzles during their passage through Edom, that
they might do no damage to the land of the dwellers there.
With these words he ended his message to the king of
Edom: " To the right and to the left of thy land may we
pillage and slaughter, but in accord with God's words, we
may not touch thy possession." But all these prayers and
pleadings of Moses were without avail, for Edom's answer
was in the form of a threat: " Ye depend upon your inheritance, upon ' the voice of Jacob ' which God answers, and I
too shall depend upon my inheritance, ' the hand and sword
of Esau.' " Israel now had to give up their attempt to reach
their land through Edom's territory, not, however, through
fear, but because God had prohibited them from bringing
war upon the Edomites, even before they had heard from the
embassy that Edom had refused them the right of passage.

The neighborhood of the godless brings disaster, as Israel
was to experience, for they lost the pious Aaron on the boundary of Edom, and buried him on Mount Hor. The cloud
that used to precede Israel, had indeed been accustomed to
level all the mountains, that they might move on upon level
ways, but God retained three mountains in the desert:
Sinai, as the place of the revelation; Nebo, as the burial-
place of Moses; and Hor, consisting of a twin mountain, as
a burial-place for Aaron. Apart from these three mountains,
there were none in the desert, but the cloud would leave little

elevations on the place where Israel pitched camp, that the sanctuary might thereupon be set up."

THE THREE SHEPHERDS

Aaron died four months after the death of his sister Miriam, whereas Moses died nearly a year after his sister. Her death took place on the first day of Nisan, and that of Moses on the seventh day of Adar in the same year. Although the death of these three did not take place in the same month, God spoke of them saying, " And I cut off the three shepherds in one month," for He had determined upon their death in one month." It is God's way to classify people into related groups, and the death of these three pious ones was not determined upon together with that of the sinful generation of wanderers in the desert, but only after this generation had died, was sealed the doom of the three." Miriam died first, and the same fate was decreed for her brothers as a consequence of her death.

Miriam's death plunged all into deep mourning, Moses and Aaron wept in their apartments and the people wept in the streets. For six hours Moses was ignorant of the disappearance of Miriam's well with Miriam's death, until the Israelites went to him, saying, " How long wilt thou sit here and weep? " He answered, " Shall I not weep for my sister, who has died? " They replied, " While thou art weeping for one soul, weep at the same time for us all." " Why? " asked he. They said, " We have no water to drink." Then he rose up from the ground, went out and saw the well without a drop of water. He now began to quarrel with them, saying, " Have I not told ye, ' I am not able to bear you myself alone'? Ye have rulers of thousands, rulers of hundreds, rulers of fifties, and rulers of tens, princes, chiefs, elders, and magnates, let these attend to your needs." Israel, however, said: "All rests with thee, for it is thou who didst lead us out of Egypt and brought 'us in unto this evil place; it is no place of seed or of figs, or of vines, or of pomegranates; neither is there any water to drink.' If thou wilt give us water, it is well, if not, we shall stone thee." When Moses heard this, he fled from them and betook himself to the Tabernacle. There God said to him: "What ails thee?" and Moses replied: "O Lord of the world! Thy children want to stone me, and had I not escaped, they would have stoned me by now." God said: "Moses, how much longer wilt thou continue to calumniate My children? Is it not enough that at Horeb thou didst say, 'They be ready to stone me,' whereupon I answered thee, 'Go up before them and I will see whether they stone thee or not!' 'Take the rod and assemble the congregation, thou and Aaron thy brother, and speak ye unto the rock before their eyes, that it give forth its water.'"

Moses now went to seek for the rock, followed by all Israel, for he did not know which was the rock out of which God had said water was to flow.[625] For the rock out of which Miriam's well flowed vanished among the rest of the rocks in such a way that Moses was not able to distinguish it among the number.[626] On the way they saw a rock that dripped, and they took up their places in front of it. When Moses saw that the people stood still, he turned around and they said to him: "How long wilt thou lead us on?" Moses: "Until I fetch ye forth water out of the rock."

The people: " Give us water at once, that we may drink."
Moses: " How long do ye quarrel? Is there a creature in
all the world that so rebels against its Maker as ye do, when
it is certain that God will give ye water out of a rock, even
though I do not know which one that may be!" The
people: " Thou wert a prophet and our shepherd during our
march through the desert, and now thou sayest, ' I know not
out of which rock God will give ye water.' "

Moses hereupon assembled them about a rock, saying to
himself: " If I now speak to the rock, bidding it bring
forth water, and it bring forth none, I shall subject myself to humiliation in the presence of the community, for
they will say, ' Where is thy wisdom?' " Hence he said to
the people: " Ye know that God can perform miracles for
ye, but He hath hidden from me out of which rock He will
let the water flow forth. For whenever the time comes that
God wishes a man not to know, then his wisdom and understanding are of no avail to him." Moses then lifted his rod
and let it quietly slide down upon the rock upon which he
laid it, uttering, as if addressing Israel, the words, " Shall
we bring you forth water out of this rock?" The rock of its
own accord now began to give forth water, whereupon
Moses struck upon it with his rod, but then water no longer
flowed forth, but blood. Moses hereupon said to God:
" This rock brings forth no water," and God instantly turned
to the rock with the question: " Why dost thou bring forth
not water, but blood?" The rock answered: " O Lord of
the world! Why did Moses smite me?" When God asked
Moses why he had smitten the rock, he replied: " That it
might bring forth water." God, however, said to Moses:

" Had I bidden thee to smite the rock? I had only said,
' Speak to it.' " Moses tried to defend himself by saying, " I
did speak to it, but it brought forth nothing." " Thou," God
replied, " hast given Israel the instruction, ' In righteousness
shalt thou judge thy neighbor '; why then, didst not thou
judge the rock ' in righteousness,' the rock that in Egypt
supported thee when out of it thou didst suck honey? Is
this the manner in which thou repayest it? Not only wert
thou unjust to the rock, but thou didst also call My children
fools. If then thou art a wise man, it does not become thee
as a wise man to have anything further to do with fools, and
therefore thou shalt not with them learn to know the land of
Israel." [627] At the same time God added, " Neither thou, nor
thy brother, nor thy sister, shall set foot upon the land of
Israel." For even in Egypt God had warned Moses and
Aaron to refrain from calling the Israelites fools, and as
Moses, without evoking a protest from Aaron, at the water
of Kadesh, called them fools, the punishment of death was
decreed for him and his brother. [628] When God had informed
Moses of the impending punishment due to him and his
brother, He turned to the rock, saying: " Turn thy blood
into water," and so it came to pass. [629]

PREPARING AARON FOR IMPENDING DEATH

As a sign of especial favor God communicates to the
pious the day of their death, that they may transmit their
crowns to their sons. But God considered it particularly fitting to prepare Moses and Aaron for impending death, saying: " These two pious men throughout their lifetime did
nothing without consulting Me, and I shall not therefore take

them out of this world without previously informing them." [630]

When, therefore, Aaron's time approached, God said to Moses: "My servant Moses, who hast been 'faithful in all Mine house,' I have an important matter to communicate to thee, but it weighs heavily upon Me." Moses: "What is it?" God: "Aaron shall be gathered unto his people; for he shall not enter into the land which I have given unto the children of Israel, because ye rebelled against My word at the waters of Meribah." Moses replied: "Lord of the world! It is manifest and known before the Throne of Thy glory, that Thou art Lord of all the world and of Thy creatures that in this world Thou hast created, so that we are in Thy hand, and in Thy hand it lies to do with us as Thou wilt. I am not, however, fit to go to my brother, and repeat to him Thy commission, for he is older than I, and how then shall I presume to go up to my older brother and say, 'Go up unto Mount Hor and die there!'" God answered Moses: "Not with the lip shalt thou touch this matter, but 'take Aaron and Eleazar his son, and bring them up unto Mount Hor.' Ascend thou also with them, and there speak with thy brother sweet and gentle words, the burden of which will, however, prepare him for what awaits him. Later when ye shall all three be upon the mountain, 'strip Aaron of his garments, and put them upon Eleazar his son, and Aaron shall be gathered unto his people, and shall die there.' [631] As a favor to Me prepare Aaron for his death, for I am ashamed to tell him of it Myself." [632]

When Moses heard this, there was a tumult in his heart, and he knew not what to do. He wept so passionately that his grief for the impending loss of his brother brought him to the brink of death himself. As a faithful servant of God, however, nothing remained for him to do, but to execute his Master's command, hence he betook himself to Aaron to the Tabernacle, to inform him of his death.

Now it had been customary during the forty years' march through the desert for the people daily to gather, first before the seventy elders, then under their guidance before the princes of the tribes, then for all of them to appear before Eleazar and Aaron, and with these to go to Moses to present to him their morning greeting. On this day, however, Moses made a change in this custom, and after having wept through the night, at the cock's crow summoned Eleazar before him and said to him: "Go and call to me the elders and the princes, for I have to convey to them a commission from the Lord." Accompanied by these men, Moses now betook himself to Aaron who, seeing Moses when he arose, asked: "Why hast thou made a change in the usual custom?" Moses: "God hath bidden me to make a communication to thee." Aaron: "Tell it to me." Moses: "Wait until we are out of doors." Aaron thereupon donned his eight priestly garments and both went out.

Now it had always been the custom for Moses whenever he went from his house to the Tabernacle to walk in the centre, with Aaron at his right, Eleazar at his left, then the elders at both sides, and the people following in the rear. Upon arriving within the Tabernacle, Aaron would seat himself as the very nearest at Moses' right hand, Eleazar at his left, and the elders and princes in front. On this day, however, Moses changed this order; Aaron walked in the centre,

Moses at his right hand, Eleazar at his left, the elders and princes at both sides, and the rest of the people following.

When the Israelites saw this, they rejoiced greatly, saying: "Aaron now has a higher degree of the Holy Spirit than Moses, and therefore does Moses yield to him the place of honor in the centre." The people loved Aaron better than Moses.[883] For ever since Aaron had become aware that through the construction of the Golden Calf he had brought about the transgression of Israel, it was his endeavor through the following course of life to atone for his sin. He would go from house to house, and whenever he found one who did not know how to recite his Shema', he taught him the Shema'; if one did not know how to pray he taught him how to pray; and if he found one who was not capable of penetrating into the study of the Torah, he initiated him into it.[884] He did not, however, consider his task restricted 'to establishing peace between God and man,' but strove to establish peace between the learned and the ignorant Israelites, among the scholars themselves, among the ignorant, and between man and wife.[885] Hence the people loved him very dearly, and rejoiced when they believed he had now attained a higher rank than Moses.

Having arrived at the Tabernacle, Aaron now wanted to enter, but Moses held him back, saying: "We shall now go beyond the camp." When they were outside the camp, Aaron said to Moses: "Tell me the commission God hath given thee." Moses answered: "Wait until we reach the mountain." At the foot of the mountain Moses said to the people: "Stay here until we return to you; I, Aaron, and Eleazar will go to the top of the mount, and shall return when we shall have heard the Divine revelation." All three now ascended.

AARON'S DEATH

Moses wanted to inform his brother of his impending death, but knew not how to go about it. At length he said to him: "Aaron, my brother, hath God given anything into thy keeping?" "Yes," replied Aaron. "What, pray?" asked Moses. Aaron: "The altar and the table upon which is the shewbread hath He given into my charge." Moses: "It may be that He will now demand back from thee all that He hath given into thy keeping." Aaron: "What, pray?" Moses: "Hath He not entrusted a light to thee?" Aaron: "Not one light only but all seven of the candlestick that now burn in the sanctuary." Moses had, of course, intended to call Aaron's attention to the soul, "the light of the Lord," which God had given into his keeping and which He now demanded back. As Aaron, in his simplicity, did not notice the allusion, Moses did not go into further particulars, but remarked to Aaron: "God hath with justice called thee an innocent, simple-hearted man."

While they were thus conversing, a cave opened up before them, whereupon Moses requested his brother to enter it, and Aaron instantly acquiesced. Moses was now in a sad predicament, for, to follow God's command, he had to strip Aaron of his garments and to put them upon Eleazar, but he knew not how to broach the subject to his brother. He finally said to Aaron: "My brother Aaron, it is not proper to enter the cave into which we now want to descend, invested in the priestly garments, for they might there become unclean; the cave is very beautiful, and it is therefore possible that there are old graves in it." Aaron replied, "Thou art right." Moses then stripped his brother of his priestly garments, and put them upon Aaron's son, Eleazar.[636]

As it would have been improper if Aaron had been buried quite naked, God brought about the miracle that, as soon as Moses took off one of Aaron's garments, a corresponding celestial garment was spread over Aaron, and when Moses had stripped him of all his priestly garments, he found himself arrayed in eight celestial garments. A second miracle came to pass in the stripping of Aaron's garments, for Moses was enabled to take off the undermost garments before the upper. This was done in order to satisfy the law that priests may never use their upper garments as undergarments, a thing Eleazar would have had to do, had Moses stripped off Aaron's outer garments first and with these invested his son.[637]

After Eleazar had put on the high priest's garments, Moses and Aaron said to him: "Wait for us here until we return out of the cave," and both entered it. At their entrance they beheld a couch spread, a table prepared, and a candle lighted, while ministering angels surrounded the couch. Aaron then said to Moses: "How long, O my brother, wilt thou still conceal the commission God hath entrusted to thee? Thou knowest that He Himself, when for the first time He addressed thee, with His own lips declared of me, 'When he seeth thee, he will be glad in his heart.' Why, then, dost thou conceal the commission God hath entrusted to thee? Even if it were to refer to my death, I should take it upon myself with a cheerful countenance."

Moses replied: " As thou thyself dost speak of death, I will acknowledge that God's words to me do concern thy death, but I was afraid to make it known to thee. But look now, thy death is not as that of the other creatures of flesh and blood; and not only is thy death a remarkable one, but see! The ministering angels have come to stand by thee in thy parting hour." [638]

When he spoke of the remarkable death that awaited Aaron, Moses meant to allude to the fact that Aaron, like his sister Miriam and later Moses, was to die not through the Angel of Death, but by a kiss from God. [639] Aaron, however, said: " O my brother Moses, why didst not thou make this communication to me in the presence of my mother, my wife, and my children? " Moses did not instantly reply to this question, but tried to speak words of comfort and encouragement to Aaron, saying: " Dost thou not know, my brother, that thou didst forty years ago deserve to meet thy death when thou didst fashion the Golden Calf, but then I stood before the Lord in prayer and exhortation, and saved thee from death. And now I pray that my death were as thine! For when thou diest, I bury thee, but when I shall die, I shall have no brother to bury me. When thou diest, thy sons will inherit thy position, but when I die, strangers will inherit my place." With these and similar words Moses encouraged his brother, until he finally looked forward to his end with equanimity.

Aaron lay down upon the adorned couch, and God received his soul. Moses then left the cave, which immediately vanished, so that none might know or understand how it had happened. When Eleazar saw Moses return alone, he said to him: " O my teacher, where is my father?" Moses replied: " He has entered Paradise." Then both descended from the mountain into the camp."⁰ When the people saw Moses and Eleazar return without Aaron, they were not at all in the mood to lend faith to the communication of Aaron's death. They could not at all credit that a man who had overcome the Angel of Death was now overcome by him. Three opinions were then formed among the people concerning Aaron's absence. Some declared that Moses had killed Aaron because he was jealous of his popularity; some thought Eleazar had killed his father to become his successor as high priest; and there were also some who declared that he had been removed from earth to be translated to heaven. Satan had so incited the people against Moses and Eleazar that they wanted to stone them. Moses hereupon prayed to God, saying: " Deliver me and Eleazar from this unmerited suspicion, and also show to the people Aaron's bier, that they may not believe him to be still alive, for in their boundless admiration for Aaron they may even make a God of him." God then said to the angels: " Lift up on high the bier upon which lies My friend Aaron, so that Israel may know he is dead and may not lay hands upon Moses and Eleazar." The angels did as they were bidden,"¹ and Israel then saw Aaron's bier floating in the air, while God before it and the angels behind intoned a funeral song for Aaron. God lamented in the words, " He entereth into peace; they rest in their beds, each one that walketh in his uprightness," whereas the angels said: " The law of truth was in his mouth, and unrighteousness was not found in his lips: he walked with Me in peace and uprightness, and did turn many away from iniquity."

THE GENERAL MOURNING FOR AARON

When Israel beheld the funeral rites prepared in honor
of Aaron by God and by the angels, they also prepared a
funeral ceremony of thirty days in which all the people, men
and women, adults and children, took part.[642] This universal
mourning had its foundation not only in Israel's emulation of
the Divine mourning and of the ceremonies arranged by
Moses and Eleazar, or in their wish to show their reverence
for the deceased high priest, but first and foremost in the
truth that the people deeply loved Aaron and deeply felt his
death. They mourned for him even more than they did later
for Moses; for the latter only a part of the people shed tears,
but for Aaron, everyone. Moses, as a judge, was obliged to
mete out justice to the guilty, so that he had enemies
among the people, men who could not forget that he had pronounced them guilty in court. Moses, furthermore, was
sometimes severe with Israel when he held up to them their
sins, but never Aaron. The latter " loved peace and pursued
peace, loved men and brought them near to the Torah." In
his humility, he did not consider his dignity hurt by offering
greetings first to even the lowliest, yes, he did not even fail in
offering his greeting when he was certain that the man before him was wicked or godless. The lament of the angels
for Aaron as one " who did turn many away from iniquity "
was therefore well justified. This kindliness of his led many
a sinner to reform, who at the moment when he was about
to commit a sin thought to himself: " How shall I be able to
lift up my eyes to Aaron's face? I, to whom Aaron was so
kind, blush to do evil." Aaron recognized his especial task as
that of the peace-maker. If he discovered that two men had

fallen out, he hastened first to the one, then to the other, saying to each: "My son, dost thou not know what he is doing with whom thou hast quarreled? He beats at his heart, rends his garments in grief, and says, 'Woe is me! How can I ever again lift up my eyes and look upon my companion against whom I have acted so?'" Aaron would then speak to each separately until both the former enemies would mutually forgive each other, and as soon as they were again face to face salute each other as friends. If Aaron heard that husband and wife lived in discord, he would hasten to the husband, saying: "I come to thee because I hear that thou and thy wife live in discord, wherefore thou must divorce her. Keep in mind, however, that if thou shouldst in place of thy present wife marry another, it is very questionable if thy second wife will be as good as this one; for at your first quarrel she will throw up to thee that thou art a quarrelsome man, as was shown by thy divorce from thy first wife." Many thousands of unions were saved from impending rupture by the efforts and urgings of Aaron, and the sons born to the couples brought together anew usually received Aaron's name, owing, as they did, their existence to his intercession. Not less than eighty thousand youths bearing his name took part in the mourning for Aaron.[643]

When Moses beheld the deep-felt sorrow of the heavenly beings and of men for Aaron, he burst into passionate weeping, and said: "Woe is me, that am now left all alone! When Miriam died, none came to show her the last marks of honor, and only I, Aaron, and his sons stood about her bier, wept for her, mourned her, and buried her. At Aaron's death, I and his sons were present at his bier to show him

the last marks of honor. But alas! How shall I fare? Who
will be present at my death? I have neither father nor
mother, neither brother nor sister,—who then will weep for
me?" God, however, said to him: "Be not afraid, Moses,
I Myself shall bury thee amid great splendor, and just as the
cave in which Aaron lies has vanished, that none may know
the spot where Aaron is buried, so too shall no mortal know
thy burial place. As the Angel of Death had no power over
Aaron, who died 'by the kiss,' so shall the Angel of Death
have no power over thee, and thou shalt die 'by the kiss.'"
Moses grew calm at these words, knowing at last that he had
his place among the blessed pious. Blessed are they, for not
only does God in person gather them to Him, but as soon as
they are dead, the angels go joyously to meet them and with
beaming faces go to greet them, saying, "Enter into
peace." [444]

The False Friends

When Moses and Eleazar returned from the mountain
without Aaron, Israel said to Moses: "We shall not release
thee from this spot until thou showest us Aaron, dead or
alive." Moses prayed to God, and He opened the cave and
all Israel saw within it Aaron, lying dead upon a bier. They
instantly felt what they had lost in Aaron, for when they
turned to look at the camp, they saw that the clouds of glory
that had covered the site of the camp during their forty
years' march had vanished. They perceived, therefore, that
God had sent these clouds for Aaron's sake only, and hence,
with Aaron's death, had caused them to vanish. Those
among Israel who had been born in the desert, having now,

owing to the departure of the clouds of glory, for the first time beheld the sun and moon, wanted to fall down before them and adore them, for the clouds had always hidden the sun and the moon from them, and the sight of them made a most awful impression upon them. But God said to them: " Have I not commanded you in My Torah: ' Take ye therefore good heed unto yourselves . . . lest thou lift up thine eyes unto heaven, and when thou seest the sun and the moon and the stars, even all the host of heaven, thou be drawn away and worship them, and serve them?' For it is God that led thee out of the furnace of Egypt, that thou mightest be the people of His inheritance." [445]

The disappearance of the clouds of glory inspired Israel with terror, for now they were unaided against the attacks of enemies, whereas none had been able to enter into the camp of Israel while the clouds covered them. This fear was not, indeed, ungrounded, for hardly did Amalek learn that Aaron was dead and that the clouds of glory had vanished, when he at once set about harassing Israel. [446] Amalek acted in accordance with the counsel his grandsire Esau had given him, for his words to his grandson had been: " In spite of all my pains, I did not succeed in killing Jacob, therefore be thou mindful of avenging me upon his descendants." " But how, alas!" said Amalek, " Shall I be able to compete with Israel?" Esau made answer: " Look well, and as soon as thou seest Israel stumble, leap upon them." Amalek looked upon this legacy as the guiding star of his actions. When Israel trespassed, saying with little faith, " Is the Lord among us, or not?" Amalek instantly appeared. Hardly had Israel been tempted by its spies wickedly to exclaim,

"Let us make a captain, and let us return into Egypt," when Amalek was upon the scene to battle with Israel. In later times also Amalek followed this policy, and when Nebuchadnezzar moved to Jerusalem in order to destroy it, Amalek took up his position one mile away from the holy city, saying: "If Israel should conquer, I should declare that I had come to assist them, but should Nebuchadnezzar be victorious, then shall I cut off the flight of the fleeing Israelites." His hopes were realized, for Nebuchadnezzar was victorious, and standing at the crossway, he cut down the fleeing Israelites, and added insult to injury by hurling invectives against God and the people, and ridiculing them.

When, after Aaron's death, Amalek no longer considered Israel dangerous, since the clouds had disappeared, he instantly set about making war upon them. Amalek did not, however, go in open warfare against Israel, but tried through craft to attain what he dared not hope for in open warfare. Concealing their weapons in their garments, the Amalekites appeared in Israel's camp as if they meant to condole with them for Aaron's death, and then unexpectedly attacked them. Not content with this, the Amalekites disguised themselves in Canaanite costume and spoke the speech of the latter, so that the Israelites might not be able to tell if they had before them Amalekites, as their personal appearance seemed to show, or Canaanites, as their dress and speech indicated. The reason for this disguise was that Amalek knew that Israel had inherited the legacy from their ancestor Isaac that God always answered their prayer, hence Amalek said: "If we now appear as Canaanites, they will implore God to send them aid against the Canaanites, and we shall slay them." But all these wiles of Amalek were of no avail. Israel couched their prayer to God in these words: " O Lord of the world! We know not with what nation we are now waging war, whether with Amalek or with Canaan, but whichsoever nation it be, pray visit punishment upon it." [647] God heard their prayer and, promising to stand by them, ordered them totally to annihilate their enemy, saying: " Although ye are now dealing with Amalek, do not treat him like Esau's other sons, against whom ye may not war, but try totally to destroy them, as if they were Canaanites." Israel acted according to this command, slaying the Amalekites in battle, and dedicating their cities to God. [648] Amalek's only gain in this enterprise was that, at the beginning of the war, they seized a slave woman who had once belonged to them, but who later passed over into the possession of the Israelites. [649]

For Israel this attack of Amalek had indeed serious consequences, for as soon as they perceived the approach of the enemy, they were afraid to continue the march to Palestine, being now no longer under the protection of the clouds, that vanished with Aaron's death; hence they determined to return to Egypt. They actually carried out part of this project by retreating eight stations, but the Levites pursued them, and in Moserah there arose a bitter quarrel between those who wanted to return to Egypt and the Levites who insisted upon the continuance of the march to Palestine. Of the former, eight tribal divisions were destroyed in this quarrel, five Benjamite, and one each of the Simeonite, Gadite, and Asherite divisions, while of the Levites one division was completely extirpated, and three others decimated in such a way that they did not recover until the days of David. The Levites were finally victorious, for even their opponents recognized that it had been folly on their part to desire to return to Egypt, and that their loss had been only a punishment because they had not arranged a mourning ceremony adequate to honor a man of Aaron's piety. They thereupon celebrated a grand mourning ceremony for Aaron in Moserah, and it is for this reason that people later spoke of this place as the place where Aaron died, because the great mourning rites took place there.[650]

The Brazen Serpent

Owing to the king of Edom's refusal to permit Israel to pass through his land, they were obliged, at the very point when they believed themselves at the end of their march, to continue it, so as to go around the land of Edom. The people, weary of the many years' marches, now became peevish, saying: "We had already been close to the promised land, and now must turn about once more! It was the same with our fathers who, close to their goal, had to turn back and roam about for thirty-eight years. Thus will it be with us!"[651] In their dejection they set about murmuring against God and Moses, "master and servant being to them as one." They complained that they were entirely thrown upon manna as a means of sustenance. This last mentioned complaint came from those in regard to whom God had vowed that they should never see the land which He had sworn unto the Patriarchs. These people could not bear the sight of the products of Palestine's soil, dying as soon as they beheld them. Now that they had arrived at the outskirts of the

promised land, the merchants brought into the camp of the
Israelites the native products, but these, unable to partake
of them, still had to continue to gather sustenance exclusively from manna.[652]

Then a voice sounding from the heavens became audible
upon earth, making this announcement: " Come hither
and behold, O ye men! Come hither and hearken, ye
creatures of flesh! In the beginning of things I cursed
the serpent with the words, ' Dust shalt thou eat,' yet it
complained not of its food. But ye, My people that I have
led out of Egypt, for whom I caused manna to rain
down from heaven, and quails to fly from the sea, and a
spring to gush forth from the abyss, ye do murmur against
Me on account of manna, saying, ' Our soul loatheth this
light bread.' Let now the serpents come, that complained
not, even though whatever food they ate tasted only of the
dust, and let them bite those who murmur though they have
a food that possesses every conceivable flavor.[653] The serpent, which was the first creature to slander its Maker
and was therefore punished, shall now punish this people,
which, not profiting by the example of the serpent's punishment, blasphemes its Creator by declaring that the heavenly
food that He sends them would finally bring them death."
The very serpents that during the forty years' march had
been burned by the cloud of glory and lay heaped up high
round about the camp, these same serpents now bit the people so terribly that their poison burned the souls of those
whom they attacked.[654]

When Moses betook himself to those who had been bitten,
hearing that they were too ill to come to him,[655] they, con-

scious of their guilt, said to him: "We have sinned, because we have spoken against the Lord and against thee;
pray unto the Lord, that He take away the serpents from
us." Such was the meekness of Moses, that he instantly
forgave the people's transgression in regard to himself, and
at once implored God's aid. God also, however, forgave
their sin as soon as they had shown penitence, and thus set
an example to man likewise to grant forgiveness when it is
requested.

As a healing for those who had been bitten, God now bade
Moses to make a serpent of brass, and put it upon a pole, that
it might come to pass that every one who was bitten might
look upon it and live. Moses did as he was bidden, and
made a serpent of brass. As soon as he hurled it on high, it
remained floating in the air, so that all might be able to look
upon it.[656] He made the serpent of brass, because in Hebrew
Nahash signifies "snake" and Nehoshet, "brass"; hence
Moses made the serpent of a substance that had a sound
similar to that of the object fashioned out of it.[657] It was
not, however, the sight of the serpent of brass that brought
with it healing and life; but whenever those who had been
bitten by the serpents raised their eyes upward and subordi-
nated their hearts to the will of the heavenly Father, they
were healed; if they gave no thought to God, they perished.[658]

Looking upon the serpent of brass brought healing not
only to those who had been bitten by serpents, but also to
those who had been bitten by dogs or other animals. The
cure of the latter was effected even more quickly than that
of the former, for a casual glance sufficed for them, whereas
the former were healed only after a long and insistent
gaze.[659]

AT ARNON

The murmurs of the people, on account of which God sent upon them the serpents, took place in Zalmonah, a place where grew only thorns and thistles. Thence they wandered on to Punon, where God's punishment overtook them.[660] In the following two stations also, in Oboth and Iye-abarim, they continued their hostile actions against God, who for this reason was full of wrath against them, and did not look upon them again with favor until they reached Arnon.[661] God's favor was instantly shown during Israel's passage through the valley of Arnon, where He wrought for Israel miracles as great as those of yore at the passage through the Red Sea. This valley was formed by two lofty mountains that lay so close together that people upon the two summits of them could converse with one another. But in passing from one mountain to the other, one had to cover a distance of seven miles, having first to descend into the valley, and then again to ascend the other mountain. The Amorites, knowing that Israel should now have to pass through the valley, assembled in innumerable multitudes, and a part of them hid in the caves, of which there were many on the slopes of the mountain, while another part of them awaited Israel in the valley below, hoping to attack and destroy them unexpectedly from above and from below in their passage through the valley. God, however, frustrated this plan, bringing it to pass that Israel did not descend into the valley at all, but stayed above, through the following miracle. For whereas the mountain on the one side of the valley was full of caves, the other consisted entirely of pointed rocks; and God moved this rocky mountain so close up to the other, that the jutting rocks of the one entered into the caves of the other, and all the Amorites that were concealed within them were crushed.

It was the rocky mountain that was moved, and not the other, for this same rocky mountain was the beginning of the promised land, and at the approach of Israel from the other mountain, which was Moabite, the land leaped to meet them, for it awaited them most longingly.

An old proverb says: " If you give a piece of bread to a child, tell its mother about it." God, likewise, wanted Israel to know the great miracles He had accomplished for their sake, for they had no inkling of the attack the heathens had planned to make upon them. God therefore bade the well that had reappeared since their stay in Beeroth to flow past the caves and wash out parts of the corpses in great numbers. When Israel now turned to look upon the well, they perceived it in the valley of the Arnon, shining like the moon, and drawing corpses with it. Not until then did they discover the miracles that had been wrought for them. Not only did the mountains at first move together to let them pass, and then again move apart, but God saved them from great peril. They now intoned a song of praise to the well that revealed to them the great miracle.[662]

When, at the passage through the Red Sea, Israel wanted to intone a song of praise, Moses did not let them do it alone, but first sang to them the song they were to sing to the Lord. For then Israel was young, and could only repeat what its teacher Moses sang before them, but when the nation reached Arnon, it was fully grown, after its forty years' march through the desert. Now the Israelites sang their own song,

saying: "O Lord of the world! It behooves Thee to work
miracles for us, whereas it is our duty to intone to Thee
songs of praise." Moses had no part in the song of praise
to the well, for the well had given occasion to his death in
the desert, and no man can be expected to sing about his
executioner. As Moses wanted to have nothing to do with
this song, God demanded that His own name also be not
mentioned in it, acting in this instance like the king who was
invited to a prince's table, but refused the invitation when he
learned that his friend was not to be present at the feast.[663]
The song to the well was as follows: "This is the well
that the Patriarchs of the world, Abraham, Isaac, and Jacob,
have digged, the princes of olden times have searched, the
heads of the people, the lawgivers of Israel, Moses and Aaron,
have made its water to run with their staves. In the desert
Israel received it as a gift, and after they had received it, it
followed Israel upon all their wanderings, to lofty mountains
and deep valleys. Not until they came to the boundary of
Moab did it disappear, because Israel did not observe the
words of the Torah." [664]

Israel sang a song to the well alone, and not to manna, because they had on several occasions railed against the
heavenly food, and therefore God said: "I do not wish ye
to find fault with manna, nor yet to have ye praise it now,"
and He would not permit them to sing a song of praise to
manna.[665]

Sihon, the King of the Amorites

The crushing of those concealed in the caves of the mountain at Arnon was only the beginning of the miracles God

wrought for Israel during their conquest of the land. It
was at Arnon, too, that Sihon, the king of the Amorites, and
his people who, hardly a month after Aaron's death, rushed
upon Israel, were completely destroyed by them.⁶⁶⁶ This
Amorite king, and likewise Og, the king of Bashan, were
sons of Ahiah, whose father Shemḥazai was one of the fallen
angels.⁶⁶⁷ In accordance with his celestial origin Sihon was a
giant whom none could withstand, for he was of enormous
stature, taller than any tower in all the world, his thigh-bone
alone measuring eighteen cubits, according to the big cubit
of that time.⁶⁶⁸ In spite of his huge size he was also fleet of
foot, wherefore he was called Sihon, " foal," to indicate the
celerity with which he moved, for his true name was Arad.⁶⁶⁹

Moses was sorely afraid of waging war against this giant,
but God put Sihon's and Og's guardian angels in chains, and
then said to Moses: " Behold, I have begun to deliver up
Sihon and his land before thee: begin to possess, that thou
mayest inherit his land." For indeed after the angels of
Sihon and his people had fallen, Moses had nothing more to
fear, for his enemies were thus delivered into his hands.⁶⁷⁰
God assured Moses that " He would begin to put the dread of
him and the fear of him upon the peoples that are under the
whole heaven," by bidding the sun to stand still during his
war against Sihon, that all the world might see that God
battled for Moses.⁶⁷¹

Moses now asked if he might before waging war send
ambassadors to Sihon to request him to permit Israel to pass
through his land. God replied: " How now! I commanded
thee, ' Rise up, contend with him in battle, begin to possess
his land!' and thou wantest to send him messengers of

peace?" Moses, however, replied: "I desire only to follow Thy example when Thou didst wish to lead Israel out of
Egypt, and yet didst send me to Pharaoh with the message
to let Israel, Thy people, pass out, even though Thou couldst
have consumed all of Egypt with one flash of lightning.
When Thou didst reveal the Torah, too, Thou didst offer it
to the heathen nations for acceptance before giving it to
Israel." God saw the justice of Moses' words, and commanded him never in the future to declare war upon a city
before previously urging the people to surrender in peace.[672]

Moses hereupon sent a missive to Sihon in which he requested him to permit Israel to pass through his land, promising him that he would see to it that the people should go
along by the king's highway, so that he need have no cause
to fear any deeds of violence upon married women, or
seductions of girls.[673] "We shall even," continued Moses,
"pay for the water that is otherwise given freely, and likewise [674] buy food-stuffs from thee at good prices." [675] This
letter to Sihon contained at its close, notwithstanding, the
communication that the Israelites would bring war upon
Sihon in case he did not permit them to pass through.
Moses' assumption, however, that Sihon should permit Israel
to pass through sounded in Sihon's ears like a summons to
the keeper of a vineyard to permit one to harvest it. Sihon's
answer therefore was as follows: "I and my brother Og
receive tribute from all the other Canaanite kings to keep
off their enemies from access to the land, and now you ask
me to give you free access to Canaan!"

War between Sihon and Moses ensued, and ended in a
brilliant victory for Israel.[676] Sihon and his son, who equaled

him in heroic strength, found their death in this fray.[677] God had so brought it to pass that Israel had no need of laboriously waging war upon one city after another in Sihon's land, He had brought all the hosts of this Amorite king together into Heshbon. When this city therefore and the hosts within it were destroyed, all the rest of Sihon's land lay open before them. Israel's victory was all the more marvellous, because Heshbon was an exceptionally well fortified city, so that, had gnats been its inhabitants, it could not have been captured by mortal means, much less so when manned by the hero Sihon and his heroic warriors.[678] This victory was made possible only by the fact that God visited them with convulsions so terrible that they rolled up and writhed in pain, unable to stand in the battle lines, so that Israel could cut them down while they were half dead from convulsive pains.[679] God also drew masks over their faces, so that they could not see plainly, and taking one another for Israelites, slew their own people.[680]

With the fall of Heshbon Israel came into possession of all the land of Sihon, with the exception of Jazer, and Moses therefore sent spies to that city. The men whom he sent there, Caleb and Phinehas, were not only capable warriors, but also pious men. They said: " Moses once sent spies who brought great misfortune upon all their generation, we will attack this city, trusting in God, and we are sure we shall not perish, because Moses has prayed for our welfare." They thereupon attacked Jazer, conquered it, and when upon the day after Moses had sent them out they returned to him, they informed him that they had conquered Jazer and slain its inhabitants.[681]

The Giant Og

The war with Sihon took place in the month of Elul. In the following month of Tishri they rested on account of the holy days, but immediately after these they set out to battle against Og.[682] This king did not hasten to his brother's aid, although he was only one day's distance from him, for he felt sure Sihon could conquer Israel without his assistance.[683] He erred in this, however, as in some other matters. In the war of the four kings against the five, it was Og who had brought to Abraham news of his nephew Lot's bondage, assuming that Abraham would surely hasten to his kinsman's aid, be killed in battle, and thus enable Og to get possession of the beautiful Sarah. God, however, leaves no man unrewarded or unpunished. To reward him for hastening with quick steps to advise Abraham of Lot's captivity, God granted him life for five hundred years, but he was eventually killed because it was only a wicked motive that had induced him to perform this service for Abraham. He did not, as he had hoped, gain Sarah, but was slain by her descendant Moses.[684]

The battle against Og took place in Edrei, the outskirts of which Israel reached toward nightfall. On the following morning, however, barely at gray dawn, Moses arose and prepared to attack the city, but looking toward the city wall, he cried in amazement, " Behold, in the night they have built up a new wall about the city!" Moses did not see clearly in the misty morning, for there was no wall, but only the giant Og who sat upon the wall with his feet touching the ground below.[685] Considering Og's enormous stature, Moses' mistake was pardonable, for as a grave-digger of later times related, Og's thigh-bone alone measured more than three parasangs. "Once," so records Abba Saul, "I hunted a stag which fled into the thigh-bone of a dead man. I pursued it and ran along three parasangs of the thigh-bone, yet had not reached its end." This thigh-bone, as was later established, was Og's.[686]

This giant never in all his days made use of a wooden chair or bed, as these would have broken down beneath his weight, but sat upon iron chairs and lay upon iron beds. He was not only of gigantic build and strength, but of a breadth also that was completely out of proportion even with his height, for his breadth was one half his height, whereas the normal proportion of breadth to height is as one to three.[687] In his youth Og had been a slave to Abraham, who had received him as a gift from Nimrod, for Og is none other than Eliezer, Abraham's steward. One day, when Abraham rebuked him and shouted at him, Eliezer was so frightened that one of his teeth fell out, and Abraham fashioned out of it a bed in which he always slept. Og daily devoured a thousand oxen or an equal number of other animals, and drank correspondingly, requiring daily not less than a thousand measures of liquids.[688] He remained in Abraham's service until Isaac's marriage, when Abraham gave him his freedom as a reward for having undertaken the labor of wooing Rebekah for his son, and of fetching her to his house. God also rewarded him in this world, that this wicked wight might not lay claim to a reward in the world to come. He therefore made a king of him.[689] During his reign he founded sixty cities, that he surrounded with high walls, the lowest of which was not less than sixty miles in height.[690]

Moses now feared to wage war against Og, not only on account of his giant strength and huge size, which Moses had now witnessed with his own eyes, but he also thought: " I am only one hundred and twenty years old, whereas he is more than five hundred. Surely he could never have attained so great an age, had he not performed meritorious deeds." [691] Moses also remembered that Og was the only giant that had escaped the hand of Amraphel, and he perceived in this a token of God's special favor toward Og.[692] Moses feared, moreover, that Israel in the recent war against Sihon might have committed sins, so that God would not now stand by them. " The pious are always afraid of the consequences of sin, and therefore do not rely upon the assurances God has made to them; " hence Moses now feared to advance upon Og even though God had promised him aid against his enemies.[693] God, however, said to him: " What matters to thee Og's gigantic stature? He is as a green leaf in thy hand,[694] his destruction has been decreed since the moment when he looked with evil eyes upon Jacob and his family when they arrived in Egypt." For even then God had said to him: " O thou wicked knave, why dost thou look upon them with an evil eye? Verily, thine eye shall burst, for thou shalt fall into their hands." [695]

Og met his death in the following fashion. When he discovered that Israel's camp was three parasangs in circumference, he said: " I shall now tear up a mountain of three parasangs, and cast it upon Israel's camp, and crush them." He did as he had planned, pulled up a mountain of three parasangs, laid it upon his head, and came marching in the direction of the Israelite camp, to hurl it upon them. But what did God do? He caused ants to perforate the mountain, so that it slipped from Og's head down upon his neck, and when he attempted to shake it off, his teeth pushed out and extended to left and right, and did not let the mountain pass, so that he now stood there with the mountain, unable to throw it from him. When Moses saw this, he took an axe twelve cubits long, leaped ten cubits into the air, and dealt a blow to Og's ankle, which caused the giant's death.[696]

This was the end of the last of the giants, who was not only last in time, but also in significance, for despite his height and strength, he was the most insignificant of the giants who perished in the flood.[697]

With Og's death all his lands fell to the lot of the Israelites without another sword's stroke, for God had so ordained it that all of Og's warriors were with him at his encounter with Israel, and after Israel had conquered these, only women and children remained in all the land. Had Israel been obliged to advance upon every city individually, they would never have finished, on account of the number of the cities and the strength of the hosts of the Amorites.[698]

Not alone Sihon and Og, the kings of the Amorites, were such giants and heroes, but all the Amorites. When Hadrian conquered Jerusalem, he boasted of his victory, whereupon Rabban Johanan, the son of Zakkai, said to him: " Boast not of thy victory over Jerusalem, for, had not God conquered it for thee, thou shouldst never have gained it.' He thereupon led Hadrian to a cave where he showed him the corpses of the Amorites, each of which was eighteen cubits, and said: " When we were worthy of victory, these fell into our hands, but now, on account of our sins, dost thou rule over us." [699]

The victory over Sihon and his hosts was as great as that over Pharaoh and his hosts, and so was the victory over Og and his hosts. Each of these victories was as important as that over the thirty-one kings that Joshua later captured, and it would well have behooved Israel to sing songs of praise to their Lord as after Pharaoh's destruction. David later made good this omission, for he intoned a song of praise in gratitude for the victory God had lent to Israel over Sihon and Og.[700]

Without direct assistance from God these victories would not have been possible, but He sent hornets upon them, and their destruction was irrevocable. Two hornets pursued every Amorite; one bit one eye, the second the other eye, and the poison of these little creatures consumed those bitten by them.[701] These hornets remained on the east side of the Jordan, and did not pursue Israel's march to the regions west of the Jordan, nevertheless they wrought great havoc among the Canaanites of the region west of the Jordan. The hornets stood on the eastern bank of the Jordan, and spat their venom across to the opposite bank, so that the Canaanites that were hit became blind and were disarmed.[702]

When God promised Moses to send an angel to Israel, he declined the offer with the words: " If Thy presence go not with me, carry us not up hence," whereupon God replied: " Thou complainest because I desire to send only an angel to assist thee to conquer the land. As truly as thou livest, I shall now send thee not even an angel, but a hornet to destroy the enemies of Israel. It is, however, for thy sake alone that I deliver the enemy into Israel's hands, and not as if Israel deserved it through their own good deeds." [703]

Og's bed, fashioned out of ivory, that measured nine arms'
length, taking the giant's arm as a standard,[704] Og had preserved in the Ammonite city Rabbah, for he knew that Israel
would penetrate neither to the iand of the Ammonites nor of
the Moabites, because God had prohibited them from coming
too close to Lot's descendants.[705] He likewise forbade them
to wage war with the Edomites; in this way Esau, a son
kind to his father Isaac, was rewarded by not having his descendants, the Edomites, molested by Israel. God said to
Israel: " In this world ye shall have no sway over the
mountain Seïr, Edom's realm, but in the future world, when
ye shall be released, then shall ye obtain possession of it.
Until then, however, beware of the sons of Esau, even when
they fear ye, much more so when ye shall dwell scattered
among them." [706]

Moses' Speech of Admonition

As Abraham before his death spoke to his son Isaac, he to
his son Jacob, and Jacob in turn to his sons, words admonishing them to walk in the ways of the Lord, so Moses also
did not depart from this world without previously calling
Israel to account for their sins, and admonishing them to
observe the commandments of the Lord. Moses' speech of
admonition had a greater effect than the revelation of the
Decalogue upon Mount Sinai, for whereas Israel, shortly
after they had said on Sinai, " We shall do according as we
have heard," transgressed by worshipping the Golden Calf,
Moses' words of admonition had left a powerful impression
upon them, and he restored them to God and the Torah.
God therefore said, " As a reward to thee because thy words

of exhortation have brought Israel to follow Me, I shall designate these words as thine, even though thou didst speak them only in execution of My command."

Moses did not, however, make his speech of exhortation to the people until after the victory of Sihon and Og, for Moses thought: "Were I to have called them to account before these victories, they would have answered, ' He is trying to recall to us our sins because he is unable to lead us into the promised land against Sihon and Og, and he is seeking our sins as an excuse.' " But after Moses had proven what he could do, he could safely venture to recall to the people their sins.[707] He now assembled all classes of Israel, the nobles as well as the common people, saying to them: "I will now give you a severe rebuke for your sins, and if any one have something to offer as an excuse, let him now advance it." In this way he shut off the possibility of their saying later on, " Had we heard the words of the son of Amram, we should have answered each word fourfold and fivefold."

Moses now recounted the ten temptations with which they tempted God: how at the Red Sea they had repented having followed Him, and had even turned back three stations on the way to Egypt; how even after the miracle that clove the Red Sea for them, they had so little faith in God as to say, " Just as at this spot we passed unharmed through the Red Sea, so also did the Egyptians in another part of it." At Marah and at Rephidim they tried God on account of the dearth of water, and as they twice rebelled against God on account of water, so also did they on account of manna. They infringed upon the two laws God had given them in regard to manna, storing it from one day to the

next, and going to gather it on the Sabbath, although God
had strictly forbidden both. On account of their lust for
flesh also they twice transgressed, murmuring for flesh at
the same time as they received manna, although manna completely satisfied their needs; and after God had granted their
wish and had sent them quails, they remained content for a
short time only, and then again demanded quails, until God
granted them that wish also. "But the worst of all," Moses
told them, "was the worship of the Golden Calf. And not
only that, but again in Paran, misled by the spies, ye transgressed in desiring to make an idol, and under its guidance
to return to Egypt."

Moses then pointed out to them that it was owing to their
sin that they had strayed about in the desert for forty years,
for otherwise God would have brought them to Palestine on
the same day as He had led them out of Egypt. He not only
reproached Israel with the sins they had committed against
God, but also with the evil they had worked Moses himself,
mentioning how they had thrown their infants into his lap,
saying, "What food hast thou for these?" [708] On this occasion it was evident how good and pious a nation was that before Moses, for all the sins he enumerated to them had been
committed not by them, but by their fathers, all of whom had
in the meantime died, yet they were silent, and made no
answer to this severe reprimand their leader gave them.[709]
Moses did not, however, merely admonish the people to walk
in the ways of the Lord, but he said to Israel: "I am near
to death. Whosoever hath learned from me a verse, a
chapter, or a law, let him now come to me and learn it anew,"
whereupon he repeated all the Torah,[710] and that, too, in the

seventy languages of the world, that not Israel alone but all the heathen peoples, too, might hear the teachings of God."[111]

BALAK, KING OF MOAB

" God allows nothing to stay unrewarded, not even a respectable word remains without its reward." The older of Lot's two daughters had called her son that was conceived in guilt, Moab, " by the father," whereas the younger, for the sake of decency, called her son Ammon, " son of my people," and she was rewarded for her sense of propriety. For when Moses wanted to overrun the descendants of Lot with war, God said to him : " My plans differ from thine. Two doves shall spring from this nation, the Moabite Ruth and the Ammonite Naomi, and for this reason must these two nations be spared."

The treatment God bade Israel accord to these two nations was not, however, uniform. In regard to Moab, God said, " Vex not Moab, neither contend with them in battle," which portended that Israel was not to wage war against the Moabites, but that they might rob them or reduce them to servitude. In regard to the sons of Ammon, on the other hand, God forbade Israel to show these descendants of Lot's younger daughter even the slightest sign of hostility, or in any way to alarm them, so that Israel did not even show themselves in battle array to the Ammonites."[112]

Israel's hostile, though not warlike, attitude toward Moab inspired these people and their kings with great fear, so much so that they seemed to be strangers in their own land, fearing as they did that they should have to fare like the Egyptians ; for the Israelites had come to Egypt as strangers, but had in time possessed themselves of the land so that the Egyptians had to rent their dwelling-places from them. Their fear was still further increased by their belief that Israel would pay no attention to God's command to them not to wage war against Lot's descendants. This assumption of theirs was based on the fact that Israel had taken possession of the kingdoms of Sihon and Og, even though these had originally been part of Ammon's and Moab's possessions.[118] Heshbon, Sihon's capital city, had formerly belonged to Moab; but the Amorites, thanks to Balaam and his father Beor's support, had taken from Moab these and some other regions. The Amorites had hired these two sorcerers to curse Moab, with the result that the Moabites were miserably defeated in the war against Sihon. "Woe to thee, Moab! Thou art undone, O people of Chemosh!" These and similar utterances were the ominous words that Balaam and his father employed against Moab.[114] Chemosh was a black stone in the form of a woman, that the Moabites worshipped as their god.[115]

As a part of Moab passed into Sihon's possession so did a part of Ammon fall into Og's hands, and because Israel had appropriated these lands, the Moabites feared they would filch from them all their land. In great alarm they therefore gathered together in their fastnesses, in which they knew themselves to be safe from Israel's attacks.[116] Their fear was in reality quite without foundation, for Israel never dreamed of transgressing God's command by waging war upon Lot's descendants. They might without compunction keep the former provinces of Moab and Ammon because they took them not from these, but from Sihon and Og, who had captured them.[117]

At this time the king of Moab was Balak, who was formerly a vassal of Sihon, and in that capacity was known as Zur. After Sihon's death he was chosen king, though he was not worthy of a rank so high. Favored by fortune, he received royal dignity, a position that his father had never filled.⁷¹⁸ Balak was a fitting name for this king, for he set about destroying the people of Israel, wherefore he was also called the son of Zippor, because he flew as swiftly as a bird to curse Israel.⁷¹⁹ Balak was a great magician, who employed for his sorcery the following instrument. He constructed a bird with its feet, trunk, and head of gold, its mouth of silver, and its wings of bronze, and for a tongue he supplied it with the tongue of the bird Yadu'a. This bird was now placed by a window where the sun shone by day and the moon by night, and there it remained for seven days, throughout which burnt offerings were offered before it, and ceremonies performed. At the end of this week, the bird's tongue would begin to move, and if pricked by a golden needle, would divulge great secrets. It was this bird that had imparted to Balak all his occult lore. One day, however, a flame that suddenly leaped up burned the wings of this bird, which greatly alarmed Balak, for he thought that Israel's proximity had destroyed his instrument of sorcery.⁷²⁰

The Moabites now perceiving that Israel conquered their enemies by supernatural means said, " Their leader had been bred in Midian, let us therefore inquire of the Midianites about his characteristics." When the elders of Midian were consulted, they replied, " His strength abides in his mouth." " Then," said the Moabites, " we shall oppose to him a man whose strength lies in his mouth as well,"

and they determined to call upon Balaam's support. The
union of Moab and Midian establishes the truth of the proverb: "Weasel and Cat had a feast of rejoicing over the
flesh of the unfortunate Dog." For there had always been
irreconcilable enmity between Moab and Midian, but they
united to bring ruin upon Israel, just as Weasel and Cat had
united to put an end to their common enemy Dog.[721]

BALAAM, THE HEATHEN PROPHET

The man whom the Moabites and Midianites believed to
be Moses' peer was none other than Laban, Israel's arch-
enemy, who in olden days had wanted to root out entirely
Jacob and all his family,[722] and who had later on incited
Pharaoh and Amalek against the people of Israel to bring
about their destruction.[723] Hence, too, the name Balaam,
"Devourer of Nations," for he was determined to devour the
nation of Israel.[724] Just at this time Balaam was at the
zenith of his power, for his curse had brought upon the
Moabites their defeat at the hands of Sihon, and his prophecy that his compatriot Balak should wear the royal crown
had just been fulfilled, so that all the kings sent ambassadors
to seek advice from him. He had gradually developed from
an interpreter of dreams to a sorcerer, and had now attained
the still greater dignity of prophet, thus even surpassing his
father, who had indeed been a prophet too, but not so notable
a one as his son.[725]

God would permit the heathens to have no ground for
exculpation, for saying in the future world, "Thou hadst
kept us far from Thee." To them, as well as to Israel, he
gave kings, sages, and prophets; but whereas the former

showed themselves worthy of their high trust, the latter proved themselves unworthy of it. Both Solomon and Nebuchadnezzar were rulers over all the world: the former built the Temple and composed many hymns and prayers, the latter destroyed the Temple and cursed and blasphemed the Lord, saying, " I will ascend above the heights of the clouds; I will be like the Most High." Both David and Haman received great treasures from God, but the former employed them to secure a site for God's sanctuary, whereas the latter with his tried to destroy a whole nation. Moses was Israel's prophet, and Balaam was prophet of the heathens: but how great a contrast between these two! Moses exhorted his people to keep from sin, whereas Balaam counselled the nations to give up their moral course of life and to become addicted to lewdness. Balaam was also different from the Israelite prophets in his cruelty. They had such pity for the nations that misfortune among the heathens caused them suffering and sorrow, whereas Balaam was so cruel that he wanted to destroy an entire nation without any cause.

Balaam's course of life and his actions show convincingly why God withdrew from the heathens the gift of prophecy.[736] For Balaam was the last of the heathen prophets. Shem had been the first whom God had commissioned to communicate His words to the heathens. This was after the flood, when God said to Shem: ' Shem, had My Torah existed among the previous ten generations, I suppose I should not have destroyed the world by the flood. Go now, announce to the nations of the earth My revelations, ask them if they will not accept My Torah." Throughout four hundred years did

Shem go about as a prophet, but the nations of the earth did not heed him. The prophets that labored after him among the heathens were Job and his four friends, Eliphaz, Zophar, Bildad, and Elihu, as well as Balaam, all of whom were descendants of Nahor, Abraham's brother, from his union with Milcah. In order that the heathens might not say, "Had we had a prophet like Moses, we should have received the Torah," God gave them Balaam as a prophet, who in no way was inferior to Moses either in wisdom or in the gift of prophecy. Moses was indeed the greatest prophet among the Israelites, but Balaam was his peer among the heathens. But although Moses excelled the heathen prophet in that God called him without any previous preparation, whereas the other could obtain Divine revelations only through sacrifices, still Balaam had one advantage over the Israelite prophet. Moses had to pray to God "to shew him His ways," whereas Balaam was the man who could declare of himself that he "knew the knowledge of the Most High." But because, in spite of his high prophetic dignity, Balaam had never done anything good or kind, but through his evil tongue had almost destroyed all the world, God vowed a vow to His people that He would never exchange them for any other people or nation, and that He would never permit them to dwell in any land other than Palestine.[111]

BALAK'S MESSENGERS TO BALAAM.

Balak now sent messengers to Balaam with the following message: "Think not that I ask thy help against Israel exclusively in my own interests, and that thou canst expect from me alone honor and rewards for thy service, but rest assured that all nations will then honor thee, that Canaanites as well as Egyptians will cast themselves at thy feet when thou shalt have destroyed Israel. This people that hath gone out of Egypt hath covered with earth Sihon and Og, the eyes that guarded the whole land, and now they are about to destroy us as well. They are not, indeed, greater heroes than we, nor are their hosts more numerous than ours, but they conquer as soon as they open their lips in prayer, and that we cannot do. Try now to see if I may not gradually become their master, so that I may at least lead a certain per cent of them to destruction, be it only a twenty-fourth part of them."

Balak himself was even a greater magician and soothsayer than Balaam, but he lacked the gift of properly grasping prophetic observations. He knew through his sorcery that he was to be the cause of the death of twenty-four thousand Israelites, but he did not know in what way Israel was to suffer so great a loss, hence he requested Balaam to curse Israel, hoping by this curse to be able to restrain Israel from entering the Holy Land.

Balak's messengers to Balaam consisted of the elders of Moab and Midian. The latter were themselves great magicians, and by their art established the truth, that should Balaam obey Balak's summons, their mission against Israel would be successful, but should he hesitate even for a moment to follow them, nothing was to be expected from him. When they now reached Balaam and he bade them stay over night to await his answer, the elders of Midian instantly returned, for they knew that they had now nothing to expect from him.⁷⁸ They said: " Is there such a father as hates his son? God is the father of Israel, He loves them. Shall He now, owing to a curse from Balaam turn His love into hatred?" [729] Indeed, had the matter depended on Balaam's wishes, he would doubtless instantly have acquiesced and followed Balak's summons, for he hated Israel more than Balak, and was much pleased with the commission of the Moabite king. The elders that Balak had sent had besides in their possession all needful instruments of magic, so that Balaam might have no excuse for not instantly following them, but Balaam had, of course, to bide his time and first find out if God would permit him to go to Balak, hence he bade the Moabite messengers stay over night, because God never appears to heathen prophets save at night. As Balaam expected, God appeared by night and asked Balaam, "Who are these people with thee?"

Balaam was one of the three men whom God put to the test and who miserably failed to pass it. When God appeared to Cain and asked, "Where is Abel thy brother?" he tried to deceive God. He should have replied, "Lord of the world! What is hidden and what is open, both alike are known to Thee. Why then dost Thou inquire after my brother?" But instead of this he replied, "I know not. Am I my brother's keeper?" God therefore said to him: "Thou hast spoken thine own sentence. The voice of thy brother's blood crieth unto Me from the ground, and now cursed art thou." Hezekiah acted like Cain when the messengers from the king of Babylon came to him, and Isaiah the prophet asked him, "What said these men? And from whence came they unto thee?" Hezekiah should have answered, "Thou art a prophet of God, why dost thou ask me?" But instead of giving this answer, he replied haughtily and boastfully, "They are come from a far country unto me, even from Babylon." On account of this haughty answer Isaiah announced to the king this prophecy: " Behold, the days come, that all that is in thine house shall be carried to Babylon; and of thy sons that shall issue from thee, they shall be eunuchs in the palace of the king of Babylon."

The scoundrel Balaam, too, should have made answer to God's question, " What men are these with thee?" by saying, " Lord of the world! Everything lies open before Thee, and nothing is hidden from Thee, why then dost Thou ask me?" But he, on the other hand, made quite a different answer and started to boast, saying to God: " Although Thou dost not distinguish me, and dost not spread my fame over the world, still the kings seek me: Balak, the king of Moab, hath sent to ask me to curse Israel." Then God said, " Because thou speakest thus, thou shalt not curse the people," and added, " O thou wicked rascal! I said of Israel, He that toucheth them, toucheth the apple of My eye,' and yet thou wishest to touch them and curse them! Therefore shall thine eye be blinded." [730] Thus Balaam became blind of one eye, as he had already been lame of one foot.[731] Balaam now perceiving that God did not wish him to curse Israel said, " If it be so, then I shall bless them." God: " They have no need of thy blessing, for they are blessed." God said to Balaam as one says to a bee: " Neither thy honey nor thy sting."

Balaam Accepts Balak's Invitation

On the following morning Balaam gave the elders of Moab his answer, saying that he would not follow Balak's call, but not betraying to them the truth, that God hath forbidden him to curse Israel. He said instead, " God said to me, ' Go not with these men, for that would be beneath thy dignity, but await nobler ambassadors.' " [732] Balaam's plan was to insult Balak, so that he should send no further messengers to him, and no one might discover that he could accomplish nothing beyond the word of God. His expectations, however, were disappointed. The ambassadors in their turn, not quite painstaking in their representation of the truth, told their king that Balaam considered it beneath his dignity to appear in their escort, making no mention of God, but speaking as if the refusal came simply and exclusively from Balaam.[733]

Balak thereupon sent more honorable ambassadors to Balaam, until he was at last obliged to admit that he could undertake nothing against God's command. Even then, it is true, he did not admit that his acceptance or his refusal of Balak's invitation depended entirely upon God, but declared that he could, if he wished, do as he chose, but did not choose to transgress God's prohibition. In his second embassy Balak promised Balaam more for his service than he had offered him the first time. Balaam's answer was as follows: " If Balak would give me his house full of silver and gold, I cannot go beyond the word of the Lord my God." These words characterize the man, who had three bad qualities: a jealous eye, a haughty spirit, and a greedy soul. His jealousy was the reason why he wanted to curse Israel, whom he envied for their good fortune; in his haughtiness, he told the first messengers the falsehood that God would not let him go with them because it would be beneath his dignity; and his avarice was expressed in his answer to the second embassy in which he not only surreptitiously mentioned Balak's gold and silver, but spoke his mind by explaining to them that their master could not adequately compensate him for his service, saying, "If Balak were to hire hosts against Israel, his success would still be doubtful, whereas he should be certain of success if he hired me!"

He did not, however, give even the second embassy a decisive answer, but said to them also, "I cannot go beyond the word of the Lord my God, to do less or more. Now therefore I pray you, tarry ye also here this night, that I may know what the Lord will speak unto me more." These words of his held unconscious prophecies: "I cannot go beyond the word of the Lord," was as much as to say that he could not put the blessings of God to Israel to naught. "Tarry ye also here this night," contained the prophecy that this second embassy would be as much disappointed as the first, for although Balaam accompanied the second messengers, still he had no power to curse Israel, but only to bless them. Finally, the words, "What the Lord will speak unto me more," held a prediction that God would bestow even more benedictions upon the Israelites through him.

"God permits man to go upon the way he chooses to go." When God appeared to Balaam the first time he said to him, "Thou shalt not go with them;" but when Balaam still did not relinquish his desire to go to Balak, God would not interfere. Hence, at His second appearance, God said to

Balaam, " If the men be come to call thee, rise up, go with them; but only the word which I speak unto thee, that shalt thou do." [784]

" Audacity prevails even before God." Balaam's steadfast insistence upon his wish wrested from God His consent to Balaam's journey to Moab.[785] He warned him of its consequences, saying to him: " I take no pleasure in the destruction of sinners, but if thou art bound to go to thy destruction, do so! Whosoever leads righteous men astray upon an evil way, will fall into the ditch of his own digging! " Balaam was misled by God's behavior toward him, and thus plunged into destruction. When God first appeared to him and asked him, " What men are these with thee? " this blasphemer thought: " God knows them not. It seems clear that there are times when He is not aware of what goes on, and I shall now be able to do with His children as I wish." Balaam was misled by God because he had with his words seduced to unchastity people who had up to his time lived in purity.[786] God's apparent change of decision, that first prohibited him from going to Balak, and then permitted him to do so, completely bewildered him, so that he thought, " God at first said to me, ' Go thou not with them,' but the second time He said, ' Go with them.' So too will He change His words, ' Curse them not,' into ' Curse them.' " Just as Balaam was confused by God, so too were the magicians that Balak had sent to him. At the first visit these had through their magic lore established that he would accept Balak's invitation, but God made him decline it; at the second time, on the other hand, they established that he would not accept the invitation, and God made him obey their summons.[787]

Balaam's Ass

Balaam could hardly await the morning, rejoicing no less than Balak's messengers at God's consent to his journey to Balak, and still hoping that he might succeed in bringing disaster upon Israel. In his haste to set out, he himself saddled his ass although he did not lack servants, whereupon God said: " O thou villain, their ancestor Abraham forestalled thee, for he too rose up early in the morning and in person saddled his ass to lead Isaac to sacrifice in fulfilment of the command that had reached him." [738]

The ass that Balaam took with him had been created on the sixth day of the creation. He had received it as a gift from Jacob, that he might not give evil counsel to Pharaoh concerning Jacob's children. It was upon his advice, nevertheless, that Pharaoh forced the Israelites to make bricks.[739] He took his two sons, Jannes and Jambres,[740] for it behooves a noble man always to have at least two companions upon any journey that he undertakes.[741]

Although God had now granted him permission to go on the journey, still His wrath was kindled when he set out. God said, " Behold, this man! He knows that I read each man's heart, and knows also that he departeth only to curse Israel." [742] This wickedness on his part had the result that even the Angel of Mercy turned against him as an enemy, standing in his way. At first the ass alone perceived the angel, and not Balaam, for God has so arranged it that human beings may not perceive the angels that surround them or else they would through terror lose their reason.[743] The ass, on the other hand, instantly perceived the angel. He at first stood in her way as she was in the middle of the road, so that she could turn aside on both sides; then she perceived him when the road narrowed, and she could turn to one side only; and finally she reached a spot where there was no road at all to which she could turn either on this side or on that. This was to teach Balaam the following lesson: if he wished to curse Abraham's children, he should have leeway on both sides, Ishmael's children and Keturah's children; if he wanted to curse Isaac's children, one side would still be open to him, Esau's children; but if he wanted to curse Jacob's children, he should never bring it to pass, for they are protected on both sides, on the one hand by Abraham and Isaac, on the other by Jacob and Levi, while God watches over them from above. " The wall on this side, and on that side," through which place he had to pass, were furthermore to indicate to him that he could not become master over Israel, who have in their possession the tables of the law, " that were written on both their sides." When the ass reached the wall that Jacob and Laban had erected as a token that they " would never pass over it for harm," she thrust her feet against it, to punish him for having broken his agreement with Jacob.⁴⁴

Balaam, who had with blows attempted to make the ass walk straight ahead, flew into a rage when she lay down altogether and would not budge from the spot, so that he smote her all the more. Then the Lord opened the mouth of the ass, and permitted her to use speech, a gift that she had possessed ever since her creation, but had not until then used.⁴⁵ She said, " What have I done unto thee, that thou hast smitten me these three times? " The first words of the ass were so chosen as to call Balaam's attention to the wick-

edness and uselessness of his undertaking against Israel;
" Three times " was to remind him that he wished to curse a
nation that " three times " in every year arranged pil-
grimages to the Lord. The ass's speech was altogether to
serve as a warning to Balaam to beware of his mouth, and
not to curse Israel. The ass, through her speaking, was to
instruct him that the mouth and the tongue are in God's
hand.

Balaam answered the ass in the language in which she
had addressed him, in Hebrew, which he did not, however, speak fluently. He said, " Because thou hast mocked
me: I would there were a sword in mine hand, for now I
had killed thee." The ass thereupon replied, " Thou canst
not kill me save with a sword in thy hand; how then wilt
thou destroy an entire nation with thy mouth! " Balaam
was silent, knowing no reply.[746] The ass did not only make
him ridiculous in the eyes of the elders of Moab that accompanied him, but she also exposed him as a liar. For when
the ambassadors asked him why he had not chosen a horse
rather than an ass for his journey, he answered that his saddle horse was in the pasture. Then the ass interrupted him,
saying, " Am not I thine ass upon which thou hast ridden all
thy life long? " Balaam: " I use thee as a beast of burden,
but not for the saddle." The ass: " Nay, upon me hast thou
ridden since thine earliest days, and thou hast always treated
me with as much affection as a man treats his wife." Balaam
had now to admit that the ass had spoken the truth.[747]

Balak's princes were much amazed at this extraordinary
miracle, but the ass died the moment she had spoken what
she had to say. God did this for two reasons, firstly because

He feared that the heathens might worship this ass were she to stay alive; and secondly because God wanted to spare Balaam the disgrace of having people point to his ass and say, " This is she that worsted Balaam." By this action it can be seen how highly God prizes the honor of pious men, if He even sought to spare the honor of this villain. It is out of consideration to mankind, also, that God has closed the mouth of animals, for were they to speak, man could not well use them for his service, since the ass, the most stupid of all animals, when she spoke, confounded Balaam, the wisest of the wise.

Balaam Runs into His Own Destruction

While all this was going on, Balaam still did not perceive that God's angel stood before him. God meant to show him that in His hand is not only the tongue of man, but his eye as well, so that as long as He chooses, man will fail to see what is directly before his nose. But God suddenly permitted Balaam to see the angel with a sword drawn in his hand, and Balaam fell flat on his face.[748] For, being uncircumcised, Balaam might not listen to the words of God or of an angel, standing erect; hence, upon perceiving the angel, who instantly began to address him, Balaam cast himself upon the ground.[749] The sword in the angel's hand did not signify that he meant to strike Balaam, for a breath from his mouth would have sufficed to kill myriads, but it was to point out the following truth to Balaam: " The mouth was given to Jacob, but to Esau and to the other nations, the sword. Thou art about to change thy profession, and to go out against Israel with his own weapon, and therefore shalt thou find death through the sword that is thy own weapon." [750]

The angel now said to Balaam: "If I have been commissioned to demand restitution from thee for the injustice thou hast offered to the ass, that can show neither meritorious deeds of her own nor of her fathers, how much the more must I stand up as the avenger of an entire nation, that have their own merits and can refer to the merits of their fathers. But to return to the ass, why didst thou smite her, that turned from the road only because she saw me and was frightened?" Balaam was a shrewd sinner, for he knew that Divine punishment could be averted only by penitence, and that the angels have no power to touch a man who, after sinning, says, "I have sinned." Hence he said to the angel, "I have sinned," but added, "I did not set out until God said to me, ' Rise up, go with them; ' and now thou sayest to me, ' Return.' But this is the Lord's way. Did He not also at first tell Abraham to sacrifice his son, and then He caused an angel to call out to him, ' Lay not thine hand upon the lad? ' It is His custom first to give a command, and then through an angel to recall it. So also did He indeed say to me, ' Go with them; ' but if it displeaseth thee, I shall turn back." [751] The angel replied: "All that I have done was to thy advantage, but if thou art bound to plunge into destruction, do so, go with these people, but destruction is decreed for all of you. Think not, however, that thou shalt do as thou wilt, for thou shalt have to say what I desire thee to speak, and to restrain what I wish to remain unuttered."

In spite of the warnings he had received from God and the angel, he was not to be restrained from taking this fatal

step, but in his hatred toward Israel still cherished the hope
that he should succeed in obtaining God's consent to curse
Israel, and he continued his journey in this happy expectation.[752]

BALAAM WITH BALAK

Whensoever God wishes to humble an evil-doer, He at first
exalts him, to fill him with pride. So too He humbled
Balaam after exalting him, for at first Balak had sent princes
of little distinction to him, whereupon God said to him,
" Thou shalt not go with them." When, however, he sent
many renowned princes to him, God said to Balaam, " Go
with them," but this journey brought him nothing but
humiliation and ruin, for he fared in accordance with the
proverb, " Pride goeth before destruction, and an haughty
spirit before a fall." God does this so that men might not
say, " Whom hath God destroyed? Surely not that insignificant person," hence God exalts sinners before their fall.[753]

When Balaam approached the Moabite boundaries, he sent
messengers to Balak to announce his arrival, and Balak went
forth to his country's border to meet him. Pointing to the
boundary lines, Balak said to Balaam: " These have been
fixed since Noah's days, that no nation might push into the
realm of another, but Israel set out to destroy the boundaries, as their attitude toward Sihon and Og shows, into whose
kingdoms they entered." [754] He then greeted him with the
words: " Did I not twice send unto thee to call thee?
Wherefore camest not thou unto me? Am I not able indeed
to promote thee to honor?" Balak unconsciously uttered a
prophecy, for in truth Balaam went hence in disgrace and

dishonor, and not covered with glory, as he could not fulfil the other's wish to curse Israel.[755] It should now have been Balaam's duty, had he really desired to be of service to the king of Moab, to say to him, " Why dost thou attempt to do what will bring thee misfortune, and finally utter ruin? " But he spoke quite differently instead, boastfully bragging with his gift of prophecy, pointing out that he was the last prophet among the heathens. " And," continued he, " I, the last prophet among the heathens, shall thus counsel thee. The ancestor of that nation erected to God an altar upon which, thrice annually, he offered up seven oxen and seven rams; do thou, then, erect seven altars, and offer up on each seven oxen and seven rams." God laughed when he heard this counsel, saying: " Every beast of the forest is Mine, and the cattle upon a thousand hills. I know all the fowls of the mountains: and the wild beasts of the field are Mine. If I were hungry, I would not tell thee: for the world is Mine, and the fulness thereof. Will I eat the flesh of bulls, or drink the blood of goats? " [756]

Balak led his guest from the border-line to the interior of the land, taking pains to show him great multitudes of the people, having bazars erected for that purpose. Pointing to these multitudes, among which there were also many children, Balak said, " Look thou, how Israel plan to destroy these multitudes of people that have done them no injury."

Balak slew for Balaam's welcome one ox and one sheep, proving the proverb, " The pious promise little and do much, the wicked promise much and do little." Balak had sent word to Balaam, saying, " I will promote thee unto very great honor; " yet when he arrived, he offered him for food

only one ox and one sheep. Suppressing his rage, Balaam
thought, " Is that all that he offers me! He will have to pay
for this to-morrow," for he instantly determined to have him
offer up many sacrifices on the following day to punish him
for having treated him in so niggardly a fashion.

BALAAM'S SACRIFICES REFUSED

On the following morning Balak took Balaam and brought
him up into the high places of Baal. For Balak was even a
greater magician and soothsayer than Balaam, who allowed
himself like a blind man to be led by him. He led him to
this spot because through his magic lore he knew that Israel
was to suffer a great misfortune upon the heights of Baal-
peor, and he thought it was to be Balaam's curse that would
effect this disaster upon them. The relation of these two
men to each other was like that between two men, one of
whom has a knife in his hand, but does not know what part
of the body to strike for slaughter, and the other knows the
part of the body, but has no knife. Balak knew the place
where disaster awaited Israel, but did not know how it was
to be brought about, whereas Balaam knew how evil is conjured up, but did not know the places set for disaster, to
which Balak had to lead him.[757] Balaam's superiority over
Balak and the other magicians lay in this, that he could accurately determine the moment in which God is wrathful, and
it was for this reason that his curse was always effective because he knew how to curse at the very instant of God's
anger. It is true that God is angry for one instant every
day, to wit, during the third hour of the day, when the kings
with crowns upon their heads worship the sun, but this mo-

ment is of infinitesimally short duration. Fully eighty-five
thousand and eighty-eight such moments make one hour, so
that no mortal save Balaam had ever been able to fix that
moment, although this point of time has its outward mani-
festations in nature, for while it lasts, the cock's comb becomes absolutely white, without even the smallest stripe of
red. God's love for Israel, however, is so great that during
the time that Balaam prepared to curse Israel, He did not
wax angry at all, so that Balaam waited in vain for the moment of wrath.[758]

Balaam now tried to obtain God's consent for Israel's curse
through sacrifices, and hence bade Balak erect seven altars
upon the high places of Baal, corresponding to the seven
altars that since Adam had been erected by seven pious men,
to wit: Adam, Abel, Noah, Abraham, Isaac, Jacob, and
Moses. When the altars had been erected, he said to God:
"Why didst Thou favor these people, if not for the sacrifices that they offered Thee? Were it not better for Thee to
be adored by seventy nations than by one?" But the Holy
Spirit answered, "'Better is a dry morsel and quietness
therewith, than an house full of sacrifices and strife.'
Dearer to Me is a dry offering of meal than all these many
flesh offerings by which thou strivest to stir up strife between Me and Israel."

Now was Balaam's fate decided, for by his conduct he put
himself into direct opposition to God, and hence his destruction was decreed,[759] and from that moment the holy spirit of
prophecy left him and he was nothing more than a magician.
For Israel's sake, however, God granted him the honor of
His revelation, but He did so grudgingly, as one loathes to

touch an unclean thing. Hence He would not permit
Balaam to come to Him, but rather appeared to Balaam.
God's different treatment of Balaam and of Moses at the
revelation is evident, for whereas the latter betook himself
to the sanctuary to hear God's words, the former received
God's revelation at any place whatsoever. It characterizes
God's attitude toward them. Two men once knocked at a
magnate's door, the one being a friend, who had a request to
make, and the other a leprous beggar. The magnate said,
" Let my friend enter, but I shall send the beggar's alms to
the door, that he may not enter and pollute my palace."
God called Moses to Him, whereas He did not desire Balaam
to come to Him, but betook Himself there.[760]

He found Balaam at the seven altars that he had erected,
and said to him, " What doest thou here? " whereupon Balaam answered, " I have erected for Thee as many altars as
the three fathers of Israel, and I have offered upon them bullocks and rams." God, however, said to him: " ' Better is a
dinner of herbs where love is, than a stalled ox and hatred
therewith.' Pleasanter to Me is the meal of unleavened
bread and herbs that the Israelites took in Egypt, than the
bullocks that thou offerest out of enmity. O thou knave, if
I wished for offerings, I should order Michael and Gabriel
to bring them to Me, thou art mistaken if thou believest that
I should accept offerings from the nations of the world, for
I have vowed a vow to accept such from Israel alone." [761]
God thereupon handed him over to an angel who entered and
settled in his throat, and would not permit Balaam to speak
when he wanted to curse Israel.[762]

Balaam Extols Israel

Balaam now turned back to Balak, who awaited him with his princes. He now wanted to begin to curse Israel, but his mouth, far from being able to utter the words, was on the contrary compelled to praise and bless Israel.[763] He said: " I found myself upon the high places, in company with the Patriarchs, and thou, Balak, hast cast me down from the heights; through thee did I lose the gift of prophecy. Both of us are ungrateful men if we wish to undertake evil against Israel, for, had it not been for their father Abraham, for whose sake God saved Lot out of the ruin of the cities, there should now be no Balak, for thou art one of Lot's descendants. And had it not been for Jacob, I, Laban's descendant, should not now be on earth, for no sons were born unto Laban until after Jacob had come into his house.[764] Thou didst bring me out of Aram to curse Israel, but it was this land that their father Abraham left, laden with blessings, and it was this land also that their father Jacob entered, laden with blessings. Shall now a curse come upon them from this land?[765] How can I curse them if he that curseth them bringeth a curse upon himself? Thou, moreover, wishest me even to curse Jacob. Hadst thou urged me to curse a nation that were only the descendants of Abraham or of Isaac, I might have been able to do so; but to curse Jacob's descendants is as bad as if a man were to come to a king and say to him, ' The crown that thou wearest upon thy head is worthless.' Would such a man be permitted to live? ' The Lord's portion is His people; Jacob is the lot of His inheritance.' ' In Israel,' said the Lord, ' will I be glorified.' How now should I curse them? How shall I curse whom

God hath not cursed? Even when they have been worthy of a curse, they have not been cursed. When Jacob went in to receive the blessings, he went in through craft and said to his father, ' I am Esau, thy firstborn.' Doth not he deserve a curse out of whose mouth issueth a lie? Yet, far from being cursed, he was even blessed. Ordinarily a legion that stirs up sedition against their king is declared guilty of death, but Israel had denied God, saying, ' These be thy gods, O Israel.' Should they not then have been destroyed? God, however, did not even at that moment withdraw from them His love, but left to them the clouds of glory, manna, and the well, even after they had adored the Calf. Howsoever often they sinned and God threatened them with a curse, still He did not say that He would bring it upon them, whereas in His promises of blessings He always tells them that He Himself would send them upon Israel. How shall I curse when God doth not curse! [766]

" Israel is a nation of whom God thought even before the creation of the world. It is the rock upon which the world is founded. For, when God was considering the scheme of the creation, He thought, ' How can I create the world if the idolatrous generation of Enosh and the generation of the flood will arouse My anger?' He was about to desist from the creation of the world, when He saw before Him Abraham's form, and He said, ' Now I have a rock upon which I can build, one upon which I can found the world.' [767] How, too, should I curse this nation that are protected and surrounded by the merits of the Patriarchs and the wives of the Patriarchs as if by lofty mountains and steep hills, so that if Israel sin, God forgives them as soon as Moses prays to Him to be mindful of the Patriarchs! [768]

" I was in error when I believed Israel could be easily attacked, but now I know that they have taken deep root in the earth, and cannot be uprooted. God forgives them many sins out of consideration for their having preserved the token of the Abrahamic covenant; and as powerless as I am to curse them alone, just as powerless am I to curse them together with another nation, for ' it is a people that shall dwell alone, and shall not be reckoned among the nations.' Israel is distinguished from all other nations by their costume, by their food, by the token of the covenant upon their bodies, and by the token upon their doorposts, wherefore God doth not judge them at the same time with other nations, for He judges the latter in the darkness of the night, but the former in bright daylight. Israel is a separate people, alone they enjoy the blessings God gives them, no other nation rejoices with Israel. So too in the Messianic time Israel will quite alone rejoice in delights and pleasures, whereas in the present world it may also partake of the universal welfare of the nations.[769]

" I am not able to accomplish anything against a nation that zealously fulfils God's commandments, and that owes its existence to the devotion with which the wives of the Patriarchs obeyed the commandments of God."[770] ' Let me die the death of the righteous, and let my last end be like his! ' " Balaam in these words spoke an unconscious prophecy, to wit, that he should be entitled to participate in the fate of the righteous, to his share in the future world, if he died the death of the righteous, a natural death, but not otherwise. He died, however, a violent death, and thus lost his share in the future world.[771]

BALAAM'S HOPES DISAPPOINTED

When Balak saw that Balaam, instead of cursing, praised and exalted Israel, he led him to the top of Pisgah, hoping that he might there succeed in cursing Israel. By means of his sorcery, Balak had discovered that Pisgah was to be a place of misfortune for Israel, hence he thought that Balaam would there utter his curse against Israel. He was, however, mistaken; the disaster that there awaited Israel was the death of their leader Moses, who died there, and God refused to grant Balaam's wish on this spot also.

God indeed appeared to Balaam, but what He said to him was: " Go again unto Balak, and bless Israel." Balaam now did not wish to return to Balak at all, to disappoint him a second time, but God compelled him to return to Balak and communicate to him the blessings of Israel. Balaam now turned back to Balak, whom he found standing by his burnt offering. But whereas on the first occasion the king had awaited Balaam, surrounded by all his princes, Balaam now saw only a few notables surrounding Balak. Most of the princes had deserted their king without awaiting Balaam, for they expected nothing further from him after the first disappointment he had caused them. Balak as well did not now receive him as kindly, but mockingly asked, " What hath the Lord spoken? " hinting in this way that Balaam was unable to say what he wished, but only what God willed.

Balaam replied to these scornful words of Balak: " Rise up, Balak. Thou mayest not be seated when God's words are spoken. God is not like a man of flesh and blood, that makes friends and disowns them, as soon as he finds such as are better than they. God is not so, for He doth not cancel the vow He had made to the Patriarchs, for He promised to bestow Canaan upon their descendants, and He fulfilleth His promise. He always fulfils what He hath promised to Israel, but allows the evil with which He threatens them to be unfulfilled as soon as they repent them of their sins. God sees not their sins, but He seeth their good deeds. Thou, Balak, sayest to me, ' Come, curse Jacob for me,' but a thief can enter a vineyard that hath a keeper only if the keeper sleeps, but ' He that keepeth Israel neither sleepeth nor slumbereth,' and how then can I enter their vineyard? If, however, thou dost think that I cannot harm Israel on account of Moses, who is their keeper, know then that his successor will be as invincible as he, for through the sound of trumpets he will overthrow the walls of Jericho.

" Thou, Balak, furthermore sayest, ' A people hath gone forth out of Egypt,' but they have not only gone forth, ' God brought them forth out of Egypt,'[772] who combines in Himself the powers of the angels and of the invisible demons.[773] Swift as the flight of a bird doth fortune as well as misfortune come upon Israel; if they sin, God suddenly plunges them down, but if they act well in the sight of the Lord, God exalts them as quickly as a cloud. Thou, Balak, hast repeatedly tried to discover in what spot thou shouldst be able to work them woe, but they will have nothing to do with sorceries, they baffle and put to naught the sorceries and prophecies of other nations by their pious deeds. When they set forth into battle, they practice no magic, but the high priest, clad in the Urim and Tummim, consults God about the outcome of the battle. There will even be a time when Israel will sit before the Lord like a pupil before his master, and will receive the revelation of the secrets of the Torah from Him, so that even the angels will consult Israel concerning the secrets revealed to them by God, for the angels are not permitted to approach God as closely as the Israelites in the Messianic time.

"There is not indeed upon the earth a nation like Israel. The last thing they do before going to sleep is to devote themselves to the study of the Torah and the fulfilment of its laws, and this also is their first occupation upon awakening. As soon as they arise, they recite the Shema' and adore God, and not until after they have done this, do they go about their business. If evil spirits come to attack them, or if disaster threatens them, they worship their God, and as soon as they utter the words, 'The Lord our God is one Lord,' the harmful spirits become powerless against them and whisper after them the words, 'Praised be the Name of the Glory of His Kingdom, for ever and ever.' When at night they retire, they again recite the Shema', whereupon the angels of the day pass on the trust of guarding them to the angels of the night, and when, upon awakening, they again worship their Lord, the angels of the night again pass them on to be guarded by the angels of the day." [114]

When Balak for the second time saw that Balaam, instead of cursing, blessed Israel, he brought him to the top of Peor, thinking that peradventure it would please God to have him curse them from thence. For by his sorcery Balak had discovered that a great disaster was to fall upon Israel on the top of Peor, and thought that this disaster might be their curse from Balaam. He was, however, mistaken in this supposition, for the disaster in that spot was none other than

Israel's sin with the daughters of Moab, and God's punishment for this.[775]

CURSES TURNED TO BLESSINGS

Balaam, on the other hand, made no further attempts to induce God to curse Israel, but thought he might be able to bring misfortune upon Israel by enumerating the sins they had committed in the desert, and in this way to conjure up God's wrath against them. But the desert had also been the place where Israel had accepted the Torah, hence the mention of the desert called up God's love instead of His wrath.[776] Balaam himself, when he let his eyes wander over the camp of Israel, and perceived how their tents were so pitched that no one might see what was going on in the homes of the others, found himself compelled to burst into praises of Israel;[777] and, under the inspiration of the prophetic spirit, the curses he had intended to speak were changed in his mouth into blessings, and he spoke of the extent and importance of the kingdom of Israel.[778] But whereas Moses blessed his people in a low, quiet voice, Balaam spoke his words of blessing in a very loud voice, so that all the other nations might hear and out of envy make war upon Israel. Balaam's blessings were therefore accounted to him not as blessings, but as curses. God said: " I have promised Abraham, ' And I will bless them that bless thee, and him that curseth thee will I curse,' hence will I account Balaam's blessings as curses." [779] And indeed all of Balaam's blessings later turned to curses, except his blessing that houses of teaching and of prayer should never be missing among Israel.[780]

The words that Balaam announced were heard by all the inhabitants of the earth, such power did God lend to his voice, for He knew that at some future time there would be a man born of woman who would pass himself for a god and would mislead all the world. Hence God permitted all the world to hear Balaam's words, that said: " God is not a man, and the man that passeth himself for God lieth. But he that will mislead the world by declaring that he will disappear for a time and then reappear will promise what he can never fulfil. Woe then to that nation that will lend ear to the man who will pass himself for God." [781] Balaam furthermore announced the events that would come to pass at the time of David's sovereignty; and also what will happen at the end of days, in the time of the Messiah, when Rome and all other nations will be destroyed by Israel, excepting only the descendants of Jethro, who will participate in Israel's joys and sorrows.[782] Yea, the Kenites are to be the ones to announce to Israel the arrival of the Messiah, and the sons of the Kenite Jonadab are to be the first at the time of the Messiah to bring offerings at the Temple and to announce to Jerusalem its deliverance.[783] This was Balaam's last prophecy. After this, the prophetic spirit left Balaam, and God in this way granted Moses' wish to reserve the gift of prophecy as a special distinction to Israel. Balaam was the last prophet of the nations.[784]

BALAAM'S WICKED COUNSEL

Although Balaam had not been able to fulfil Balak's wish and curse Israel, still he did not leave him before giving him advice as to how he might bring ruin to Israel, saying:

" The God of this people loathes unchastity; but they are very eager to possess linen garments. Pitch tents, then, and at their entrances have old women offer these articles for sale. Induce them in this way to enter the interior of the tents where they will be surprised by young harlots, who will seduce them to unchastity, so that God may punish them for their sin." [185]

" Throw the stick up in the air it will always return to its original place." The Moabite nation that owes its existence to the illegal relations of Lot with his daughter could not deny its origin, and followed Balaam's counsel to tempt Israel to unchastity. They pitched tents, filled them with pretty women, whom they provided with valuable things, and had old women take up their posts at the doors of the tents, whose task it was to lure the passing Israelites into the interior. If an Israelite passed to buy something of the Moabites, the old women at the entrance to the tent would thus address him, " Dost thou not wish to buy linen garments that were made in Bet-Shan? " Then they would show him a sample of the goods, and name the price, and finally add, " Go within, and thou wilt see wares still more beautiful." If he went within, he was received by a young woman who was richly adorned and perfumed, who would at first set for him a price much lower than the value of the goods, and then invite him to do as if he were at home, and to choose the article he liked best. While he sat there, he was treated with wine, and the young woman invited him to drink with the words: " Why do we love ye while you hate us? Are we not all descendants of one man? Was not Terah our ancestor as much as yours? If thou wilt not eat of our sacrifices or what we have cooked, here are calves and fowl that thou mayest slaughter in accordance with thy law." But as soon as the Israelite had allowed himself to be persuaded to drink, he was absolutely in the hands of the shameless woman. Intoxicated with wine, his passion for the woman was soon kindled, but she agreed to satisfy his desires only after he had first worshipped Peor, the god of the Moabites. Now the worship of this idol consisted in nothing else than the complete baring of the body, hence the Israelites, seeing no evil in it, declared themselves willing to follow the summons of the Moabite women; and in this way they were seduced both to unchastity and to idolatry by the Moabite women. At first the men were ashamed and committed this whoredom with the Moabite women in secret, but they soon lost this feeling of shame and betook themselves two by two to their lewd actions.[786]

Israel's moral degeneration is to be partly explained by this, that the place where they found themselves was apt to tempt them to lewdness. For there are springs whose waters have various effects upon those who partake of them. One kind of water strengthens, another weakens; one makes beautiful, another makes ugly; one makes chaste, another brings about lewdness. Now there was in Shittim, where the Israelites then dwelt, the "Well of Lewdness," out of which the inhabitants of Sodom had erstwhile fetched water, but from which, since the destruction of the sinful cities, no one had drunk, and for this reason the people had until then been chaste. But Israel, as soon as they tasted of this water, gave up their chaste manner of life. This disastrous spring will lose its force only in the Messianic time when God will cause it to dry up.[787]

Phinehas, Zealous for God

When the people's shamelessness became more and more widespread, God commanded Moses to appoint judges to punish the sinners, and as it was difficult to discover these through the agency of witnesses, God marked them by causing the cloud of glory that lay spread over the camp of Israel to disappear from the sinners. Those that were not covered by the cloud of glory were thus clearly marked as sinners.[788] God appointed as judges and executioners the seven myriads eight thousand six hundred officers of the people, giving them the order that each of them execute two sinners.[789] These carried out Moses' command and stoned the sinners, whose corpses then hung upon the gallows for a few minutes. This was the legal punishment, for these sinners had not only committed whoredom with the women of Moab, but had worshipped the Moabite idol Peor; and idolatry is punishable with death by stoning.[790]

While the judges administered their stern offices, the tribe of Simeon approached their prince, Zimri, and said to him, " People are being executed, and thou sittest still as if nothing were going on." He thereupon took with him twenty-four thousand men, and betook himself to Cozbi, Balak's daughter, and without considering God or men, he requested her in the presence of many people to yield herself to him, to satisfy his evil desires. Now Balak had ordered his daughter Cozbi to employ her beauty only for the sake of enticing Moses, thinking, " Whatever evil may be decreed by God against Israel, Moses will be brought to naught, but if my daughter should succeed in seducing him to sin, then all Israel will be in my hand." Hence Cozbi said to Zimri:

" My father ordered me to be obedient to the wishes of
Moses alone, and to none other; for he is a king, and so is
my father, and a king's daughter is fit for none but a king."
Zimri, however, replied: " I am a greater man than Moses,
for he is chief only of the third tribe in Israel, whereas I am
prince of the tribe of Simeon, the second of the Israelite
tribes, and if thou wilt, I will convince thee that I am a
greater man than Moses, for I will take thee to myself in his
presence, without paying attention to his prohibition."

Zimri then seized Cozbi by the locks of her hair, and
brought her before Moses, whom he then addressed as follows: " Tell me, son of Amram, is this woman permitted
me, or is she forbidden me? " Moses said, " She is forbidden to thee." Zimri answered: "Art thou really the faithful
expounder of the Torah, whose reliability God praised with
the words, ' He is faithful in all Mine house?' How then
canst thou assert that she is forbidden to me, for then thy
wife would be forbidden to thee, for she is a Midianite like
this woman, and this one is a noble woman of a noble family,
whereas thy wife is the daughter of an idolatrous priest."
At these words, Moses, Eleazar, and the elders began to weep,
for they knew not how to make answer to Zimri's insolent
words, nor what they could do to restrain this sinner from
the accomplishment of his sin. God said to Moses: " Where
is thy wisdom? Thou didst need to utter only one word, and
Korah and all his company were swallowed by the earth.
Canst thou now do nothing better than to weep? " The
Holy Spirit exclaimed at Moses' perplexity and silence,
" The stouthearted are spoiled, they have slept their sleep." [791]

God, who calls the pious to strict account, punished Moses

for the lack of decision that he displayed on this occasion, by leaving his burial-place unknown to mankind.[792] While Moses and other pious men were irresolute and deliberated whether or not Zimri deserved death, Phinehas said to Moses: " O my great-uncle, didst thou not teach me, when thou didst return from Mount Sinai, that it was the zealot's task for the sake of God's law to slay those who commit unchastity with non-Jewish women?" Phinehas took the liberty of pointing out the law to his teacher Moses who had forgotten it, because, " when God's name is profaned, no man should consider the respect due to a teacher," wherefore Phinehas thought now only of establishing God's law, and in doing this it was necessary to recall it to Moses' mind. Moses indeed did not take it at all amiss, but said to Phinehas, " Let the reader of the letter be its bearer also," words by which he called upon Phinehas himself to visit punishment upon the sinners.[793]

Phinehas was now for a time in doubt whether he should dare to punish the sinners, for it was to be expected that he would eventually meet his death in this way, being one against two, Zimri and his mistress Cozbi. When, however, the plague that God had sent upon Israel on account of their sins spread more and more rapidly, Phinehas determined to risk his life in trying to kill the sinners. " For," said he to himself, " the horse goes willingly into battle, and is ready to be slain only to be of service to its master. How much more does it behoove me to expose myself to death in order to sanctify God's name!"[794] He found himself all the more impelled to act thus because he could not well leave the punishment of the sinners to others.

He said: "The tribe of Reuben can effect nothing in this instance, because their grandsire Reuben was himself suspected of an unchaste action; nothing is to be expected from the tribe of Simeon, for it follows the sinful example of its prince Zimri; the tribe of Judah cannot well be of use in this matter, because their grandsire Judah committed unchastity with his daughter-in-law Tamar; Moses himself is doomed to impotence because his wife Zipporah is a Midianite woman. Hence there remains nothing but for me to interpose." [195]

TWELVE MIRACLES

Phinehas now, prepared at the risk of his own life to punish Zimri for his sin, left the house of teaching where he had until now debated the case of Zimri with Moses and all other pious men, and had himself provided with a lance, having none with him because no armed man may enter a house of teaching. That his weapon might not betray him, he detached the upper iron part of the lance and hid it in his bosom, and leaned upon the wooden shaft as if it were a staff.[796] When he reached the house where Zimri and Cozbi were giving extravagant play to their passions, the people said to him, "Whence, Phinehas, and whither?" He replied, "Do ye not know that the tribe of Levi is always to be found where the tribe of Simeon is?" Then they permitted him to enter the house, but said, "It seems that even the Pharisees now permit intercourse with the heathen women." When Phinehas had entered, he drew his lance, "and thrust both of them through, the man of Israel, and the woman through her belly." [797]

Phinehas's fear that these two might attack him was not realized, for God performed no less than twelve miracles for Phinehas, which not only made it impossible for the sinners to attack him, but also showed the people that his action found favor in the sight of the Lord. The first miracle was that an angel would not allow the sinful couple to separate when Phinehas surprised them; the second miracle was that the angel stopped their mouths so that they could not cry out for help; the third miracle was that Phinehas's lance struck the man's and the woman's pudenda; the fourth miracle was that the upper, iron part of the lance extended, so that Phinehas could at one thrust pierce the man as well as the woman; the fifth miracle was that Phinehas's arm was sufficiently strong to lift both upon the point of his lance; the sixth miracle was that the wooden shaft of the lance sustained the weight of two persons; the seventh miracle was that the two bodies remained poised upon the lance and did not fall off; the eighth miracle was that the angel turned the shameless pair around, so that all might see that Phinehas had surprised them *in flagranti;* the ninth miracle was that no blood flowed from them although they had been thrust through, or else Phinehas would have been polluted; the tenth miracle was that the shameless couple did not give up the ghost so long as Phinehas bore them upon the point of his lance, as he would otherwise have been polluted by their corpses; the eleventh miracle was that the angel raised the doorposts of the room so that Phinehas might pass through with the sinners upon the point of his lance, and the twelfth miracle was that when the tribe of Simeon prepared to avenge Prince Zimri's death upon Phinehas, the angel sent a plague upon them, so that they were impotent against him.[798]

Phinehas was not, however, content with having punished the sinners, but tried also to reconcile God with Israel. He threw the two dead bodies upon the ground, saying to God, " Why, alas! Hast Thou on account of the sins of these two slain twenty-four thousand Israelites! " For this was the number that had been snatched away by the plague that God had sent upon Israel for their sins. The angels now wanted to plunge Phinehas into death for his bold words, but God bade them desist, saying, " Leave him in peace, he is a zealot, the son of a zealot, and an appeaser of wrath, the son of an appeaser of wrath." [799]

PHINEHAS REWARDED

While God expressed His entire satisfaction with Phinehas's act, it found many adversaries among Israel, who would scornfully call after him, " Behold, this man, the grandson of one who fattened calves to offer them up to an idol, daring to slay a prince among Israel! " This spiteful remark referred to the fact that Phinehas was descended on his mother's side not only from Joseph, but from Jethro also who, before his conversion to Judaism, had been a priest of idols. God therefore said to Moses, " Phinehas the son of Eleazar, the son of Aaron the priest, hath turned My wrath away from the children of Israel, hence I offer him My greeting of peace, for it was he who, zealous for My sake, preserved the seed of Abraham." The reason God designated Phinehas as the son of Eleazar and the grandson of Aaron was that He wanted to stop the mouths of Phinehas's detractors, who pretended that he was nothing but a grand-son of the heathen priest Jethro, ignoring the fact that he was at the same time the grandson of Aaron, the high priest before the Lord.[800]

God was not content with the greeting of peace, but bade Moses tell Phinehas: " With thy mouth hast thou defended Israel, therefore as thy priest's portion shalt thou receive the jawbone of animals; with thy lance didst thou aim at the bellies of the shameless couple, hence shalt thou receive the bellies of the animals; and as with thy arm thou didst labor to slay the sinners, so for thy portion shalt thou receive the shoulder of the animals. As, moreover, thou didst strive to make peace among mankind, so shalt thou bestow the priestly blessing upon My children, and bless them with peace." [801] As a reward for his pious deed Phinehas was appointed by God as a priest with all the rights of priesthood, that en-abled him to lay claim to the twenty-four tributes to priests.[802]

But the highest reward to Phinehas was that God granted him everlasting priesthood. For Phinehas is none other than the prophet Elijah. His task it is to make atonement for Israel, and without tasting of death, he constantly discharges the duties of his everlasting priesthood until the resurrection of the dead, offering up daily two sacrifices for the children of Israel, and upon the skins of these animals recording the events of each day.[803] God furthermore said to Phinehas: " Thou hast in this world established peace between Me and Israel; in the future world also shalt thou establish peace between Me and them." He was therefore destined to be the forerunner of the Messiah to establish before his coming peace on earth.[804]

When Israel addicted themselves to an immoral life at Shittim, the nations of the world rejoiced greatly, for they knew that God had distinguished Israel before all other nations, and had given them the Torah, only because their life had been moral. " Now," said they, " the crown has been taken from Israel's head, their pride is departed, for now they are no better than we." God, however, raised up Israel from their fall by sending the plague upon the sinners at Shittim, and thus purified Israel from them, so that they could again, as of yore, be proud of their family purity, through which they had been distinguished from all other nations.

God therefore ordered them to take a census, to show in this way that Israel remained true to the traditions of their ancestor Abraham by keeping their family life pure.[805] This census showed that several tribes had lost entire divisions since the time that passed between the entrance of Israel into Egypt, and their entrance into the promised land. Among the tribes that had perished were such as had already lost their lives in Egypt, those, namely, who had died during the days of darkness because they were such sinners that they did not want to leave Egypt. But heaviest of all were the losses in the tribes of Benjamin and of Simeon, for in the battle between the Levites and the other tribes after Aaron's death, when the latter, for fear of the Canaanites, wanted to return to Egypt, the Benjamites lost no less than seven divisions. All of the twenty-four thousand men that died from the plague at Shittim belonged, however, to the tribe of Simeon which, at the end of the march through the desert, had dwindled down to less than half its number.

The tribe of Dan, on the other hand, had turned out to be very fruitful, for, whereas at the entrance into Egypt it had consisted of only one division, it later exceeded in number all the other tribes, except the tribe of Judah.[806]

THE DAUGHTERS OF ZELOPHEHAD

But there was another purpose beside that of establishing Israel's family purity in taking the census at Arbot-Moab. For when God at the exodus from Egypt put His people into Moses' hands, He entrusted them to him after having counted them, and now when Moses was about to depart from this world, he wanted to return the flock that God had entrusted to him, truly numbered, into God's hand.[807]

After the number of the nation had been determined, God ordered Moses to divide the promised land among them according to their numbers.[808] Jacob had indeed upon his death-bed determined what parts of the land were to fall to the lot of each tribe, but in order that the tribes might not quarrel among themselves, God decreed that the assignments be made by lot.[809] After the conquest of the land Joshua and Eleazar saw to the drawing of lots. On this occasion the miracle came to pass that whenever Eleazar drew a lot from the urn, the lot itself announced the words, " I am the lot of Thus-and-So." In this way was avoided the possibility of having the malcontents declare that Eleazar had, at the drawing of lots, been partial to his friends and had assigned to them the lots they wished for.[810]

When Zelophehad's daughters, that had lived piously and wisely like their father and their ancestors, heard that the land was being divided among the male members of the tribe, but not among the female, they took counsel together, discussing what they could do, so that they might not find themselves come out empty-handed. They said: " God's love is not like the love of a mortal father; the latter prefers his sons to his daughters, but He that created the world extends His love to women as well as to men, ' His tender mercies are over all His works.' " They now hoped that God would take pity on them and give them their share of the promised land, which they loved with as great devotion as their grandsire Joseph, who had upon his death-bed exhorted his children to transfer his body to the Holy Land.[311]

Being wise and learned, they waited for a propitious time to lay their case before Moses, an opportunity which they found when Moses in the house of teaching recited the law concerning the levirate marriage. They now advanced and said: " If we are as good as our brothers, then do we lay claim to our father's inheritance, and to his share of the land; but if we are not to be considered as sons, then should our mother have to marry her brother-in-law, as our father has left no issue, since we do not count." [312] They furthermore pointed out that their father had been neither one of the spies nor one of Korah's followers, who had, owing to their sins, lost claim to their share of the land,[313] but that he had found his death when a number of men, in spite of Moses' warnings, had presumed to storm the mountain occupied by the Amalekites and the Canaanites.[314] " Had our father," continued they, " left behind him a son, and the latter were now also dead, then should we lay no claim to inheritance if this son had left a living child, were it even a daughter; but as we are our father's only descendants, give us, we pray, ' a possession among the brethren of our father.' "

The fervent longing of these women to have a share in the Holy Land shows how much better and more pious were the women of this generation than the men. The latter said, " Let us make a captain, and let us return to Egypt," whereas the women said, " Give us a possession among the brethren of our father." [515] But not only during the rebellion that was kindled by the spies did the women remain true to Moses and to their God, but on other occasions also it was they who tried to build up what the men had torn down. At the worship of the Golden Calf, too, they tried to restrain the men from sin, hence it was the men only that had to die in the desert because they had been tempted to rebellion by the spies, whereas the women entered into the promised land. [516] Among them also there was even to be found a woman as old as Jochebed—the daughter of Levi by his union with Otah—who survived her sons Moses and Aaron, as well as her daughter Miriam, and who was permitted to enter the promised land at the age of two hundred and fifty years. [517]

The daughters of Zelophehad did not bring their request directly to Moses, but at first urged their plea before the lowest officers, the captains of tens. These, however, said: " This is an important matter since it touches upon laws of inheritance, hence it does not become us to decide this matter; greater men than we must settle it." Hence they sent them to the captains of fifties. When these saw that out of consideration for them the captains of tens would not pass judgment, they sent the daughters of Zelophehad on to the captains of hundreds, that were their superiors. But these too, out of consideration for the higher judges, would not settle this matter, and so the daughters of Zelophehad came to the captains of thousands, who sent them to the princes of the tribes, until they came at last to the highest authority, to Moses. Now Moses might well have decided this case without further ado, but in his meekness he thought, " There is still a higher authority than I, to wit, God," and he bade them await God's judgment.[818] The answer that he received from God was as follows: " The daughters of Zelophehad have the law on their side, for what they desire is in accordance with the law that was written in heaven by Me; give them therefore their father's inheritance, and also two parts of their grandfather Hepher's possessions, for their father Zelophehad was his firstborn and was therefore entitled to a double share." [819]

The daughters of Zelophehad, who in spite of their years —the youngest of them had attained forty—had not yet been married, now entered into wedlock, and according to God's bidding that Moses communicated to them, they married their uncle's sons, although they were free to marry whomsoever they chose.[820]

" God works good through the good, and evil through the evil." The chapter of the laws of God that was published by Moses as an addition to the incident of Zelophehad's daughters would have been given without them also, but God rewarded these women for their piety by making them the direct occasion of this chapter of the law.[821] At the same time this case of these women was to teach several lessons to Moses. He who, since he had been made God's messenger to the people, had lived apart from his wife was not to grow too conceited on account of the sacrifice he had made to his sacred calling; hence in the last year of his life there appeared before him the daughters of Zelophehad, who of their own accord had not married because they had not found mates that they considered suitable. Then, too, Moses could not answer the legal question that the daughters of Zelophehad presented to him, and had to ask God's counsel, which was a second lesson to Moses. At the appointment of the elders, Moses earnestly told them, " The cause that is too hard for ye, bring it to me, and I will hear it," and in punishment of these boastful words God so brought it to pass that he could give no answer to this request of the women, whereupon God said to him, " Didst not thou say, ' the cause that is too hard for ye, bring it to me? ' and now thou canst not properly settle this legal question of the women."

A similar punishment for a similar offense was visited upon David who, well aware of his erudition, said, " The laws of the Torah do I grasp as easily and as quickly as songs." God then said, " As truly as thou livest, thou shalt hereafter forget a Biblical law that even the school children know." So, too, it came to pass that when he had the Holy Ark fetched from Gibeah to Zion, he forgot the Biblical instruction that the Ark may be carried only upon the shoulder, and had it lifted upon a wagon. Then occurred the miracle that the Ark leaped of itself into the air, whereas the oxen that pulled the wagon fell down, whereupon Uzzah, to whom the transportation of the Ark had been entrusted, stretched out his hand to prevent the Ark from falling and himself fell dead upon the ground, for " a sin that is committed in ignorance of the law is accounted as if it had been intentional."

Uzzah should have been mindful of the law that the Ark was not to be lifted upon a cart, hence his punishment. God thereupon said to David, " Didst thou not say, ' Thy statutes have been my songs?' and thou hast not even mastered the words of the Bible, ' Unto the sons of Kohath he gave none : because the service of the sanctuary belonged unto them; they bare it upon their shoulders.' "

THE APPOINTMENT OF JOSHUA

When Moses heard God's decision in the case of the daughters of Zelophehad, which turned out in their favor so that they inherited their father's property, he thought, " This is a propitious time to urge a plea before the Lord, for if daughters are to inherit their father, then must my sons inherit my office." [822] He then began to pray to God that his successors, who, he hoped, were also to be his descendants, might be worthy leaders of their people. He said: " O my Lord, before whom come the spirits of all human beings, so that Thou knowest the spirit of each—whose spirit is proud, and whose spirit is meek; whose spirit is patient and whose spirit is restive; mayest Thou set over Thy community a man who is gifted with strength, with wisdom, with beauty, and with decorum, so that his conduct may not give offense to the people.[823] O Lord of the world! Thou knowest each man's views, and knowest that each man has a view of his own, hence, as I am about to depart from this world, I pray Thee, appoint a leader over them that will know how to deal with each man according to his views." [824]

Moses, being a truly pious man, thought when he saw his end approach, not of himself, but of the welfare of the community, for whom he implored a good and worthy leader.[325] Hence he furthermore said to God: " Let not my successor share my fate, for although I accepted the guidance of the people only after long hesitation, owing to Thy urgings and requests, still I shall not be permitted to lead them into the promised land. Mayest Thou then deal differently with my successor than Thou hast dealt with me, and permit him not only to lead the people in the desert, but to take them into the promised land.[326] He, however, shall be a man ' which may go out before them,' who, unlike the kings of the heathens, that send their legions to war but themselves remain at home, shall himself lead Israel to war. But he shall also be a man ' which may come in before them ; ' may it be granted him to see the number of those returning from war no less than that of those going into war. O Lord of the world ! " continued Moses, " Thou hast led Israel out of Egypt, not to punish them for their sins, but to forgive them, and Thou hast not led them out of Egypt that they may be without leaders, but that they may indeed have leaders. I insist, therefore, that Thou shouldst tell me whether or not Thou wilt grant them a leader."

This is one of the five occasions upon which Moses implored God to give him an answer to his question. When he saw that his appearance before Pharaoh only occasioned him to bring greater and greater cruelties upon Israel, he said to God, " Tell me if Thou wilt now deliver them, or not." He also demanded God's answer to the question, " Shall I now fall into their hands or not ? " when at Rephidim, on account of the dearth of water, he was threatened by the people. The third occasion was when he prayed to God

for Miriam's recovery, and said, " Tell me, wilt Thou heal
her or not?" And lastly when, after long and fervent
prayer, he asked God whether he should be permitted to
enter into the Holy Land, he said, " Let me know if I am to
enter the Holy Land or not." [827]

God fulfilled this wish of Moses, saying: " Thou hast
now requested to be informed concerning thy immediate successor.   I shall do more than this, and show thee all the
judges and prophets that I will allow to arise for My children from now on to the resurrection of the dead."   Then He
showed Moses his successor Joshua, his successor's successor, Othniel, and all the other judges and prophets.   Then
God added these words: " Of all these that I have shown
thee, each will have his individual spirit and his individual
knowledge, but such a man as thou now wishest for thy successor, whose spirit is to embrace in itself the spirits of sixty
myriads of Israel, so that he may speak to each one of them
according to his understanding, such a man as this will not
arise until the end of time.   The Messiah will be inspired
with a spirit that in itself will embrace the spirits of all
mankind.

But now, concerning thy immediate successor, know
then that he that watcheth the fig tree shall eat of its
fruits, and he that waiteth upon his master will be promoted
to honor, and thy sons shall not inherit the leadership because
they concerned themselves little with the Torah.   Joshua
shall be thy successor, who served thee with devotion and
showed thee great veneration, for at morn and eve he put up
the benches in thy house of teaching and spread the carpets
over them; he served thee as far as he was able, and Israel

shall now know that he will therefore receive his reward.[828] Take then Joshua, a man such as thou didst wish as a successor, whom thou hast proven, and who knows how to deal with people of every tendency, ' and lay thy hand upon him.' Give him an opportunity, while thou art still alive, to speak in public and to pronounce the law, so that Israel may not after thy death contemptuously say of thy successor, ' As long as his teacher was alive, he dared not pronounce judgment, and now he wishes to do so!' [829] Although Joshua, who is not of thy kin, is to be thy successor, I shall nevertheless be mindful of the law that ' no inheritance shall remove from one tribe to another tribe,' for the dignity of leadership is to be reserved for thy family; Joshua ' shall stand even before Eleazar the priest, thy brother's son, who shall ask counsel for him according to the judgment of the Urim.' " [830]

After Moses in kindly words had induced Joshua to accept the leadership after his death, pointing out to him the great rewards that in the future world await the leaders of Israel, ' he took Joshua, and set him before Eleazar the priest, and before all the congregation,' that all might thereafter acknowledge him as his successor.[831] He then bade Joshua, who had been sitting on the floor like all the rest, rise and seat himself upon a bench beside him. Joshua seated himself with the words, " Blessed be the Lord that hath through Moses bestowed the Torah upon Israel." [832] Moses honored Joshua furthermore by interrupting his discourse as soon as Joshua entered the house of teaching, and resuming it only when he had taken his seat.[833] Moses also bade a herald proclaim throughout all the camp, " This man Joshua is worthy of being appointed by God as His shepherd." [834]

Moses distinguished Joshua not because God had ordered him to do so, but because he was sincerely glad to pass his dignity on to him, just as a father is glad to leave his possessions to his son. So, too, whereas God had bidden Moses to lay only one hand upon Joshua's head and in this way put his honor upon him, Moses fulfilled God's command by laying both his hands upon Joshua, and by this action bestowed upon him not only insight and understanding, but also a radiant countenance like that of Moses, from whose face issued rays like those of the sun. In giving all these qualities to Joshua, Moses lost nothing. Moses' wisdom was like a torch, whereas Joshua's may be compared to a candle only, and just as a torch loses none of its intensity if a candle is lighted therefrom, so little was Moses' wisdom diminished by the wisdom he gave to Joshua.[335] The rays, too, that emanated from Joshua's countenance were weaker than those from Moses', and not until the crossing of the Jordan did they attain their full intensity, so that upon beholding them, "the people feared him as they feared Moses."[336]

Joshua's appointment by God as Moses' successor had been Moses' most cherished wish, but he had not ventured to give expression to it, for he was mindful of the punishment God had sent over him when he had entreated Him to send Aaron instead of himself to deliver Israel out of Egypt, and from that time he feared to make any proposals whatsoever to God. He was like the child who had once been burned by a coal, and then seeing a brightly sparkling jewel, took it to be a burning coal, and dared not touch it.[337]

MOSES' LEGACY TO JOSHUA

After Moses had announced Joshua as his successor before all the congregation, he disclosed to him that the course of his own life was run, and that he would now depart to his fathers. As his inheritance he gave to Joshua a book of prophecy, which Joshua was to anoint with cedar-oil, and in an earthen vessel to lay upon the spot that from the creation of the world God had created for it, so that His name might there be invoked. This book contained in brief outline the history of Israel from the entrance into the promised land to the establishment of God's kingdom upon earth, when, in wrath and indignation on account of His children, the Lord will rise from His Throne of power and proceed from His holy dwelling.

When Joshua heard the words of Moses as they are written in his Holy Scriptures, he rent his garments and fell at Moses' feet, who, himself in tears, yet comforted him. Joshua, however, said: "How canst thou comfort me concerning the bitter word that thou hast spoken, which abounds in sobs and tears, that thou art to depart from thy people? What place will receive thee? What monument will point to thy grave? Or who will dare to remove thy corpse from one place to another as if it were an ordinary mortal's? All dying men receive a grave upon earth according to their rank, but thy grave extends from sunrise to sunset, from South to North; all the world is thy tomb. Thou goest. Who now, O master, shall care for this people? Who shall take pity upon them and be a guide upon their way? Who shall pray for them incessantly, that I may lead them into the land of their fathers? How shall I provide food for them according to their wish, or drink according to their desire? From the beginning they numbered sixty myriads, and now, thanks to thy prayers, they have greatly multiplied. Whence shall I draw insight and understanding to give them judgment and counsel? Even the kings of the Amorites, hearing that we desire to attack them, will say, ' Let us now set out against them, for there is now no longer among them the many-sided, incomprehensible and sacred spirit, worthy of the Lord, the ever-faithful master of the word, the Divine prophet of all the world, the most consummate master of this age. If now our enemies once more transgress before the Lord, they will have no defender to offer up prayers for them before God, as Moses had done, the great messenger who at all hours of the day kneeled down and prayed, lifting up his eyes to Him who rules all the world, and constantly reminding Him of His covenant with the Patriarchs, and appeasing Him with invocations.' For thus will the Amorites speak saying, ' He is no longer among them; arise then and let us wipe them from the face of the earth.' But what then, O my lord Moses, will become of this people? "

When Joshua had spoken these words, he cast himself once more at Moses' feet. Moses seized his hand, raised him to a seat before them, and answered him, saying: " Do not underestimate thyself, O Joshua, but be light of heart, and pay heed to my words. All the nations that dwell in the universe hath God created, and us also. Them and us did He foresee from the beginning of the creation of the universe even unto the end of the world, and He overlooked nothing, even down to the smallest, but He at the same time foresaw and foredoomed everything. All that was to happen in this universe did God foresee and foredoom, and lo! it cometh to pass. He appointed me for them and for their sins, that for them I might make prayer and exhortation. Not for my fitness or my strength was I chosen, but only through the grace of His mercy and His long-suffering. For I assure thee, Joshua, not on account of the excellence of this people wilt thou destroy the heathens; all the fastnesses of heaven and the foundations of the universe were created and approved by God, and are beneath the ring of His right hand. Those, therefore, that maintain and fulfil God's commandments thrive and prosper, but those who sin and neglect the commandments will not receive the promised possessions, and will be punished by the heathens with many plagues. But that He should wholly destroy or abandon them is impossible, for God will step forth, who foresaw everything even to eternity, and whose covenant is firmly founded, in accordance with the oath which He swore to the Patriarchs. Then the hands of the angel will be filled and he will be appointed chief, and he will forthwith avenge them of their enemies." [838]

Moses' Last Campaign

Balaam's prophecy, " He shall not lie down until he eat of the prey, and drink the blood of the slain," was very quickly fulfilled. Shortly before his death, before he lay down to everlasting sleep, it was granted Moses to rejoice in the death of Balaam and the five Midianite kings allied to him.[839] Israel's sinful profanation at Shittim, occasioned by Balaam's wicked advice, sorely smote Moses' heart. God had appointed Moses as lord of the angels, who through fire and cloud had to step aside to make room for him and let him pass, yea, at his appearance they rose from their seats to do him honor. As he had power over the angels, so too did he rule the sea, which he clove at will and then commanded to resume its former guise, and the treasures of hail, which he employed to send hail over the Egyptians. Now this man, who was sovereign over the angels and over the forces of nature, could only weep when Israel committed whoredom with the daughters of Moab and Midian. To comfort Moses, God now said: " As truly as thou livest, thou shalt not depart out of this world until thou shalt have avenged those who tempted Israel to sin. ' Avenge the children of Israel of the Midianites: afterward shalt thou be gathered unto thy people.' " [840] God at the same time reproached Moses for his despair and lack of energy at Shittim, saying: " When all the tribes of Israel, save the tribe of Levi, were against thee, thou didst not then lack courage to stand up against all the people on account of the worship of the Golden Calf; how much more then at Shittim, when all Israel save only one tribe, the tribe of Simeon, were on thy side, shouldst thou have proven thyself sufficiently strong to keep back the sinners from their sin! " [841]

When Moses received the command to wage war upon the people that had tempted Israel to sin, he said to God: " Yesterday didst Thou say to me, ' Vex not Moab,' and now Thou sayest, ' Avenge the children of Israel.' " God, however, replied: " When I said, ' Vex not Moab,' I named these people after their grandsire, the son of Lot, but now that through their own fault they have lost the claim to kind treatment from Israel, I shall no longer think of their grandsire Abraham's kinsman, but shall call them Midianim, ' they that lost their claim.' " [842]

Lot's descendants now not only had no further claims to exemption, but a command was given to Moses to treat them with still greater hostility than the other nations. Until then it had been Israel's duty not to fight against a city of the heathens unless they had first proclaimed peace to it and the heathens had refused to accept it, but now they were instantly to proceed to hostility; and whereas they had formerly been prohibited from destroying the trees that surrounded a city, they were now ruthlessly to destroy all that lay in their path. This wrath of God against those who had tempted Israel to sin was justified, for " the tempter to sin is worse than the murderer, since he who slays another robs him of this world alone, but he that tempts another deprives him of this world and the world beyond." Two nations, the Egyptians and the Edomites, attacked Israel with the sword, but God nevertheless said, " Thou shalt not abhor an Edomite; thou shalt not abhor an Egyptian." The Moabites and Ammonites, on the other hand, tempted Israel to sin, hence God's word concerning them was as follows: " An Ammonite or Moabite shall not enter into the assembly of the Lord, even to the tenth generation." [843]

Israel received the command to make war upon the Midianites at the same time as that to fight the Moabites, but whereas Moses at once waged war against Midian, it was not until David's time that a relentless war was waged against Moab. There were several reasons why the Midianites were to receive their punishment before the Moabites. Firstly, Moab's hatred against Israel was not quite without foundation, for although the Israelites had not attacked them in war, still they had inspired them with great fear by pillaging the Moabite region, hence the Moabites tried by every means to be rid of Israel. Midian, on the other hand, had no cause for undertaking hostilities against Israel, and yet they not only joined the Moabites, but outdid them in their hatred against Israel. Furthermore Moab wanted to kill Israel, but Midian wanted to tempt them to sin, which is worse than death.[844] The delay in punishing Moab also corresponded in other ways to God's plan, for the Moabite Ruth was destined to become the mother of the dynasty of David, hence God said to Israel: " Wait yet a while in this matter of the war against the Moabites: I have lost something valuable among them. As soon as I have found it, ye shall avenge yourselves of them." [845]

God indicated that the war against Midian would be Moses' last in these words, "Avenge the children of Israel of the Midianites: afterward shalt thou be gathered unto thy people." The connection between the war and Moses' death is as follows. When God announced to Moses that he was to die on this side the Jordan, Moses implored God with the words: " O Lord of the world! Is it right that death should so soon overtake me, that have seen Thy ways, Thy actions, and Thy path?" God replied, saying: "Moses, if a long life were better for men, surely I should not then have permitted thy ancestors to taste of death; but it is better for thee if thou art taken from this world than if thou wert to remain in it." Moses was not, however, satisfied with this answer from God, whereupon God said: "Well then, thou mayest live many years longer, yea, thou shalt live even to a

thousand years, but know thou that Israel will not then conquer their foes, and that Midian will not be brought under
their yoke." In this way was Moses made to yield by God,
for he thought, " Whether I die to-day or to-morrow matters little, for death will come to me at last. I would rather
see Israel conquer their foes and bring Midian under their
yoke than that I should live longer." God therefore bade
Moses avenge Israel of the Midianites, if he was thereupon
ready to die.[846]

Moses then thought: " I know that if I were now to go
into battle against the Midianites, the people would declare
that I wished for my own death, since God made it dependent upon the punishing of the Midianites, and my life is assured me as long as ever I wish to put it off." This consideration did not, however, determine him, for, fully aware that
his enterprise of war would hasten his death, he nevertheless
set about the execution of this war as soon as God commanded him. Wherever the execution of a Divine command,
or the possibility of furthering Israel's cause was concerned,
Moses gave no thought to himself, even though it touched
his life. Not so Joshua. When he came to Canaan, he
thought: " If I wage an incessant war upon the Canaanites,
I shall certainly die as soon as I shall have conquered them,
for Moses also died immediately after his conquest of Midian." He therefore proceeded very slowly in his conquest
of the Holy Land, so that he might be sure of a long life.
But, " however many thoughts there may be in man's heart,
God's word prevails," and whereas Joshua hoped to become
very aged, he died ten years before the time God had
originally allotted to him, for, although he would otherwise

have attained his master's age, he now died at the age of a
hundred and ten.[847]

THE COMPLETE ANNIHILATION OF MIDIAN

Whereas Moses, disregarding the expected consequences
of the war upon himself, gladly went into battle, Israel did
not want to obey his summons to war. The people of whom
Moses had on one occasion said, " They be almost ready to
stone me," when they now learned that their leader Moses
was to die at the end of this war, tried to evade it, saying
that they preferred to forego impending victory rather than
to lose their leader, and each one hid himself, so as not to
be picked out for this war. God therefore bade Moses cast
lots to decide their going into battle, and those whose lots
were drawn had to follow the call to arms even against their
will. Moses' summons to battle was as follows: "Arm ye
men from among you for the war, to execute the Lord's vengeance on Midian." Moses spoke of the Lord's revenge,
whereas God designated this war against Midian as Israel's
revenge. For Moses said to God: "Lord of the world! If
we had worshipped the stars and planets, the Midianites
should not have hated us, they hate us only on account of
the Torah and the commandments that Thou hast given us,
hence must Thou avenge Thyself of them." [848]

Moses did not in person lead the war against Midian, for
he was mindful of the proverb, " Cast no stone into the well
from which thou hast drawn water," and he who as a fugi-
tive from Egypt had sought refuge in Midian, did not wish
to make war upon that land. He relinquished the leadership of the people to Phinehas, for " he that beginneth a

good deed shall also complete it," and it was Phinehas who had begun God's war against the Midianites by slaying the princess Cozbi, Zimri's mistress, hence the task of completing this war fell to his lot. Phinehas, as a descendant of Joseph, had, moreover, a special reason for wishing to take revenge upon the Midianites, as those had been Midianites who had sold Joseph as a slave in Egypt.[849]

The forces under Phinehas's command consisted of thirty-six thousand men, one third to take active part in battle, one third to guard the baggage, and one third to pray, whose duty it was in the course of battle to implore God to lend victory to the warriors of Israel. Moses passed on to Phinehas not only the Holy Ark, which Israel always takes into battle, but also the Urim and Tummim, that he might, if necessary, consult God.[850] Outside of this Phinehas also received the gold plate of the mitre from the high priest's forehead, for Moses said to him: "The knave Balaam will by means of his sorceries fly into the air, and will even enable the five Midianite kings to fly with him, therefore shall ye hold up to them the plate of pure gold upon which is engraved God's name, and they will fall to earth." They did as Moses commanded, and truly Balaam and the five kings fell to earth. They then executed Balaam according to the four forms prescribed by the Jewish laws. They hanged him, kindled a fire beneath the gallows, struck off his head with a sword, and then dropped him from the gallows into the fire below.[851]

Although Israel undertook the war against Midian upon God's bidding, to take vengeance for the wrong that had been done them, still their method of warfare was most humane. They attacked the cities of the Midianites from three sides only, so as not entirely to cut off flight. Victory was on the side of Israel, into whose possession fell the cities with all their temples, idols, and palaces. The same fate overtook all the five kings of Midian. All were slain alike just as all had made a common cause of the wish to destroy Israel. Balaam who had come to Midian from his home in Mesopotamia in order to receive his reward for his counsel not to fight Israel, but to tempt them to sin, instead of a reward, met with death at the hands of the Jews.[852]

The Gruesome End of Balaam

This arch-magician at first tried to escape Israel's power by sorcery. For when he saw Phinehas and the leaders of the hosts of Israel, he flew into the air,[853] a feat which he accomplished by magic arts, but particularly through the assistance of his wizard sons, Jannes and Jambres. At the sight of Balaam flying high in the air, Phinehas shouted to his army, " Is there any one among us who is able to fly after this villain? " The Danite Zaliah, a past master in the art of sorcery, followed this summons, and flew high into the air. Balaam, however, surpassed him, and took a path in the air on which Zaliah could not follow, and after the former had soared through five different layers of air, he had quite vanished from Zaliah's ken, who knew not what to do. Phinehas, however, came to his aid. By means of a magical invocation he dispelled the clouds that covered Balaam, and then Zaliah forced Balaam to descend to earth and appear before Phinehas.[854] He began to implore Phinehas to spare his life, promising never again to try to curse Israel, but Phinehas replied: " Art not thou the Aramean

Laban who tried to destroy our father Jacob? Then thou
didst pass on to Egypt to destroy Jacob's seed, and when they
removed from Egypt thou didst incite the wicked Amalek to
harass us, and now thou didst attempt to curse Israel. But
when thou sawest that thy endeavor to curse them was without avail, since God would not hear thee, thou gavest Balak
the despicable advice to deliver up the daughters of his land
to prostitution, and thereby to tempt Israel to sin, and wert
in part successful, for twenty-four thousand Israelites died
in consequence of their sin with the daughters of Moab. In
vain therefore dost thou plead that thy life be spared." He
then ordered Zaliah to kill Balaam, admonishing him, however, to be sure not to kill him through the holy name of
God, as it does not befit so great a sinner to meet his
death in such a way. Zaliah now tried in vain to kill Balaam, for through his magic wiles he was proof against every
weapon, until Phinehas at last gave Zaliah a sword on both
sides of which was engraved a serpent, with the words, " Kill
him with that to which he belongs—through this he will die,"
and with this sword Balaam was killed.[855]

His corpse was not buried, but his bones rotted, and from
them arose several species of harmful snakes, that bring
disaster to human beings; and even the worms that devoured
his flesh were turned into snakes. The magicians made use
of these snakes for three different types of enchantment, for
the heads, the bodies, and the tails, had each a different
effect. One of the questions that the Queen of Sheba put
to Solomon was how to withstand these three different kinds
of enchantment, and the wise king knew even this secret,
which he then imparted to her.[856]

The Victorious Return from the War

After the close of the campaign against Midian, the warriors returned with rich spoils to the camp of Israel, but they were such pious and honorable men that they did not lay claim to the booty, but rendered it all up, so that it might be impartially divided among all.[857] As they were honest and conscientious in their relations between man and man, so likewise were they very strict in their observance of religious statutes. Throughout the time of war not a single one of them neglected even the slightest religious ceremony, were it only to put on the phylactery of the forehead before that of the arm.[858] But they were especially careful never again to be tempted by the Midianite women. If they entered a house to take its treasures from it, they did so in pairs, one blackening the faces of the women, and the other seizing their ornaments. In vain would the Midianite women cry, " Are we not creatures of God, that ye treat us thus? " whereupon the Israelites would say, " Were not ye the cause that so many of us found their death? " Justly therefore could these pious men say to Moses: " Thy servants have taken the sum of the men of war which are under our charge, and not one among us had committed a sin or an unchaste action. We have therefore brought the Lord's oblation to make atonement for our souls." Moses thereupon said in surprise, " Ye contradict yourselves, what need of atonement is there if no man among you is guilty of sin? " They replied: " It is true, our teacher Moses, two by two did we approach the women, one blackening their faces, and the other taking off their ear-rings, but even though we committed no sin with the Midianite women, still the heat of passion was kindled in

us when we took hold of the women, and therefore by an
offering do we seek to make atonement." Moses thereupon
set out to praise them, saying: "Even the common men
among you are filled with good and pious deeds, for a man
that was under conditions that enabled him to sin, but con-
trolled himself, has done a pious deed, not to speak of the
pious and chaste men among you whose pious deeds are
legion." [859]

As among those who had been slain in Midian there was a
Jewish apostate, the warriors were polluted, and hence might
not enter the camp, but had to stay without. Moses in his
meekness did not, however, wait for them to come to him,
but hastened to them. When, however, he heard that they
had killed only the men but not the women, his wrath was
kindled against the leaders of the army, for, "Upon the leaders falls the blame for the faults of the people." He reproached them, pointing out to them that it had been the
women who really had brought disaster upon Israel at
Shittim. But Phinehas replied: "Our teacher Moses, we
acted according to thy instructions, thou didst bid us only
'avenge ourselves of the Midianites,' but madest no mention
of the women of Midian." [860] Moses then ordered them to execute all the women of the Midianites that were ripe for marriage, but to spare the young girls. In order to determine the
difference in age, all were led past the gold plate of the mitre
on the high priest's forehead, and this had the effect of
making those who had been doomed to death grow pale. [861]

In punishment for Moses' outburst of anger God caused
him to forget to communicate to the soldiers outside the
camp the laws of purification. These were then announced

by Eleazar, Aaron's son. It was not, however, proper for him to pronounce a law in the presence of his teacher Moses, and he was accordingly punished for his lack of reverence to his teacher Moses. God had previously said that whenever Joshua wanted to inquire of God, he was "to stand before Eleazar the priest, and inquire of him by the judgment of the Urim and Tummim." But this did not come about. In all his long career, Joshua had no need of asking Eleazar's counsel, so that the latter lost the honor that had been intended for him.[862]

The occasion that led to the war against Midian had been Israel's seduction by the Midianite women, but these had succeeded only by having first intoxicated the sinners with wine. Phinehas, to make sure that this might not be repeated in the future, put the earthly as well as the heavenly ban upon all those who should drink the wine of the heathens, for the latter used it only as libations to their idols and for immoral purposes. In pronouncing this ban, he called upon the Ineffable Name and upon the holy writing of the two tables against its transgressors.[863]

WEALTH THAT BRINGETH DESTRUCTION

God gave three gifts to the world, wisdom, strength, and wealth. If they come from God, they are a blessing, otherwise they bring ruin. The world had two great sages, Balaam among the Gentiles, and Ahithophel among the Jews, but both of these, on account of their wisdom, lost this world as well as the world beyond. There were two great heroes in the world, Samson in Israel, and Goliath among the Gentiles, but both met death on account of their strength.

There were two wealthy men in the world, Korah among the Jews, and Haman among the Gentiles, and both perished on account of their wealth. A similar fate overtook the two and a half tribes that stayed on the hither side of the Jordan. These had grown very rich in cattle through the spoils of the Midianites, and therefore preferred the pasture land on the hither side of the Jordan as their inheritance. But later on their wealth brought them destruction, because, choosing on account of their wealth of cattle to separate themselves from their brethren, they were afterwards the first that were driven from their dwelling place into exile.[864]

How intent these people were upon their possessions is shown in the words with which they presented their wish to Moses, saying, "We will build sheepfolds here for our cattle, and cities for our little ones," showing that they rated the cattle higher than their children, for they thought of the animals before they considered their children. Moses did not indeed call them to account for this, but showed them in unmistakable words that it was their duty first to consider men and then animals, by saying in his reply to these tribes, "Build you cities for your little ones, and folds for your sheep." [865]

The land which these tribes had selected was indeed of great excellence, as even the names of the cities indicate. One was called Ataroth, "garlanded with fruits;" a second, Dibon, "flowing with honey;" a third, Jazer, "help," for its possession was a great help to those who owned it. Three other cities in this region that were named on account of the excellence of the soil were: Nimrah, "gaily colored," for the ground of this city was gaily colored with fruits; Sebam,

" perfume," whose fruits scattered a fragrance like perfume; and Nebo, " produce," because it was distinguished for its excellent produce.[866] This last mentioned city, like Baal-meon, did not retain its name when it passed into Israel's possession, for they wanted to have no cities that bore the names of idols, and therefore gave them new names.[867] Many another town as well received a new name from the Israel-ites, just as Nobah gave his own name to the city of Kenath that he had gained by arms, hoping in this way to immor-talize his name, for he had no children. His name was, how-ever, not preserved in this way, for after the death of the conqueror, the old name of Kenath returned again.[868]

It was among the possessions of these two and a half tribes also that Moses shortly before his death founded the cities of refuge. Moses in this instance illustrates the proverb, " Whosoever loves pious deeds, never has enough of them." Although God had told Moses that he would never cross to the other side of the Jordan, he still insisted upon at least determining the site for the asylum in the region of the East Jordan. God gave Moses the law concerning the cities of refuge in accordance with Israel's wish. For the people said to God : " Lord of the world ! Thou didst promise us a long course of life as a reward for fulfilling the commandments, but supposing now that a man hath slain another uninten-tionally, and the avenger of the blood slays him, he will die before his time." God then said to Moses : " As truly as thou livest, they speak wisely. Appoint therefore several cities for cities of refuge, ' that the manslayer might flee thither, which slayeth his neighbor unawares.' " Moses re-joiced greatly at this statute, and instantly set about its exe-

cution, for " he that hath tasted of a food knoweth its flavor,"
and Moses who had erstwhile been obliged to flee on account
of having slain an Egyptian, knew the feelings of the man
who is pursued on account of a manslaughter that he had
committed unawares.[869]

MOSES' DEATH IRREVOCABLY DOOMED

When God in wrath against Moses and Aaron vowed,
" Therefore ye shall not bring this assembly into the land
which I have given them," Moses forbore to implore God to
do away with this sentence, acting in accordance with the
precept, " Do not attempt to dissolve thy neighbor's vow in
the moment he hath made it." Moses waited forty years
before he approached God with the request to permit him to
enter the promised land with Israel.[870] This occurred when
he had received God's command to appoint Joshua as his
successor, for he now perceived that God had actually resolved to execute His sentence.[871] For although God had ten
times decreed that Moses was to die in the desert, still Moses
had not troubled much about it, even when the resolution had
been sealed in the heavenly court. He thought: " How often
did Israel sin, and yet, when I prayed for them, He annulled
the punishment He had decreed; surely God should accept
my prayer, if I—a man who never sinned—should pray to
Him." [872] Moses had also a special reason for assuming that
God had changed His determination concerning him, and
would now permit him to enter the promised land, for he had
been permitted to enter the part of Palestine lying on this
side the Jordan, the land of Sihon and of Og, and from this
he reasoned that God had not irrevocably decreed punish-

ment for him, and that it might therefore now be **recalled.**[873]
He was strengthened in this assumption by the fact that
after the conquest of the east-Jordanic region God revealed
to him the instructions as to how the land was to be divided,
and it seemed to him as if he were in person to carry out
these instructions. He was, however, mistaken, for shortly
after these laws had been revealed to him, God informed him
that he was to look upon the promised land from Mount
Abarim, as he should never enter it.[874]

When God saw that Moses was not much concerned about
the impending punishment, He sealed the command He had
issued against him, and swore by His Ineffable Name that
Moses should not march into the land. Moses thereupon
put on sackcloth, threw himself upon the ashes, and prayed
not less than fifteen hundred prayers for the annulment of
the Divine resolve against him. He drew a circle about himself, stood in the center of it, and said, " I will not move from
this spot until judgment shall have been suspended." Heaven
and earth, as well as all the forms of creation, trembled and
said, " Perhaps it is God's wish to destroy this world, to
create a new universe." But a voice sounded from heaven
and said: " God's wish to destroy the world has not yet
come, the commotion in nature is due to this that ' in God's
hand is the soul of all living things and the spirit of all
flesh,' even the spirit of the man Moses, whose end is now at
hand."

God then bade them proclaim in heaven, and in all the
celestial courts of justice, that they should not accept Moses'
prayers, and that no angel was to carry Moses' prayer to
Him, because Moses' doom of death had been sealed by

Him. God quickly called before Him the Angel Akraziel, who is the celestial herald, and bade him proclaim the following in heaven: " Descend at once and lock every single gate in heaven, that Moses' prayer may not ascend into it." Then, at Moses' prayer, trembled heaven and earth, all the foundations thereof and the creatures therein, for his prayer was like a sword that slashes and rends, and can in no wise be parried, for in it was the power of the Ineffable Name that Moses had learned from his teacher Zagzagel, the teacher and scribe of the celestial beings. But when the Galgalim and Seraphim saw that God did not accept Moses' prayer, and without taking consideration of him did not grant his prayer for longer life, they all opened their mouths, saying: " Praised be the glory of the Lord from its place, for there is no injustice before Him, no forgetfulness, no respect of persons toward the small or the great." [875]

Moses' Prayer for Suspension of Judgment

Moses began his long but fruitless prayer by saying: " Lord of the world! Consider how much I had to bear for the sake of Israel until they became the people of Thy claim and of Thy possession. I suffered with them, shall I not then take part in their rejoicing? Look Thou, by forbidding me to enter the promised land, Thou givest the lie to Thy Torah, for it says, ' In his day thou shalt give the laborer his hire.' Where, then, is my hire for the forty years during which I labored for the sake of Thy children, and for their sake suffered much sorrow in Egypt, in the desert, and at the giving of the Torah and the commandments? With them I suffered pain, shall not I behold their good fortune as well?

But Thou tellest me that I may not cross the Jordan! All the time that we were in the desert I could not sit quietly in the academy, teaching and pronouncing judgment, but now that I should be able to do so, Thou tellest me that I may not." [876]

He continued: " May the mercy in Thee precede Thy justice, so that my prayer may be answered, for I well know that ' there is no mercy in justice.' [877] Thou Thyself didst tell me when I asked Thee how Thou didst conduct the world, ' I owe nothing to any creature, and what I do for them is a free gift on My part,' therefore as a free gift, grant now my prayer to me. [878] Thou Thyself didst point out to me that it is Thy desire that people should pray to Thee to cancel punishment that was laid upon them. When Israel committed that terrible sin, the worship of the Golden Calf, Thou didst say to me, ' Let Me alone, that I may destroy them, and blot out their name from under heaven.' I then thought, ' Who can restrain God, that He should say, " Let Me?" It is plain that He desires me to pray for His children ; ' and I prayed, and was answered. The prayer of the individual for the community was answered, but not so the prayer of the community for the one individual! Is it because I called Israel, ' rebels?' But in this I only followed Thy example, for Thou too didst call them, ' the sons of rebellion.' [879]

" Thou didst call me, as well as Leviathan, thy servant; I sent up prayers to Thee, and Leviathan likewise, and him didst Thou answer, for Thou madest a covenant with him that Thou keepest, but the covenant that Thou madest with me Thou breakest, for Thou didst say, ' Die in the mount whither thou goest up.' In the Torah Thy words are: ' If the servant

shall plainly say, I love my master, my wife, and my children; I will not go out free: then his master shall bring him
unto the judges; and he shall serve him for ever.' I implore
Thee now, 'hear my cry, O God; attend unto my prayer.'[880]
Thou art not in the position of a judge of flesh and blood
who, when granting a prayer, has to consider that he may
be compelled by his superior to repeal his answer, Thou canst
do what Thou wilt, for where on earth or in heaven is there
one so mighty that he can do such deeds as Thine in Egypt,
or who can perform such mighty deeds as Thou didst at the
Red Sea?[881] I pray Thee, therefore, let me behold the land
that, in spite of the slander of the spies, I praised, and Jerusalem and the Temple also.[882]

"When, in answer to the proposition Thou madest me to
go into Egypt and deliver Israel, I said, 'I can not do it,
for I made a vow to Jethro never to leave him,' Thou
didst release me from that vow. O Lord of the world!
As then Thou didst absolve me of my vow, saying, 'Go,
return into Egypt,' so do Thou now absolve Thyself from
Thy vow, and permit me to enter the land of Israel."
Then God answered: "Thou hast a master to absolve thee
from thy vow, but I have no master."[883] Moses then said:
"Thy judgment against me reads that I shall not as king
enter the promised land, for to me and to Aaron Thou didst
say, 'Ye shall not bring this assembly into the land which I
have given them.' Permit me then, at least, to enter it as a
common citizen." "That," said the Lord, "is impossible.
The king shall not enter it degraded to the rank of a common citizen." "Well, then," said Moses, "if I may not even
go into the land as a common citizen, let me at least enter

into the promised land by the Paneas Grotto, that runs from
the east bank to the west bank of the Jordan." But this request, too, God denied him, saying, " Thou shalt not go from
this bank of the Jordan to the other." " If this request also
is to be denied me," begged Moses, " grant me at least that
after my death my bones may be carried to the other side of
the Jordan." But God said, " Nay, not even thy bones shall
cross the Jordan." [884] " O Lord of the world! " exclaimed
Moses, " If Joseph's bones were permitted to be carried into
the promised land, why not mine? " God replied, " Whosoever acknowledges his country shall be buried therein, but
whosoever does not acknowledge his country shall not be
buried therein. Joseph pledged allegiance to his country
when he said, ' For indeed I was stolen away out of the land
of the Hebrews,' and therefore also does he deserve to have
his bones brought to the land of Israel, but thou didst in
silence hear the daughters of Jethro say to their father, ' An
Egyptian delivered us out of the hands of the shepherds,'
without correcting them by saying, ' I am a Hebrew; ' and
therefore shall not even thy bones be brought into the land
of Israel." [885]

Moses furthermore said to God: " O Lord of the
world! With the word, ' Behold ' did I begin Thy praise,
saying, ' Behold, the heaven and the heaven of heavens is the
Lord's,' and with that very word, ' Behold,' dost Thou seal
my death, saying, ' Behold, thy days approach that thou must
die.' " God replied to this: " A wicked man in his envy
sees only the profits, but not the expenditures of his neighbor. Dost thou not recall that when I wanted to send thee
to Egypt, thou didst also decline My request with the word,

Behold,' saying, ' Behold, they will not believe me.' Therefore did I say, ' Behold, thy days approach that thou must
die.' " ³⁰⁶   " As furthermore," continued God, " thou didst
say to the sons of Levi when they asked thy forgiveness,
' Enough, ye take too much upon ye, ye sons of Levi,' so too
shall I answer thy prayer for forgiveness, ' Let it suffice thee;
speak no more unto Me of this matter.' "

"O Lord of the world!" again pleaded Moses, "Wilt
not Thou recall the time when Thou didst say to me, ' Come
now, therefore, and I will send thee unto Pharaoh, that
thou mayest bring forth My people the children of Israel
out of Egypt.' Let them be led by me into their land as I
led them out of the land of bondage." But to this also
God found a reply: " Moses, wilt not thou recall the time
when thou didst say to Me, ' O my Lord, send, I pray Thee,
by the hand of him whom Thou wilt send?' ' With the
measure that a man uses, shall measure be given him.' ³⁵⁷
I announced death to thee with the word, ' Behold,' saying,
' Behold, thy days approach that thou must die,' because I
wanted to point out to thee that thou diest only because thou
art a descendant of Adam, upon whose sons I had pronounced death with the word, ' Behold,' saying to the angels:
' Behold, the man is become as one of us, to know good and
evil; and now, lest he put forth his hand, and take also of
the tree of life, and eat, and live forever.' " ³⁵⁸

Moses then said, " O Lord of the world! To the first
man didst Thou give a command that could easily be obeyed,
and yet he disobeyed it, and thereby merited death; but I
have not transgressed any of Thy commandments." God:
" Behold, Abraham also, who sanctified My name in the world,

died." Moses: "Yea, but from Abraham issued Ishmael,
whose descendants arouse Thy anger." God: "Isaac, also,
who laid his neck upon the altar to be offered as a sacrifice to
Me, died." Moses: "But from Isaac issued Esau who will
destroy the Temple and burn Thy house." God: "From
Jacob issued twelve tribes that did not anger Me, and yet he
died." Moses: "But he did not ascend into heaven, his feet
did not tread the clouds, Thou didst not speak with him face
to face, and he did not receive the Torah out of Thy hand."
God: "'Let it suffice thee; speak no more unto Me of this
matter,' speak not many words, for only 'a fool multiplieth
words.'" Moses: "O Lord of the world! Future generations will perchance say, 'Had not God found evil in Moses,
He would not have taken him out of the world.'" God:
"I have already written in My Torah, 'And there hath not
arisen since a prophet in Israel like unto Moses.'" Moses:
"Future generations will perhaps say that I had probably
acted in accordance with Thy will in my youth, while I was
active as a prophet, but that in my old age, when my prophetic activities ceased, I no longer did Thy will."

Moses: "Lord of the world! Let me, I pray, enter into the
Land, live there two or three years, and then die." God: "I
have resolved that thou shalt not go there." Moses: "If I
may not enter it in my lifetime, let me reach it after my
death." God: "Nay, neither dead nor alive shalt thou go
into the land." Moses: "Why this wrath against me?"
God: "Because ye sanctified Me not in the midst of the
children of Israel." Moses: "With all Thy creatures dost
Thou deal according to Thy quality of mercy, forgiving them
their sins, once, twice, and thrice, but me Thou wilt not for-

give even one single sin!" God: "Outside of this sin of
which thou art aware, thou hast committed six other sins
with which I have not until now reproached thee. At the
very first, when I appeared to thee, thou didst say, 'O my
Lord, send I pray Thee, by the hand of him whom Thou wilt
send,' and didst refuse to obey My command to go to Egypt.
Secondly thou didst say, 'For since I came to Pharaoh to
speak in Thy name, he hath evil entreated this people;
neither hast Thou delivered Thy people at all,' accusing Me
thereby of having only harmed Israel, instead of aiding
them. Thirdly didst thou say, 'If these men die the common death of all men, then the Lord hath not sent me,' so
that thou didst arouse doubts among Israel if thou wert really
My ambassador. Fourthly didst thou say, 'But if the Lord
make a new thing,' doubting if God could do so. Fifthly
didst thou say to Israel, 'Hear now, ye rebels,' and in this
way didst insult My children. Sixthly didst thou say, 'And
behold, ye are risen up in your fathers' stead, an increase of
sinful men.' Were Abraham, Isaac, and Jacob, Israel's
fathers, perchance sinful men, that thou didst thus address
their children?" Moses: "I only followed Thy example,
for Thou, too, didst say, 'The censers of these sinners.'"
God: "But I did not characterize their fathers as sinners."

Moses: "O Lord of the world! How often did Israel sin
before Thee, and when I begged and implored mercy for
them, Thou forgavest them, but me Thou wilt not forgive!
For my sake Thou forgavest the sins of sixty myriads, and
now Thou wilt not forgive my sin?" God: "The punishment
that is laid upon the community is different from the punishment that is laid upon the individual, for I am not so severe

in my treatment of the community as I am in dealing with
an individual. But know, furthermore, that until now fate
had been in thy power, but now fate is no longer in thy
power." [889] Moses: "O Lord of the world! Rise up from the
Throne of Justice, and seat Thyself upon the Throne of
Mercy, so that in Thy mercy, Thou mayest grant me life,
during which I may atone for my sins by sufferings that
Thou shalt bring upon me. Hand me not over to the sword
of the Angel of Death. If Thou wilt grant my prayer, then
shall I sound Thy praises to all the inhabitants of the earth;
I do not wish to die, ' but live and declare the works of the
Lord.' " God replied: " ' This is the gate of the Lord; the
righteous shall enter into it,' this is the gate into which the
righteous must enter as well as other creatures, for death
had been decreed for man since the beginning of the
world." [890]

Moses, however, continued to importune God, saying:
" With justice and with mercy hast Thou created the world
and mankind, may mercy now conquer justice. In my youth
Thou didst begin by showing me Thy power in the bush of
thorns, and now, in my old age, I beseech Thee, treat me not
as an earthly king treats his servant. When a king of flesh
and blood has a servant, he loves him so long as he is young
and strong, but casts him off when he is grown old. But
Thou, ' cast me not off in the time of old age.' Thou didst
show Thy power at the revelation of the Ten Commandments, and Thy strong hand in the ten plagues that Thou
didst bring upon Egypt. Thou didst create everything, and
in Thy hand doth it lie to kill and to give life, there is none
who can do these works, nor is there strength like Thine in

the future world. Let me then proclaim Thy majesty to the coming generations, and tell them that through me Thou didst cleave the Red Sea, and give the Torah to Israel, that throughout forty years Thou didst cause manna to rain from heaven for Israel, and water to rise from the well." For Moses thought that if his life were spared, he should be able everlastingly to restrain Israel from sin and to hold them forever in faith to the one God. But God said: "'Let it suffice thee.' If thy life were to be spared, men should mistake thee, and make a god of thee, and worship thee." "Lord of the world!" replied Moses, "Thou didst already test me at the time when the Golden Calf was made and I destroyed it. Why then should I die?" God: "Whose son art thou?" Moses: "Amram's son." God: "And whose son was Amram?" Moses: "Izhar's son." God: "And whose son was he?" Moses: "Kohath's son." God: "And whose son was he?" Moses: "Levi's son." God: "And from whom did all of these descend?" Moses: "From Adam." God: "Was the life of any one of these spared?" Moses: "They all died." God: "And thou wishest to live on?" Moses: "Lord of the world! Adam stole the forbidden fruit and ate of it, and it was on this account that Thou didst punish him with death, but did I ever steal aught from Thee? Thou Thyself didst write of me, 'My servant Moses, who is faithful in all Mine house.'" God: "Art thou worthier than Noah?" Moses: "Yes; when Thou sentest the flood over his generation he did not beg Thy mercy for them, but I did say to Thee, 'Yet now, if Thou wilt forgive their sin; and if not, blot me, I pray Thee, out of Thy book which Thou hast written.'"

God: " Was it I perchance, that counselled thee to slay the Egyptian?" Moses: " Thou didst slay all the firstborn of Egypt, and shall I die on account of one single Egyptian that I slew?" God: " Art thou perchance My equal? I slay and restore to life, but canst thou perchance revive the dead?" [891]

GOD TRIES TO COMFORT MOSES CONCERNING HIS DEATH.

That Moses might not take his approaching end too much to heart, God tried to comfort him by pointing out to him that in his lifetime he had received such distinctions from his Creator as no man before him, and that still greater distinctions awaited him in the future world. God said: " Dost not thou remember the great honor I showed thee? Thou didst say to Me, ' Arise,' and I arose; thou saidst, ' Turn about,' and I turned about; for thy sake too did I invert the order of heaven and earth, for the order of heaven it is to send down dew and rain, and earth's order is it to produce bread, but thou didst say to Me, ' I do not wish it so, but bid heaven to send down bread, and earth to bring forth water,' and I acted in accordance with thy wish; I caused bread to rain from heaven, and the well ' sprung up.' Thou didst say, ' If the Lord make a new thing, and the ground open her mouth, and swallow them up, then ye shall understand that the Lord hath sent me,' and I fulfilled thy wish, and it swallowed them. I had also spoken, ' He that sacrificeth unto any god, save unto the Lord only, shall be utterly destroyed,' but when Israel sinned with the Golden Calf and I meant to deal with them according to My words, thou wouldst not let Me, saying: ' Pardon, I pray Thee, the iniquity of this people,' and

I forgave them as thou didst ask Me. More than this, the Torah is named after Me, it is the Torah of the Lord, but I named it after Thy name, saying, ' It is the Torah of My servant Moses.' The children of Israel also are named after Me, ' for unto Me the children of Israel are servants; they are My servants,' but I called them after thy name. I distinguished thee still more, for just as there is neither food nor drink for Me, so also didst thou stay in heaven forty days and forty nights, and in all that time, ' didst neither eat bread, nor drink water.' I am God, and see, ' I made thee a god to Pharaoh ; ' I have prophets, and thou hast a prophet, for I said to thee, ' and Aaron, thy brother, shall be thy prophet.' Again, no being may see Me, and thee too did I make so that ' the people were afraid to come nigh thee,' and as I said to thee, ' thou shalt see My back : but My face shall not be seen,' so too did the people see the back of thee. I glorified the Torah with twenty-two letters, and with all these letters did I glorify thee. I sent thee to Pharaoh, and thou didst lead Israel out of Egypt; through thee did I bestow the Sabbath upon Israel, and the law of circumcision ; I gave thee the Ten Commandments, I covered thee with the cloud, I gave thee the two tables of stone, which thou didst break; I made thee unique in the world; I gave thee the Torah as an inheritance, and honored thee more than all the seventy elders."

Moses had to acknowledge that extraordinary marks of honor had been his. He said : " Lord of the world! Thou didst set me on high, and didst bestow upon me so many benefits that I cannot enumerate one of a thousand, and all the world knows how Thou didst exalt me and honor me, and all the world knows as well that Thou art the One God, the only One in Thy world, that there is none beside Thee, and that there is nothing like Thee. Thou didst create those above and those below, Thou art the beginning and the end. Who can enumerate Thy deeds of glory? Do one of these, I beseech Thee, that I may pass over the Jordan." God said: " ' Let it suffice, speak no more unto Me of this matter.' [892] It is better for thee to die here, than that thou shouldst cross the Jordan and die in the land of Israel. There in a tomb fashioned by men, on a bier made by men, and by the hands of men wouldst thou be buried; but now shalt thou be buried in a tomb fashioned by God, on a bier made by God, and shalt be buried by the hands of God.[893] O My son Moses, much honor has been stored up for thee in the future world, for thou wilt take part in all the delights of Paradise, where are prepared three hundred and ten worlds, which I have created for every pious man that through love of Me devoted himself to the Torah. And as in this world I appointed thee over the sixty myriads of Israel, so in the future world shall I appoint thee over the fifty-five myriads of pious men. Thy days, O Moses, will pass, when thou art dead, but thy light will not fade, for thou wilt never have need of the light of sun or moon or stars, nor wilt thou require raiment or shelter, or oil for thy head, or shoes for thy feet, for My majesty will shine before thee, My glory will clothe thee, My splendor will shelter thee, My radiance will make thy face beam, My sweetness will delight thy palate, the carriages of My equipage shall serve as vehicles for thee, and one of My many sceptres upon which is engraved the Ineffable Name, one that I had employed in the creation of the world, shall I give to thee, the image of which I had already given thee in this world." ^{***}

THE INTERCESSIONS FOR MOSES

When Moses saw that God lent no ear to his prayers, he sought to invoke God's mercy through the pleadings of others. "To everything there is a season, and a time to every purpose under the heaven." So long as the course of Moses' days had not yet been run, everything was in his power, but when his time was over, he sought for some one to appeal to God's mercy for him. He now betook himself to Earth and said: "O Earth, I pray thee, implore God's mercy for me. Perhaps for thy sake will He take pity upon me and let me enter into the land of Israel." Earth, however, replied: "I am 'without form and void,' and then too I shall soon 'wax old like a garment.' How then should I venture to appear before the King of kings? Nay, thy fate is like mine, for 'dust thou art, and unto dust shalt thou return.'"

Moses then betook himself to the Heavens, and said: "I pray you, implore God's mercy for me, for through you perchance will He take pity upon me and let me enter into the land of Israel." The Heavens, however, replied: "Before imploring God's mercy for thee, we must first do so for ourselves, for 'the heavens are not clean in His sight,' and 'the heavens shall vanish away like smoke.'"

Moses hastened to Sun and Moon, and implored them to intercede for him with God, but they replied: "Before we pray to God for thee, we must pray for ourselves, for 'the moon shall be confounded, and the sun ashamed.'"

Moses then took his request to the Stars and the Planets, but these, too, replied: "Before we venture to plead for thee, we must plead for ourselves, for 'all the host of heaven shall be dissolved.'"

Moses then went to the Hills and the Mountains, beseeching them, "Pray appeal to God's mercy for me," and they, too, replied: "We too have to implore God's mercy for ourselves, for He said, 'The mountains shall depart, and the hills be removed.'"

He then laid his plea before Mount Sinai, but the latter said: "Didst thou not see with thine eyes and record in the Torah that, 'Mount Sinai was altogether in smoke, because the Lord descended upon it in a fire?' How then shall I approach the Lord?"

He then went to the Rivers, and sought their intercession before the Lord, but they replied: "'The Lord made a way in the sea, and a path in the mighty waters.' We cannot save ourselves out of His hand, and how then should we aid thee?"

Then he went to the Deserts, and to all the Elements of Nature, but in vain sought to secure their aid. Their answer was: "All go unto one place; all are of the dust, and turn to dust again."

The Great Sea was the last to which he brought his request, but it replied: "Son of Amram, what ails thee today? Art not thou the son of Amram that erstwhile came to me with a staff, beat me, and clove me into twelve parts, while I was powerless against thee, because the Shekinah accompanied thee at thy right hand? What has happened, then, that thou comest before me now pleading?" Upon being reminded of the miracles that he had accomplished in his youth, Moses burst into tears and said, " Oh, that I were as in months past, as in the days when God preserved me!" And turning to the sea, he made answer: " In those days, when I stood beside thee, I was king of the world, and I commanded, but now I am a suppliant, whose prayers are unanswered." [895]

When Moses perceived that Heaven and Earth, Sun and Moon, Stars and Planets, Mountains and Rivers turned a deaf ear to his prayers, he tried to implore mankind to intercede for him before God. He went first to his disciple Joshua, saying: " O my son, be mindful of the love with which I treated thee by day and by night, teaching thee mishnah and halakah, and all arts and sciences, and implore now for my sake God's mercy, for perhaps through thee He may take pity upon me, and permit me to enter the land of Israel." Joshua began to weep bitterly, and beat his palms in sorrow, but when he wanted to begin to pray, Samael appeared and stopped his mouth, saying, " Why dost thou seek to oppose the command of God, who is ' the Rock, whose work is perfect, and all whose ways are judgment?' " Joshua then went to Moses and said, " Master, Samael will not let me pray." At these words Moses burst into loud sobs, and Joshua, too, wept bitterly.

Moses then went to his brother's son, Eleazar, to whom he said: " O my son, be mindful of the days when God was angry with thy father on account of the making of the Golden Calf, and I saved him through my prayer. Pray now thou to God for me, and perhaps God will take pity upon me, and let me enter into the land of Israel." But when Eleazar,

28

in accordance with Moses' wish, began to pray, Samael appeared and stopped his mouth, saying to him, " How canst thou think of disregarding God's command? " Then Eleazar reported to Moses that he could not pray for him.

He now tried to invoke Caleb's aid, but him, too, Samael prevented from praying to God. Moses then went to the seventy elders and the other leaders of the people, he even implored every single man among Israel to pray for him, saying: " Remember the wrath which the Lord nursed against your fathers, but I brought it to pass that God relinquished His plan to destroy Israel, and forgave Israel their sins. Now, I pray ye, betake yourselves to the sanctuary of God and exhort His pity for me, that He may permit me to enter into the land of Israel, for ' God never rejects the prayer of the multitude.' "

When the people and their leaders heard these words of Moses, they broke out into mournful weeping, and in the Tabernacle with bitter tears they entreated God to answer Moses' prayer, so that their cries rose even to the Throne of Glory. But then one hundred and eighty four myriads of angels under the leadership of the great angels Zakun and Lahash descended and snatched away the words of the suppliants, that they might not reach God. The angel Lahash indeed tried to restore to their place the words which the other angels had snatched away, so that they might reach God, but when Samael learned of this, he fettered Lahash with chains of fire and brought him before God, where he received sixty blows of fire and was expelled from the inner chamber of God because, contrary to God's wish, he had attempted to aid Moses in the fulfilment of his desire. When

Israel now saw how the angels dealt with their prayers, they went to Moses and said, " The angels will not let us pray for thee." [896]

When Moses saw that neither the world nor mankind could aid him, he betook himself to the Angel of the Face, to whom he said, " Pray for me, that God may take pity upon me, and that I may not die." But the angel replied: " Why, Moses, dost thou exert thyself in vain? Standing behind the curtain that is drawn before the Lord, I heard that thy prayer in this instance is not to be answered." Moses now laid his hand upon his head and wept bitterly, saying, " To whom shall I now go, that he might implore God's mercy for me? "

God was now very angry with Moses because he would not resign himself to the doom that had been sealed, but His wrath vanished as soon as Moses spoke the words: " The Lord, the Lord, a God full of compassion and gracious, slow to anger, and plenteous in mercy and truth; keeping mercy for thousands, forgiving iniquity and transgression and sin." God now said kindly to Moses: " I have registered two vows, one that thou art to die, and the second that Israel is to perish. I cannot cancel both vows, if therefore thou choosest to live, Israel must be ruined." " Lord of the world! " replied Moses, " Thou approachest me artfully; Thou seizest the rope at both ends, so that I myself must now say, ' Rather shall Moses and a thousand of his kind perish, than a single soul out of Israel! ' But will not all men exclaim, ' Alas! The feet that trod the heavens, the face that beheld the Face of the Shekinah, and the hands that received the Torah, shall now be covered with dust! ' " God replied: " Nay, the people will say: ' If a man like Moses, who ascended into heaven, who was a peer of the angels, with whom God spoke face to face, and to whom He gave the Torah—if such a man cannot justify himself before God, how much less can an ordinary mortal of flesh and blood, who appears before God without having done good deeds or studied the Torah, justify himself?' I want to know," He added, " why thou art so much aggrieved at thy impending death." Moses: " I am afraid of the sword of the Angel of Death." God: " If this is the reason then speak no more in this matter, for I will not deliver thee into his hand." Moses, however, would not yield, but furthermore said, " Shall my mother Jochebed, to whom my life brought so much grief, suffer sorrow after my death also?" God: " So was it in My mind even before I created the world, and so is the course of the world; every generation has its learned men, every generation has its leaders, every generation has its guides. Up to now it was thy duty to guide the people, but now the time is ripe for thy disciple Joshua to relieve thee of the office destined for him." [897]

MOSES SERVES JOSHUA

Moses now said to himself: " If God has determined that I may not enter the land of Israel, and I am thus to lose the reward for the many precepts that may be observed only in the Holy Land, for no other reason than because the time has come for my disciple Joshua to go to the front of Israel and lead them into the land, then were it better for me to remain alive, to enter the land, and relinquish to Joshua the leadership of the people." What now did Moses do? From the first day of Shebat to the sixth of Adar, the day before his death, he went and served Joshua from morning until evening, as a disciple his master. These thirty-six days during which Moses served his former disciple corresponded to the equal number of years during which he had been served by Joshua.

The way in which Moses ministered to Joshua was as follows. During this period he arose at midnight, went to Joshua's door, opened it with a key, and taking a shirt from which he shook out the dust, laid it near to Joshua's pillow. He then cleaned Joshua's shoes and placed them beside his bed. Then he took his undergarment, his cloak, his turban, his golden helmet, and his crown of pearls, examined them to see if they were in good condition, cleaned and polished them, arranged them aright, and laid them on a golden chair. He then fetched a pitcher of water and a golden basin and placed them before the golden chair, so that Joshua upon awakening might find water wherewith to wash himself. He then caused Joshua's rooms, which he had furnished like his own, to be swept and put into order, then ordered the golden throne to be brought in, which he covered with a linen and a woolen cloth, and with other beautiful and costly garments, as is the custom with kings. After all these preparations had been made, he bade the herald proclaim: "Moses stands at Joshua's gate and announces that whosoever wishes to hear God's word should betake himself to Joshua, for he, according to God's word, is the leader of Israel."

When the people heard the herald, they trembled and shook, and pretended to have a headache, so that they might not have to go to Joshua. Every one of them said, in tears,

"Woe to thee, O land, when thy king is a child!" But a voice from heaven resounded, crying, "When Israel was a child, then I loved him," and Earth, too, opened her mouth, and said, "I have been young, and now am old, yet have I not seen the righteous forsaken."

While the people refused to lend ear to the herald's summons, the elders of Israel, the leaders of the troops, the princes of the tribes, and the captains of thousands, of hundreds, and of tens appeared at Joshua's tent, and Moses assigned to each his place according to his rank.

In the meantime approached the hour when Joshua was wont to arise, whereupon Moses entered his room and extended his hand to him. When Joshua saw that Moses served him, he was ashamed to have his master minister to him, and taking the shirt out of Moses' hand, and dressing himself, trembling, he cast himself at Moses' feet and said: "O my master, be not the cause wherefore I should die before half my time is done, owing to the sovereignty God has imposed upon me." But Moses replied: "Fear not, my son, thou sinnest not if thou art served by me. With the measure wherewith thou didst mete out to me, do I mete out to thee; as with a pleasant face thou didst serve me, so shall I serve thee. It was I that taught thee, 'Love thy neighbor as thyself,' and also, 'Let thy pupil's honor be as dear to thee as thine own.'" Moses did not rest until Joshua seated himself upon the golden chair, and then Moses served Joshua, who still resisted, in every needful way. After he was through with all this, he laid upon Joshua, who still resisted, his rays of majesty, which he had received from his celestial teacher Zagzagel, scribe of the angels, at the close of his instruction in all the secrets of the Torah.

When Joshua was completely dressed and ready to go out, they reported to him and to Moses that all Israel awaited them. Moses thereupon laid his hand upon Joshua to lead him out of the tent, and quite against Joshua's wish insisted upon giving precedence to him as they stepped forth. When Israel saw Joshua precede Moses, they all trembled, arose, and made room for these two to proceed to the place of the great, where stood the golden throne, upon which Moses seated Joshua against his will. All Israel burst into tears when they saw Joshua upon the golden throne, and he said amid tears, " Why all this greatness and honor to me? " [898]

In this way did Moses spend the time from the first day of Shebat to the sixth of Adar, during which time he expounded the Torah to the sixty myriads of Israel in seventy languages.

THE LAST DAY OF MOSES' LIFE

On the seventh day of Adar, Moses knew that on this day he should have to die, for a heavenly voice resounded, saying, " Take heed to thyself, O Moses, for thou hast only one more day to live." [899] What did Moses now do? On this day he wrote thirteen scrolls of the Torah, twelve for the twelve tribes, and one he put into the Holy Ark, so that, if they wished to falsify the Torah, the one in the Ark might remain untouched. Moses thought, " If I occupy myself with the Torah, which is the tree of life, this day will draw to a close, and the impending doom will be as naught." God, however, beckoned to the sun, which firmly opposed itself to Moses, saying, " I will not set, so long as Moses lives." [900] When

Moses had completed writing the scrolls of the Torah, not
even half the day was over. He then bade the tribes come
to him, and from his hand receive the scrolls of the Torah,
admonishing the men and women separately to obey the
Torah and its commands. The most excellent among the
thirteen scrolls was fetched by Gabriel, who brought it
to the highest heavenly court to show the piety of Moses,
who had fulfilled all that is written in the Torah. Gabriel
passed with it through all the heavens, so that all might witness Moses' piety. It is this scroll of the Torah out of which
the souls of the pious read on Monday and Thursday, as well
as on the Sabbath and holy days.

Moses on this day showed great honor and distinction to
his disciple Joshua in the sight of all Israel. A herald passed
before Joshua through all the camp, proclaiming, " Come
and hear the words of the new prophet that hath arisen for
us to-day! " All Israel approached to honor Joshua. Moses
then gave the command to fetch hither a golden throne, a
crown of pearls, a royal helmet, and a robe of purple. He
himself set up the rows of benches for the Sanhedrin, for the
heads of the army, and for the priests. Then Moses betook
himself to Joshua, dressed him, put the crown on his head,
and bade him be seated upon the golden throne to deliver
from it a speech to the people. Joshua then spoke the following words which he first whispered to Caleb, who then announced it in a loud voice to the people. He said : " Awaken,
rejoice, heavens of heavens, ye above; sound joyously,
foundations of earth, ye below. Awaken and proclaim aloud,
ye orders of creation; awaken and sing, ye mountains everlasting. Exult and shout in joy, ye hills of the earth, awaken

and burst into songs of triumph, ye hosts of heaven. Sing
and relate, ye tents of Jacob, sing, ye dwelling places of
Israel. Sing and hearken to all the words that come from
your King, incline your heart to all His words, and gladly
take upon yourselves and your souls the commandments
of your God. Open your mouth, let your tongue speak,
and give honor to the Lord that is your Helper, give
thanks to your Lord and put your trust in Him. For He is
One, and hath no second, there is none like Him among the
gods, not one among the angels is like Him, and beside Him
is there none that is your Lord. To His praise there are no
bounds; to His fame no limit, no end; to His miracles no
fathoming; to His works no number. He kept the oath that
He swore to the Patriarchs, through our teacher Moses. He
fulfilled the covenant with them, and the love and the vow He
had made them, for He delivered us through many miracles,
led us from bondage to freedom, clove for us the sea, and
bestowed upon us six hundred and thirteen commandments."

When Joshua had completed his discourse, a voice resounded from heaven, and said to Moses, " Thou hast only
five hours more of life." Moses called out to Joshua, " Stay
seated like a king before the people!" Then both began to
speak before all Israel; Moses read out the text and Joshua
expounded. There was no difference of opinion between
them, and the words of the two matched like the pearls in a
royal crown. But Moses' countenance shone like the sun,
and Joshua's like the moon.

While Joshua and all Israel still sat before Moses, a voice
from heaven became audible and said, " Moses, thou hast
now only four hours of life." Now Moses began to implore

God anew: " O Lord of the world! If I must die only for
my disciple's sake, consider that I am willing to conduct
myself as if I were his pupil; let it be as if he were high
priest, and I a common priest; he a king, and I his servant."
God replied: " I have sworn by My great name, which ' the
heaven and heaven of heavens cannot contain,' that thou shalt
not cross the Jordan." Moses: "Lord of the world! Let
me at least, by the power of the Ineffable Name, fly like
a bird in the air; or make me like a fish transform my two
arms to fins and my hair to scales, that like a fish I may
leap over the Jordan and see the land of Israel." God: " If
I comply with thy wish, I shall break My vow." Moses:
"Lord of the world! Lead me upon the pinions of the
clouds about three parasangs high beyond the Jordan, so
that the clouds be below me, and I from above may see the
land." God replied: " This, too, seems to Me like a breaking of My vow." Moses: "Lord of the world! Cut me
up, limb by limb, throw me over the Jordan, and then revive me, so that I may see the land." God: " That, too,
would be as if I had broken My vow." Moses: " Let me
skim the land with my glance." God: " In this point will I
comply with thy wish. ' Thou shalt see the land before
thee; but thou shalt not go thither.' " God thereupon
showed him all the land of Israel, and although it was a
square of four hundred parasangs, still God imparted such
strength to Moses' eyes that he could oversee all the land.
What lay in the deep appeared to him above, the hidden was
plainly in view, the distant was close at hand, and he saw
everything.[901]

MOSES BEHOLDS THE FUTURE

Pointing to the land, God said: " ' This is the land which I sware unto Abraham, unto Isaac, and unto Jacob, saying, I will give it unto thy seed; ' to them did I promise it, but to thee do I show it." But he saw not only the land. God pointed with His finger to every part of the Holy Land, and accurately described it to Moses, saying, " This is Judah's share, this Ephraim's," and in this way instructed him about the division of the land. Moses learned from God the history of the whole land, and the history of every part of it. God showed it to him as it would appear in its glory, and how it would appear under the rule of strangers. God revealed to him not only the complete history of Israel that was to take place in the Holy Land, but also revealed to him all that had occurred and that was to occur in the world, from its creation to the Day of Judgment, when the resurrection of the dead will take place Joshua's war with the Canaanites, Israel's deliverance from the Philistines through Samson, the glory of Israel in David's reign, the building of the Temple under Solomon, and its destruction, the line of kings from the house of David, and the line of prophets from the house of Rahab, the destruction of Gog and Magog on the plain of Jericho, all this and much more, was it given Moses to see. And as God showed him the events in this world, so too did he show him Paradise with its dwellers of piety, and hell with the wicked men that fill it.[902]

The place whence Moses looked upon the Holy Land was a mountain that bore four names: Nebo, Abarim, Hor, and Pisgah. The different appellations are due to the fact that the kingdoms accounted it as a special honor to themselves if they had possessions in the Holy Land. This mountain was divided among four kingdoms, and each kingdom had a special name for its part.⁹⁰⁸ The most appropriate name seems to be Nebo, for upon it died three sinless nebi'im, "prophets," Moses, Aaron, and Miriam.

To this mountain, upon God's command, Moses betook himself at noon of the day on which he died. On this occasion, as upon two others, God had His commands executed at noon to show mankind that they could not hinder the execution of God's orders, even if they chose to do so. Had Moses gone to die on Mount Nebo at night, Israel would have said: "He could well do so in the night when we knew of nothing. Had we known that he should go to Nebo to his death, we should not have let him go. Verily, we should not have permitted him to die, who led us out of Egypt, who clove the sea for us, who caused manna to rain down and the well to spring up, who bade the quails to fly to us, and performed many other great miracles." God therefore bade Moses go to his grave on mount Nebo in bright daylight, at the noon hour, saying, "Let him who wishes to prevent it try to do so."

For a similar reason did Israel's exodus from Egypt take place in the noon hour, for, had they departed at night, the Egyptians would have said: "They were able to do this in the darkness of the night because we knew nothing of it. Had we known, we should not have permitted them to depart, but should have compelled them by force of arms to stay in Egypt." God therefore said: "I shall lead out Israel at the noon hour. Let him who wishes to prevent it try to do so."

Noah, too, entered the ark at the noon hour for a similar reason. God said: "If Noah enters the ark at night, his generation will declare: 'He could do so because we were not aware of it, or we should not have permitted him to enter the ark alone, but should have taken our hammers and axes, and crushed the ark.' Therefore," said God, "do I wish him to enter the ark at the noon hour. Let him who wishes to prevent it try to do so."

God's command to Moses to betake himself to Mount Nebo, and there to die, was couched in the following words: "'Get thee up into this mountain of Abarim.' Death for thee means not destruction, but elevation. 'Die in the mount whither thou goest up;' go up all alone, and let no one accompany thee. Aaron's son Eleazar accompanied him to his tomb, but no man shall witness the distinction and reward that await thee at thy death. There shalt thou be gathered to thy people, to the fathers of Israel, Abraham, Isaac, and Jacob, and to thy fathers, Kohath and Amram, as well as to thy brother Aaron and thy sister Miriam, just as Aaron thy brother died in mount Hor, and was gathered unto his people." For when Aaron was to die, Moses drew off one by one his garments, with which he invested Aaron's son Eleazar, and after he had taken off all his garments, he clothed him in his death robe. Then he said to Aaron: "Aaron, my brother, enter the cave," and he entered. "Get upon the couch," said Moses, and Aaron did so. "Close thine eyes," and he closed them. "Stretch out thy feet," and Aaron did so, and expired. At sight of this painless and peaceful death, Moses said: "Blessed is the man that dies such a death!" When therefore Moses' end drew nigh, God said: "Thou shalt die the death that thou didst wish, as peacefully and with as little pain as thy brother Aaron." [904]

Moses Meets the Messiah in Heaven

Moses received still another special distinction on the day of his death, for on that day God permitted him to ascend to the lofty place of heaven, and showed him the reward that awaited him in heaven, and the future. The Divine attribute of Mercy appeared there before him and said to him: "I bring glad tidings to thee, at which thou wilt rejoice. Turn to the Throne of Mercy and behold!" Moses turned to the Throne of Mercy and saw God build the Temple of jewels and pearls, while between the separate gems and pearls shimmered the radiance of the Shekinah, brighter than all jewels. And in this Temple he beheld the Messiah, David's son, and his own brother Aaron, standing erect, and dressed in the robe of the high priest. Aaron then said to Moses: "Do not draw near, for this is the place where the Shekinah dwells, and know that no one may enter here before he have tasted of death and his soul have been delivered to the Angel of Death."

Moses now fell upon his face before God, saying, "Permit me to speak to Thy Messiah before I die." God then said to Moses: "Come, I shall teach thee My great name, that the flames of the Shekinah consume thee not." When the Messiah, David's son, and Aaron beheld Moses approach them, they knew that God had taught him the great name, so they went to meet him and saluted him with the greeting: "Blessed be he that cometh in the name of the Lord."

Moses thereupon said to the Messiah: "God told me that Israel was to erect a Temple to Him upon earth, and I now see Him build His own Temple, and that, too, in heaven!" The Messiah replied: "Thy father Jacob saw the Temple that will be erected on earth, and also the Temple that God rears with His own hand in heaven, and he clearly understood that it was the Temple God constructed with His own hand in heaven as a house of jewels, of pearls, and of the light of the Shekinah, that was to be preserved for Israel to all eternity, to the end of all generations. This was in the night when Jacob slept upon a stone, and in his dream beheld one Jerusalem upon earth, and another in heaven. God then said to Jacob, ' My son Jacob, to-day I stand above thee as in the future thy children will stand before Me.' At the sight of these two Jerusalems, the earthly and the heavenly, Jacob said: ' The Jerusalem on earth is nothing, this is not the house that will be preserved for my children in all generations, but in truth that other house of God, that He builds with His own hands.' But if thou sayest," continued the Messiah, "that God with His own hands builds Himself a Temple in heaven, know then that with His hands also He will build the Temple upon earth."

When Moses heard these words from the mouth of the Messiah, he rejoiced greatly, and lifting up his face to God, he said, " O Lord of the world! When will this Temple built here in heaven come down to earth below?" God replied: " I have made known the time of this event to no creature, either to the earlier ones or to the later, how then should I tell thee?" Moses said: " Give me a sign, so that out of the happenings in the world I may gather when that time will approach." God: "I shall first scatter Israel as with a shovel over all the earth, so that they may be scattered among all nations in the four corners of the earth, and then shall I ' set My hand again the second time,' and gather them in that migrated with Jonah, the son of Amittai, to the land of Pathros, and those that dwell in the land of Shinar, Hamath, Elam, and the islands of the sea."

When Moses had heard this, he departed from heaven with a joyous spirit. The Angel of Death followed him to earth, but could not possess himself of Moses' soul, for he refused to give it up to him, delivering it to none but God Himself.[905]

The Last Hours of Moses

When Moses had finished looking upon the land and the future, he was one hour nearer to death. A voice sounded from heaven and said, " Make no fruitless endeavors to live, for thou hast now in this world only three hours of life." Moses, however, did not desist from prayer, saying to God: " Lord of the world! Let me stay on this side the Jordan with the sons of Reuben and the sons of Gad, that I may be as one of them, while Joshua as king at the head of Israel shall enter into the land beyond the Jordan." God replied: " Dost thou wish Me to make as naught the words in the Torah that read, ' Three times in the year all thy males shall appear before the Lord God?' If Israel sees that thou dost not make a pilgrimage to the sanctuary, they will say, ' If Moses, through whom the Torah and the laws were given to us, does not make a pilgrimage to the sanctuary, how much less do we need to do so!' Thou wouldst then cause nonobservance of My commandments. I have, furthermore, written in the Torah through thee, 'At the end of every seven years, in the set time of the year of release, when all Israel is come to appear before the Lord thy God, in the place which He shall choose, thou shalt read this law before all Israel in their hearing.' If thou wert to live thou shouldst put Joshua's authority in the eyes of all Israel to naught, for they would say, ' Instead of learning the Torah and hearing it from the mouth of the disciple, let us rather go to the teacher and learn from him.' Israel will then abandon Joshua and go to thee, so that thou wouldst cause rebellion against My Torah, in which is written that the king shall read before all Israel the Torah in the set time of the year of release." [908]

In the meanwhile still another hour had passed, and a voice sounded from heaven and said: " How long wilt thou endeavor in vain to avert the sentence? Thou hast now only two hours more of life." The wicked Samael, head of the evil spirits, had eagerly awaited the moment of Moses' death, for he hoped to take his soul like that of all other mortals, and he said continually, " When will the moment be at hand when Michael shall weep and I shall triumph? " When now only two hours remained before Moses' death, Michael, Israel's guardian angel, began to weep, and Samael was jubilant, for now the moment he had awaited so long was very close. But Michael said to Samael: " ' Rejoice not against me, mine enemy: when I fall, I shall arise; when I sit in darkness, the Lord shall be a light unto me.' Even if I fell on account of Moses's death, I shall arise again through Joshua when he will conquer the one and thirty

29

kings of Palestine. Even if I sit in darkness owing to the destruction of the first and second Temples, the Lord shall be my light on the day of the Messiah."

In the meanwhile still another hour had passed, and a voice resounded from heaven and said, "Moses, thou hast only one hour more of life!" Moses thereupon said: "O Lord of the world! Even if Thou wilt not let me enter into the land of Israel, leave me at least in this world, that I may live, and not die." God replied: "If I should not let thee die in this world, how then can I revive thee hereafter for the future world? Thou wouldst, moreover, then give the lie to the Torah, for through thee I wrote therein, ' neither is there any that can deliver out of My hand.'" Moses continued to pray: "O Lord of the world! If Thou dost not permit me to enter into the land of Israel, let me live like the beasts of the field, that feed on herbs, and drink water, let me live and see the world: let me be as one of these." But God said, "Let it suffice thee!" Still Moses continued: "If Thou wilt not grant me this, let me at least live in this world like a bird that flies in the four directions of the world, and each day gathers its food from the ground, drinks water out of the streams, and at eve returns to its nest." But even this last prayer of his was denied, for God said, "Thou hast already made too many words." [907]

Moses now raised up his voice in weeping, and said, "To whom shall I go that will now implore mercy for me?" He went to every work of creation and said, "Implore mercy for me." But all replied: "We cannot even implore mercy for ourselves, for God ' hath made everything beautiful in its time,' but afterward, ' all go unto one place, all are of the

dust, and all turn to dust again,' ' for the heavens shall vanish away like smoke, and the earth shall wax old like a garment.' "

When Moses saw that none of the works of creation could
aid him, he said : " He is ' the Rock, His work is perfect, for
all His ways are judgment: A God of faithfulness and without iniquity, just and right is He.' "

When Moses saw that he could not escape death, he called
Joshua, and in the presence of all Israel addressed him as
follows : " Behold, my son, the people that I deliver into thy
hands, is the people of the Lord. It is still in its youth, and
hence is inexperienced in the observance of its commandments ; beware, therefore, lest thou speak harshly to them,
for they are the children of the Holy One, who called them,
' My firstborn son, Israel '; and He loved them before all
other nations." But God, on the other hand, at once said to
Joshua : " Joshua, thy teacher Moses has transferred his
office to thee. Follow now in his footsteps, take a rod and
hit upon the head, ' Israel is a child, hence I love him,' and
' withhold not correction from the child.' " [908]

Joshua now said to Moses : " O my teacher Moses, what
will become of me? If I give to the one a share upon a
mountain, he will be sure to want one in the valley, and he to
whom I shall give his share in the valley will wish it to be
upon a mountain." Moses, however, quieted him, saying,
" Be not afraid, for God hath assured me that there will be
peace at the distribution of the land." Then Moses said:
" Question me regarding all the laws that are not quite clear
to thee, for I shall be taken from thee, and thou shalt see
me no more." Joshua replied, " When, O my master, by

night or by day, have I ever left thee, that I should be in doubt concerning anything that thou hast taught me?" Moses said, "Even if thou hast no questions to ask of me, come hither, that I may kiss thee." Joshua went to Moses, who kissed him and wept upon his neck, and a second time blessed him, saying, "Mayest thou be at peace, and Israel be at peace with thee." [909]

THE BLESSING OF MOSES

The people now came to Moses and said, "The hour of thy death is at hand," and he replied: "Wait until I have blessed Israel. All my life long they had no pleasant experiences with me, for I constantly rebuked them and admonished them to fear God and fulfil the commandments, therefore do I not now wish to depart out of this world before I have blessed them." [910] Moses had indeed always cherished the desire of blessing Israel, but the Angel of Death had never permitted him to satisfy his wish, so shortly before dying, he enchained the Angel of Death, cast him beneath his feet, and blessed Israel in spite of their enemy, saying, "Save Thy people, and bless Thine inheritance: feed them also, and bear them up for ever." [911]

Moses was not the first to bestow blessings, as former generations had also done so, but no blessing was as effective as his. Noah blessed his sons, but it was a divided blessing, being intended for Shem, whereas Ham, instead of being blessed, was cursed. Isaac blessed his sons, but his blessings led to a dispute, for Esau envied Jacob his blessing. Jacob blessed his sons, but even his blessing was not without a blemish, for in the blessing he rebuked Reuben and called him to account for the sins he had committed. Even the number of Moses' blessings excelled that of his predecessors. For when God created the world, He blessed Adam and Eve, and this blessing remained upon the world until the flood, when it ceased. When Noah left the ark, God appeared before him and bestowed upon him anew the blessing that had vanished during the flood, and this blessing rested upon the world until Abraham came into the world and received a second blessing from God, who said, " And I will make of thee a great nation, and I will bless them that bless thee, and curse him that curseth thee." God then said to Abraham: " Henceforth it no longer behooves Me to bless My creatures in person, but I shall leave the blessings to thee: he whom thou blessest, shall be blessed by Me." Abraham did not, however, bless his own son Isaac, in order that the villain Esau might not have a share in that blessing. Jacob, however, received not only two blessings from his father, but one other besides from the angel with whom he wrestled, and one from God; and the blessing also that had been Abraham's to bestow upon his house went to Jacob. When Jacob blessed his sons, he passed on to them the five blessings he had received, and added one other. Balaam should really have blessed Israel with seven benedictions, corresponding to the seven altars he had erected, but he envied Israel greatly, and blessed them with only three blessings. God thereupon said: " Thou villain that begrudgest Israel their blessings! I shall not permit thee to bestow upon Israel all the blessings that are their due. Moses, who has ' a benevolent eye,' shall bless Israel." And so, too, it came to pass. Moses added a seventh blessing to the six benedictions with which Jacob had

blessed his twelve sons. This was not, however, the first
time that Moses blessed the people. He blessed them at the
erection of the Tabernacle, then at its consecration, a third
time at the installation of the judges, and a fourth time on
the day of his death.[912]

Before bestowing his blessing upon Israel, however, Moses
intoned a song in God's praise, for it is fitting to glorify
God's name before asking a favor of Him, and as Moses was
about to ask God to bless Israel, he first proclaimed His
grandeur and His majesty.[913]

He said: " When God first revealed Himself to Israel to
bestow the Torah upon them, He appeared to them not from
one direction, but from all four at once. He ' came from
Sinai,' which is in the South, ' and rose from Seïr unto them,'
that is in the East; ' He shined forth from mount Paran,'
that is in the North, ' and he came from the ten thousands of
holy ' angels that dwell in the West.[914] He proclaimed the
Torah not only in the language of Sinai, that is Hebrew, but
also in the tongue of Seïr, that is Roman, as well as in Paran's
speech, that is Arabic, and in the speech of Kadesh, that is
Aramaic, for He offered the Torah not to Israel alone, but to
all the nations of the earth. These, however, did not want to
accept it, hence His wrath against them, and His especial
love for Israel who, despite their awed fear and trembling
upon God's appearance on Sinai, still accepted the Torah.[915]
Lord of the world! " continued Moses, " When Israel shall
have been driven out of their land, be mindful still of the
merits of their Patriarchs and stand by them, deliver them in
Thy mercy from ' the yoke of the nations,' and from death,
and guide them in the future world as Thou didst lead them
in the desert." [916]

At these words Israel exclaimed, " The Torah that Moses brought to us at the risk of his life is our bride, and no other nation may lay claim to it."[917] Moses was our king when the seventy elders assembled, and in the future the Messiah will be our king, surrounded by seven shepherds, and he will gather together once more the scattered tribes of Israel."[918] Then Moses said: " God first appeared in Egypt to deliver His people, then at Sinai to give them the Torah, and He will appear a third time to take vengeance at Edom, and will finally appear to destroy Gog."[919]

After Moses had praised and glorified God, he began to implore His blessings for the tribes. His first prayer to God concerned Reuben, for whom he implored forgiveness for his sin with Bilhah. He said: " May Reuben come to life again in the future world for his good deed in saving Joseph, and may he not remain forever dead on account of his sin with Bilhah. May Reuben's descendants also be heroes in war, and heroes in their knowledge of the Torah." God granted this prayer and forgave Reuben's sin in accordance with the wish of the other tribes, who begged God to grant forgiveness to their eldest brother.[920] Moses at once perceived that God had granted his prayer, for all the twelve stones in the high priest's breastplate began to gleam forth, whereas formerly Reuben's stone had given forth no light.[921]

When Moses saw that God had forgiven Reuben's sin, he at once set about trying to obtain God's pardon for Judah, saying, " Was it not Judah that through his penitent confession of his sin with his daughter-in-law Tamar induced Reuben, too, to seek atonement and repentance? " The sin for which Moses asked God to forgive Judah was that he had never redeemed his promise to bring Benjamin back to his father. Owing to this sin, his corpse fell to pieces, so that its bones rolled about in their coffin during the forty years' march in the desert. But as soon as Moses prayed to God, saying, " Hear, Lord, the voice of Judah," the bones joined together once more, but his sin was not quite forgiven, for he was not yet admitted to the heavenly academy. Therefore Moses continued to pray : " Bring him in unto his people," and he was admitted. It did not, indeed, benefit him, for in punishment of his sin, God brought it to pass that he could not follow the discussions of the scholars in heaven, much less take part in them, whereupon Moses prayed : " Let his hands be sufficient for him," and then he no longer sat as one dumb in the heavenly academy. But still his sin was not quite forgiven, for Judah could not succeed in being victorious in the disputes of the learned, hence Moses prayed, " And Thou shalt be an help against his adversaries." It was only then that Judah's sin was quite forgiven, and that he succeeded in disputes with his antagonists in the heavenly academy.[922]

As Moses prayed for Judah, so too did he pray for his seed, and especially for David and the royal dynasty of David. He said : " When David, king of Israel, shall be in need, and shall pray to Thee, then, ' Hear, Lord, his voice, and Thou shalt be an help against his adversaries,' ' bring him ' then back ' to his people ' in peace ; and when alone he shall set out into battle against Goliath, ' let his hands be sufficient for him, and Thou shalt be an help against his adversaries.' " Moses at the same time prayed God to stand by the tribe of Judah, whose chief weapon in war was the bow, that their 'hands might be sufficient,' that they might vigorously and with good aim speed the arrow.

As Moses had never forgiven Simeon their sin with the daughters of Moab, he bestowed upon them no blessing, but this tribe also was not quite forgotten, for he included this tribe in his blessing for Judah, praying to God, that He might hear Judah's voice whenever he should pray for the tribe of Simeon when they should be in distress, and that furthermore He should give them their possession in the Holy Land beside Judah's. [928]

Simeon and Levi " drank out of the same cup," for both together in their wrath slew the inhabitants of Shechem, but whereas Levi made amends for his sin, Simeon added another new one. It was the Levites who, in their zeal for God, slew those that worshipped the Golden Calf; it was a Levite, Phinehas, moreover, who in his zeal for God slew the wicked prince of the tribe of Simeon, and his mistress. Hence Moses praised and blessed the tribe of Levi, whereas he did not even consider Simeon with a word.

His words first referred to Aaron, prince of the tribe of Levi. He said: " Well may Thy Urim and Tummim belong to Aaron, who ministered services of love to Thy children, who stood every test that Thou didst put upon him, and who at the ' waters of rebellion ' became the victim of a wrong accusation." God had then decreed against Aaron that he was to die in the desert, although not he, but Moses had trespassed against Him, saying to Israel, " Hear now, ye rebels." As Aaron, prince of the tribe of Levi, when Israel was still in Egypt, declaimed passionately against the people because they worshipped idols, so too all the tribe of Levi stood up

by God's standard when Israel worshipped the Golden Calf
in the desert, and slew the idolaters, even if they were their
half-brothers or their daughters' sons.   The Levites also
were the only ones who, in Egypt as in the desert, remained
true to God and His teachings, did not abandon the token of
the covenant, and were not tempted to rebellion by the spies.
" Hence," continued Moses, " shall the Levites be the only
ones from whose mouth shall issue judgment and instruction for Israel. ' They shall put incense ' in the Holy of
Holies, ' and whole burnt offerings upon His altar.'   Their
sacrifices shall reconcile Israel with God, and they themselves
shall be blessed with earthly goods.   Thou, Lord, ' smitest
through the loins of them that rise up against them,' that
dispute the priestly rights of this tribe, Thou didst destroy
Korah, and they ' that hated them,' like king Uzziah, ' shall
not rise again.' [924]   ' Bless, Lord, the substance ' of the Levites
who give from the tithes that they receive one-tenth to the
priests.   Mayest Thou accept sacrifice from the hands of the
priest Elijah upon mount Carmel, ' smite the loins ' of his
enemy Ahab, break the neck of the latter's false prophets, and
may the enemies of the high priest Johanan rise not again." [925]

" Benjamin," said Moses, " is the beloved of the Lord,
whom He will always shield, and in whose possession the
sanctuary shall stand, in this world as well as in the time of
the Messiah, and in the future world." [926]

Moses blessed Joseph's tribe with the blessing that their
possession might be the most fruitful and blessed land on
earth ; dew shall ever be there, and many wells spring up.
It shall constantly be exposed to the gentle influences of sun
and moon, that the fruits may ripen early. " I wish him," said

Moses, " that the blessings given him by the Patriarchs and the wives of the Patriarchs may be fulfilled." And so, too, it came to pass, for the land of the tribe of Joseph possessed everything, and nothing within it was lacking. This was the reward to Joseph for having fulfilled the will of God that was revealed to Moses in the bush of thorns; and also because as king of Egypt he treated his brothers with high honors although they had thrust him from their midst. Moses furthermore blessed Joseph by promising him that, as he had been the first of Jacob's sons to come to Egypt, he was also to be the first in the future world to appear in the Holy Land. Moses proclaimed the heroism of Joseph's seed in the words: " As it is a vain thing to try to force the firstling bullock to labor, so little shall Joseph's sons be yoked into service by the empires; as the unicorn with his horns pushes away all other animals, so, too, shall Joseph's sons rule the nations, even to the ends of the earth. The Ephraimite Joshua shall destroy myriads of heathens, and the Manassite Gideon thousands of them." [927]

Zebulun was the tribe that before all the other tribes devoted itself to commerce, and in this way acted as the agent between Israel and the other nations, selling the products of Palestine to the latter, and foreign wares to the former. Hence the blessing that Moses bestowed upon them. " ' Rejoice, Zebulun, in thy going out ' on commercial enterprises; at thy instance shall many nations pray upon the sacred mountain of the Temple and offer their sacrifices." For the people that came into Zebulun's realms on matters of business used to go from thence to Jerusalem to look upon the sanctuary of the Jews, and many of them were converted

through the grand impression that the life in the holy city
made upon them. Moses furthermore blessed this tribe by
giving them an estate by the sea, which might yield them
costly fish and the purple shell, and the sand of whose shores
might furnish them the material for glass. The other tribes
were therefore dependent upon Zebulun for these articles,
which they could not obtain from any one else, for whosoever attempted to rob Zebulun of them, was doomed to bad
luck in business. It is the " Sea of Chaifa " also, within
Zebulun's territory, where all the treasures of the ocean were
brought to shore; for whenever a ship is wrecked at sea, the
ocean sends it and its treasures to the sea of Chaifa, where
it is hoarded for the pious until the Judgment Day.[928] One
other blessing of Zebulun was that it would always be victorious in battle, whereas the tribe of Issachar, closely bound
up with it, was blessed by its distinction in the "tents of
learning." For Issachar was " the tribe of scholars and of
judges," wherefore Moses blessed them, saying that in " the
future time," Israel's great house of instruction as well as the
great Sanhedrin would be located in this tribe.[929]

The tribe of Gad, dwelling on the boundary of the land of
Israel, received the benediction that in " the future time " it
would be as strong in battle as it had been at the first conquest of Palestine, and would hereafter stand at the head of
Israel on their return to the Holy Land, as it had done on
their first entrance into the land. Moses praised this tribe
for choosing its site on this side the Jordan because that place
had been chosen to hold Moses' tomb. Moses indeed died
on mount Nebo, which is Reuben's possession, but his body
was taken from Nebo by the pinions of the Shekinah, and

brought to Gad's territory, a distance of four miles, amid the lamentations of the angels, who said, " He shall enter into peace and rest in his bed." [980]

Dan, who like Gad had his territory on the boundary of the land, was also blessed with strength and might, that he might ward off the attacks of Israel's enemies. He was also blessed in receiving his territory in the Holy Land in two different sections of it. [981]

Naphtali's blessing read: " O Naphtali, satisfied with favor, and full with the blessing of the Lord: possess thou the west and the south." This blessing was verified, for the tribe of Naphtali had in its possession an abundance of fish and mushrooms, so that they could maintain themselves without much labor; and the valley of Gennesaret furthermore was their possession, whose fruits were renowned for their extraordinary sweetness. But Naphtali was blessed not with material blessings only, but also with spiritual; for it was the great house of instruction at Tiberias to which Moses alluded when he said of Naphtali, " he is ' full with the blessings of the Lord.' " [982]

Moses called Asher the favorite of his brethren, for it was this tribe that in the years of release provided nourishment for all Israel, as its soil was so productive that what grew of its own accord sufficed to sustain all. But Moses blessed Asher in particular with a land rich in olives, so that oil flowed in streams through Asher's land. Hence Moses blessed him with the words: " The treasures of all lands shall flow to thee, for the nations shall give thee gold and silver for thine oil." He blessed Asher moreover with many sons, [983] and with daughters that preserved the charms of youth in their old age. [984]

As Moses uttered eleven benedictions, so likewise did he compose eleven psalms, corresponding to the eleven tribes blessed by him.[935] These psalms of Moses were later received into David's Psalter, where the psalms of Adam, Melchizedek, Abraham, Solomon, Asaph, and the three sons of Korah also found their place.[936] Moses' first psalm says, " ' Thou turnest man to destruction; and sayest, Return, ye children of men,' and forgivest the forefather of the tribe of Reuben who sinned, but returned again to God." Another one of Moses' psalms reads, " He that dwelleth in the secret place of the most High shall abide under the shadow of the Almighty," which corresponds to the tribe of Levi that dwelled in the sanctuary, the shadow of the Almighty. To the tribe of Judah, whose name signifies, " Praise the Lord," belongs the psalm, " It is a good thing to give thanks unto the Lord." The psalm: " The Lord is apparelled with majesty," is Benjamin's, for the sanctuary stood in his possession, hence this psalm closes with the words, " Holiness becometh Thine house, O Lord, forevermore." The psalm: " O Lord, Thou God to whom vengeance belongeth; Thou God to whom vengeance belongeth, shine forth," was composed by Moses for the tribe of Gad; for Elijah, a member of this tribe, was to destroy the foundations of the heathens, and to wreak upon them the vengeance of the Lord. To the tribe of learned men, Issachar, goes the psalm: " O come, let us sing unto the Lord: let us make a joyful noise to the rock of our salvation," for it is this tribe that occupy themselves with the Torah, the book of praise.[937]

MOSES PRAYS FOR DEATH

Moses still had many other blessings for every single tribe, but when he perceived that his time had drawn to a close, he included them all in one blessing, saying,⁹³⁸ " Happy art thou, O Israel: Who is like unto thee, a people saved by the Lord, the shield of thy help, and that is the sword of thy excellency! " With these words he at the same time answered a question that Israel had put to him, saying, " O tell us, our teacher Moses, what is the blessing that God will bestow upon us in the future world? " He replied: " I cannot describe it to you, but all I can say is, happy ye that such is decreed for ye! " Moses at the same time begged God that in the future world He might restore to Israel the heavenly weapon that He had taken from them after the worship of the Golden Calf. God said, " I swear that I shall restore it to them." ⁹³⁹

When Moses had finished his blessing, he asked Israel to forgive his sternness toward them, saying: " Ye have had much to bear from me in regard to the fulfilment of the Torah and its commandments, but forgive me now." They replied: " Our teacher, our lord, it is forgiven." It was now their turn to ask his forgiveness, which they did in these words: " We have often kindled thine anger and have laid many burdens upon thee, but forgive us now." He said, " It is forgiven."

In the meanwhile people came to him and said, " The hour has come in which thou departest from the world." Moses said, " Blessed be His name that liveth and endureth in all eternity! " Turning to Israel, he then said, " I pray ye, when ye shall have entered into the land of Israel, remember me still, and my bones, and say, 'Woe to the son of Amram that ran before us like a horse, but whose bones remained in the desert.'" Israel said to Moses: "O our teacher, what will become of us when thou art gone?" He replied: "While I was with ye, God was with ye; yet think not that all the signs and miracles that He wrought through me were performed for my sake, for much rather were they done for your sake, and for His love and mercy, and if ye have faith in Him, He will work your desires."⁴⁰ 'Put not your trust in princes, nor in the son of man, in whom there is no help,' for how could ye expect help from a man, a creature of flesh and blood, that cannot shield himself from death? Put, therefore, your trust in Him through whose word arose the world, for He liveth and endureth in all eternity. Whether ye be laden with sin, or not, 'pour your heart before Him,' and turn to Him." Israel said: "'The Lord, He is God; the Lord, He is God.' God is our strength and our refuge."⁴¹

Then a voice sounded from heaven and said, "Why, Moses, dost thou strive in vain? Thou hast but one-half hour more of life in the world." Moses, to whom God had now shown the reward of the pious in the future world, and the gates of salvation and of consolation that He would here-after open to Israel, now said: "Happy art thou, O Israel: who is like unto thee, a people saved by the Lord!" He then bade farewell to the people, weeping aloud. He said: "Dwell in peace, I shall see ye again at the Resurrection," and so he went forth from them, weeping aloud. Israel, too, broke into loud lamentations, so that their weeping ascended to the highest heavens.

Moses took off his outer garment, rent his shirt, strewed

dust upon his head, covered it like a mourner, and in this
condition betook himself to his tent amid tears and lamentations, saying: " Woe to my feet that may not enter the land
of Israel, woe to my hands that may not pluck of its fruits!
Woe to my palate that may not taste the fruits of the land
that flows with milk and honey!" ⁹⁴²

Moses then took a scroll, wrote upon it the Ineffable
Name, and the book of the song, and betook himself to
Joshua's tent to deliver it to him.⁹⁴³ When he arrived at
Joshua's tent, Joshua was seated, and Moses remained standing before him in a bowed attitude without being noticed by
Joshua. For God brought this to pass in order that Moses,
on account of this disrespectful treatment, might himself
wish for death. For when Moses had prayed to God to let
him live, were it only as a private citizen, God granted his
prayer, saying to him, " If thou hast no objection to subordi-
nating thyself to Joshua, then mayest thou live," and in accordance with this agreement, Moses had betaken himself to
hear Joshua's discourse.

The people who had gathered as usual before Moses' tent
to hear from him the word of God, failed to find him there,
and hearing that he had gone to Joshua, went there likewise,
where they found Moses standing and Joshua seated.
" What art thou thinking of," they called out to Joshua,
" that thou art seated, while thy teacher Moses stands before
thee in a bowed attitude and with folded hands?" In their
anger and indignation against Joshua, they would instantly
have slain him, had not a cloud descended and interposed
itself between the people and Joshua. When Joshua noticed
that Moses stood before him, he instantly arose, and cried in

tears: " O my father and teacher Moses, that like a father didst rear me from my youth, and that didst instruct me in wisdom, why dost thou do such a thing as will bring upon me Divine punishment?" The people now besought Moses as usual to instruct them in the Torah, but he replied, " I have no permission to do so." They did not, however, cease importuning him, until a voice sounded from heaven and said, " Learn from Joshua." The people now consented to acknowledge Joshua as their teacher, and seated themselves before him to hear his discourse. Joshua now began his discourse with Moses sitting at his right, and Aaron's sons, Eleazar and Ithamar, at his left. But hardly had Joshua begun his lecture with the words, " Praised be God that taketh delight in the pious and their teachings," when the treasures of wisdom vanished from Moses and passed over into Joshua's possession, so that Moses was not even able to follow his disciple Joshua's discourse. When Joshua had finished his lecture, Israel requested Moses to review with them what Joshua had taught, but he said, " I know not how to reply to your request!" He began to expound Joshua's lecture to them, but could not, for he had not understood it. He now said to God: " Lord of the world! Until now I wished for life, but now I long to die. Rather a hundred deaths, than one jealousy." [944]

SAMAEL CHASTISED BY MOSES

When God perceived that Moses was prepared to die, He said to the angel Gabriel, " Go, fetch Me Moses' soul." But he replied, " How should I presume to approach and take the soul of him that outweighs sixty myriads of mortals!" God then commissioned the angel Michael to fetch Moses' soul, but he amid tears refused on the same grounds as Gabriel. God then said to the angel Zagzagel, " Fetch Me Moses' soul!" He replied, "Lord of the world! I was his teacher and he my disciple, how then should I take his soul!"⁰⁴⁵ Then Samael appeared before God and said: "Lord of the world! Is Moses, Israel's teacher, indeed greater than Adam whom Thou didst create in Thine image and Thy likeness? Is Moses greater, perchance, than Thy friend Abraham, who to glorify Thy name cast himself into the fiery furnace? Is Moses greater, perchance, than Isaac, who permitted himself to be bound upon the altar as a sacrifice to Thee? Or is he greater than Thy firstborn Jacob, or than his twelve sons, Thy saplings? Not one of them escaped me, give me therefore permission to fetch Moses' soul." God replied: " Not one of all these equals him. How, too, wouldst thou take his soul? From his face? How couldst thou approach his face that had looked upon My Face! From his hands? Those hands received the Torah, how then shouldst thou be able to approach them! From his feet? His feet touched My clouds, how then shouldst thou be able to approach them! Nay, thou canst not approach him at all." But Samael said, " However it be, I pray Thee, permit me to fetch his soul!" God said, " Thou hast My consent."⁹⁴⁶

Samael now went forth from God in great glee, took his sword, girded himself with cruelty, wrapped himself in wrath, and in a great rage betook himself to Moses. When Samael perceived Moses, he was occupied in writing the Ineffable Name. Darts of fire shot from his mouth, the radiance of his face and of his eyes shone like the sun, so

that he seemed like an angel of the hosts of the Lord, and
Samael in fear and trembling thought, " It was true when
the other angels declared that they could not seize Moses'
soul ! "

Moses, who had known that Samael would come, even
before his arrival, now lifted his eyes and looked upon
Samael, whereupon Samael's eyes grew dim before the
radiance of Moses' countenance. He fell upon his face,
and was seized with the woes of a woman giving birth,
so that in his terror he could not open his mouth. Moses
therefore addressed him, saying: " Samael, Samael! ' There
is no peace, saith my God, to the wicked!' Why dost
thou stand before me? Get thee hence at once, or I shall
cut off thy head." In fear and trembling Samael replied:
" Why art thou angry with me, my master, give me thy
soul, for thy time to depart from the world is at hand."
Moses: " Who sent thee to me? " Samael: " He that
created the world and the souls." Moses: " I will not
give thee my soul." Samael: " All souls since the creation
of the world were delivered into my hands." Moses: " I
am greater than all others that came into the world, I have
had a greater communion with the spirit of God than these
and thou together." Samael: " Wherein lies thy pre-
eminence? " Moses: " Dost thou not know that I am the
son of Amram, that came circumcised out of my mother's
womb, that at the age of three days not only walked, but
even talked with my parents, that took no milk from my
mother until she received her pay from Pharaoh's daughter? When I was three months old, my wisdom was so
great that I made prophecies and said, ' I shall hereafter from

God's right hand receive the Torah.' At the age of six months I entered Pharaoh's palace and took off the crown from his head. When I was eighty years old, I brought the ten plagues upon Pharaoh and the Egyptians, slew their guardian angel, and led the sixty myriads of Israel out of Egypt. I then clove the sea into twelve parts, led Israel through the midst of them, and drowned the Egyptians in the same, and it was not thou that took their souls, but I. It was I, too, that turned the bitter water into sweet, that mounted into heaven, and there spoke face to face with God! I hewed out two tables of stone, upon which God at my request wrote the Torah. One hundred and twenty days and as many nights did I dwell in heaven, where I dwelled under the Throne of Glory; like an angel during all this time I ate no bread and drank no water. I conquered the inhabitants of heaven, made known their secrets to mankind, received the Torah from God's right hand, and at His command wrote six hundred and thirteen commandments, which I then taught to Israel. I furthermore waged war against the heroes Sihon and Og, that had been created before the flood and were so tall that the waters of the flood did not even reach their ankles. In battle with them I bade sun and moon to stand still, and with my staff slew the two heroes. Where, perchance, is there in the world a mortal who could do all this? How darest thou, wicked one, presume to wish to seize my pure soul that was given me in holiness and purity by the Lord of holiness and purity? Thou hast no power to sit where I sit, or to stand where I stand. Get thee hence, I will not give thee my soul."

Samael now in terror returned to God and reported Moses'

words to Him. God's wrath against Samael was now kindled, and He said to him: "Go, fetch Me Moses' soul, for if thou dost not do so, I shall discharge thee from thine office of taking men's souls, and shall invest another with it." Samael implored God, saying: "O Lord of the world, whose deeds are terrible, bid me go to Gehenna and there turn uppermost to undermost, and undermost to uppermost, and I shall at once do so without a moment's hesitation, but I cannot appear before Moses." God: "Why not, pray?" Samael: "I cannot do it because he is like the princes in Thy great chariot. Lightning-flashes and fiery darts issue from his mouth when he speaks with me, just as it is with the Seraphim when they laud, praise and glorify Thee. I pray Thee, therefore, send me not to him, for I cannot appear before him." But God in wrath said to Samael: "Go, fetch Me Moses' soul," and while he set about to execute God's command, the Lord furthermore said: "Wicked one! Out of the fire of Hell wast thou created, and to the fire of Hell shalt thou eventually return. First in great joy didst thou set out to kill Moses, but when thou didst perceive his grandeur and his greatness, thou didst say, 'I cannot undertake anything against him.' It is clear and manifest before Me that thou wilt now return from him a second time in shame and humiliation."

Samael now drew his sword out of its sheath and in a towering fury betook himself to Moses, saying, "Either I shall kill him or he shall kill me." When Moses perceived him he arose in anger, and with his staff in his hand, upon which was engraved the Ineffable Name, set about to drive Samael away. Samael fled in fear, but Moses pursued him, and when he reached him, he struck him with his staff, blinded him with the radiance of his face, and then let him run on, covered with shame and confusion. He was not far from killing him, but a voice resounded from heaven and said, " Let him live, Moses, for the world is in need of him," so Moses had to content himself with Samael's chastisement.[447]

God Kisses Moses' Soul

In the meanwhile Moses' time was at an end. A voice from heaven resounded, saying: " Why, Moses, dost thou strive in vain? Thy last second is at hand." Moses instantly stood up for prayer, and said: " Lord of the world! Be mindful of the day on which Thou didst reveal Thyself to me in the bush of thorns, and be mindful also of the day when I ascended into heaven and during forty days partook of neither food nor drink. Thou, Gracious and Merciful, deliver me not into the hand of Samael." God replied: " I have heard thy prayer. I Myself shall attend to thee and bury thee." Moses now sanctified himself as do the Seraphim that surround the Divine Majesty, whereupon God from the highest heavens revealed Himself to receive Moses' soul. When Moses beheld the Holy One, blessed be His Name, he fell upon his face and said: " Lord of the world! In love didst Thou create the world, and in love Thou guidest it. Treat me also with love, and deliver me not into the hands of the Angel of Death." A heavenly voice sounded and said: " Moses, be not afraid. ' Thy righteousness shall go before thee; the glory of the Lord shall be thy rearward.' "
With God descended from heaven three angels, Michael,

Gabriel, and Zagzagel. Gabriel arranged Moses' couch, Michael spread upon it a purple garment, and Zagzagel laid down a woolen pillow. God stationed Himself over Moses' head, Michael to his right, Gabriel to his left, and Zagzagel at his feet, whereupon God addressed Moses: " Cross thy feet," and Moses did so. He then said, " Fold thy hands and lay them upon thy breast," and Moses did so. Then God said, " Close thine eyes," and Moses did so. Then God spake to Moses' soul: " My daughter, one hundred and twenty years had I decreed that thou shouldst dwell in this righteous man's body, but hesitate not now to leave it, for thy time is run." The soul replied: " I know that Thou art the God of spirits and of souls, and that in Thy hand are the souls of the living and of the dead. Thou didst create me and put me into the body of this righteous man. Is there anywhere in the world a body so pure and holy as this is? Never a fly rested upon it, never did leprosy show itself upon it. Therefore do I love it, and do not wish to leave it." God replied: " Hesitate not, my daughter! Thine end hath come. I Myself shall take thee to the highest heavens and let thee dwell under the Throne of My Glory, like the Seraphim, Ofannim, Cherubim, and other angels." But the soul replied: " Lord of the world! I desire to remain with this righteous man; for whereas the two angels Azza and Azazel when they descended from heaven to earth, corrupted their way of life and loved the daughters of the earth, so that in punishment Thou didst suspend them between heaven and earth, the son of Amram, a creature of flesh and blood, from the day upon which Thou didst reveal Thyself from the bush of thorns, has lived apart from his wife. Let me therefore remain where I am." ⁹⁴⁸ When Moses saw that his soul refused to leave him, he said to her: " Is this because the Angel of Death wishes to show his power over thee? " The soul replied: " Nay, God doth not wish to deliver me into the hands of death." Moses: " Wilt thou, perchance, weep when the others will weep at my departure? " The soul: " The Lord ' hath delivered mine eyes from tears.' " Moses: `` Wilt thou, perchance, go into Hell when I am dead? " The soul: " I will walk before the Lord in the land of the living." When Moses heard these words, he permitted his soul to leave him, saying to her: " Return unto thy rest, O my soul; for the Lord hath dealt bountifully with thee." ⁹⁴⁹ God thereupon took Moses' soul by kissing him upon the mouth.⁹⁵⁰

Moses' activity did not, however, cease with his death, for in heaven he is one of the servants of the Lord.⁹⁵¹ God buried Moses' body in a spot that remained unknown even to Moses himself. Only this is known concerning it, that a subterranean passage connects it with the graves of the Patriarchs.⁹⁵² Although Moses' body lies dead in its grave, it is still as fresh as when he was alive.⁹⁵³

The Mourning for Moses

When Moses died, a voice resounded from heaven throughout all the camp of Israel, which measured twelve miles in length by twelve in width, and said, " Woe! Moses is dead. Woe! Moses is dead." All Israel who, throughout thirty days before Moses' decease, had wept his impending death now arranged a three months' time of mourning for him.⁹⁵⁴ But Israel were not the only mourners for Moses. God Himself wept for Moses, saying, "Who will rise up for

Me against the evil-doers? Who will stand up for Me against the workers of iniquity?" Metatron appeared before God and said: "Moses was Thine when he lived, and he is Thine in his death." God replied: "I weep not for Moses' sake, but for the loss Israel suffered through his death. How often had they angered Me, but he prayed for them and appeased My wrath." The angels wept with God, saying, "But where shall wisdom be found?" The heavens lamented: "The godly man is perished out of the earth." The earth wept: "And there is none upright among men." Stars, planets, sun, and moon wailed: "The righteous perisheth, and no man layeth it to heart," and God praised Moses' excellence in the words: "Thou hast said of Me, 'The Lord He is God: there is none else,' and therefore shall I say of thee, 'And there arose not a prophet in Israel like unto Moses.'" [955]

Among mortals, it was particularly Jochebed, Moses' mother, and Joshua, his disciple, that deeply mourned Moses' death. They were not indeed certain if Moses were dead, hence they sought him everywhere. Jochebed went first to Egypt and said to that land, "Mizraim, Mizraim, hast thou perchance seen Moses?" But Mizraim replied, "As truly as thou livest, Jochebed, I have not seen him since the day when he slew all the firstborn here." Jochebed then betook herself to the Nile, saying, "Nile, Nile, hast thou perchance seen Moses?" But Nile replied, "As truly as thou livest, Jochebed, I have not seen Moses since the day when he turned my water to blood." Then Jochebed went to the sea and said, "Sea, sea, hast thou perchance seen Moses?" The sea replied, "As truly as thou livest, Jochebed, I have not seen him since the day when he led the twelve tribes through me." Jochebed thereupon went to the desert and said, "Desert, desert, hast thou perchance seen Moses?" The desert replied, "As truly as thou livest, Jochebed, I have not seen him since the day whereon he caused manna to rain down upon me." Then Jochebed went to Sinai, and said, "Sinai, Sinai, hast thou perchance seen Moses?" Sinai said, "As truly as thou livest, Jochebed, I have not seen him since the day whereon he descended from me with the two tables of the law." Jochebed finally went to the rock and said, "Rock, rock, hast thou perchance seen Moses?" The rock replied, "As truly as thou livest, I have not seen him since the day when with his staff he twice smote me." [956]

Joshua, too, sought his teacher Moses in vain, and in his grief for Moses' disappearance he rent his garments, and crying aloud, called ceaselessly, "'My father, my father, the chariot of Israel and the horsemen thereof.' 'But where shall wisdom be found?'" But God said to Joshua: "How long wilt thou continue to seek Moses in vain? He is dead, but indeed it is I that have lost him, and not thou." [957]

SAMAEL'S VAIN SEARCH

Samael, the Angel of Death, had not heard that God had taken Moses' soul from his body and received it under the Throne of Glory. Believing that Moses was still among the living, he betook himself to Moses' house in order to seize his soul, for he feared to return before God without having executed His command to take Moses' soul. He did not, however, find Moses in his accustomed place, so he hastened into the land of Israel, thinking, "Long did Moses pray to be permitted to enter this land, and perhaps he is there." He said to the land of Israel, " Is Moses perchance with thee? " But the land replied, " Nay, he is not found in the land of the living."

Samael then thought: " I know that God once said to Moses, ' Lift up thy rod and divide the sea,' so perhaps he is by the sea." He hastened to the sea and said, " Is Moses here? " The sea replied: " He is not here, and I have not seen him since the day when he clove me into twelve parts, and with the twelve tribes passed through me."

Samael then betook himself to Gehenna asking, " Hast thou seen Moses, the son of Amram? " Gehenna replied, " With mine ears have I heard his cry, but I have not seen him."

He betook himself to Sheol, Abaddon, and Ṭiṭ-ha-Yawen, to whom he said, " Have ye seen the son of Amram? " They replied: " Through Pharaoh, king of Egypt, have we heard his call, but we have not seen him."

He betook himself to the Abyss and asked, " Hast thou seen the son of Amram? " The answer arose, " I have not seen him, but heard indeed his call."

He asked Korah's sons, that dwell within the Abyss, " Have ye seen the son of Amram? " They replied, " We have not seen him since the day upon which at Moses' bidding the earth opened its mouth and swallowed us."

He betook himself to the clouds of glory and asked, " Is Moses perchance with you? " They answered, " He is hid from the eyes of all living."

He went to the heavens and asked, " Have ye seen the son of Amram? " The answer was, " We have not seen him since at God's command he mounted to us to receive the Torah."

He hastened to Paradise, but when the angels that guard its gates beheld Samael, they drove him away and said, " Wicked one! Wicked one! ' This is the gate of the Lord; the righteous shall enter into it.' " Samael thereupon flew over the gates of Paradise at a height of four thousand parasangs, descended into Paradise and asked Paradise, " Hast thou perchance seen Moses? " Paradise answered, " Since in Gabriel's company he visited me to look upon the reward of the pious, I have not seen him."

He went to the tree of life, but even at the distance of three hundred parasangs, it cried out to him: " Approach me not." He therefore asked from afar, " Hast thou seen the son of Amram? " The tree replied, " Since the day on which he came to me to cut him a staff, I have not seen him."

He betook himself to the tree of the knowledge of good and evil, and said, " Hast thou seen the son of Amram? " The tree replied, " Since the day on which he came to me to get a writing reed, wherewith to write the Torah, I have not seen him."

He betook himself to the mountains with his query. These replied, " Since he hewed the two tables out of us, we have not seen him."

He went to the deserts and asked, " Have ye seen the son of Amram? " These replied, " Since he has ceased to lead Israel to pasture upon us, we have not seen him."

He betook himself to mount Sinai, for he thought God had formerly commanded Moses to ascend it, and that he might now be there. He asked Sinai, " Hast thou seen the son of

Amram?" Sinai said, "Since the day on which out of God's right hand he received the Torah upon me, I have not seen him."

He betook himself to the birds and said, "Have ye seen Moses?" They replied, "Since the day whereon he separated the birds into clean and unclean we have not seen him."

He went to the quadrupeds and asked: "Have ye seen Moses?" They answered: "Since the day on which he determined which beasts might be eaten, and which might not, we have not seen him." [958] The answer of the birds and beasts referred to the day on which God assembled all the species of animals, led them before Moses, and instructed him which of these were clean and which were not, which might, and which might not be eaten. [959]

Samael then betook himself to the "Court of the Dead," where the angel Dumah guards the souls of the deceased, and asked this angel, "Hast thou seen the son of Amram?" He replied: "I heard the words of lamentation for him in heaven, but I have not seen him."

He betook himself to the angels and asked, "Have ye seen the son of Amram?" These made the same reply as Dumah, and advised him to go to the mortals, who might possibly give him information concerning Moses' whereabouts.

He betook himself to the mortals and asked, "Where is Moses?" These replied: "Our teacher Moses is not like human beings. He is the peer of the angels of ministry, for he ascended into heaven and dwelt in heaven like the angels, 'he hath gathered the wind in his fists' like an angel, and

God took his soul to Himself in the place of His sanctity. What connection then hast thou with the son of Amram?" [000]

MOSES EXCELS ALL PIOUS MEN

The special distinction that God granted to Moses at his death was well merited, for Moses outweighed all other pious men.[961] When Moses died, Adam appeared and said, "I am greater than thou, for I was created in God's image." But Moses replied: "I am nevertheless superior to thee, for the glory that thou didst receive from God was taken from thee, whereas I retained the radiance of my face forever."

Noah then said to Moses: "I am greater than thou, for I was preserved out of the generation of the flood." Moses replied: "I am superior to thee, for thou didst save thyself alone, and hadst not the power to save thy generation, but I saved myself and also saved my generation at the time when they transgressed with the Golden Calf."

Abraham said to Moses, "I am greater than thou, for I fed the wanderers." Moses: "I am superior to thee, for thou didst feed the uncircumcised whereas I fed the circumcised; and thou, moreover, didst feed them in a land of habitations, whereas I fed Israel in the desert."

Isaac said to Moses: "I am greater than thou, for I bared my neck upon the altar and beheld the Face of the Shekinah." Moses replied: "Still am I superior to thee, for thou didst indeed behold the Face of the Shekinah, but thine eyes grew dim, whereas I talked with the Shekinah face to face, and yet neither did mine eyes grow dim nor my strength wane."

Jacob said, " I am greater than thou, for I wrestled with the angel and conquered him." Moses replied: " Thou didst wrestle with the angel upon thy territory, but I mounted to the angels into their own territory, and still they feared me." [962]

Joseph said to Moses, " I am greater than thou, for my master's wife could not tempt me to sin." Moses replied: " Still am I superior to thee, for thou didst restrain thyself from a strange woman, whereas I abstained from intercourse with my own wife." [963]

The degree of Moses' superiority over the other pious men can be seen by the following. Adam died because he had been seduced by the serpent, whereas Moses fashioned a serpent out of brass at sight of which everyone that had been bitten by a snake recovered. Noah offered a sacrifice to God that was accepted, but he himself was not admitted to God's presence. When Moses, on the other hand, offered a sacrifice in Israel's name, God said to him, " Know that twice daily I shall dwell with ye." Abraham had been the cause for Israel's bondage in Egypt, for that was the punishment for his words, " ' Whereby shall I know that I shall inherit ' the land?" Moses, on the other hand, it was that delivered Israel out of Egyptian bondage. Jacob indeed conquered in his struggle with the angel, but the blow that the angel dealt him put Jacob's thigh out of joint forever, whereas Moses inspired the angels with such fear that as soon as they beheld him in heaven, they fled.

But Moses not only surpassed all other human beings, he surpassed also the entire creation that God had brought forth in six days. On the first day God created light, but

Moses mounted into heaven and seized the spiritual light, the Torah. On the second day God created the firmament, whereby He decreed that the earth was not to enter the realm of the firmament, nor the firmament the realm of earth, but Moses scaled the firmament even though he belonged to earth. On the third day God created the sea, but as soon as the sea caught sight of Moses, it retreated before him affrighted. On the fourth day God created the sun and the moon to illuminate the earth, but Moses said to God: " I do not wish sun and moon to give light to Israel, Thou Thyself shalt do so," and God granted his prayer. On the fifth day God created the animals, but Moses slaughtered whatever animals he wanted for Israel's needs. When, therefore, God laid all the objects of creation on one side of the scales, and Moses upon the other, Moses outweighed them.[964] Moses was justly called, " the man of God," for he was half man and half God.[965]

But not in this world alone was Moses the great leader and teacher of his people, he shall be the same in the future world, in accordance with the promise God made him shortly before his death. God said: " Thou that didst lead My children in this world, shalt also lead them in the future world.[966]